Islam and Contemporary European Literature

Islam and Contemporary European Literature

Carool Kersten

Edinburgh University Press is one of the leading university presses in the UK. Publishing new research in the arts and humanities, EUP connects people and ideas to inspire creative thinking, open new perspectives and shape the world we live in. For more information, visit www.edinburghuniversitypress.com.

Edinburgh University Press Ltd
13 Infirmary Street, Edinburgh EH1 1LT

Typeset in 10.5/13 pt Sabon LT Pro
by Cheshire Typesetting Ltd, Cuddington, Cheshire

A CIP record for this book is available from the British Library

ISBN 978 1 4744 9267 6 (hardback)
ISBN 978 1 4744 9269 0 (webready PDF)
ISBN 978 1 4744 9270 6 (epub)

EU Authorised Representative:
Easy Access System Europe
Mustamäe tee 50, 10621 Tallinn, Estonia
gpsr.requests@easproject.com

Contents

Acknowledgements

Looking back at the gestation of this book made me realise that it has been almost a decade in the making, with some aspects going back even further than that. This has only been possible thanks to the generosity of the Department of Theology & Religious Studies and the Faculty of Arts & Humanities at my previous place of work, King's College London, in granting me research leave during the academic years 2015–16 and 2018–19, as well as for the final semester of employment in 2022. I have also benefited from my association with the Institute of Philosophical & Religious Studies at the Science and Research Centre Koper in Slovenia, where my involvement in the projects *Between Politics and Ethics: Towards a New World Culture of Hospitality and Non-Violence* (2013–16) and *Liminal Spaces: Areas of Cultural and Societal Cohabitation in the Age of Risk and Vulnerability* (2019–25) have had a direct bearing on the research for this book.[1] For this I want to thank in particular the Institute's director, Lenart Škof, for his appreciation of, confidence in and sustained support for my scholarship. I am also grateful to the Catholic University of Leuven for appointing me Research Professor in Islamic Studies in the Faculty of Theology and Religious Studies.[2] Over the years, I have learned much from the comments and suggestions of colleagues, fellow scholars and friends specialised in comparative literature or in geographical areas that are outside of my own areas of expertise. Especially valuable have been the readings of individual chapters by Ziad Elmarsafy, Cecilie Endresen, Ana Jelnikar, Dilyana Mincheva, Klaus von Stosch and Anja Zalta. Of course, all remaining errors or imperfections remain my sole responsibility.

Roermond, August 2024

A Note on Translation and Transliteration

As this book is written in English, I have relied on English translations of the books by authors discussed in this volume where and when these have been available. The main reason for this decision is that although I can read French and German in the original, I do not know Spanish, Albanian or Serbo-Croat. While I will be the first to admit that there is such a thing as 'lost in translation', in this case I consider this approach to the use of translated texts acceptable, because this book is about Islamic references and themes in contemporary European literature, not an examination of linguistic fidelity as such. Similarly, although this book is entitled *Islam and Contemporary European Literature*, it is also not a philological examination. Consequently, in transliterating names and terms from the Arabic, Persian or (Ottoman) Turkish I will follow the choices made by the authors concerned; in other instances I have opted for a simplified version of the system used in the *International Journal of Middle Eastern Studies* (IJMES), dispensing with diacritics. This will suffice for those competent in these languages to determine the exact spelling, while other readers need not be distracted by too complicated a typography.

About the issues that are proper to religion – I learned more from Adorno's Minima Moralia *than from Muhammad.*

Navid Kermani, *Between Quran & Kafka*, x

A text is not immutable, but open, carrying events and words along in its stream picked up from both lived experience and fiction.

Abdelwahab Meddeb, *Talismano*, 205

Freedom and isolation will be the reward of the creator immersed to his eyebrows in a multiple, frontierless culture.

Juan Goytisolo, *Forbidden Territory*, 23–4

Even the Koran is dangerous if you use God's words about sinners to refer to those who decide who the sinners are. You will regret a thousand times what you say, but rarely what you keep silent. I had known that wisdom when I had not needed it.

Meša Selimović, *Death and the Dervish*, 147

Only literature can put you in touch with another human spirit, as a whole, with all its weaknesses and grandeurs, its limitations, its pettiness, its beliefs; with whatever it finds moving, interesting, exciting and repugnant.

Michel Houellebecq, *Submission*, 6–7

There is no such thing as chance in the world of Oriental Studies.

Mathias Énard, *Compass*, 72

Introduction: Studying Islam through Literature

The idea for this book was triggered by the acute refugee and migrant crisis erupting along Europe's borders in 2015. It was caused by a conflux of two migration streams, the first consisting of refugees fleeing conflict zones in the Eastern and Southern Mediterranean and elsewhere in the Muslim world, and the other representing a more sustained pattern of economic migrants from the also predominantly Muslim countries in North and West Africa. Although it may no longer be front-page news, the perception of this as a crisis situation on European soil, or a threat to the social-political fabric of Europe, has remained a key issue in the European public space over the decade that has passed since. The impact of this influx of what are perceived as Muslim outsiders has led to a dramatic and radical resetting of the social-cultural engineering exercise known as multiculturalism. It is a consequence of the growing polarisation between its advocates (including the often self-proclaimed spokespersons on behalf of Muslims) and their detractors (populist politicians exploiting and actively feeding the phenomenon of Islamophobia). Both camps operate on the basis of collective identity formations grounded in religious communitarianism and ethno-religious nationalism respectively. The purpose of the present project is to suggest literary writings as an alternative way of formulating counter-narratives to the strong identity politics dominated by such reductive interpretations. In this regard, I like Rebecca Gould's formulation when making a case for extending the postcolonial field of subaltern studies to her specialist field of the Islamicate literatures in the Caucasus, on account of its potential for opening up 'a space for generating new meanings, new ways of seeing, and new ways of being to readers around the world'.[1] I share the view that such a redirection of perspective contains promising prospects of providing more illustrative, and therefore compelling, examples of the importance of recognising and acknowledging the individual and its multiple belongings for successful human cohabitation in an increasingly interconnected world. To that end, the literary texts in question will be read as personal interpretations of religion, *in casu* Islam (but often in relation to other traditions, qualified as 'religious' or 'secular'), on the part of their authors. While the current project continues to have the same intellectual-historical pretensions as my earlier work as a scholar of Islam, moving attention from academic philosophical writings to literature constitutes what I call a shift from abstraction to sublimation.

Quarrying literary writings for connections between religious references, individual storytelling and fiction ties in with Paul Ricoeur's notion of narrative identity. Originating in his 1980s *Time and Narrative* trilogy, the idea was further unpacked in *Oneself as Another* (1992), and then applied to religious questions in *Figuring the Sacred* (1995). In these latter two books, the philosopher made way for the Christian thinker Paul Ricoeur. Without wanting to make any sort of comparison with one of the giants of twentieth-century philosophy, I consider this book project to be an experiment in making references to religion in literary texts the object of study from the viewpoint of a scholar of Islam. An additional incentive for pursuing this angle is the question of whether the use of Islamic referents in literary texts mirrors the religious turn in philosophy signalled by Hent de Vries in 1999. Central figures in reformulating philosophical questions by using religious vocabulary are Italian philosophers like Giorgio Agamben and Gianni Vattimo.[2] I will return to these later in this Introduction where I address the epistemological aspects of the present investigation.

By taking contemporary European literature as an alternative domain for articulating Muslim individuality and senses of selfhood, or for reflecting on otherness by authors from non-Muslim backgrounds, I venture into – for me at least – largely uncharted territory where it concerns the academic study of Islam.[3] A useful entry-point for situating this project in the wider context of studying religions through literature is an article from 1998 by Eric Ziolkowski, a scholar of religions specialised in the reception history of the Bible. In 'History of Religions and the Study of Religion and Literature: Grounds for an Alliance', he recalls the aesthetic sensibilities and literary interests of those nineteenth- and twentieth-century scholars, such as Max Müller and Rudolf Otto, Émile Durkheim and Gerardus van der Leeuw, who founded and shaped the field of academic inquiry that is referred to as Comparative Religion, History of Religions, or even Science of Religion (*Religionswissenschaft*). Their mission to 'break down walls between disciplines' made Ziolkowski realise that the 'affinities between the world's religions and its arts and literature is an unappreciated legacy of the history of religions', and that literature 'furnishes a boundless range of what Ninian Smart calls "world-view analysis in fictional form"' (309–10). Globally-minded scholars of religion, meanwhile, can help improve the study of religion and literature by liberating literary theory and hermeneutics from its Eurocentric and theological confinements, because 'neither the religious nor the aesthetic need be construed reductively as a product of the other' (311). To that end, Ziolkowski advocates a fusion of horizons in the Gadamerian sense, to the extent that the proposed alliance between scholarship in religion and literature rests on a 'conceptualization that would allow hermeneutical reflections from both fields to be combined' (313).

For the purposes of this book, I take Islamic referents very broadly. In fact, it would be more accurate to speak of 'references to Islam and Muslims'. Also, I wish to immediately add the caveat that I will not deal with confessional texts as expressions of personal piety. The authors discussed in this book have also drawn on hagiographies and other devotional material, but I will read their use of such sources with the objective of trying to establish the considerations, motivations or reasons for selecting such materials – this in order to move closer to answering questions as to the writers' purposes with those choices. As an academic researcher, I therefore treat references to Islam and the Muslim world as data for analysis and interpretation to the extent that they contribute to the knowledge about religion rather than religious knowledge.

Conceived as the first part of a two-volume book project on Islamic referents in contemporary world literature, this book concentrates on European authors from Muslim and non-Muslim backgrounds who have contributed to this nexus between literature and religion. Historical antecedents for Islamic themes in European literature are manifold and can be traced back to the Middle Ages. Composed in the eleventh century but set during the reign of Charlemagne, the *Song of Roland* tells the story of a Frankish military leader battling the Saracens – the medieval term for the eighth-century Arab conquerors of the Iberian Peninsula; thirteenth-century translations of *The Book of Mohammed's Ladder* into Romance languages influenced Dante's *Divine Comedy*; in seventeenth-century France, the playwright Jean-Baptiste Racine wrote *Bajazet*, a piece of theatre set at the court of the Ottoman Sultans; half a century later, Montesquieu alluded to Islamic themes in an epistolary novel criticising despotism, entitled *Persian Letters*; while his fellow Enlightenment thinker Voltaire wrote the controversial play *Fanaticism or Mahomet the Prophet*. Of more recent date are John Buchan's adventure novel *Greenmantle* from 1916, about a Jihadist conspiration set in the First World War, and *Alamut* (1938), a romance by the Slovene writer Vladimir Bartol, featuring the Ismaili sect that became known as the 'Assassins'. This literary history also begs the question as to whether there is something like an 'Euro-Islam', a term that began circulating in the first decade of the new millennium.[4]

So far, I have used the words 'Europe' and 'European' without question or qualification, that is, with the implicit assumption that it is clear what we are talking about. In her recent, wide-ranging but very readable book *How the World Made the West*, the historian and archaeologist Josephine Crawley Quinn shows how what is now a supposedly clear geographic denotation has a long history of ambiguity. This comes twenty years after fellow historian Nancy Bisaha noted, in her *Creating East and West*, a study of depictions of Muslims and Islam by Renaissance humanists, that it was only in the fifteenth century that Aeneas Silvius Piccolomini (1405–64), the later Pope Pius II, coined the adjective 'European'. She goes on to argue the following:

> This shift substantially expanded the discourse of East and West, allowing humanists and others to think and speak of themselves, their ways of life, their learning and arts as belonging to a larger, coherent collective. It is crucial to note that Aeneas's sense of this cultural unity arose from a perception of opposition to the Turks and 'Asia' – not from any genuine sense that European countries shared many strong similarities beyond religion and a common language of Latin among the elite.[5]

It is ironic that both Bisaha and Quinn interrogate the terms 'European' and 'Europe' in books with the word 'West' in the title. While carefully unpacking the etymology of these two cognates, they have unquestionably equated them with the West, leaving differences between the 'old continent' and (former) settler colonies in the 'New World' unaddressed.[6]

Outline and Conceptual Framing

I have no intention of providing an encyclopaedic coverage of Islamic referents in contemporary European literature. The various chapters provide only keyhole views of how Islam and Muslims feature in literary texts, but the diverse and divergent insights they offer do have the pretension of being representative of the variety in Islamic referents found in European literatures. The selection includes authors from different generations writing in both major and minor European languages. Two chapters give impressions from the geographical areas where, in the past, Muslims established a centuries-long presence on the continent: the Iberian Peninsula and those parts of South-Eastern Europe that were conquered by the Ottoman Turks. The sequence of chapters is not chronological, either in terms of the authors' lives or the appearance of their writings, or with respect to the themes with which they engage and the periods they describe. As a matter of fact, as my account progresses, I will actually go back in time, only to end with some of the most recent, and in some instances very controversial, novels featuring Muslims and Islam.

The first three chapters revolve around single authors for whom Islam and the Muslim world remained a sustained interest throughout their writing careers. It concerns two individuals with Muslim roots whose engagement with their Islamic heritage or legacy is not tied down to a specific time or place, but who themselves are nonetheless firmly embedded in the cultural spaces of the German language and the Francophone milieu respectively. The title of the first chapter, 'West-Eastern Affinities', is taken from an essay collection by Navid Kermani, which in turn is an obvious nod to Johann Wolfgang von Goethe's *West-Eastern Divan* (1819). Not only did this German polymath seriously engage with Persian poetry, and indeed with the wider cultural achievements of the Muslim world, but he also engaged with Islam's main sacred text, the Qur'an.[7] Moreover, it was also Goethe who coined the term 'world literature' (*Weltliteratur*). A German writer with Iranian roots, Navid Kermani has been the recipient of many literary prizes and other accolades, while his growing standing as a public intellectual is reflected by an invitation to address the German parliament (*Bundestag*) on the occasion of the sixty-fifth anniversary of the country's constitution in 2014. He also shares my academic background as a scholar of Islam, thus creating an additional and personal east–west affinity that definitely also played a part in my selecting him for this book. The double genealogies in the second chapter refer to the multiple cultural belongings of Abdelwahab Meddeb. Although his academic specialisation is in the field of comparative literature, thanks to his Tunisian lineage of religious scholars Meddeb was also familiar with traditional Islamic learning. After his migration to France, he was engaged in myriad cultural activities: aside from creative writing, he also worked as a translator and publisher, and as a producer and presenter of radio programmes, as well as working as an academic, teaching at universities in France and abroad, and co-editing a volume on the history of Jewish–Muslim relations. Chapter 3 gravitates around the Muslim presence in the Western parts of the historical *Dar al-Islam* or Abode of Islam, in Arabic referred to as *al-Andalus* where it concerns the Iberian Peninsula, or *Maghreb* when it also encompasses North West Africa. At one point the most translated Spanish writer after Cervantes, Juan Goytisolo was not an academically trained orientalist, but as he became increasingly concerned with the cultures on the southern shores of the Mediterranean, he did acquire a command of Moroccan colloquial Arabic (*darija*), and later also studied Turkish. His lifelong critique of the hegemonic aspects of contemporary Spanish culture and politics was initially informed by Marxism, but became increasingly oriented towards the hybridity of the Iberian Peninsula's premodern cultural-historical experiences during a Muslim presence that lasted from the early eighth to the end of the fifteenth century. Islam-related themes have dominated his writings since the 1970s, expanding from the Muslim West to also include novels, essays and reportage about the Eastern Mediterranean and Caucasus. The next chapter moves from the western reaches of the Muslim world to encounters with Islam on the south-eastern edge of Europe. Coverage is also expanded from single authors to three writers from Albania and the former Yugoslavia who have made the region's Ottoman past the subject of their creative writings. Although the historical novels set in his native Bosnia during Ottoman times earned Ivo Andrić the Nobel Prize for Literature, he being a Catholic Croat by origin his approach is definitely that of an outsider. But also, the affinities with Islam of the Bosniak Meša Selimović and Albania's Ismail Kadare are ambiguous at best. The final chapter features two winners of France's most prestigious literary award, the Prix Goncourt. Although their work proceeds from very different angles, there are nonetheless thematic convergences in Mathias Énard's and Michel Houellebecq's concerns with Islam and Muslims. Belonging to the same generation as Navid Kermani, as an Arabist and Persianist by training Énard also shares a comparable academic background with the German author. In line with his reputation as one of the most controversial figures on the international writing scene, Houellebecq seems to flaunt an anti-intellectual attitude. However, despite the notoriety he has achieved as a supposed Islamophobe, a closer reading of Houellebecq's several novels featuring Islam and Muslims not only leaves a more ambiguous impression, but also evinces serious reading and research belying an alleged lack of erudition.

I am conscious that the above outline leaves me open to two criticisms. First of all, the absence of women writers in the selection. The reason for that has to do with the development of this project. The research turned up such a wealth of material that the originally-conceived single volume will be expanded to two separate monographs. The second volume, which will present global coverage, will feature women writers.[8] Other readers may question the omission of authors writing in English. This is not an oversight but an intentional choice and conscious decision. Partly motivated by the fact that, with Brexit, the UK has chosen to no longer consider itself as a part of Europe, it is also borne out by the orientation of many anglophone authors from Muslim backgrounds towards their origins in Britain's former colonies in South Asia and Africa. Moreover, the writings of South Asians have certainly already received extensive coverage in the context of area studies, as well as the generic fields of postcolonial and subaltern studies. Again, authors from Asian and African backgrounds will be part of the other volume on world literature.

A study with a scope as wide as the present book requires an accretive conceptual structure that can accommodate the different themes and genres, geographical coverage and varying backgrounds of the selected authors. Instead of a constrictive framework, the following sections are best understood as a map for situating the various case studies in a wider landscape of ideas, showing how the thematic concerns and religious referents branch off as part of a rhizomatic network of philosophies and theories. For the interpretative template and the theoretical underpinnings holding these chapters together, I return to some of the ideas and notions that informed my earlier research and the concepts I have used in that work, augmented with some new insights I have gained since then. These concepts include cultural hybridity and third space, cosmopolitanism and enlightened or affirmative Orientalism. As for the epistemological dimensions of this intellectual-historical research, in my first endeavour, *Occupants of the Third Space* (2009), later published as *Cosmopolitans and Heretics: New Muslim Intellectuals and the Study of Islam* (2011), I applied these concepts in combination with the hermeneutics of Paul Ricoeur, whose charitable or generous interpretations leave room for accommodating other developments in contemporary thinking, including postmodern philosophies and postcolonial theory, which I have continued to explore since then.[9]

Cultural Hybridity as Positionality: Liminality, In-betweenness, *Entre-deux*

With respect to cultural hybridity, I find what I have learned from contributions by Norbert Bugeja and Ludmila Peters particularly useful for the present purposes, not least because their critiques of cultural hybridity form part of their work as scholars of literature. In the introduction to his *Postcolonial Memoir in the Middle East*, entitled 'Rethinking the Liminal', the Maltese poet and postcolonial studies specialist Norbert Bugeja takes issue with those elaborations of cultural hybridity and liminality (from the Latin *limen*, 'threshold') by postcolonial theorists that remain 'part of a metropolitan discourse serving to reify global power relations and the spread of Western liberalism under the guise of a subversive ethos, a concept at once relational and exclusivist, ostensibly dissident but also, at heart, deceptively reactionary'.[10] Interrogating the lack of analytical and philosophical rigour and grounding of what he calls post-structuralist 'metaphors of dispersal' (2), Bugeja singles out a text with which I too have engaged on an earlier occasion. In *The Location of Culture* (1994), Homi Bhabha coined the term 'Third Space' to refer to cultural hybridity as a subversive force and give currency to what Bugeja paraphrases as 'the rhetoric of the "Transformative Power of the In-Between"' (3). To Bugeja's mind, discourses of liminality such as Bhabha's, while 'disarticulating the perceived authenticity of national, ethnic, religious, or identitarian narratives' (11), at the same time harbour the peril of depoliticising historically situated concerns for liberation and emancipation. Still, that does not lead Bugeja to dismiss the potentially empowering virtues of the liminal altogether:

> While it is patently impossible to generalise a theory of liminal or ambivalent spaces – which accounts for Bhabha's inevitable recourse to abstraction – it is very possible to outline those salient properties which render a liminal literary consciousness relevant within a particular political and cultural scenario. (12)

Instead of using the postcolonial theory of Homi Bhabha, Norbert Bugeja proposes a reformulation that goes back to its earlier conceptualisation by such anthropologists as Victor Turner. Turner's understanding of liminality can be properly deployed in questioning the existing dominant global order along the lines of political and social critics as different as Theodore Adorno, Noam Chomsky, Edward Said and Slavoj Žižek. Turner identified liminality as the middle stage in a three-tiered structure of rites of passage; a transitory phase, and therefore necessarily ambiguous and subversive. By interpreting liminality as anti-structural 'seedbeds of cultural creativity' (7), in line with the contingencies of societies' underlying norms and values, in his seminal study *From Ritual to Theatre* (1982), Turner singled out literary texts as spaces where such anti-structural liminality can find expression. Liminality is also part of a process, constituting an intermediate stage preceding the reconstitution phase, that is to say, the 'subject's re-incorporation into the prevalent normative body' (28). As some of the case studies will show, several of the authors discussed in this book have used creative writing to challenge hegemonic discourses of normativity, but also as an emancipatory device for the acceptance of otherness.

A more charitable reading of Bhabha's theorising of cultural hybridity and liminality is provided in Ludmila Peters' *Religion als Diskursive Formation* (*Religion as Discursive Formation*, 2020). A Germanist and scholar of comparative literature, Peters too pushes back against the complicity of Middle Eastern writers with what Bugeja called 'the expansion of Western metropolitan criticism and self-serving forms of Eurocentric thought'.[11] With the help of notions taken from Stuart Hall, such as 'unclean concept' and 'subversive force', instead of employing it as an analytical tool, Peters argues that cultural hybridity can be reinterpreted as an aesthetic praxis of dislocation, thus salvaging Homi Bhabha's cultural hybridity as a polemic metaphor to challenge the binary thinking that informs the 'dialectical logic of identity' of other postcolonial theorists, including that of Edward Said.[12]

The pitfalls of postcolonial theories of cultural hybridity signalled by Bugeja and Peters therefore do not disqualify the use of the figure of the in-between. In fact, alternative formulations of the *limen* as threshold or as in-betweenness have also been put forward by the Iranian philosopher Daryush Shayegan.[13] In *Cultural Schizophrenia* (1997), he connects the state of in-between (*entre-deux* in the author's original French) with the 'narration of a hypothetical "I"' to reveal the contradictions affecting this narrative ego on the level of the individual, and how the resulting schizophrenia leads to false consciousness in the political domain.[14] Shayegan's use of the psycho-pathological term 'schizophrenia' suggests a connection with the Capitalism and Schizophrenia project of the post-structuralist philosophers Gilles Deleuze and Felix Guattari. Explicit references to their seminal *A Thousand Plateaus* (1980), and to Deleuze's equally important *Difference and Repetition* (1968), are deferred to one of Shayegan's later publications, a collection of short essays published under the title *La lumière vient de l'Occident*. Translating as *The Light Comes from the Occident*, this must not be taken as a provocative inversion of the adage *ex oriente lux*, in the sense of a triumphant celebration of European Enlightenment thinking or an implied superiority of Western rationality. Quite the contrary: the title alludes to a treatise by the Persian mystic and philosopher Sohrawardi (Persian rendition of Shihab al-Din al-Suhrawardi, 1154–91).[15] Nicknamed *al-Maqtul* – 'the Slain One' – on account of his death while imprisoned in Aleppo, and also to distinguish him from two other Sufis named al-Suhrawardi, he was the founder of a school of intuitive wisdom known as Illuminationism (*ishraq*). Shayegan's provocation therefore consists precisely in calling into question the dominant epistemologies associated with Eurocentric modernity. In *The Light Comes from the Occident*, he also trades the notion of cultural schizophrenia for 'polyphrenic consciousness'.[16] In sections with the telling titles 'Harlequin Identity' and 'Zones of Hybridization', his discussions of 'double displacement' (140) and 'double decentering' (170) contain references to Tzvetan Todorov's dual phenomena of acculturation and deculturation and to Gilles Deleuze's rhizome (145). Shayegan also identifies the *entre-deux* with the Persian notion of the *barzakh*, the state of limbo in which the human soul initially finds itself after death, and with yet another Persian notion: *nâ kojâ âbâd*, or 'nowhere land' (217). This is a metaphor that stands for the world of images and archetypes between the domains of the intelligible and sensible around which gravitates his illuminationist episteme.[17]

Cosmopolitanism: Rooted and Worldly

Aside from Homi Bhahba's Third Space, in earlier research I have also engaged the writings of sociologist Ulrich Beck on second modernity and realistic cosmopolitanism; the examinations of the cultural dynamics between the cosmopolitan and the local by the anthropologist Ulf Hannerz; and the comparative cosmopolitanisms of the intellectual historian and literary scholar Bruce Robbins.[18]

The latter's attention to local inflections resonates with the notion 'rooted cosmopolitanism'.[19] The term as such was introduced in 1992 by the then editor of *Dissent*, Mitchell Cohen, but its conceptual prequel can already be found in Ulf Hannerz's article 'Cosmopolitans and Locals in World Culture' (1990). As Sidney Tarrow explains in his book *The New Transnational Activism* (2005), on the back of the changing world order following the collapse of the Communist bloc in Eastern Europe, rooted cosmopolitanism was further developed through interventions by philosophers, political scientists and sociologists like Anthony Kwame Appiah, Craig Calhoun, David Held, Martha Nussbaum and Jeremy Waldron, bringing together cognitive and relational views, including cosmopolitanism's connection with patriotism. The reason for adopting it here is the potential creative leap that can result from the interactive 'encounter between local socialization and a newer different reality'.[20] In fact, the link between philosophical thinking about cosmopolitanism, Islam and contemporary literatures becomes manifestly clear from the opening pages of Waldron's 'Minority Cultures and the Cosmopolitan Alternative' (1992), where this leading philosopher of law uses Salman Rushdie's defence of his controversial novel *The Satanic Verses* (1988) as his own 'point of departure to explore the vision of life, agency, and responsibility that is implicit in this affirmation of cosmopolitanism'.[21] Waldron places Rushdie's claim for personal freedom in the wider context of the debates between liberals and communitarians. He defends the author's choice against rigid liberal interpretations by the likes of Dworkin and Rawls: 'A choice running rampant, and pluralism internalised from the relations *between* individuals to the chaotic coexistence of projects, pursuits, ideas, images, and snatches of culture *within* an individual' (754). In the same breath, Waldron also invokes Rushdie's essay 'In Good Faith' to reject the claim made by communitarians, such as Alasdair Macintyre, Michael Sandel, Charles Taylor and Michael

Walzer, that people need to take part 'in the substantive life of a particular community as a source of meaning, integrity, and character' (754). The particular advantage of an alternative – cosmopolitan – vision is that it enables us 'to think a little more grandly about the scale on which community and friendship are available for the constitution of the individual and the sustenance of friendship and interdependence' (777), in other words, to cater for the possibility of multiple belongings. Waldron's use of Rushdie's cosmopolitan ideal acts as a counterpoint to the homogeneity that underpins nineteenth-century ethnic nationalism and that has also been implicitly adopted by communitarians and identitarians alike to forge their strong – but deceptively reductive – identity claims. Rooted cosmopolitanism offers 'a richer, more honest, and more authentic response to the world in which we live than a retreat into the confined sphere of a particular community' (788).

Rooted cosmopolitanism has therefore also a bearing on the literary counter-narratives to Islamic communitarianism pursued in the case studies of this book. These are not read as frivolous manifestations of diversity or plurality, but taken seriously as exponents of creatively addressing fundamental questions of human dignity. In this respect, it is important to take into account that such acts of individual creativity are instances of cultural production that do not take place in a vacuum, while simultaneously recognising that any given cultural heritage is a composite of disparate elements of varied provenance, and that any given social setting remains exposed to. and can avail itself of, a multitude of cultural material. It is in articulating this dialectic dynamic that a rooted understanding of cosmopolitanism, grounded in what Waldron calls an interdependence thesis based on the Aristotelian notion of the human as a *zoon politikon* (a political, and therefore social, animal), can enact its mediating function.

In a much shorter reflection, published eight years later under the title 'What Is Cosmopolitan?' (2000), Waldron wants to dispel the misunderstanding that had arisen from his earlier article, namely that a cosmopolitan lifestyle is incompatible with remaining immersed in a particular culture. For that purpose, he returns to Kant's notion of the cosmopolitan right, which must be understood 'not so much as a substantive thesis of what the law ought to be, but as a way of designating an area of human life and interaction with which law, right and justice ought to be concerned'.[22] Waldron points at the connection made by Kant between the outward circumstance of the earth's spherical shape and the human disposition to wander, travel, explore and settle new regions. However, this innate human curiosity about how others live is not just offset by a shortfall in taking these others seriously in their very alterity, but also by 'the temptation to plunder and conquer, and exploit, enslave, or even exterminate others' (237). Thus the idea of the cosmopolitan right was primarily understood as a set of constraints governing what a people was entitled to do in the course of this process as they came alongside strangers, or what they were entitled to do when strangers came closer to them. As a jurist and philosopher of law, Waldron is interested in the consequences of the cosmopolitan right for civic responsibilities: in a mobile and migratory world, this notion is bound to have 'interesting implications for social and political organization' (239).

At this point, it is instructive to digress for a moment into *The Passage West* by the Italian political and social philosopher Giacomo Marramao. Subtitled *Philosophy After the Age of the Nation State*, this study introduces the concept of a 'cosmopolitanism of difference': the product of a set of push-and-pull factors that form a 'conjunctive-disjunctive hyphen between the global and the local [where] one finds the key to interpreting the proliferation of fundamentalisms and the politics of identity'.[23] Drawing together the notions of *mundus* and *globus* as the origins of the French-Italian and Anglo-Saxon cognates of continental *mondialisation/mondializzazione* and oceanic *globalisation* respectively, Marramao's cosmopolitanism of difference distinguishes between, on the one hand, a spheric geometric conceptualisation of globalisation that informs cartography and atlases and, on the other, an anthropological understanding of mondialisation concerned with inhabitants of that sphere, with humankind. However, both represent a passage of Western universalism to a new vision of spatiality and time. Marramao's cosmopolitanism of difference also undermines projections of an all-encompassing, yet at the same time very Eurocentric, notion of Empire as advocated by radical leftist ideologues such as Hardt and Negri. According to Marramao, a more attentive analysis of the ideas they borrowed from Deleuze and Guattari should also have led Hardt and Negri to the conclusion that 'in the space comprised by this new techno-political and socio-cultural interdependence, the web of power appears to be without a summit and without a centre' (39). This has resulted in a transition from territorially-oriented nation-modernity to a world-modernity:

> The more modernity expands, spreading the economics and aesthetics of the commodity on a global scale, the more Western society is permeated by cultural 'alterity'. [...] the two-pronged optic underlying the thesis of the passage to the Occident will be translated, through the theoretical programme of a universalism of difference, into a revival and 'transvaluation' of the cosmopolitan paradigm of the modern. (15–16)

Although Marramao remains wedded to the modernity project and seeks to offset the drawbacks of postmodernism along the lines of Alain Touraine's radical revision of the structuralist presuppositions of French sociology and Ulrich Beck's earlier-mentioned notion of a Second Modernity (20), I suggest that Marramao's advocacy of a cosmopolitanism of difference finds its postcolonial and postmodern refraction in Hamid Dabashi's notion of worldly cosmopolitanism (or cosmopolitan worldliness, as he sometimes also calls it). As a specialist in the intellectual history of the Muslim world in premodern times, Dabashi saw this particular cosmopolitan disposition exhibited in the literary humanism of the classical Persian poets, whose writings later also captured the imagination of European thinkers from the Enlightenment era and writers from the age of Romanticism.[24] This worldly cosmopolitanism forms but one component in a long-term philosophical project that culminated in what Dabashi refers to as a hermeneutics of alterity. As I have already unpacked many of Dabashi's ideas elsewhere, here I will only rehearse its main points.

Towards a Hermeneutics of Alterity

Situated in the interstices of the intellectual history of Islam, cultural criticism and political engagement, the writings of Hamid Dabashi bring together several of the strands of thought I have touched on earlier in this Introduction. Aside from explicit references to post-structuralists, such as Gilles Deleuze and his Italian fellow 'philosopher of difference' Gianni Vattimo, Dabashi's hermeneutics also bears a family resemblance to Paul Ricoeur's Hermeneutics of the Self, developed in the latter's *Oneself as Another* and applied in his writings on religion found in *Figuring the Sacred* – albeit it with a twist, in the sense that Dabashi directs the gaze at a fusion of horizons missing from the myopic vision of most European hermeneuticians and post-structuralists. Dabashi has laid out the trajectory towards this hermeneutics of alterity in three books. The first, *Islamic Liberation Theology* (2008), presents the project's blueprint. This book grew out of earlier historical studies on the history of Shi'a thinking until the modern era and on the eleventh-century Persian legal scholar, philosopher, mystic and poet Hamadhani.[25]

In the second volume, *Post-Orientalism* (2009), Dabashi seeks to replace the collapsed and obsolete dichotomous world-view of a binary 'West versus the Rest' opposition.[26] In this book, Dabashi offers what he calls an Islamic liberation geography; an alternative that provides a better fit for a world that is not only post-colonial and post-modern, but also post-Islamist, post-Western and – indeed – post-Orientalist.[27] European imperialism and Islamist reactions to it were two sides of the same coin: a functional opposition that worked for two centuries, but that must now be considered as outdated. There is a remarkable parallel between the collapsing of these binaries in Dabashi's *Post-Orientalism* and what Gianni Vattimo wrote in a chapter in *The End of Modernity*, entitled 'Hermeneutics and Anthropology', where he criticised Richard Rorty's understanding of cultural anthropology as overly Eurocentric.[28] As a result of the relentless Europeanisation and westernisation of the world, which also continues in our postcolonial times, Vattimo argues that non-Western cultures have been turned into construction sites of 'hybrid traces and residues contaminated by modernity'. These construction sites of 'third world societies and the ghettos of industrial societies' (158) are none other than Dabashi's post-Orientalist and post-Western world where metropole and colony, centre and periphery intermingle.[29] However, the inherent violence of this dichotomy has not yet dissipated. Quite the contrary: instead of dissolving, violence has proliferated, except that it is now structured in accordance with newly emerging globalised social systems. The essays in *Post-Orientalism* are therefore also a double critique of Western and Muslim thinking, which forms the hallmark of Dabashi's hermeneutical concerns.

Finally, there is *Being a Muslim in the World* (2013), which offers what I propose calling a new ethos for today's decentred world, where in fact the phrase 'towards a hermeneutics of alterity' is used as the title for that book's conclusion (158–60). Dabashi's hermeneutics of alterity offers a counter-narrative to the identity politics that have shaped both European thinking since the Enlightenment and the oppositional reactions by Muslims emerging in the course of the age of high imperialism:

> That hermeneutics of alterity, which I propose has always been definitive of Islamic intellectual history and worldly experiences, has been categorically eclipsed and compromised by the politics of identity imposed on Muslims under colonial duress, and in that state of colonial duress, Muslims themselves have been instrumental in that fateful transmutation of their own collective integrity. 'Islam' has never been a reduction of Muslims to what the Sunnis and the Shi'is have thought of each other, or what mystics and philosophers have said about each other. Islam has been the metamorphic sublimation of the constellation of those dialectics, and never the tribal reductionism of that constellation to one sect or another. Islam has been a hermeneutics of alterity sublated to a gestalt view of Muslims of themselves.[30]

Dabashi's trilogy forms an interlocking set of thoughts and ideas, which not only stand in opposition to the identity politics of the modern era, but also offer an alternative to the underlying strong truth claims of what Dabashi refers to as the 'metaphysics of identity'. In that sense, Dabashi's hermeneutics of alterity also mirrors the weakening strategies which Gianni Vattimo devised for his 'ontology of decline', where epistemological, political and theological concerns come together to forge a new ethics focusing on 'beings' rather than 'Being'.[31] In fact, Dabashi directly borrowed Vattimo's notion of 'weak thought' to develop his own alternative regime of knowledge exhibiting the kind of epistemological modesty, intellectual humility even, needed for opposing the strong, yet reductive, theses of identity politics and the underlying equally over-confident truth claims of the metaphysics of identity.[32] By way of illustration, I refer to the parallel between Vattimo and Dabashi's idiosyncratic interpretations of the theological notions of kenosis and theodicy. In its original Pauline meaning, kenosis refers to the emptying out of God into world through the figure of Jesus Christ. Vattimo calls this transformation of transcendence into immanence a 'weakening' of God, who is no longer absolute in the sense that such an incarnation of the divine in human form constitutes a non-violent way of revelation promoting emancipation and justice. As a hermeneutics of open possibility and becoming, 'weak thought' takes kenosis as an enduring process continuing to this day through the constant rereading of scripture and re-interpretation of its revelation.[33] Similarly, Dabashi does not use the term 'theodicy' in the conventional sense of the word: as an explanation for evil in the world. Instead, he reads it as radical difference or alterity, allowing for shades and shadows of truths, rather than the certainties associated with the absolute truth claims grounded in a metaphysics of identity that can only think in terms of binary oppositions and thus lead to the kind of othering that underlies dichotomous world-views.[34]

Other Weakening Strategies: Nomad Science and Nomadic Thinking

The use of Vattimo's 'weak thought' also attunes Dabashi's hermeneutics of alterity to another alternative regime of knowledge laid out by Deleuze and Guattari in a part of *A Thousand Plateaus* entitled 'Treatise on Nomadology'.[35] Their idea of a 'nomad science' has since been adopted under the name 'nomadic thinking' by the Italian-Australian philosopher and theorist of feminism Rosi Braidotti in *Nomadic Subjects* (2011) and in *After Cosmopolitanism* (2012), or as '*pensée nomade*' (nomad thought) by Daryush Shayegan in *The Light Comes from the Occident*, which carries the subtitle *The Re-Enchantment of the World and Nomad Thought*.

This figure of the nomad is employed metaphorically, in the sense that the pastoral peoples inhabiting the deserts of the Middle East stand for a generic way of thinking that can be traced back to the emergence of the monotheist religions in that part of the world.[36] It stands in opposition to sedentary thinking, which refers to those epistemes or regimes of knowledge that have dominated throughout written human history. Deleuze and Guattari have also employed the alternative designation 'minor science', which stands in contrast to state, royal or even imperial sciences. The latter are defined by such characterisations as ideal, exact, organised and formalised, circular and fixed in terms of their essence, whereas the former is described as vagabond and vague, yet rigorous and consistent, round and possessing a morphological essence. Sedentary thinking or royal science is associated with the theorematic thinking of Euclid, whereas nomad science is problematic and Archimedean in orientation.[37] So what Deleuze and Guattari want to present are two different conceptualisations of what constitutes reliable knowledge, which are nonetheless ontologically located in a single field of interaction, where

> royal science continually appropriates the content of vague or nomad science while nomad science continually cuts the contents from royal science loose [...] nomad science is not a simple technology or practice, but a scientific field in which the problem of these relations is brought about and resolved in an entirely different way than from the point of view of royal science. (405)

Nomad and sedentary thinking are also situated in different conceptualisations of space called smooth and striated respectively. Again, striated and smooth spaces do not refer to the conditions of the landscape in a specific geographical area. Like nomad and sedentary, these are again metaphors for the contexts in which particular ways of thinking occur. Deleuze and Guattari associate the sedentary striated space with chess as a game of regulated warfare with identifiable front-lines and battlefields, whereas the smooth space of the nomads has more affinity with Japanese board game of go: a war without confrontation or retreat – no battles, no front-lines even, but pure strategy. Striated space is a closed domain with walls and roads between enclosures and is regarded as relative and global, while the smooth habitat of the nomad is open, and described as both absolute and local.[38]

Describing the nomad as 'the deterritorialized par excellence' (421), within the framework of the present examination of the Islamic contexts of religious referents in literature, Deleuze and Guattari make two important observations: first of all, that 'nomads and migrants can mix in many ways' (419), and that 'those who joined Mohammed at Medina had a choice between a nomadic or bedouin pledge, and a pledge of hegira or emigration' (420), although it was also the case that already 'early Islam favored the theme of the hegira, or migration over nomadism' (423). And yet, even a 'monotheistic religion, at the deepest level of its tendency to project a universal or spiritual State over the entire ecumenon, is not without ambivalence or fringe areas' (423). Secondly, with a tip of the hat to George Bataille's *The Accursed Share*, Deleuze and Guattari go on to explain:

> We are referring to religion as an element of the war machine and the idea of holy war as the motor of that machine. The *prophet*, as opposed to the state personality of the king and the religious personality of the priest, directs the movement by which a religion becomes a war machine and passes over to the side of such a machine. It has often been said that Islam, and the prophet Mohammed, performed such a conversion of religion and constituted a veritable esprit de corps: in the formula of Georges Bataille, 'early Islam, a society reduced to the military enterprise.' This is what the West invokes in order to justify its antipathy toward Islam. Yet the Crusades were a properly Christian adventure of this type. (423, original italics)[39]

In *The Light Comes from the Occident*, Daryush Shayegan elaborated his understanding of nomad thought in tandem with the earlier-mentioned Deleuzian notion of the rhizome.[40] He suggests that Deleuze used this figure in an earnest attempt not so much to dig for the foundations of European philosophy as we know it, but rather to uproot the metaphysical justifications for its tree of knowledge, and to present the rhizome as an alternative for this prevailing arboreal model of thinking.

Critical as she is of 'dominant visions of the subject, identity and knowledge', in Rosi Braidotti's *Nomadic Subjects*, philosophical nomadism functions as a counter-discourse too.[41] Rhizomatic in itself as it grows organically from a cluster of interrelated ideas and capable of entering into a series of interdisciplinary connections with other discourses, nomadic thinking 'challenges the separation of critique from creativity and of reason from the imagination' (13). However, as the title of her book already betrays, Braidotti is primarily concerned with nomadic subjectivity. Her configuration of the nomad is not metaphorical, but a 'transformative account of the self'. Without considering it antithetical to other philosophical traditions, but rather as an alternative creative space of becoming, Braidotti envisages a 'relocation of identities on new grounds that account for multiple belongings' of what she calls a 'nonunitary vision of the subject' (10). In the opening chapter of the essay collection *After Cosmopolitanism*, entitled 'Becoming World', Braidotti 'splits open the classical idea of cosmopolitanism' (36) and reworks it into a 'nomadic form of reflexive cosmopolitanism' (37). Moving away from ahistorical Eurocentrism towards an alternative genealogy of universalism inspired by Ulrich Beck's *Cosmopolitan Vision* and his notion of Second Modernity, she insists:

> A nomadic cosmopolitan philosophy can sustain the contemporary subjects in the efforts to relate more actively to the changing world in which they try to make a positive difference. [...] The key method is an ethics of respect for

> diversity that produces mutually interdependent nomadic subjects and thus constitutes communities across multiple locations and generations. (59)

Whereas this understanding of cosmopolitanism as 'becoming world' demands a decentring of the human as a sovereign subject, and while this move beyond humanist individualism 'entails the criticism of narrow-minded self-interests, intolerance and xenophobic rejection of others' (36), its transposition of notions like 'hybridity, nomadism, diasporas, creolisation processes into means of re-grounding claims to connections and alliances among different constituencies' (47) can produce a 'philosophy of radical immanence and affirmative belonging' (56) geared towards the pursuit of hope and attentive to the interconnection between self and community in the name of a new humanism.

Retrieving Literary Humanism and Worldly Cosmopolitanism: A New Rhetorical Device

With his hermeneutics of alterity, Hamid Dabashi too points at a new humanism. It was already noted earlier that Hamid Dabashi regarded Persian literary humanism as the supreme premodern embodiment of a disposition of worldly cosmopolitanism.[42] In the chapter 'The Muslim Cosmopole' from *Being a Muslim in the World*, under the heading 'Retrieving the literary', Dabashi rehearses this again in order to work towards a new – contemporary – worldly imagination. Just as Gianni Vattimo noted that an ontology of decline needs a new dialect with its own grammar and syntax, so Hamid Dabashi's hermeneutics of alterity requires a new idiom too. To elucidate this a bit further, I invoke one more passage from Giacomo Marramao, where he criticises the persistent Eurocentrism of substantive communitarianism, procedural liberalism, and the rational ethics underlying Habermas's theory of communicative action:

> It is not the dialogic-discursive elaboration of singular and collective experiences so much as narrative elaboration. Only through the elaboration of effectively lived singular and collective experiences can values escape the closed, self-referential schema of principles [...]. The philosophical implications of such a proposal should now be clear. It is as much a case of overcoming the abstract, 'logocentric' idea that assigns normative primacy to discursive rationality as it is a case of overcoming its specular opposite that refers the entire horizon of experiences to diverse and incommunicable islands of the symbolic.[43]

In a similar vein, Hamid Dabashi envisions for his hermeneutics of alterity a new rhetorical device that defies schematisation and categorisation:

not oppositional but appositional, because there is no east or west; contrapuntal and centrifugal in its challenges to the centripetal tendencies of Islam's own dogmatic nomocentric juridicalism, which suppressed both the logocentric interests of Islamic philosophy and the anthropocentric focus of mysticism with their shared openness to cultural heteroglossia.[44]

Theologies of Immanence and Becoming

Aside from being the progenitor of nomad thought, in a lecture series from 1956–7, later published as *What Is Grounding?* (2015), and in the book *Pure Immanence: Essays on a Life* (2001), Gilles Deleuze pursued various other lines of thought that have had a bearing on postmodern thinking about religion, whether articulated in terms of antifoundationalism or theologies of immanence and becoming.

His findings concerning the connection between ground and principle in *What Is Grounding?* are not only relevant for Deleuze's own thinking about religion: they also inform Dabashi's hermeneutics of alterity. From his examination of the great systemic thinkers Leibniz, Kant and Hegel, and of the subsequent critiques by Husserl and Post-Kantians, Deleuze concluded that – unlike theology – philosophy 'cannot [...] take in the idea of creation' (168). Another finding engendered by this genealogy is the importance of poetry; more specifically, the ambition of the German Romantic writers to produce a '"philosophy", not a psychology of the imagination' (169). Interpreted as a purely creative dynamics, it is, Deleuze concludes, 'not about discovering the other world and essence beyond appearance. The task of philosophy is to discover what appears. Essence no longer has anything to do with philosophy' (172). In his introduction to *Pure Immanence*, John Rajchman calls this Deleuze's empiricist conversion: 'It is about saying yes to what is singular and yet impersonal about living; and for that one must believe in the world and not in the fictions of God or the self that Hume thought derived from it' (18).

In *Deleuze and the Naming of God*, Daniel Barber takes Nietzsche's link between God and the power of imagination as the 'capacity to generate a world' as Deleuze's 'theopolitical' point of departure.[45] Aside from echoing Dabashi's hermeneutics of alterity and its concomitant disposition of cosmopolitan worldliness, this particular understanding of immanence also resonates with other scholars working in the interstices of philosophy and theology, such as John Caputo (spectral hermeneutics), Kevin Hart (non-metaphysical theology), Richard Kearney (the god-who-may-be) and Mark C. Taylor (deconstructive a/theology). Although Caputo, Hart and Taylor primarily engage with continental philosophy and Christian theology, there is a remarkable parallel in Taylor's take on theodicy and the earlier-mentioned interpretation by Dabashi, as becomes manifestly clear from the juxtaposition of the following two passages:

> In Western theology, theodicy is usually understood as the vindication of divine justice and holiness in the face of what seems to be obvious evil. Although theodicy appears to express predominantly theological concerns, it is actually motivated by essentially anthropological interests. Claims to the contrary notwithstanding, the issue that theodicy addresses is less the holiness and justice of God than the intelligibility, hospitality, and coherence of man's [original emphasis] world.[46]

> Theodicy in this sense is not accounting for any 'evil' in the world, but the presence of diversity, alterity, shades and shadows of truth [...] Theodicy of liberation liberates Islam itself, before anything else, from the dogged dogmatism of its nomocentric juridicalism having brutally supressed its own logocentric and homocentric domains in Islamic philosophy and mysticism.[47]

The similarity between these two interpretations of theodicy extends beyond the theological into the literary. Recognising that 'when the book is normative, theology tends to be systematic [...] or even scientific', Taylor goes on to argue that, since modern theology has moved beyond normativity and beyond the 'omnipresent logos [...] that structures the systematic theologian's book', there is no other option for the theologian than to become a 'writer'.[48] In *Being a Muslim in the World*, Dabashi too notes that in order to 'be searching for God in all the right places [...] what we need is not a political argument, but a hermeneutic imagination in excavating key concepts from our moral and intellectual heritage'.[49]

Meanwhile, Dabashi's agenda for pushing Islamic legalism, with its nomocentric bias and metaphysical logocentrism, from its pedestal in favour of Sufism's anthropocentric interest in the imaginary finds a counterpart in Kevin Hart's affinity with mysticism as the challenger to metaphysical theologies (Hart 1991), whereas, in a chapter entitled 'In the World: Between Secular and Sacred' from *Anatheism: Returning to God after God* (2011), Richard Kearney not only discusses contemporary Muslim intellectuals such as Mohammed Abid al-Jabri, Mohammed Arkoun, Hasan Hanafi and Abdolkarim Soroush, but also invokes scholars and writers from the classical era of Islam, such as Biruni, Ghazali, Hafiz, Ibn Arabi and Rumi.

Orientalism: Critique and Affirmation

Unavoidable in the case of a book about Islam (or rather Muslims) and Europe are a few words on Orientalism and Edward Said's landmark book with that title from 1978. In its intention, *Orientalism* was a critique, a structuralist analysis of the study of non-Western cultures in terms of power and politics.[50] That such an approach can invite the very essentialism it seeks to criticise is ironically borne out by the uncritical reception of the book by some as the gospel truth, all too often accompanied by an admiration for its author that borders on hagiography. That this was not what the author envisaged is borne out by the careful qualification of his understanding of Orientalism in the book's Introduction, and the nuances articulated in an article that was published seven years later under the title 'Orientalism Reconsidered'. In this regard it is also instructive to read the new afterword to the re-issue of *Orientalism* in 1995. Said's robust, at times belligerent and hostile, responses to the detractors of his book shows that *Orientalism* was indeed intended first and foremost as a critique of colonial policymaking in Europe vis-à-vis the Muslim world, and the Arab world in particular. Consequently, *Orientalism* has its blind spots. These have been sympathetically, and at times satirically, criticised in Daniel Varisco's *Reading Orientalism: Said and the Unsaid* (2007); combatively opposed by Robert Irwin in *For the Lust of Knowing: The Orientalists and their Enemies* (published in the USA as *Dangerous Knowledge: Orientalism and its Discontents*, 2006); used for signalling a constructive alternative (based on Homi Bhabha's interpretation of hybridity); called 'affirmative Orientalism' by Richard King in his *Orientalism and Religion: Postcolonial Theory, India and 'The Mystic East'* (1999); or complemented by a survey of Orientalist scholarship in German, which Said indeed only touches on in passing.[51] Edward Said would be hard-pressed not to agree with most of these responses, even with a hostile critic like Robert Irwin's advocacy for a more generous appreciation of the individual scholarship that lies at the basis of Orientalism as a field of academic inquiry. In fact, he has not only acknowledged the importance of this individuality, but has also self-identified as a professional 'humanist' (9) in the tradition of Giambattista Vico and Erich Auerbach (one of the few Germans featuring in *Orientalism*), qualifying the 'best Orientalist work' as 'humanistic scholarship' (258).[52] Said's view of all cultural production as first and foremost the work of people (not peoples, as Josephine Quinn recently noted) makes him also an opponent of both Islamism (331) and 'gloating and uncritical nationalism' (338). As a scholar of comparative literature and erudite aesthete, he would be appreciative of studying Islam and Muslims in the postcolonial age through the lens of contemporary literature.

Only someone who believes in the Highest can throw stones all the way up to Heaven.

Navid Kermani, *The Terror of God*, 134

I know of no other poem, Western or Eastern, that seizes the essence of Islam as easily and at the same time with such rich ambiguity as Goethe's succinct, poetically elegant 'Talismans'.

Navid Kermani, *Between Quran & Kafka*, 89

Not Goethe with his learned Diwan or Rückert with his artistic Ghazals, no, Hölderlin, who is not particularly interested in the Orient, is the Sufi of German literature, the eccentric, the fool, the ridiculed, all the way to the outcry, to the burn-out, to dissolution. The others write about mysticism, he embodied it [...]

Navid Kermani, *Über den Zufall*, p. 63

Chapter 1

West-Eastern Affinities

A writer from a Muslim background who dares to claim that he has learned more about the most fundamental questions concerning religion from one of the founders of the Frankfurt School than from the Prophet Muhammad is bound to have something interesting to say about Islam. This is especially so when he also happens to have an academic background as an Orientalist.

Navid Kermani (b. 1967) was born in Siegen, Germany as the fourth son of Iranian immigrant parents who saw a brighter future in Germany than in their home country. Instead of following the family tradition and becoming a physician, he decided for the humanities, studying Arabic and Islam, as well as philosophy and drama, in Cologne, Cairo and Bonn. As a teenager he had already begun writing for newspapers, including the reputable *Frankfurter Allgemeine Zeitung*. Although he completed postgraduate and post-doctoral studies in Islam, instead of pursuing an academic career Kermani opted for an existence as what is called a *freier Schriftsteller* (freelance writer) in German. Since then, he has developed into a very versatile author, producing novels, short stories and plays, as well as reflective prose, including literary and art criticism, travel writing, reportage and opinion pieces. He is the recipient of more than twenty awards, honours and prizes; his standing as a public intellectual was affirmed in 2014, when he was invited to address the federal parliament on the occasion of the 65th anniversary of the German constitution. His speech left such an impression that it even led to – somewhat exaggerated – speculations about Kermani's possible candidacy for the Republic's presidency.[1] Navid Kermani is often associated with migrant literature, but does not consider himself a part of that. Carrying both German and Iranian passports and feeling at home in both cultures, he associates his self-admitted imperfect command of Persian with the spoken word and the intimacy of family, but regards the German language as his literary *Heimat*. Emphasising the universality of the Enlightenment project, Kermani advocates replacing ethno-nationalism and its sinister excesses with constitutional and cultural patriotism.[2] His double belonging as a German writer with Iranian-Islamic roots exercises a strong influence on both his appreciation of German literature and his attitude towards identity politics – especially its religious components. Illustrative in this regard is the remark that, as a writer, he considers himself 'as German as Kafka' – who, after all, was a Jew from Prague writing in German.[3] In the essay collection *Between Quran & Kafka: West-Eastern Affinities*, Kermani explains it thus:

> The Quran and Kafka really did designate two poles between which my writing oscillates: revelation and literature; religious and aesthetic experience; the history of the Islamic and the German-speaking cultures; the Orient and the Occident. But the Quran in particular, and Kafka's works in particular, were important points of reference to me for many years. (16)

Obviously intended as a tribute to Goethe's *West-Eastern Divan*, this reference to two poles seems to carry a whiff of binary thinking or a dichotomous world-view, but that is not the case.[4] Reading the connections between his belonging to two cultures through the lenses of Homi Bhabha or Daryush Shayegan's interpretations of cultural hybridity, or the rooted cosmopolitanism originating with Ulf Hannerz, Navid Kermani's attitude towards Germany and Islam, religion and Europe, is best understood organically or rhizomatically.

Navid Kermani's first two books were Islam-related academic studies based on his doctoral dissertation on the aesthetic experience of the Qur'an and a post-doctoral study (known in German as *Habilitation*) of theodicy. Published commercially as *Gott ist schön* (1999) and *Der Schrecken Gottes* (2005), they were later released in English translation under the titles *God is Beautiful* (2015) and *The Terror of God* (2011).[5] Because Kermani's approach to Islamic studies is not just historical-philological but literary-critical as well, and because their influence has carried over into his own literary writings, both publications also merit attention in the context of the present book.[6]

The Qur'an as Literature

For *God is Beautiful: The Aesthetic Experience of the Quran*, Kermani was awarded the Ernst Bloch Prize. By taking the Qur'an as a literary text, he treads in the footsteps not only of classical religious scholars, but also of (near-)contemporary Muslim academics and intellectuals such as Amin al-Khuli, Muhammad Khalafallah and Nasr Hamid Abu Zayd, as well as scholars from non-Muslim backgrounds, including Angelika Neuwirth.[7] In this context, Navid Kermani has also been instrumental in introducing Abu Zayd and his work to Western audiences.[8] Elements of Abu Zayd's groundbreaking use of structural linguistics and semiotics in his analyses of the Qur'an have found their way into Kermani's *God Is Beautiful*. In order to demonstrate that this is not a modern or profane imposition, Kermani also draws on the composition doctrine of the Persian grammarian and literary theorist Abd al-Qahir al-Jurjani (1009–78). Moreover, the aesthetic experience of the Qur'an's so-called 'inimitability' (*'i'jāz*) does not just rest in its structural composition and poetics, it also has an auditory component. Both aspects form an integral part of the Qur'an as a religious phenomenon, in which the aesthetic-literary is closely bound up with theological-doctrinal. Using the notions of collective and cultural memory developed by the French philosopher Maurice Halbwachs and the German Egyptologist Jan Assmann to explain the workings of the Qur'an text and how it affected Muslim audiences since Islam's earliest beginnings, Kermani drives home an important point in his engagement with literature and religion, the enduring normative and formative force exercised by myth:

> Whoever regards fiction and reality in terms of a rigid duality, not only fails to recognize the cultural–historical and religious–phenomenological significance of even the most subjective and improbable testimonies of faith, but also of reports on the reception of the Qur'an.[9]

The disconnect signalled by Kermani between aesthetics and truth is a modern phenomenon that has no equivalents in earlier epochs, when there was a persistent structural relation between life, values and aesthetic means. In this regard, Kermani finds it instructive to make an excursion into the notion of *Sprachmagie* or 'the magic of language'. That it cannot be dismissed as archaic or obsolete is attested by the interest it commanded among intellectuals as different as Gershom Scholem, Ernst Cassirer or Walter Benjamin, either interpreting it as a positive foundation for theological *Sprachmystik* or reading it negatively as a linguistic-analytical critique of a Wittgensteinian disenchantment of language. Hellenic, ancient Persian and Eastern cultures remained in awe of language, as did the Muslims after the early formative period of their cultures' first audiences came to an end. A post-Enlightenment re-appreciation of the magic of language on the part of the German Romantics was also retained by certain modern-day writers from both Muslim and non-Muslim backgrounds.[10] Others who recognised this regression into a kind of remythologisation of language and the return to the magical also included two of Kermani's favourite philosophers,

Theodor W. Adorno and Max Horkheimer. However, Kermani singles out Franz Kafka as the 'most prophetic' (84) among modern writers who attempted to find words that had not been emptied of meaning and turned into clichés. With a nod to Umberto Eco, Kafka's novels and stories are also presented as emblematic of those literary works that have been emphatically designed as 'open' texts (134). This particular reference parallels the suggested openness of revealed texts advocated not only by present-day non-Muslim Arabists, such as Norman Calder and John Wansbrough, but also by certain scholars from Islam's classical age, such as the earlier-mentioned grammarian al-Jurjani or his fellow Persian Abu-'l-Qasim al-Zamakhshari (d. 1143), who made his name as a *mufassir* or exegete of the Qur'an. Kermani argues that this is 'not a theological dilemma, but rather a necessary implication of a message sent by God' (131). To my mind, Kermani's mention of Wansbrough's comparison of the Qur'an with a torso, and Calder's likening it to a Chinese painting, as illustrations of this suggested incompleteness of a revealed text resonate with Dabashi's reliance on Vattimo's interpretation of kenosis as an invitation to a never-ending interpretation of scripture.[11]

In order to avoid any false parallels between Christian and Muslim understandings of scripture, it is important to recognise a fundamental difference. In terms of theological doctrine, Muslims take the Qur'an as the *verbatim* revealed word of God, whereas the Hebrew Bible and the Gospels are historical accounts written by humans. This ontological difference has had implications for both the canonisation and translation of the source texts, and – with this – the literary appreciation of scripture. To illustrate this distinction, Kermani draws on a diachronic cross-section of Christian views of the Bible, ranging from the church fathers, via the reformers Luther and Calvin, to theologians and philosophers such as Nicolaus Zinzendorf, Johann-George Hamann and Maurice Blondel, all of whom rejected the use of adorned or ornamental speech. When it comes to religion, simplicity and clarity should be the rule, so that the divine message is transmitted unambiguously. This substantive approach was only challenged during the Enlightenment and in liberal Christian theology, when aesthetics was allowed into the Christian tradition.

In the Islamic context the opposite is the case. This is why Kermani suggests that *'i'jāz* should not be translated as 'inimitability', but rather as an 'incapacitation' or 'annihilation' of any attempt to compete with the Qur'an's linguistic and poetic excellence (240). The superiority of its language – not only captured in its formal composition but also in the auditory experience of the Qur'an (after all, its literal meaning translates as 'that which is recited') – is to be taken as 'a kind of aesthetic proof of God, which does not have its parallel in the cultural sphere of the West' (241).[12] Aside from its aesthetics, hearing the Qur'an has an epistemological aspect as well: 'it is *sami'a* (hearing), not so much *qara'a* (reading), that leads to the cognitive act (*'aqala*)' (173), Kermani says. In this respect, it is also worth mentioning that Kermani adopts Paul Valéry's suggestion about comparing a poem to a musical score for his argument that 'the Qur'an is a good example of poetry being the transition from speech to music, and that the fluidity of a text only unfolds in its sounds' (183). This reliance on (near-)contemporary intellectuals with musical interests, such as Valéry and Adorno, also serves to set Kermani's approach to Islamic studies apart from those of scholars who lack such sensibilities and who remain tone-deaf as a result of their privileging of the written word alone in the study of scripture. In a wider sense, accepting the absolute dominance of the subjective in all aesthetic experience also helps to counteract the academic skepsis that dominates much scholarship on Islam: 'Does not the collective subjective experience of an audience constitute an objectivity that is more verifiable, and scientifically more convincing, than judgements of taste made by European philologists under their desk lamps?' (243), Kermani rhetorically asks. Any remaining doubt as to where his own affinities lie is dispelled by the following passage:

> As a book, talisman, calligraphy, recitation, or quote, in traditional Muslim everyday life, revelation becomes what Kenneth Cragg has called 'a sort of accompaniment to life, in the musical sense of the word – the theme by which the believer is articulate, like the singer in the song'. (224)

I will return to this point in the next chapter, where I will signal a meeting of minds between Navid Kermani's scholarly examination of the aesthetic experience of the Qur'an and Abdelwahab Meddeb's novel *Talismano*, underscoring once more that for many Muslims the initial encounter with scripture is auditory.[13]

God Is Beautiful already prefigures some of Kermani's concerns in his later literary writings. In the book's penultimate chapter, he addresses the Prophet Muhammad's objection to being likened to a poet.[14] The reason for his dislike of poetry was the Arabs' tendency to associate poetic inspiration with being possessed by a *jinn*, the Arabic term for demonic entities of pre-Islamic origin, and also the source word for the English genie. Its derivative *majnun* (possessed by a *jinn*) nowadays carries the connotation of madness or insanity in a pathological sense of the word, but it also means being 'love-crazed', as in the countlessly retold seventh-century tale of Leila and Majnun.[15] What cannot be denied either is how 'Muslim representations of revelation (*waḥy*) point up astonishing parallels with theories of inspiration and the essence of the artist', formulated by German Enlightenment thinkers and Romantics as part of their so-called *Genieästhetik* (the English translation 'aesthetics of genius' (316) does not quite capture the German original). Whereas Friedrich Schiller suggested that both divine and artistic inspiration derived from the same kind of naivety, Goethe, Herder and Kant stressed that it also requires elements of deliberateness and necessity. The most compelling formulation of *Genieästhetik*, however, Kermani detected in Friedrich Schelling's transcendental idealism, which argues that the unity of conscious and unconscious, subjective and objective, free and necessary activity is not just given by nature, but requires a knowing subject who is aware of this. This makes the work of art a product of free activity and a higher necessity. Schelling's distinction between art as a trade-like skill that can be acquired and poetry as a naturally given ability also reflects the difference between prophets and poets: 'The way philosophy relates to art according to Schelling resembles that of reason and revelation for many Muslim thinkers' (333). While the thin line between aesthetic genius and madness – think of the poet Hölderlin, the composer Schumann or the philosopher Nietzsche – brings us back to the Prophet Muhammad's reservations against poets, the fact remains that 'a whole series of qualities, which modern European intellectual history reserves for artists, Muslim imagination attributes to the Messenger of God' (319).

Theodicy as a Counter-theology of Heretical Piety

The final chapter of *God Is Beautiful* also anticipates Kermani's next academic book, which examines theodicy through a comparative study of the biblical story of Job and the Persian poet Farīd al-Dīn 'Aṭṭār of Nishapur (d. c. 1221). The latter figure is introduced in a section already entitled 'The terror of God'. At face value, the awe-inspiring and terrifying aspect of God appears to be diametrically and irreconcilably opposed to divine beauty. However, they are actually inseparable, as Rudolf Otto has tried to capture with the phrase *mysterium tremendum et fascinans*.[16] The Islamic equivalent is found in the twin notions of majesty (*jalāl* in Arabic) and beauty (*jamāl*), and their parallel effects of fear (*khawf*) or terror *hayba* (terror), and joy (*faraḥ*) or bliss (*surūr*). As Sufism is regarded as one of the prime outlets for the manifestation of these concepts, this is an opportune point for a momentary digression into the place of Sufism within the wider Islamic tradition.[17]

This concerns, especially, the question as to whether Sufism (*tasawwuf*) can be considered an Islamic variant of mysticism. Although this has indeed been a matter of debate among scholars of Islam, Navid Kermani does use the terms interchangeably – as do many reputable specialists in the field.[18] When doing so, however, a few points need to be kept in mind. First of all, it is important to recognise the Christian connotations attached to the English term 'mysticism' and its equivalents in other European languages. In contrast to Christian meditations on divine love as embodied in the Christ figure, Sufism refers to spiritual practices that are directed inward, aiming at knowing the divine by letting go of ego and the notion of self. This is often formulated as repressing the *nafs* – the Arabic-Islamic term for the lower, or animalist, desirous, part of the human soul, in order to open the way towards the transcendent, and the experience of divine love.[19] Being conscious of these specifics also helps to avoid essentialising Sufism or reducing it to some kind of perennialism. Equally important is to avoid a dichotomous understanding of Sufism as the supposedly binary opposite of what the historian Marshall Hodgson called 'sharia-minded' understandings of Islam.[20] Quite the contrary; observing the acts of worship (*ʿibādāt*) and adhering to the basic tenets of the faith (*ʿaqīda*) are prerequisites for being able to pursue the mystical path (*tarīqa*). Also, Sufi saints, or what Muslims refer to as 'the Friends of God' (*Awliyāʾ Allāh*), have developed their own epistemological apparatus, producing a massive corpus of texts on what in Arabic and Persian are called *maʿrifa* or *ʿirfan*. Often translated as gnosis – intuitively acquired knowledge – or esotericism, the resulting regime of knowledge is distinct from but not opposed to *ʿilm*, discursive knowledge dependent on external, transmitted sources (*naql*) and the faculty of reason (*ʿaql*). Sufi epistemology must be regarded as complementary, helping the believer to access domains that cannot be comprehended rationally and captured discursively.[21]

In *The Terror of God*, Kermani does not limit himself to how Job and Attar confronted and responded to human suffering. Here too, he extends his engagement to other literary figures and intellectuals, believers and atheists, from both East and West. From the beginning, the question of how God's omnipotence, divine qualities of love and justice can be reconciled with suffering and evil is set up with references to Persian and European writers and thinkers, such as Ibn al-Rawandi and Sadegh Hedayat, Heinrich Heine, Georg Büchner and Ernst Bloch. Kermani's examination is premised on his dissatisfaction with the 'best of possible worlds' thesis put forward by both Muslim and European thinkers, such as al-Ghazali and Leibniz. Kermani proposes a different attitude towards suffering. A restoration of the biblical practice of lamenting the pain and misery inflicted on humankind is not enough. Instead, Kermani advocates a more confrontational approach. Not satisfied with merely challenging and quarrelling with God about what remains of His justice in the face of human suffering, he insists on translating such expressions of discontent into un uprising – rebellion even – against God. Such a reaction to theodicy is in effect what in the subtitle of the book is called a 'metaphysical revolt'. In *The Terror of God*, Kermani presents such a response as a heretical formulation of a counter-theology by the most pious, holding God accountable for the suffering in the world.[22] Kermani's exposition parallels the earlier-mentioned idiosyncratic interpretation of theodicy by Mark C. Taylor, while his use of terms like revolt and quarrelling with God (*hadern mit Gott*) also echo Dabashi's characterisation of Shiʿism as a 'religion of protest'.[23]

While Attar is the book's central figure, *The Terror of God* also pays attention to the biblical figure of Job (Ayyub in the Qur'an) and the Job motif in Islam, as well as Attar's relationship with the Jewish tradition (242ff).[24] In comparison to other classical Persian poets, there is little certain biographical information about Attar. Attar lived at the time of the first Mongol invasions, and Kermani has compared his eventual disappearance with the occultation of the twelfth Shiʿa Imam.[25] Even though Goethe barely mentions him in his *West-Eastern Divan*, and in spite of his frequent omission from the usual list of the Seven Greats, alongside Firdausi, Hafiz, Jami, Omar Khayyam, Rumi, Saadi or Sanaʿi, Kermani considers Attar one of the greatest poets in Persian.[26] Known first and foremost for the parable *The Conference of the Birds* (*Mantiq al-Tayr*) and for a hagiographic collection of thirty-nine Sufi life-stories, entitled *Biographies of the Saints* (*Tadhkirat-ul-Awliyā*), Attar is thought to have written a total of 114 literary works – the same number as there are chapters in the Qur'an. In *The Terror of God*, Kermani presents a close reading of a text called *The Book of Suffering* (*Mosibat-Nameh*), crediting the Orientalist Helmut Ritter with unlocking what is 'very likely one of the darkest works in world literature' (48).[27] Kermani goes on to note that the erudition displayed in Ritter's book on Attar, *The Ocean of the Soul* (1955), was so overwhelming that since then hardly any scholar has dared to venture into a penetrating study of Attar. Not to be intimidated, Kermani writes:

> What remains to be discovered is that Attar stands not only between Sanaʿi and Rumi, but also between Sophocles (d. ± 404 BC) and Schopenhauer (d. 1860), that he is related to Abu Aʿla al-Maʿarri (d. 1058) and Omar Khayyam, but also to Büchner and Beckett. As obvious as the specific Sufi connotations and allegorical potential of his verses may be, at the same time they unfold – often

even literally – existential, metaphysical or social meanings, that can be understood both historically and universally. (49–50)

Composed as a frame story that follows the Sufi practice of the forty-day retreat (*khalwa*), Attar narrates a wanderer's journey through the Cosmos in forty stages.[28] Kermani analyses the structure and themes of Attar's *Book of Suffering*, an account of rigorous self-examination, by pointing out parallels, affinities and shared concerns with the seventeenth-century mystic Blaise Pascal and the nineteenth-century German philosopher Arthur Schopenhauer, but also by signalling the contrasts with the alleged heresies of Sufis such as Abu Yazid al-Bistami (804–74) and Husayn ibn Mansur al-Hallaj (858–922). After reflecting on the End of Times and yearning for annihilation, Attar ends his account with the wanderer sinking into the ocean of his own soul. In the final chapter, however, there is a twist, as the wanderer's apparently subdued acceptance of fate is replaced by the words of a defiant poet, who challenges and confronts God about humankind's fate of suffering. Senseless or unjust misery 'has been treated in world literature as the actual reason for unbelief, or more accurately: the inability to believe, the loss of faith – "the rock of atheism", as George Büchner (d. 1837) called suffering' (32). This is not what happens in Attar's book. While his religious furore sets Attar apart from many modern-day literary writers, he nonetheless rejects the various options developed in the Abrahamic religions to absolve God of the responsibility for evil and suffering. Holding God accountable is not an expression of unbelief or a move towards atheism, however. On the contrary, it reflects a deep belief in and love for God or, as Kermani puts it: 'Only those who believe in the most High can throw stones all the way into Heaven' (172). Within the Islamic context, this religiously sanctioned charge against God is primarily found in the mystical or Sufi tradition, and it is therefore no coincidence that Attar employs either the figure of the anonymous ascetic or that of the madman to level these accusations. What Attar presents is also an instance of what Heinrich Heine identified as the third possible response to suffering in the world – besides justifying or rejecting, even denying the existence of, God. Here Kermani signals a 'turn toward the utopian' (68), thus bringing the philosopher Ernst Bloch (1885–1977) into the picture. The expression 'metaphysical revolt' in the subtitle may have been borrowed from Albert Camus, but it is Bloch who provided Kermani with the arguments for his own interpretation of reacting to theodicy in terms of rising up against God and formulating a counter-theology:

According to Bloch, completely a-religious atheism conflicts with the changeability of the world. That which is does not have to be everything. For Bloch,

> resistance per se has a religious moment, because it presumes the utopia of another world than the existing one. Although it is not so that wherever there is religion there is also hope, but in his book *Atheism in Christianity*, he wrote the reverse in italics: '*Where there is hope, there also is religion.*' (34)

That Bloch forms a suitable interlocutor for such an conversation across cultures and religions will be taken up again in the final chapter of the present book, where the unpacking of a seemingly minor text, in which Aristotle is refracted through the lenses of medieval Muslim philosophers, shows not only how the Marxist philosopher tore down both the East/West binary and a dichotomous view projecting pre-modern versus modern thought, but where the translator also recalls remarks by Max Scheler and Siegried Kracauer that Bloch was 'running amok with God' or 'fornicating with God'.[29]

To underscore his own interpretation of the rebellion against God as an expression of faith, not a turning away from God as atheists do, Kermani actually challenges Bloch's reading of the Book of Job and its implications for Muslim interpretations of the metaphysical revolt. Kermani disagrees with Bloch's assertion that the eventual surrender by a rebellious 'primordial Job' (*Urhiob*) is an addition by latter-day editors of the biblical text corpus. Rebellion runs like a red thread though the Hebrew Bible. Even when one disregards such text-historical arguments, 'a schematic breaking-down into a rebellious and docile Job is not convincing from a substantive perspective' (152). The Book of Job wants to retain the contradictory effects produced by misery; 'it is not an instance of engaged literature, but rather a complex composition of conflicting motifs, which do not cancel each other out' (153). A reading that is more attentive to this ambivalence is all the more important for dispelling the impression, an implicit consequence of Bloch's suggestion, that the absence of Job's rebellion against God in the Qur'an can simply be explained by Islam's submissive mentality. For a correct appreciation it is necessary to consider the specific textuality of the Qur'an. In contrast to the biblical account, the Qur'an reduces the story of Job to the aspect of endurance. Job laments but does not accuse; in fact, he barely speaks. Compared with that in the Bible, the Qur'anic relationship between God and humankind is presented in a more uniform manner. As the Qur'an is considered the verbal word of God, there is no talking to or about God. Kermani also highlights another contrast. Whereas Christian doctrine has increasingly suppressed the Job motif, in the Islamic tradition it has gradually grown in prominence: 'Not least because the rebellion against God returns early and all the more distinctly when Muslims began to discuss God theologically' (167). Disregarding the Qur'anic restrictions,

Kermani credits the Sufis in particular with restoring the biblical Job motif in its fullest sense. That is why Attar's *Book of Suffering* is neither a denial of religion nor a call to heresy. What Ernst Bloch has failed to take into account is that lamentation and rebellion are an integral part of faith. Theologically and spiritually, they are turned into a liturgical motif, as evinced by the Psalms and mystical texts alike: 'Job is not punished for his protest – he is abundantly compensated' (210):

> Neither Bible nor Attar call for blasphemy, rather they present the rising up against God as an intimate, perhaps even the most intimate moment of faith. [...] It is this dialectical moment that Bloch fails to recognise when he sees the original 'authentic' Job only as a rebel. (211)

Owing to this blind spot on the part of Bloch, Kermani concludes that Attar's *Book of Suffering* would validate only the first part of Marxist philosopher's famous sentence that '*only an unbeliever can be a good believer*', and that Attar could not care less about the second part: '*Only a believer can be a good unbeliever*' (212).[30] Reiterating his earlier assertions concerning text-critical and substantive engagements with the biblical Book of Job, in Kermani's estimation, '*The Book of Suffering* brings into sharper focus that rising up against God actually presumes a rebel's proximity to Him. Thus, the rebellion of the most pious is rooted in this figure of thought' (213). This brings us back to the utopian turn in the epilogue of *The Book of Suffering*, which – in spite of all misery and suffering – clings to the prospect of fulfilment, salvation and happiness. One could indeed sink into the Ocean of the Soul, since no ordinary human can ever reach its shores, but what remains between life and death, however, is exactly that manoeuvring space for reconciliation found in the grand aesthetic designs of the modern. As examples, Kermani points at the writings of Kafka and Pessoa, and the philosophies of Adorno and Benjamin. Also, Horkheimer's ideas on aesthetics and Sadegh Hedayat's novel *The Blind Owl* (another text to be encountered again in a later chapter) resonate with *The Book of Suffering* and the mystic's forty-day journey, pointing up 'the 20th-century's returning figure of thought [...] of holding on, in principle, to the possibility of salvation' (71).[31]

The Literary Writings of Navid Kermani

Navid Kermani's earliest literary publications coincide with his post-doctoral research on theodicy in Islamic contexts. First to appear was *Buch der von Neil Young Getöteten* (*The Book of Those Slain by*

Neil Young): a memoir published in 2002 that blurs the line between autobiography and fiction. This phenomenon, which scholars consider a key characteristic of contemporary literature, is a recurring feature in Kermani's literary production.[32] Torsten Hoffmann and Ludmila Peters, two scholars who have studied Kermani's oeuvre extensively and intensively, refer to such hybrid texts as 'autofiction' or 'meta-autobiography'.[33] Drawing on the work of the French writer and critical theorist Serge Doubrovsky and the Americanist and comparativist Ansgar Nünning, they focus on the distinction between historical and narrative truth: while autobiography connects life and self with writing, meta-autobiography explores the gaps between life and writing.[34] In this liminal genre, the so-called 'autobiographical pact' between author/narrator/protagonist and reader is destabilised by lifting it to a metafictional level, effectively shifting literary writings from mimicking reality towards 'self-reflection on forms of autobiographical writing'.[35] Although *The Book of Those Slain by Neil Young* is not about Islam as such, the title does contain a faint hint. It was inspired by a Sufi text Kermani had discovered when working on his study of the aesthetics of the Qur'an. In *The Book of Those Slain by the Qur'an* (*Kitab fihi qatla al-Qur'an*), the exegete Abu Ishaq al-Thaʿlabi (d. 1035) writes about the diverse ways in which hearing the Qur'an recited can affect listeners, even to the extent of bringing about lethal excitement or shock.[36] It was not the beauty of the Qur'an text that affected these audiences so much, but rather the impact of verses depicting hell fire, or referring to the Day of Judgement, to the imminent test of faith and to the threat of God's punishment, that made 'those Slain by the Qur'an' into examples of the utmost piety.[37] Al-Thaʿlabi did not offer any explanation for these subjective experiences.

Divine Love and Worldly Eroticism

For that, one must consult treatises by theorists of mysticism discussing the notion of mystical fear, for example the Afghan scholar Khawja Abdullah al-Harawi al-Ansari (1006–89), to whom Kermani turns in his first collection of short stories, published in 2004 under the title *Vierzig Leben* (*Forty Lives*). While the title invites a comparison with the forty-stage cosmic journey of Attar's *Book of Suffering*, the paratext refers explicitly to al-Ansari's compendium for spiritual guidance entitled *Stations of the Wayfarers*. Also known as the 'Sage of Herat', al-Ansari belonged to the Hanbali School of Law, known for its strict adherence to the literal meaning of the Qur'an and the Traditions of the Prophet.[38]

This led Kermani's former teacher and renowned Sufi expert Annemarie Schimmel to volunteer the following suggestion:

> The traditional idea that Hanbali rigorism and mystical emotion are mutually exclusive can no longer be maintained [...] Perhaps it was precisely the strict adherence to the outward letter of the God-given law and the deep respect for the divine word that enabled Anṣārī and his fellow Hanbalites to reach deeper understanding of the secrets of the revelation.[39]

Such contrast also strikes a chord with the catholicity of Kermani's attempts to reconcile divine beauty with the terrifying aspects of God, synthesising a unity in line with the core Islamic doctrine of *tawḥīd* – the absolute oneness of God. Characterised as 'a terse Sufi classic' and allegedly dictated by al-Ansari when he was already struck by blindness, *Stations of the Wayfarers* was conceived as a mnemonic device with a hierarchical structure reflecting progressing levels of religious insight and spiritual attainment. In *Forty Lives*, Kermani uses it as a template for organising the various themes explored in his brief portrayals of forty individuals.[40] Al-Ansari's stations numbered one hundred in total, broken down into thematic sections, which are in turn divided into three levels or stages of spiritual attainment: novices, the elite, and the elite of the elite.[41] In the ten stations of the final section, where the seeker or wayfarer's progression culminates in the all-absorbing acute aware of God's unity and unicity (*tawḥīd*), al-Ansari emphasises 'the theme of annihilation with no attempt at the end to balance it with subsistence', as is common to most other Sufi doctrines.[42] This sole focus on annihilation, or extinction of the self (*fanā'*), cancelling out subsistence or continuance of the self (*baqā'*), evinces al-Ansari's 'preference for intensity of expression over precision in meaning [and] disregard for theoretical self-reflection'.[43] It finds a parallel in Kermani's literary writings, where he too 'stresses the ambiguity of God, which is sometimes forgotten in theology'.[44]

For *Forty Lives*, Kermani actually selected the sixth section in *Stations of the Wayfarers*, called the 'conditions', beginning with love, which corresponds to Ansari's 61st station and which he considered 'the last station where the vanguard of the novices meets with the rear of the elite'.[45] This is followed by jealousy (62), yearning (63), agitation (64), thirst (65), ecstasy (66), fear (67), confusion (68), lightning (69) and taste (70).[46] These function as shibboleths for the forty keywords of Kermani's own making under which the partially fictionalised biographical episodes are presented and woven into 'a web of connections between individuals, representing the tensions and contradictions that are inherent to these relations'.[47] The resulting confrontation with the subjectivity, inauthenticity and ambiguities of storytelling are not intended as some a kind of postmodern project, but simply the consequence of an attempt to faithfully present the way life is. The very brief, but detailed, accounts are not so much short stories as vignettes of concrete individual experiences. They seem to hint at Kermani's interest in the thought of Theodor Adorno, who had already noted in his 1933 inaugural lecture at the Institute of Social Research that 'the mind is indeed not capable of producing or grasping the totality of the real, but it may be possible to penetrate the detail, to explode in miniature the mass of merely existing reality'.[48]

As was already the case with *Those Slain by Neil Young*, in *Forty Lives* too, religious referents remain for the most part implicit. However, the thematic concerns that preoccupied Kermani in his academic writings on aesthetics and theodicy in Islamic contexts continue to shine through in both these literary exercises in life-writing. And yet, when dealing with the challenges, uncertainties and randomness that seem to determine the human condition, there are also more calculated allusions. For example, the name of the protagonist in the opening episode was not created on a whim. The story's opening paragraph explains that Dariush Nicolai Oetmuller's family name establishes him as the son of a German father, while his first and middle name refer to the Iranian-Georgian origins of his mother. There might even be more to it than that. Selecting an indeed quintessentially Persian name like Dariush may seem obvious, but it will also be recalled that Daryush Shayegan, the philosopher mentioned in the Introduction, was of Iranian-Georgian extraction. Dedicated to Kermani's academic mentor, the Arabist and scholar of Islam Stefan Wild, the first story, presented under the header 'Hope', narrates the unrequited love of a besotted and cuckolded Dariush. It connects the protagonists of this contemporary piece of life-writing with the earlier-mentioned ancient Arabian tale of Layla and Majnun, but with the female counterpart recast into that of an abusive 'gold digger'. Other stories include quotations from the Qur'an, such as the so-called Light Verse (Q. 24:35), and the observation that who kills one soul, it is as if he killed the whole of humanity, while he who saves one life, it is as if he saved all humankind (Q. 5:32). There are also contemplations and reflections on the religious significance of the number one, the use of water as a religious metaphor by Persian Shiʿi Muslims, and linguistic and orthographic aspects of the Arabic and Persian languages, as well as references to the poet Rumi, the Apostle Paul, and the interest of Sufis in the figure of Jesus.[49]

In his second collection of short stories, with the definitely more religious sounding title *Thou Shalt*, Kermani continues his explorations of life's ambiguities under the contrasting aspects of divine and worldly love. Ten of its stories are presented under headings referring to the Ten Commandments of the Bible. When *Thou Shalt* was reissued, almost a decade after its initial publication in 2005, as part of an omnibus, Kermani had replaced the original opening story with a retelling of the story of Hosea. The Hebrew Bible counts Hosea among the so-called twelve Minor Prophets, but in the Christian Old Testament he has a book in its own right. In the Islamic tradition, allusions to the figure of Hosea are made in Qur'an commentaries and other forms of religious scholarship. Considered a 'prophet of doom', Hosea is instructed to marry the harlot Gomer, leaving their offspring, Jezreel (named after the bloodstained valley in northern Palestine), Lo-Ruhamah ('Unloved' or 'Pitied-on') and Lo-Ammi ('Not My People'), tainted. In most interpretations this union between Hosea and Gomer stands as a metaphor for God's enduring relationship with the unfaithful people of Israel.

In a comparative study of *Thou Shalt* and one of Kermani's later novels, *Love Writ Large*, Karolin Machtans suggests that Kermani's retelling of the Hosea story serves to contextualise the power dynamics and incidents of betrayal that mar the relationships between the couples featuring in the other stories of *Thou Shalt*. 'Fantasies of omnipotence and frenzied jealousy, passion and utter dependency' are introduced to make the case that 'divine love can only be accessed through an experience of worldly love, which of course is far from selfless'.[50]

Most significant in terms of its religious references is the eleventh and final story. At the same time, it is also the most disconcerting. Much longer than the preceding chapters, it is not presented under any one of the Ten Commandments, but carries a quotation from Exodus 20.20.[51] Kafkaesque in both its narrative style and in the unfolding of the plot, the closing story features a nameless autodiegetic narrator, who gives an account of how a sadomasochist homoerotic relation between himself, a scholar of religion, and a more senior colleague (remaining equally nameless) turns increasingly violent.[52] From references to his observation of prayer times and other religious obligations, verses from the Qur'an, depictions of Judgement Day, and an enigmatic note containing a quotation from one of the hadith collections, it can be deduced that the older academic came from a Muslim background. In what reads like a statement from a police investigation into the older academic's eventual disappearance, the narrator insists that suicide can be ruled out on account of the former's piety. With a nod to *The Terror of God*, the story goes on to explain that, rather than suffering from a crisis of faith, the professor simply did not trust God, considering him deceitful:

> During our lifetime, God gives us a sense of what could be a consolation – even if it was just the consolation of not-being – just in order to torture us with desire. Since life was just a foretaste of death, he was scared to death of dying; this was exactly how he said it in all seriousness.[53]

Although his photosensitivity had forced him into a reclusive lifestyle, the professor was 'neither a monk, nor ascetic' (333). The narrator corroborates this by citing the following observations from the professor:

> Religion is one thing. The other is life itself, and then especially women and sex, and things like that, as I have already mentioned.
>
> only sexual sensations enable human beings – or at least him, Mr. Professor – to step out of time for a few seconds and that this communication between two bodies surpassed any verbal or general mental understanding. (344–5)

The narrator goes on to explain that his colleague had made himself a subject of scholarly investigation, turning his own experiences, sexual feelings and fantasies into empirical material. Taking the Buddhist premise that life is suffering as his starting point, he had no inhibitions whatsoever in discussing his most intimate feelings and painful personal experiences, because 'the worse [it gets], the more authentic the life' (334). In pursuit of ever new sexual stimuli, the professor – despite repeated assurances that he was not gay – managed to convince his younger colleague to enter into a homosexual liaison, the colleague later recounting the increasingly abusive nature of their interactions in explicit detail.

Given their profession, the conversations between the two scholars often turned to religion. Kermani lets the narrator return to the story of Hosea with which *Thou Shalt* began. Highlighting the neglect of this prophet on the part of Bible exegetes, the narrator expands on the professor's erudition. Moving between examples from the Greek and Latin, Arabic, Hebrew and Aramaic, even Persian and Sanskrit, to illustrate the challenges associated with translating scripture, the professor expresses reservations towards modern-day practices in scriptural exegesis. He deplores the concessions made by contemporary scholars, who only managed to avoid fundamentalist interpretations by denying that religion has any relevance for present-day society. In the same vein, the professor was of the opinion 'that all translations ought to be prohibited, because they only distorted and played down [Scriptures' significance]' (361). At this point, Job makes a comeback too:

> One only had to study the Hebrew text of the Book of Job in order to establish how the translator had reinterpreted a word that actually means

> 'avenger' as 'saviour', simply to make it exegetically more acceptable and also to announce [the coming of] Jesus Christ. (361)

Continuing his rant against the 'scandalous history of bible redaction', the professor moves on to the canonisation of the Gospel, noting that the 'corruption of Christianity' had already begun with the 'biggest swindle in the history of theology': the depiction and interpretation of the miracle of Pentecost.[54] Sufficient grounds, therefore, to forgive God for definitively turning away from humankind.

The combination of explicit sexual description with the use of sacred scripture is not merely intended to shock and provoke; Kermani is too serious a writer for that. It serves to criticise the dichotomous attitudes governing the relation between religion as lived experience and as a field of scholarly inquiry, by exposing the 'self-deception and hypocrisy' of scholars who make a living from scriptural exegesis, but whose personal lifestyles stand in stark contrast to the religious teachings they purportedly study. In illustrating that 'the perversion lies in the instrumentalisation of religion, in its potential for justification and self-justification', Kermani's approach is ecumenical to the extent that he takes examples from both the Christian and Islamic traditions.[55]

Thou Shalt was met with dismay by scholars of religion and theologians of Muslim and non-Muslim backgrounds alike. While the Iranian-born Qur'anic Studies expert Hamideh Mohagheghi was unable the finish the book, it was an uncomfortable read for the Catholic theologian Klaus von Stosch as well.[56] Although he has been instrumental in bringing Navid Kermani to the attention of the German reading public, he considered the comparison between theodicy and the eroticism of human love unacceptable, and its derailment in violence unbearable.[57] *Thou Shalt* can be more profitably approached by an alternative reading through the lens of the 'indecent theology' developed by Marcella Althaus-Reid.[58] Grafted onto her earlier study of the influence of Paul Ricoeur's hermeneutical circle on the formation of liberation theologies, Althaus-Reid's Christology bears a family resemblance to Gianni Vattimo's understanding of kenosis, in the sense that it too speaks of an emptying out of God into the world through incarnation, but emphatically also in human sexuality.[59] Although embedded in Christian theology, given Kermani's ecumenical framework of religious references, Althaus-Reid's excavation and positive reinterpretation of sexuality can nonetheless be fruitfully employed in reading his writings on the religion–sexuality nexus.[60]

Another Freudian Twist: The Death Drive in Navid Kermani's Novels

In his first novel, published in 2007 as *Kurzmitteilung* (*Text Message*), Navid Kermani shifts from *eros* to *thanatos* (death drive), connecting the darker side of lust which he had explored in *Thou Shalt* to mortality and death.[61] Kermani's preoccupation with death in *Text Message* continues in his opus magnum, *Dein Name* (*Your Name*). Both texts include references to the ritual Islamic funeral prayers.[62] However, where in *Text Message* the protagonist (again named Dariush) confesses that his habitual use of the *fatiha*, the opening sura of the Qur'an, 'has nothing to do with piety', the much longer meditation in *Your Name* describes the *takbir* – the exclamation 'God is great!'– as giving structure to the prayers for the dead.[63] While in this last novel the mere invocation of God's name 'spreads through the body like a heat pack', in *Text Message* Dariush almost laconically latches on to 'the Fatiha as a piece of driftwood, too small to keep me afloat'.[64] However, notwithstanding the fact that both novels use death as a leitmotif, they are fundamentally different: in *Text Message*, the deceased is a fictional character, while *Your Name* eulogises real people. What unites them, however, is a 'basic belief that one ought not to accept dying'. [65] Kermani's exclamation that 'it is death that gives life to the novel I am writing' reminds one of the metaphysical revolt he had earlier explored in *The Terror of God*.[66]

Awarded both the 2012 von Kleist Prize and the 2014 Joseph Breitbach Prize, *Your Name* is the product of a low point in Kermani's personal life brought about by the relentless pressure and stress under which a freelance writer and public intellectual must work in an economy that sees culture as a commodity. In this respect, *Your Name* can be read as 'a counter-testimony, a rebuttal of the neoliberal demand that the expressive voice sacrifices itself on the altar of productivity'.[67] A massive tome running to 1,200 pages in small print, *Your Name* presents a mosaic of life-writing, in which the autofiction of an autodiegetic author named Navid Kermani blends with his earlier concerns and interests as a writer. On a later occasion, Kermani himself has described *Your Name* as an exercise in data collection, 'an archive, from which later individual and self-contained albums emerged, which can actually not so easily be separated, but rather grew like branches out of a tree'.[68] Spin-offs from this large book project that have appeared in print so far include a collection of lectures published under the title *Über den Zufall* (*On Coincidence*), the travelogue *State of Emergency*, and a meditation on Christianity on the basis of art and imagery: *Wonder Beyond Belief: On Christianity*.[69]

A meandering meditation traversing Kermani's academic publications and early literary writings, as well as his reportage and travelogues, *Your Name* gravitates around his grandfather's autobiography, a piece of life-writing which was rejected by publishers because it was only about dead people.[70] Kermani uses the manuscript, running like a red thread throughout his own book, to weave together his family history with reflections on his own marriage, and readings in literature and religions, as well as political events and intellectual-religious developments in twentieth-century Iran. The outcome is what Helga Druxes characterises as a 'convoluted epos' composed of an 'amalgam of genres that cannot be categorised'.[71] However, drawing on recent scholarly research on autobiographical writing, Torsten Hoffmann characterises the 'hybrid text-form' of *Your Name* as an example of autofiction, in which Kermani as autodiegetic author shifts the writing of a novel as 'mimesis of reality' towards a reflection on the conflict between how life is lived and how it is written about.[72] While Ludmila Peters also characterises Kermani's novels as meta-autobiographies, I have reservations regarding her characterisation of *Your Name* as a multi-layered work operating on four levels consisting of: (1) a series of twenty-one obituaries; (2) the narrator's everyday life; (3) the grandfather's memoirs; (4) a metafictional exposition on the art of writing and literary production.[73] To my mind, it suggests too much of a hierarchical structure, whereas the narrative makes continuous sideway shifts that go back and forth between the different genres.

The continuing relevance and literary purport of Kermani's scholarly work on Qur'anic aesthetics and theodicy in Islamic contexts is already demonstrated at the beginning of *Your Name*. Both *The Terror of God* and *God Is Beautiful* are explicitly mentioned in the first and third obituaries respectively, in which Kermani notes the importance of a study of Job and Heinrich Heine by the Hungarian writer Istvan Eörsi (1931–2005) and confesses his earlier unfair treatment of the intellectual historian Friedrich Niewöhner (1941–2005). Unaware of the latter's reputation as an expert on Jewish and Islamic thought and background as a former director of the Goethe Institute and university lecturer in the Iranian city of Shiraz, Kermani is embarrassed to learn not only of Niewöhner's appreciative review of *God Is Beautiful*, but also his contributions as a German-Jewish Orientalist to the study of Judaism, Christianity and Islam within their own Eastern contexts and in connection with the cultures of Europe.[74] Kermani dedicated the last-but-one obituary to the scholar who had been the subject of his earliest academic publications, Nasr Hamid Abu Zayd:

> After the death of Nasr Hamid Abu Zaid, I realized that there are not many people of whom we can say with certainty that without them our life would have been fundamentally different. Most of the people we mourn had always been there or have shaped particular life stages, we connect with them our own everyday-life or incisive events. Perhaps they have, without being aware of it, switched a point, which our train is about to pass. Abu Zaid has put me on track. (1,162)

Kermani goes on to explain how, when studying Arabic in Cairo during his early twenties, he began to understand what the Qur'an was all about; that it is not just a book one opens and reads for guidance, verifiable stories, or useful information. It was Abu Zayd who explained that the scripture's significance lies in both its artful recitation, which Kermani admired, and its rhetorical use – and abuse – for preaching hell and damnation, which he abhorred.

Religion also features prominently in the grandfather's autobiography, which was dedicated to the scholar Hossein Ali Rasched and ended with a passage from *Sura an-Nisā'* (The Women): 'O ye who believe! Stand out firmly for justice, as witnesses to Allah, even as against yourselves, or your parents, or your kin, and whether it be against rich or poor: for Allah can best protect both'.[75] Pious, but suspicious of human hierarchies, Kermani's grandfather mistrusted the Islamic revolution which took place two or three years before his death.[76] Kermani also learns that his great-grandfather had been a big landowner and an important religious scholar. Described as 'open-minded, pious and firmly convinced of the Islamic principles' (62), this Ayatollah Hossein Kermani had jumped to the defence of his sister's son-in-law, who had converted to Babism:

> Even for open-minded believers of his generation, the Babis, from which Baha'ism emerged, were an erring sect, manipulated by the colonial powers. In contrast to Christians, Jews and Zoroastrians, this kind of tolerance could not be justified on basis of the Qur'an, which explicitly excludes post-Islamic religions. (63)

The Babi and Baha'i question recurs several times in his grandfather's memoirs, which contain two lengthy chapters entitled 'Freedom of religion and the activities of Baha'i students' and 'Why I did not become Baha'i' (350). This discovery took Kermani by surprise, not just because Bahaism was never discussed in his family, but also because Iranian history books seldom mention the wide influence this new religion has exercised on the country's westernised elites. He was therefore also relieved to learn that, despite serving for more than thirty years as Isfahan's Chief Justice, his great-grandfather had not been involved in the persecution of the Baha'is. In fact, as a sympathiser of the 1905–11 Constitutional Revolution, Ayatollah Kermani would become one of the leading opponents of Agha Najafi (1846–1914), the wealthy cleric who had been the chief instigator of the anti-Baha'i pogroms of 1903.[77]

Throughout *Your Name*, Kermani also profiles several other religious scholars with dissenting opinions or whose conduct seems out of step with that of the stereotypical cleric – or at least what were considered conventionally appropriate behaviour and habits or acceptable doctrinal convictions in the wake of the Islamic reformism that sought to repress the sort of ambiguities that had been characteristic of the Islamic tradition for centuries.[78] From his grandfather's autobiography, he also learns that it was not uncommon for *'ulamā'*, such as great-grandfather Kermani and his colleague Agha Seyyed Abdolhassan Tabnejad, to use intoxicants.[79] Educated in Beirut, Cairo, Damascus and the Iraqi centre of Shi'a learning, Najaf, this Seyyed Tabnejad was an authority on the poetry of Rumi, who – after having turned his back on the law – had 'dedicated his life to love' (398). Illustrative of Tabnejad's own spiritual inclinations is a story about the last wishes he expressed while on his deathbed. After ordering that his extensive library should be distributed among those who would be capable of understanding it, he requested that, after his passing, a friend travel to the city of Arak, where he had maintained a retreat during the years he had served there as a judge. Located in a flower garden, it was a place where he could completely lose himself:

> I became empty, completely forgetting about myself, yes, I became a flower myself, I became one with all that lives. The flowers taught me to understand what the blessed al-Hallaj had meant when he said: 'I am God'; what the blessed Bayezid had meant, when he said: 'Praise be upon me'. (414)

The reason for asking his friend to go there was to set right a grave injustice the Seyyed had committed against a groomsman, whose donkey had eaten the flowers in the garden. Not wanting to punish an innocent animal, he had beaten the groomsman instead. The friend was to find that man and compensate him: 'whatever it costs, make him happy' (414).

As a piece of life-writing connecting autofiction with literary explorations of love, death and mortality, *Your Name* is also an exercise in consciously constructed intertextuality, especially in relation to those key figures from German literature in which Kermani had an abiding interest. At the time of writing *Your Name*, Kermani also delivered the prestigious 2010 Frankfurt Poetry Lectures, which were subsequently published under the title *On Coincidence: Jean Paul, Hölderlin and the Novel, Which I Am Writing*. Here too, Kermani continues to reflect on the complex narrative strategies employed in *Your Name*.

(Re)turn to Sufism

Jean Paul (pen name of Johann Paul Friedrich Richter, 1763–1825) and Friedrich Hölderlin (1770–1843) are key literary figures of German Romanticism. Despite similarities in their family backgrounds and education, and notwithstanding the fact that they resided near each other and shared common acquaintances, it appears the two never met in person. Moreover, no two authors writing at the time could have been more different than Jean Paul and Hölderlin. Although an admirer of both, Kermani expresses a preference for Jean Paul, whose – often humorous – novels and stories deal with the mundane aspects of everyday life, describing in great detail concrete, human experiences that are grounded in reality. Hölderlin's poetry, by contrast, is the epitome of abstraction, which would explain why a philosopher like Martin Heidegger was attracted to him. Although Kermani professes a greater affinity with the outlook and oeuvre of Jean Paul, for the present purpose, his interpretation of the writings of Hölderlin is more relevant. Both *Your Name* and *On Coincidence* contain two similar passages, describing the literary significance of the Tübinger poet, as well as signalling a family resemblance between Hölderlin's religious disposition and Sufism:

> German literati may disparage Goethe, Schiller, Rilke, Celan or Thomas Mann, it is even tolerated to dismiss Kleist and Kafka with a shrug, but nobody finds Hölderlin crap. [...] Of all people, this prematurely deranged eccentric, whom Goethe constantly brushed off, is the canonical German poet.[80]

> Not Goethe with his learned Diwan or Rückert with his artistic Ghazals, no, Hölderlin, who was not particularly interested in the Orient, is the Sufi of German literature, the eccentric, the fool, the ridiculed, all the way to the outcry, to the burn-out, to dissolution. While others write about mysticism, he embodied it.[81]

It is Hölderlin who enables Kermani to open up an Islamic – or more specifically, a Sufi – perspective on German literature. Admitting the brilliance of Hölderlin's *Hyperion, or the Hermit in Greece* for packing so much philosophy and history of ideas into one work, he struggles to reconcile the metaphysical dimensions of Hyperion's pain with his own more mundane worries: an ailing wife, a marriage that is on the rocks, a looming divorce. It is only when reaching the fourth volume of Hölderlin's collected work that it starts to dawn on Kermani:

> The lover does not surrender to anyone, he gives himself up: not a sacrifice, because it implies, sacrificing to an opposite, but rather a dissolution in an

> opposite, and thus an annihilation for the sake of healing: 'die before you do' as the prophet said.[82]

The affinity of Hölderlin's way of writing with Sufism actually echoes what is found in all forms of mysticism. It emerges from Hölderlin's simultaneous progression towards and regression from 'Christian – and therefore personalist – understandings of the Holy to the abstraction of the wholly Other, a pure pneuma, that no longer is but that also is not yet subject'.[83] Aside from hinting at Heidegger's ontological thinking and employing the vocabulary of Rudolf Otto and Karl Barth, Kermani also quarried the idiom of Sufism.[84] Thus he draws a parallel between the Sufi twin notions of *fāqid* (the one who loses) and *wājid* (the one who finds) and Hölderlin's aphorisms: for example, where he speaks of 'a forgetting of all existence, a silencing of our being, when we feel we've found everything'.[85] Turning again to *Hyperion*, Kermani writes:

> Whereas Hyperion always proves to be a dreamer, for whom the fierceness of his love has something liberating, something cathartic; making him face the world, the struggle for success and fame, with an even greater sense of selfishness, it is Diotima who remains behind: Transformed, reaching the *baghâ fi l-fanâ*,[86] what is indeed tragically interpreted as 'remaining in annihilation,' as the Sufis called it, or holy sobriety, as Hölderlin himself calls the state after ecstasy.[87]

Kermani's reading of Hölderlin through the lens of Sufism is unpacked further in *On Coincidence*, where Hölderlin's poem 'Elegy' is related to both twentieth-century poetry and to Persian poets of the classical era: 'Here sounds for the first – and perhaps for the last – time in the German language the [word] ach!, like the *ay!* of the Spanish poets, or the *ey!* of Hafis and Rumi.'[88] In his fourth and fifth lectures, Kermani explores theo-poetics in Hölderlin's *The Death of Empedocles*, which he characterises as a didactic Sufi poem.[89] After establishing that 'from God's perspective, death is the most common [experience]: Everybody dies', whereas 'from the human perspective, we are never so individual as in our dying moment', Kermani concludes:[90]

> Empedocles does not simply kill himself: He throws himself into a volcano, uniting with God as nature, in annihilation – aesthetically by falling silent – he finally wins back unity as eternity: 'There is no I but me', as Sohrawardi reformulated the Islamic Creed in the twelfth century. (195)[91]

Further references to medieval Sufism and the Islamic tradition in general are found in Kermani's novel *Große Liebe* (*Love Writ Large*) and in the essay collection *Between Quran & Kafka*, which both appeared in 2014. Composed of one hundred very brief chapters, ranging in length from a single paragraph to a maximum of two and a half pages, *Love Writ Large* tells the story of the autodiegetic author's first schoolyard love, covering the one hundred days from his first sighting of the beloved up until their break-up. The decision to break this story down into one hundred episodes, and intersperse them with tales about Arab and Persian Sufi saints, conjures up comparisons with the earlier-mentioned *Stations of the Wayfarers* of Abdullah al-Ansari.

The secondary literature on *Love Writ Large* has been selective in its references to the Sufis featuring in this novel, focusing primarily on Muhyiddin Ibn Arabi (1165–1240).[92] Not noticed by literary analysts, but playing a role only second to Ibn Arabi, is Baha-e Walad (d. 1230), the father of Rumi. A theologian and mystic in his own right, in Annemarie Schimmel's estimation 'the influence of his ideas, as yet set forth in his *Maʿārif*, on the formation of Jalāluddīn's thought still remains to be analysed fully'.[93] A close reading of *Love Writ Large* shows that Kermani's references encompass a veritable roll call of central figures from the history of Sufism. It includes key contributors from the formative period of Sufi history, such as Dhul-Nun al-Misri (d. 859), an Egyptian whose real name was Thaubān ibn Ibrahīm and who is credited with formulating 'for the first time a theory of *maʿrifa* or intuitive knowledge of God'.[94] Also cited are the earlier-mentioned Abu Yazid al-Bistami (rendered as Bayazid Bestami) and al-Hallaj, both of whom became famous – or rather, notorious – for their often outrageous exclamations made in a state of rapture.[95] Known in Arabic as *shaṭaḥāt*, these ecstatic outcries were both admired and condemned. Al-Hallaj's teachers Sahl al-Tustari (d. 896) and Abu'l-Qasim al-Junayd (d. 899) are mentioned too.[96] Featuring in the initiation chains of many Sufi orders, al-Junayd advocated the vow of poverty, ascetic practices (*zuhd*) and sobriety (*saḥw*), and was therefore opposed to intoxication (*sakr*). Small wonder, then, that he condemned the behaviour and exclamations of al-Bistami and his former student al-Hallaj. Junayd's most important contribution, however, was the definition of the different stages or stations which the initiate had to pass to attain annihilation or *fanā'* (annihilation). According to Schimmel, reaching *fanā'* is not the ultimate, but rather *baqā'* is, as '"remaining", a new life in God'.[97] For this, Kermani coined the German phrase *bleiben im entwerden*, because, as his late teacher Schimmel explained, 'The German term *Entwerden*, as used by the medieval mystics, is closer to its meaning than words like "annihilation", "being naughted", or "passing away", since it is the opposite of "becoming", *werden*'.[98]

No less controversial than his martyred friend al-Hallaj, but escaping execution himself, Abu Bakr al-Shibli (d. 945) was a former judge, who left office to become one of the most respected Sufis of his time. But he was also an eccentric; according to Kermani 'he was committed at least twenty-two times to mental asylums'.[99] In his effort to become close to God, he was pathologically jealous of those condemned to hell because of the attention they received from his Beloved. Kermani interprets this an affirmation that 'jealousy does not begin with despair, but already with [the stage of] rapture'.[100] The other Abu Bakr included in *Love Writ Large* also did not suffer a violent death: Abu Bakr al-Wasiti (d. c. 932) reflected the sober disposition favoured by Junayd, and it surprised Kermani that someone with such a subdued character and uneventful life as al-Wasiti was yet capable of such statements as 'mercy is found in all divine qualities, except love'.[101] *Love Writ Large* also makes brief mention of several important latter-day Sufis, such as Hodschwiri (Kermani's rendition of the name of Ali al-Hujwiri, d. 1071), Ruzbehan Baqli (Rūzbihān Baqlī, 1128–1209) and Abdulkarim Dschili (Abd al-Karim al-Jili, 1365–1424/8).[102] The first two of this trio came from the Persianate part of the Muslim world. A native of Ghazna in Afghanistan and author of a treatise called *Kashf al-Maḥjūb* (*Unveiling of the Concealed*), Hujwiri was a contemporary of Abdullah Ansari, who ended his days in Lahore, in present-day Pakistan, where his shrine is still an important site of pilgrimage.[103] Baqlī of Shiraz is considered the 'third name in the chain of the great love mystics of Iran'– alongside Ahmad Ghazali (brother of Abu Hamid al-Ghazali) and 'Ayn al-Qudāt Hamadhānī.[104] His most renowned text is entitled *Kashf al-Asrār* (*Unveiling of Secrets*).[105] Al-Jili, meanwhile, is most renowned for systematising the theoretical work of Ibn Arabi, in particular how his emanation theory is exhibited in the concept of the 'Perfect Human' (*al-insān al-kāmil*).[106] Kermani further explores the divine love–worldly love nexus with frequent quotations from the Persian rendition of the story of Leila and Majnun by Nizami (1141–1209) and references to Fachroddin Eraqi (Fakhruddin 'Irāqī, d. 1289) and his *Lama'āt*, or Flashes, a collection of poems inspired by the theosophy of Ibn Arabi.[107]

As the novel's autodiegetic author, Kermani himself also makes an important point about this connection between metaphysical and erotic love. The Sufi tradition frequently employed human love stories and even erotic metaphors to help believers visualise divine love; in *Love Writ Large*, that order is reversed. Here religious experiences and imagery are used to capture the magnitude of the narrator-protagonist's first love affair, or as Kermani puts it: '[While] they are concerned with the creator, I am concerned with the creature'.[108] This last point about the connection between creator and created also features in Henry Corbin's reading of Najm al-Din Kubra (1145–1220/1), to which Kermani referred in *Wonder Beyond Belief*:

> Nadschmeddin Kobra's [Kermani's spelling] understanding of the relation between God and Human is absolutely not as that of father and son, creator and creature. He regards it as the relationship between a lover and a beloved, in which both are creatively involved, whereby the humankind is not just created by God, but God, in turn, owes his existence to humankind. Henry Corbin [...] substitutes the notion of humankind as the son with that of the 'Creative Feminine'. (246)[109]

Contrary to what the title *Wonder Beyond Belief: On Christianity* suggests, Kermani's 'freely associative meditations' (292) on the art-historical legacy of the Judaeo-Christian tradition also extend into the Islamic world. Kermani takes, for example, the Venetian panels with Hieronymus Bosch's four visions of the Hereafter to make connections with the Light Verse (Q. 24:35) in the Qur'an and with the influence of Empedocles' theology of light on the light-mysticism of Najm al-Din Kubra, an honorific that translates as 'Star of the Religion' (245–6):[110]

> Henry Corbin went so far as to equate the loss of the metaphysical dimension in modern civilization with the loss of the North [Star]. The compass still connected the sense of direction tangibly to matter, nowadays the Polar Star, and with that a sense of above and below, hardly plays any role anymore. (248–9)

With all these copious references, expansions and digressions, Kermani shows that Sufism is an accretive and cumulative tradition – multifaceted and built up over centuries, firmly embedded within the wider Islamic tradition as an integral part of its body of traditional religious learning. Thus, a novel like *Love Writ Large* also works as a primer on Islam for the uninitiated reader. Moreover, I also conclude that Kermani's writings on Sufism on closer inspection clearly betray the influence of Annemarie Schimmel. This concerns her renowned history of Sufism, *Mystical Dimensions of* Islam and her study of Persian poetry in *A Two-Colored Brocade*, as well as her translation of Henry Corbin's *The Man of Light in Iranian Sufism*.[111] With some qualification, it also affirms Ludmila Peters' characterisation of Kermani's accounts of things religious as those of a 'scholar rather than as a believer'.[112] Peters is not implying that Kermani is an unbeliever or irreligious, because elsewhere she writes that 'the main motive of Kermani's work is the present-day relation between human and God, which manifests itself as *religion*, religious, mystical experience or divine love'.[113] However, what *Love Writ Large* narrates about the Sufi experience does not rest on the experiential knowledge of a practitioner or initiate: 'authority is therefore not derived from own immediate experience, but from the transmission of such experience'.[114] Also, the prominent place occupied by Ibn Arabi in *Love Writ Large* rests therefore on his role as an authority figure in transmitting theoretical insights relevant to the Sufi experience, through both direct quotations and theoretical elaborations attributed to key texts he has produced, such as *Bezels of Wisdom* (*Fusūs al-Ḥikam*), *Interpreter of Ardent Desires* (*Tarjumān al-Ashwāq*) and *Meccan Openings* (*Al-Futūḥat al-Makkiya*).[115]

Ibn Arabi is also a source for reflections on the more technical Sufi vocabulary related to the stations or stages of attainment, which often come as twin notions, such as the earlier-mentioned *fanā'* and *baqā'*.[116] Others terms that are discussed include the relation between breath (*nafas*) and soul (*nafs*) based on their etymological commonality and connection with the sighing or moaning (*tanaffus*) of the desperate lover.[117] Another terminological pair with such a respiratory connection is *qabḍ wa basṭ*, or the 'contraction and expansion' of the soul. Taken from a phrase in the second sura of the Qur'an, Sufis have integrated it into the sequence of stations to be traversed in the course of their forty-day retreats or forty-year meditations. Together they constitute the two basic dispositions in which the dialectical unfolding of the mystical – if not all experience – is completed.[118] Kermani goes on to explain how Ibn Arabi used it to describe the soul's premonition of things before they reach the outward senses:

> Thus, contraction and expansion are also heralds of love, even before it actually occurs. Ibn Arabi went even further, describing the intensity, the uncompromising stubbornness of juvenile infatuation – and expressly only this! – as comparable, as akin, not just symptomatically, to the 'drowning' (*istighrāq*) of the mystic, as the overflowing love of the divine. (13)

Usually translated as the contraction and expansion of the soul, it can indeed also be interpreted as reflecting opposite emotions or sensations, such as depression–exhilaration and trepidation–relief. Contraction and expansion are not only discussed in *Love Writ Large*; Kermani returns to it in his address to the 2013 annual conference of the German Goethe Society, which was later included in the essay collection *Between Quran & Kafka*. Published under the title 'Breathing God' (*Gott-Atmen*), in this essay Kermani selects the poem 'Talisman' from Goethe's *West-Eastern Divan* to argue that – aside from its physiological causality as the most basic life force (where contraction and expansion also correspond to diastole and systole, the two phases of the cardiac cycle) – 'the breath is the foundational religious experience, which we can neither deny nor confirm'.[119] To underscore this point, Kermani cites twice the same stanza from the poem that has captured so concisely yet elegantly the essence of Islam:

> In every breath we breathe two graces share
> The indraught and the outflow of the air;
> That is a toil, but this refreshment brings;
> So marvellous are our life's comminglings.
> Thank God when thou dost feel His hand constrain,
> And thank when He releases Thee again.[120]

When we compare this with what Kermani said about Goethe in his Frankfurt Poetry Lectures from 2010, it seems to me that Goethe's approach appeals to Kerman's own tendency towards an academic rather than experiential engagement with religion, whereas the example of Hölderlin serves as an illustration of the disposition that is required for being initiated into Sufi practice.[121]

Kermani's academic rather than experiential approach to Sufism, and indeed religion in general, can also be concluded from his excursion in *Love Writ Large* on the writings of Aldous Huxley and Robert Zaehner.[122] Kermani sides with the latter's criticism of Huxley's *The Doors of Perception*.[123] According to Zaehner, the 'oceanic feeling' associated with the loss of the sense of one's subjectivity and self, brought about by Huxley's own experiments with narcotics, 'is fundamentally different from the experience of God as testified by both Christian and Islamic mystics'.[124] At the same time, Zaehner's *Mysticism, Sacred and Profane* affirms Kermani in his conviction that 'corporeal love provides an appropriate, actually the most suitable, parable for the mystical experience'.[125] He goes on to observe that it is not the comparison that is blasphemous, 'but the degradation of the one and only act, which makes humankind equal to God'. However, since 'all higher religions recognize sexual union as something sacred', this also explains why adultery and sexual debauchery are condemned under all circumstances.[126] Taking into account Kermani's other writings about sexuality, which caused such consternation for some commentators, I suggest that the destabilising effects of a liminal genre, such as meta-autobiography, offer a useful tool for making sense of such incongruities. Similarly, Homi Bhabha's interpretation of cultural hybridity too can usefully be applied to Kermani's writings – not just to his literary output – but also to his political essays, reportage and travelogues. As these have been competently covered elsewhere by other scholars, and because the focus of this book is on religious references in literature, these writings will only be dealt with to the extent that is helpful for understanding and appreciating Kermani's engagement with Islam and Muslims in his literary output.[127]

Navid Kermani as Public Intellectual

Navid Kermani sees himself first and foremost as a German literary writer, but when it comes to religious questions, he also identifies as a son of pious Muslim parents and a bilingual citizen of the world drawing as much from the Bible as from Islamic sources. In the introduction to *Between Quran & Kafka*, Kermani explains it thus:

> In my parental house there was also a degree of, what one could indeed call, cosmopolitanism; grounded – just like in Judaism – in the religious tradition: The Qur'anic teaching, that every nation has a prophet in its own tongue, [but also] that God's ways are as numerous as the breaths of human. (10)

He goes on to note that this cosmopolitanism is more prevalent among Jewish authors writing in German than others, tying in with his earlier-mentioned self-description of being as German as Kafka. It was also confirmed by a message, which Kermani received after his commemorative address to the German parliament. In this communication he was hailed as 'the most prodigious successor' of the Jewish cosmopolitans of the nineteenth century.[128] Reflecting on the compliment, Kermani realised that he had indeed 'grown up with German literature and intellectual history, but only occasionally with its present', in the sense that he belongs to a lineage that 'runs out with the Second World War or, at the latest, the Frankfurt School', therefore legitimising the rhetorical question as to whether 'this did not echo the nineteenth and early twentieth centuries rather than an Oriental origin'.[129] Like Kafka, Kermani is an exponent of a wider phenomenon: the specific self-consciousness that German literature had been providing to Europe's smaller countries and miniature states. Quoting from Deleuze and Guattari's *Kafka: Toward a Minor Literature*, Vera Stegman notes:

> A minor literature doesn't come from a minor language; it is rather that which a minority constructs within a major language. But the first characteristic of minor literature in any case is that in it language is affected with a high coefficient of deterritorialization.[130]

According to Kermani, this last point was a result of the German conceptualisation of the Enlightenment as a European rather than a nationalist project. Also, luminaries such as Friedrich Schlegel and Thomas Mann had argued that Germans were 'the cosmopolitans of European culture', and that a 'tendency toward the cosmopolitan was essentially inseparable from the German sense of nationhood'.[131] Kermani's advocacy of the constitutional patriotism mentioned at the beginning of this chapter is grounded in this kind of German 'Enlightenment fundamentalism'.[132] The most important historical antecedent Kermani finds in the writings of another assimilated Jew: The later poems of Heinrich Heine, which he describes as stylistically indebted to both East and West, and 'subversively religious', where they seek to introduce the perspective of the vanquished and repressed into German literature.[133] While this invites drawing a parallel with the concern in Shiʿa Islam for the so-called *mustadaʿifīn*, or 'wretched of the earth', Kermani himself suggests considering Jewish cosmopolitans as representing an Enlightenment project that secularises the universal love of Jesus into the idea of equality. But he is more adamant in concluding the following:[134]

> In any case, however, along with the Judaeo-Arabic heritage of the Enlightenment, Heine and scholars of Judaism after him felt a duty to uncover its Islamic heritage as well. And it would be a good thing if Muslim authors today, whether religious or not, would reciprocate by standing up for Europe's Jews.[135]

Religious Belonging: Between Individuality and Solidarity

Clearly, Kermani embraces an ecumenical attitude towards religious questions, but how does the Islamic element or Muslim aspect fit into this multi-layered individual identity? As far as his literary writings are concerned, the first clues are already contained in Kermani's first novel.

Dariush, the narrator-protagonist in *Text Message*, is a successful German event manager of Iranian origin. While he expresses an interest in his home country's culture and in Persian literature, his attitude towards his ancestral religion seems outright hostile: 'Islam has always gone on my nerves. It was all bigotry to me'.[136] This would then also explain an assertion like this one:

> I lacked the ambition of my Iranian or Turkish contemporaries to study Islam, so as to become acquainted with my own culture, my own identity! [...] The Persian language course at the community college sufficed as an excuse to identify with something else than Germany.[137]

While Dariush's profile resembles that of Navid Kermani in some respects, it differs from him in others. This strikes me as another writing strategy to destabilise perceptions of identity and religious belonging. The ambiguity that characterises the day-to-day conduct of members of any faith community towards their own religious tradition is also addressed in *Who Is We? Germany and its Muslims*. A collection of political essays first published in 2009, it was reissued in 2017 in order to include Kermani's 2015 memorial address for the victims of the Charlie Hebdo attack. At several instances, Kermani underscores that identity formations are per definition reductionist: it is a 'definition of something that in reality is much more diverse, ambivalent and porous' (17). Affirming that he is indeed a Muslim, but at the same time also many other things, he states that it is important to realise that 'not everything I do has to do with my religion' (17). That this conclusion is not to be taken lightly becomes clear from the warning a few pages later: 'Every personality is composed of many different and contingent identities [...]. It becomes dangerous as soon as one identity is considered determinant' (26).

How does Kermani see this individual religious belonging fitting in with the kind of 'unpatriotic patriotism' that is shaped by Enlightenment ideals of citizenship and cultural affinity rather than ethnicity?[138] In both *Who Is We?* and *Text Message*, being Muslim is situated within the context of Europe's multiculturalism: more specifically, its seeming demise in the wake of the atrocities perpetrated by radicalised Islamist activists. In *Text Message*, this last point is limited to cursory references to the 9/11 and to 7/7 attacks in the USA and London, and to Dariusch's explicit disdain for suicide bombers.[139] Closely related to this is the latter's growing annoyance with constantly being taken for an Arab, as well as a more general feeling of not quite fitting in with German society; a discomfort, he discovers, shared by other Iranian Muslims: 'Germans take me for an Arab or an Italian, Iranians recognise each other ten metres away' (433). It is actually after being hired to organise an event about Iranian culture that Dariush becomes more consciously aware of living in one cultural environment, while also being rooted in another: 'If I had not received the offer to conceptualise the festival, I too would have lost my last link with the Orient. Not that I feel comfortable as a German' (406). Then, a few pages further, 'I drink German beer, the only upside of being German' (416). His involvement in the government-sponsored festival also leads to further irritation with the miscomprehensions by the German mainstream of what is Islamic and what is not:

> Do you want a dialogue with Islam, or do you want art, literature, music? I had asked the officials at the Ministry of Culture. If you want a dialogue, just invite a bunch of Mullahs and put them next to a priest. However, if you want culture, then please do not call it *Islamic*. The Fundamentalists are doing that already. (407)

These challenges and dilemmas are unpacked in *Who Is We?*. The central theme of this book is the growing distrust between Muslims and non-Muslims. This is not just putting the fabric of German society under immense pressure; for many, the outright polarisation between assertive and vocal proponents of political Islam, at one end of the spectrum, and populist politicians feeding – and feeding off – Islamophobia, at the other, has turned the concept of and the very term 'multiculturalism' into an outright profanity. According to Kermani, both phenomena – Islamism and right-wing populism – are manifestations of political and social dissatisfaction on the part of the middle classes in the Muslim world and in the West respectively, each with its own dynamics. The actual conflict about religion and politics is unfolding inside the Islamic world itself, where the return to what is perceived as the pristine Islam contained in the Qur'an and Traditions of the Prophet is actually an utterly modern phenomenon: 'there is no more radical break with the past than by those groups who want to return to it'.[140] Europe faces a different challenge. In marked contrast to the singular way in which secularisation has unfolded in Western Europe, in the rest of the world religion has never been absent from public life. However, this does not make Western Europe immune to that particular identity discourse. In view of its religious apathy, Kermani suggests that if Europe wants to create an inclusive sense of 'we', it is no longer Christianity that can provide the adhesive for gluing together a shared identity; instead, one should look at the legacy of the Enlightenment and its concomitant secularity. Another issue that needs resolving is the engagement with Europe's main interlocutor, Islam and its adherents:

> In Western Europe, the other, which one always needs to define oneself, is not only, but first and foremost, Islam. It is no coincidence that the multiculturalism debate has in fact become debate about Muslims – not *with* Muslims by the way, but mostly *about* Muslims. (36, original italics)

An additional irritant for Kermani in this regard is the fact that 'hardly any scholars of Islam are taking part in these debates' (37). Aside from scholarly participation, including the involvement of intellectuals from Muslim backgrounds, Kermani emphasises the role of artists, musicians and literary writers in highlighting the complex composition of identity formations. That also means exposing its inherent contradictions, of which Kermani considers himself to be the very embodiment:

> A large part of what is now considered Islamic culture, the masterpieces of poetry, architecture, visual arts, music, mysticism and philosophy, have not only absorbed external influences – no, many of its values and motives openly contradict the norms prescribed by the Qur'an, but without being considered heretical by most. (113)

Aside from acting as cultural brokers, artists and writers are also court jesters: 'Anyone who is even a little bit familiar with Oriental literatures, knows that it teems with fools, who drag everything, really everything, through the dirt: Including God, the Mullahs, and rulers' (46). Such mockery is not a frivolous exercise, however: 'Differentiation does not mean simplification, and certainly not trivialization' (88) – that is to say, playing down the serious challenges ahead. 'My task as an author is to criticize, more exactly to exercise self-criticism, and in my case to be applied as much to the European as to the Islamic culture' (95).

In his reportages from the Muslim world, Kermani extends and expands this gaze beyond Germany and Europe. In his first travelogue, published under the ironic title of *Beautiful New Orient*, Kermani already signals the dangers of dehumanising the other:

> Underlying this is the logic of *homo sacer*, called to mind by Giorgio Agamben and Slavoj Žižek, in order to draw attention to a new development in international politics. According to ancient Roman law, the *homo sacer* is someone whose blood can be shed with impunity, comparable to the Germanic outlaw. (152)[141]

Kermani has seen this logic at work with regard to Palestinians and non-combatants in Afghanistan, as well as separatists in the northern Indonesian province of Aceh and recipients of humanitarian aid in Bosnia and Rwanda, but it also applies to undocumented migrants in Europe and North America, or the slum dwellers in many cities throughout the developing world. This dehumanisation is also the reason for my objection to the English title of Kermani's volume of travel writings: *State of Emergency*. Translated back into German, 'state of emergency' would read *Notzustand*; this is something entirely different from the original German title. The only correct translation of *Ausnahmezustand* is 'state of exception', which is also the concept developed by the philosopher Carl Schmitt in his notorious *Political Theology*, and on which Agamben and Žižek have based their elaborations of *homo sacer*.

Concluding Remarks

The thematic concerns of Navid Kermani's early scholarly work continue to inform both his literary output and his political engagement. The inherent ambiguity of identity formations runs like a red thread through his entire work. In that sense, Kermani's West-Eastern affinities are not explicitly breaking the binary; instead they are put to work creatively and productively. His scholarship in Islam is developed in conversation with the Frankfurt School and the Tübingen philosopher Ernst Bloch, a reading of Friedrich Hölderlin that looks for traces of Sufism, and association with Franz Kafka, to discover what it means to be a cultural German. All this makes for non-reductive and critical readings of his dual heritage as a German Muslim with Iranian roots.

Navid Kermani's academic interests in the place of aesthetics and theodicy, or – to use his own words – divine beauty and terror in Islamic contexts, have continued to feed into his oeuvre as a literary writer. While Islamic referents are explicit in his earliest short stories, they became less prominent and more implicit in some of his subsequent work, only to return in his literary essays and the novel *Love Writ Large*, which appeared a decade after his literary debut. Most explicit references concern Sufi authors from the tenth to the thirteenth century, overlapping with what the historian of Islam Marshall Hodgson has called the classical Islamic civilisation of the high caliphate and the Muslim ecumene of the middle period.

Kermani's interest in divine love and in worldly or human love, evident from his borrowings from Sufi texts, and in eroticism and the death drive, as well as his politically engaged writings, must not be understood in terms of binary opposites. Instead of a dichotomy being posited between this-worldly and other-worldly Islam, reflections on the beauty and terror of God, or on twin terms from the Sufi tradition such as *fanāʾ wa baqāʿ*, *qabḍ wa basṭ* and *wājid wa fāqid*, are more accurately understood as two sides of the same coin.

In Kermani's writings, Islamic references do not stand in isolation; rather, they feature alongside or together with borrowings from Judaeo-Christian tradition, whether they concern Muslim readings of the biblical Book of Job, meditations on Christian art, or the decision to write an introduction to a study of the figure of Jesus by the philosopher, and later prime minister of Iran, Mehdi Bazargan. The catholicity of Kermani's religious interests also goes hand in hand with meditations on selfhood and the formulation of 'counter theologies'. These turn his literary output also into instances of idiosyncratic interpretations of religion, accommodative of the multiple belongings of the individual, but often at odds with the positions of what the guardians of the tradition perceive as dogma. Not concerned with establishing or finding doctrinal certainties, Kermani's selection of historical antecedents resembles the alternative history of Islamic religious thought explored by Thomas Bauer in *A Culture of Ambiguity*. In terms of epistemology, Kermani's open-ended reflections on individual experiences and his willingness to accept ambivalence evince affinities with the nomad and weak thought of Deleuze and Guattari, Shayegan and

Vattimo, and therefore also their condensation in Hamid Dabashi's hermeneutics of alterity.

Kermani's cultural-religious interests and socio-political positions reflect a cosmopolitan disposition that has also coloured his aesthetic sensibilities and ethical outlook as a German literary writer and public intellectual with Iranian Muslim roots. Thus, Kermani's West-Eastern affinities do not reflect the binary opposites of a dichotomous world-view. Instead they have a better fit with Homi Bhabha and Stuart Hall's use of cultural hybridity as an 'unclean concept' and 'subversive force', carving out a third space or 'in-between', from which to view the world as the complex individuals we are, or – as Kermani once formulated it himself – as 'someone, who is often called a novelist, but otherwise son, father, man, friend, neighbour or traveling salesman, now and then grandson, regular reporter, then again Orientalist, one year the number ten, in some places Navid Kermani and most recently poetologist'.[142]

Those *who adopted Islam practiced more calligraphy than they did painting.*

Abdelwahab Meddeb, *Talismano*, 113.

When the image is banned, the letter is exalted.

Abdelwahab Meddeb, *Phantasia*, p. 20.

It is in passage and migration, it is in the in-between where that which can actualise those energies which turned nomadism and Sufism into the juncture of the Spirit was established.

Abdelwahab Meddeb, *L'exil occidental*, 11.

Chapter 2

Double Genealogies

One year before Navid Kermani's birth, Abdelwahab Meddeb (1946–2014) left his native Tunisia for France, where he remained the rest of his life. Like Kermani, Meddeb combined artistic and academic pursuits to satisfy his interests in the multifarious aspects of Islam's civilisational heritage: writing novels, poetry and essays, translating Islamic texts, founding journals, and serving as a professor of comparative literature at universities inside and outside France. After 9/11 and subsequent atrocities elsewhere, Meddeb became an increasingly vocal and combative commentator on things Islamic: not only producing critical studies, essays and opinion pieces on the politics and intellectual state of affairs in the Muslim world, but also hosting a long-running radio show, *Cultures d'islam*.[1] Meddeb's writings about these issues must not be considered in isolation or as distinct phases in his intellectual and artistic development. Quite the contrary: these political concerns and artistic interests compound and overlap, forming a multi-layered aggregate of an increasingly rich engagement with the cultural legacies of East and West, and with developments in the contemporary world. In many respects, Abdelwahab Meddeb's multifaceted intellectualism parallels that of Navid Kermani, inviting a comparison between the latter's academic rather than experiential approach to the Islamic heritage and the former's self-identification as a Muslim atheist, which apparently formed no obstacle to his advocacy for a critical Islam.

Whereas Navid Kermani's literary and scholarly interests appear to make him a somewhat isolated figure in a family largely consisting of physicians, Abdelwahab Meddeb came from a long line of Islamic religious scholars; both his father and grandfather were graduates of the Zaytuna Mosque University in Tunis, one of the oldest surviving centres of Islamic learning in North Africa.[2] Abdelwahab, however, was sent to Collège Sadiki – an elite Francophone *lycée*, or secondary school. Founded in 1875 by the nineteenth-century Ottoman administrator and reformer Khayr al-Din Pasha, the school has produced successive generations of modern Tunisia's leading intellectuals and politicians. After enrolling at the University of Tunis, where he obtained the equivalent of a Bachelor's degree in modern literature (1967), Meddeb went to Paris for further study at the Sorbonne, obtaining another undergraduate degree in art history and archaeology (1969), followed by a postgraduate degree in literature (1970).

With this migration to Paris, Abdelwahab Meddeb found himself in the global metropole of Francophony, or what Pascale Casanova called the 'Greenwich meridian of literature'.[3] At the time, the city stood on the brink of the watershed year 1968, marked by rising anti-Vietnam War protests, and the assassinations of Martin Luther King and Robert Kennedy on the other side of the Atlantic. In Europe too, university campuses were turned into cauldrons of protest against the political and intellectual establishment. Many students and intellectuals, including future Meddeb collaborators such as Christian Jambet, began embracing ideologies of the radical left, in particular Maoism. One of the effects of this student activism was the foundation of Meddeb's future place of work, the University of Paris X-Nanterre, but first Meddeb pursued a career in publishing. Beginning as a reader with Seuil, he went on to become a literary consultant and commissioning editor at Éditions Sindbad, a publishing house specialising in translations from the Arabic and Persian. In this period Meddeb completed his two novels, *Talismano* and *Phantasia*, began writing poetry inspired by Ibn Arabi's theosophy, and translated selections from the rapturous poems of the Sufi al-Bistami.

Bilingualism and the Francophone Maghrebian Literary Milieu

At the time of Meddeb's birth, the Maghreb countries were still French colonies. Only in the course of the ensuing decade and a half did Tunisia, Morocco and Algeria attain their political independence.[4] This makes Meddeb part of the first generation of Maghrebian writers to have matured in the postcolonial era. In studies of the Francophone Maghrebian milieu, he is mentioned alongside contemporaries such as Assia Djebar (1936–2015), Nabile Farès (1940–2016) and Tahar Ben Jelloun (b. 1944), as well as intellectuals from the preceding generation, such as his fellow Tunisian Albert Memmi (1920–2020) and the Algerian Mohamed Dib (1920–2003). Meddeb's most important interlocutor – if not directly, than at least virtually – was the Moroccan critic, novelist and playwright Abdelkébir Khatibi (1938–2009), who was one of the first to write about his early literary writings. As a trained sociologist, Khatibi also theorised the concepts of a 'plural Maghreb' and 'radical bilingualism'.[5] Samia Mehrez contrasts this latter notion with the more passive 'colonial bilingualism' of earlier generations of writers from the Maghreb, whose output was still constrained by literary models of the dominant colonial language.[6] Authors like Abdelkébir Khatibi and Abdelwahab Meddeb distinguished themselves by foregrounding 'the individual at the expense of the collective experience'.[7] More self-aware as persons and writers, Meddeb and his generation seized the initiative. Intent on capturing what 'was lost to the West, to modernity, with the collapse of the Moslem empire in Spain', they embarked on an intellectual and artistic *reconquista* of their own.[8]

This attention to the individual is also reflected in Abdelwahab Meddeb's doctoral thesis, which he completed in 1990 at the University Aix-Marseille. Submitted under the title *Écriture et double généalogie* (1991), this examination of a simultaneous belonging to the Francophone and Islamic cultural worlds established Meddeb's academic credentials. Appointed *maître de conferences* (associate professor) in comparative literature at the University of Paris X-Nanterre in 1996, he was eventually promoted to full professor seven years later, after successful defending his habilitation in front of a jury that included the historian of Islam Mohammed Arkoun and the philosopher Jean-Luc Nancy.[9] As a publisher and writer Meddeb emphatically identified as an exponent of this border-crossing Francophone Maghrebian literature. Aside from his continued involvement with Éditions Sindbad, he also acted as co-editor of the cultural magazine *Cahiers Intersignes* (1992–4) and as consultant for UNESCO, advising the organisation on issues related to Islam and the Arab world, as well as curating an exhibition on Islamic art. In 1995, he founded another journal under the name *Dédale*. A publishing house named after a fictional mariner from the Abbasid era and a journal with a title that translates into English as *Labyrinth* can be taken as emblematic pinpoints on the map of Meddeb's own meandering journey through the cultural heritages of East and West.[10]

For a North African fluent in both French and Arabic, positioning oneself vis-à-vis this bilingualism and finding one's bearings in the cultural landscape called world literature continued to be a challenge. Having to cope with similar challenges of dispersal, exile and alienation as their predecessors, Meddeb's generation forged a 'tenuous alliance of the archaic and the postmodern', in order to overcome the dissonance between the calligraphic writing of the Qur'anic of their native Islamic tradition and such advances in the Western humanities through the introduction of new fields of investigation such as semiotics.[11] In their attempts to salvage a sense of collective selfhood, while simultaneously bracing themselves for the future, contemporary writers with roots in the Maghreb search for 'the hidden potentialities of the past and reflect the many complex realities of the present' (65).[12] Meddeb in particular has criticised reactionary Islamists, conservative academics and technocrats alike for their futile quest for authenticity (*aṣāla*) and their dismissal of the present-day Maghreb as either historically retarded or decadent. Meddeb has tried to offset their lack of appreciation for its cultural distinctiveness by appealing to the history of the region's popular culture as a source for creatively representing the Maghrebian cultural experience. For this, he and other like-minded writers quarried both Berber and wider African oral traditions, as well as the 'glorious archaic knowledge, namely pre-Islamic poetry, Arab and Islamic philosophy, and literature'.[13]

The literary output of Meddeb's generation is indeed indebted to both postcolonial theory and postmodern philosophies of difference. Aside from betraying a 'preoccupation with writing as a creative trace' of various cultural influences, there is also the epistemic ambition to take an 'eclectic and syncretic rather than mimetic approach to reality and knowledge'.[14] Cognisant of this challenge, Khatibi insisted:

> The major responsibility of French-Arab intellectuals is to articulate a new notion of history that deconstructs the simplistic binaries (civilized–savage, colony–metropolis, religion–secularism) of the colonial period.[15]

Echoing Vattimo and Dabashi's criticisms of Rorty and Levinas, this involves a double critique: deconstructing the dominant logocentrism and ethnocentrism of the West, as well as the discourses of self-perception in the Arab world.[16] This fusion of the postmodern (read: post-structuralist deconstruction) and the archaic (read: the traditional Arabic-Islamic heritage) produces what Hedi Abdel-Jaouad has characterised as a 'literature of syncretism, eclecticism and synthesis' that is at odds with the established historical canon – which, to my mind, is more accurately phrased in the plural, since it extends to both the Islamic and Western canons.[17] Writing in 1991, Abdel-Jaouad went on to characterise the literary output of this campaign as 'a discourse of alterity at the antipodes of both Western metaphysics and Islamic theology that is a repudiation of the idea of centrism' (63).[18] Three decades later, this still resonates with Idriss Jebari's article about a special issue of *Les temps modernes*, for which Khatibi and Meddeb were invited to act as guest editors.[19] Published in 1977 as *Du Maghreb*, Meddeb's contribution, entitled 'On the Maghreb as an Aesthetic Experience', in which he argued for a rewriting of the region's cultural history in order to discern its alterity, demonstrated a 'remarkable self-awareness and readiness to confront his own positionality', which is also in line with Khatibi's suggestion that radical ruptures with dominant discourses are best effectuated by working from the margins.[20] This is also an appropriate point to briefly digress into an intervention by Pascale Casanova. As part of her theorising about world literature, she has signalled that the question to ask is not 'whether peripheral writers borrow from the centre, or whether or not literary traffic flows from centre to periphery; it is the restitution, to the subordinated of the literary world, of the forms, specificities and hardships of their struggles'.[21] And yet, her own conclusion in this regard is rather sobering:

> Multiculturalist enthusiasms have led others to assert that the relation between centre and periphery has now been radically reversed and that the world of the periphery will henceforth occupy the central position. In reality, the effects of this pacific and hybridized fable are to depoliticize literary relations, to perpetuate the legend of the great literary enchantment and disarm writers from the periphery who are seeking recognition strategies that would be both subversive and effective.[22]

Cautioning against too much optimism regarding the achievements of multiculturalism and the advances in postcolonial theory, Casanova's interrogation of the relationship between the centre and the periphery also has a counterpart in Vattimo and Dabashi's criticisms of obsolete binary world-views that continue to retain currency also among postmodern thinkers, reflecting an ironic persistence of Western intellectual hegemony.[23]

Mediterranean Ecumene: The Novels of Abdelwahab Meddeb

Abdelwahab Meddeb's first novel, *Talismano*, was initially released in 1979 by Christian Bourgois, and then reissued by Éditions Sindbad in 1987. By then Meddeb had already written a second novel, appearing under the title *Phantasia* (1986, republished by Seuil in 2003). Literary critics and scholars of comparative literature hailed both novels as examples of postcolonial avant-garde writing in French and as founding texts of bilingualism. A closer examination of the titles shows, however, that they cannot be confined to that narrow binary, because the titles *Talismano* and *Phantasia* are neither French nor Arabic in origin, but Italian and Greek respectively, thus complicating the implied dichotomous tendencies of Arabic–French bilingualism. Looking into the etymology of the word 'talisman', Ourdia Djedid points at its Greek origin (*télesma*), its subsequent occurrence in Arabic (*ṭilasm*) and its eventual adoption by the Romance languages (*talisman*, *talismano*). For Abdelkébir Khatibi, the Italian language stands for hedonistic playfulness, 'paradisiacal language [...] far removed from the violent contradiction between French and Arabic', while Ronnie Scharfman has suggested that, because of Italy's geographical location between Tunisia and France, everything associated with it as a country 'functions as a transitional object'.[24] Highlighting the plural origin of this 'travelling word' as an indication of displacement and decentring, it can also be taken as an instance of 'Pan-Mediterraneanism' or 'Mediterranean ecumenism'.[25] The title of Meddeb's second novel has similar Mediterranean associations, in this case with the Italian and Spanish use of the word *fantasia* for the mock-battle performances at festive occasions by horsemen in North and West African countries, which can be traced back to the region's early Berber settlers, known as the Numidians. The origin of the word, however, is the Greek *phantasia*. Reflecting on its Arabic equivalent *khayāl*, Ziad Elmarsafy suggests that 'one could, without stretching the translation too much, translate *phantasia* by the word "idol" or "idolatry"'.[26] Aside from pointing back to one of the dominant themes in *Talismano*, as an exercise in intertextuality, the juxtaposition of the Arabic and Greek equivalents extends all the way to one of Meddeb's poems that is included in the posthumous collection *Portrait du poète en soufi*. Linking the Greek and Arabic words as well as explicating the Greek connection with a reference to an earlier overseer of the translation school in early Abbasid Baghdad, the polymath and philosopher al-Kindi (d. 873 CE), Meddeb wrote:

> this is how it is described by Kindî
> first philosopher of the Arabs
> who learned from the Greeks
> what *phantasia* means
> giving it the meaning of *khayêl*.[27]

For her unpacking of the notion of phantasia, Suzanne Gauch returned to the Stoics of Hellenic antiquity, who conceptualised it as 'comprehensive and accurate representation'.[28] She therefore interprets the title as ironic, because the intention of Meddeb's early novels is to call into question the possibility of any fixed and particular identities associated with either east or west. Gauch further illustrates this shift in the meaning of *fantasia* with a comparison of the picturesque in colonial painting from the early 1800s to the emerging menace of violent Islamism in the world today.[29] Meddeb's use of '*Phantasia*' is therefore closer to Henry Corbin's creative imagination than to its original meaning in ancient Greek philosophy. Instead of returning to the ancient Stoics, Thomas Connolly takes up Augustine's distinction between *corporalia phantasmata* (corporeal phantasms) and *phantasmata splendida* (glittering fantasies) to foreground Abdelwahab Meddeb's 'extensive engagement with Christian – specific Roman Catholic – culture, theology, and aesthetics', which is not confined to the novel *Phantasia*, but permeates much of his later writings and activities as well.[30]

Despite both novels' significance as contributions to postcolonial world literature, an English translation of *Talismano* only appeared in 2011, while *Phantasia* remains untranslated. This may be partly due to the fact that both books are, at one and the same time, captivating but challenging reads, not fitting easily into the category of the novel if this is taken in a conventional sense of the word. As Ziad Elmarsafy recently suggested:

> Although both *Talismano* and *Phantasia* are described by their publishers as novels, Meddeb's writing constantly tests the laws of the genre. In an astute reading of Meddeb's literary originality, Pierre Joris proposes that they be called *récits* – narratives and recitals – both in Blanchot's sense of 'nonnovel' and following Corbin's idea of the Sufi narrative as a visionary recital, 'un récit visionnaire' (Joris 2009: 13; Corbin 1999). Furthermore, adds Corbin, these narratives do not aim to mirror the world in a realistic sense. Rather, they serve as tales of initiation for their readers, preparing them for spiritual itineraries similar to those that they narrate (1991: 1.xxii). Nor indeed are these texts mere allegories that put the reader in the position of the spectator: these texts produce events in which readers participate.[31]

Where *Talismano*'s story revolves around the main character's peregrinations through Meddeb's native Tunis, *Phantasia* is set in his adopted home town of Paris, taking the reader on a journey around the city's museums and art galleries. Conjuring up parallels with Baudelaire's or Benjamin's flâneur, Meddeb even coined a neologism for such wanderings through the labyrinthine alleyways of Tunis's inner city: *médiner* – from the Arabic word for city, *medina*.[32]

Conceiving of narration as collages, Meddeb's use of tropes, such as wandering (*errance*), and concomitant figures of literary arabesque, has been characterised as a 'subversive poetics', which Samia Mehrez defined as

> [a] poetics that seeks to create a new literary space for the bilingual, postcolonial writer. It is a space that subverts hierarchies, whether they be linguistic or cultural; where separate systems of signification and different symbolic worlds are brought together in a relation of perpetual interference, interdependence

> and intersignification. By so doing, this subversive poetics not only challenges our conventions of reading and writing, but it also questions the structuring of institutions of learning and disciplinary boundaries.[33]

In the hands of Abdelwahab Meddeb, this subversive poetics turns the constraints of bilingualism into a field of what Mehrez calls risky opportunities, because the reader as 'the other' who is not familiar with the full range of connotations of the metaphors employed by the autodiegetic author 'might fail at decoding the text'.[34] In fact, Meddeb admits as much himself when he titled an autobiographical sketch included in an essay collection published some twenty years later 'Errant et Polygraphe': The French *errant* can be variously translated as wanderer, vagabond, or nomad. *Polygraphe* is trickier: according to the Larousse Dictionary it can refer to a non-specialist author writing about a variety of topics, but also to a polygraph or lie detector.[35]

Elsewhere, the language used by Meddeb in both *Talismano* and *Phantasia* has been described as vertiginous and hallucinatory – or, as a student of the *Talismano* translator Jane Kuntz phrased it, 'French on LSD'.[36] Dina al-Kassim has drawn a parallel with the prose poems of Joris-Karl Huysmans from the latter's decadent period that preceded his return to Catholicism. She goes on to speculate that Meddeb would approve of such a comparison, because of their similar views of moribund modernity.[37] The comparison is all the more intriguing, because Huysmans also features very prominently in Michel Houllebecq's controversial novel *Submission*, which will be discussed in the final chapter of this book.[38]

However, the biggest challenge facing translators of Meddeb's novels is the poetic licence taken with both French and Arabic grammar and lexicography. This is probably one of the reasons why these novels have been primarily examined by literary comparativists working in North African or Mediterranean studies. Where Islamic referents are acknowledged, they are often only mentioned in passing and not studied systematically. This was certainly the case in the 1980s and 1990s; only in 2010 did a greater scholarly interest in the novels' Islam-related themes becomes detectable. It is probably no coincidence that this attention occurred at the same time as Meddeb's increasingly combative non-fiction writing directed against political Islam. In view of this relative negligence, it makes sense to first take stock of Islamic and other relevant religious references in *Talismano* and *Phantasia*, in order to tease out dominant themes that merit a more detailed discussion.

Talismano opens with a brief prologue and closes with an epilogue, in which the narrator's observation that 'history is nothing but words and ghosts, sex restrained or intense, in all haste, borders reconciling the myth of a fleeting self' (5) dovetails with his final address to his readers: 'We have confided through writing, but without giving you a foothold' (261).[39] Whereas the opening remark is reminiscent of Navid Kermani's preoccupations with eros and thanatos, the novel's ending prefigures Meddeb's *L'Exil Occidental*, a collection of autobiographically coloured essays named after a treatise by the central figure of the so-called philosophy of illumination (*ḥikmat al-Ishrāq*, in Arabic), the twelfth-century Shihab al-Din al-Suhrawardi, who is also briefly mentioned by Navid Kermani.[40]

Wedged between this prologue and epilogue are three parts bearing provocative and suggestive titles. In the first, 'Return Prostitution', Meddeb uses the sexual dimensions of funerary practices in pre-Islamic North Africa and ritual prostitution at Sufi shrines in the Maghreb to challenge and actually embarrass the political and religious elites' 'narrow, lawyerly turn of mind', through which they have sought to repress other fertile alternatives by forming 'a common front to exorcise our symbolic fear that any diversities might survive on their own' (17).[41] This also affords Meddeb, as the autodiegetic narrator, an opportunity to invoke controversial figures from the history of Sufism, such as al-Hallaj and Suhrawardi, as well as making a first hint at the Prophet Muhammad's miraculous Night Journey (*isra'*). In the next part, entitled 'Idol Ghetto', a sorceress named Saïda and two goldsmiths-cum-alchemists – the Jew Ya'qūb and Master Mahmūd – fashion an effigy from the body parts of dug-up corpses, turning this Monster of Frankenstein-like creature into an idol that clearly flies in the face of mainstream Islamic doctrine and practice. This second session is interspersed with the narrator's reflections on calligraphy and theoretical digressions into the art of writing and religious imagery. It also features the novel's eponymous talisman, drawing not only on Islamic symbols, but also on Chinese ideograms. With its alleged hidden powers, the talisman too can be considered an object of idolatry. The storylines of the first two parts come together in 'Otherworld Procession', a thinly disguised revolt against the autocratic regime of Tunisia's founding President Habib Bourguiba, who was still governing the country at the time of writing.[42] It features a diverse cast of religious and literary figures from both the Muslim world and Europe – among them al-Ghazali, Ibn Arabi, Rumi and Yunus Emre, as well as Miguel Cervantes, Constantine Cafavy and Herman Hesse. Towards the end, several nineteenth- and early twentieth-century proponents of the modernisation of the Muslim world make an appearance too.

A hallucinatory narrative similar to *Talismano*, Meddeb's second novel, *Phantasia*, is set in Paris, giving centre stage to the city's Beaubourg district. While more confined in geographical terms, the story's ten chapters offer a chronological journey that opens up a much wider historical panorama. Although a slimmer volume, *Phantasia* features meditations on the origins of monotheism in Mesopotamia, going back to its Sumerian heritage and the figure of Abraham, while using the scandalously rapturous exclamations by early Sufis and contemplations of Renaissance art to make a connection between Islam and Christian incarnation theology. The narrative also contains reflections on Christian–Muslim confrontations, including the fall of Constantinople (1453), the *Reconquista* of Granada (1492) and the sea battle between the Holy League and the Ottomans at Lepanto (1571): three historical milestones signposting the definitive separation between the northern – Christian – and southern – Muslim – shores of the Mediterranean in early modern times. Written in the early 1980s, *Phantasia* also incorporates impressions left by landmark events affecting the Muslim world at that time: the Islamic revolution in Iran and the Soviet invasion of Afghanistan in 1979, as well as the 1981 assassination of the Egyptian President Sadat. These herald the emergence of increasingly intolerant manifestations of political Islam that would become a major concern of Meddeb's writings in the new millennium.[43]

In the first two chapters of *Phantasia*, Meddeb turned to the Qur'an. A citation from Sura Yusuf and a meditation on the so-called *ḥurūf muqaṭ'āt*, or 'disjoined letters', found at the beginning of several Qur'an chapters are introduced as 'verbal incarnations' articulating how writing 'drifts from one language to the other'.[44] The narrator insists that this last formulation translates as his own double – bilingual – genealogy. Echoing the Christian doctrine of incarnation, most specifically the line from the Gospel of John where 'the Word was made flesh', the first phrase reads as an intentional provocation.[45] This leads up to what, in terms of Islamic references, can be considered *Phantasia*'s two core chapters. Featuring several dozens of quotations from scripture and tracings of the ancient Mesopotamian origins of monotheism, Meddeb ventures yet another provocative comparison:

> The Qur'an situates itself *alongside* the Bible. It is *as* the Bible. It repeats a similar discourse in another language. It founds monotheism in Arabic.[46]

Where *Talismano*'s epilogue briefly points at *L'Exil Occidental*, references to exile abound in the third chapter of *Phantasia*. The next chapter elaborates this further by recounting the narrator's dream experience, which features again the biblical figure of Joseph, jinns, and Dante's *Divina Commedia*. Chapter 5 serves as a transition for another exposé about the end of the Mediterranean as a space for cultural cross-pollination as Europe moved from Renaissance to early modernity. Meddeb's concern about the antagonism between the monotheisms around the Mediterranean leads to a diatribe against the dichotomous world-view of Islam versus the West, in Chapter 6. Pitching increasingly assertive and openly violent forms of Islamism against Islamophobic responses from Europe and America, this new binary appears to be paradigmatic for the post-Cold War global order. In tracing historical occurrences of such animosities, Meddeb uses the image of communicating vessels: 'The capture of Constantinople is answered with the fall of Granada' (95). To illustrate that this had not always been the case, and that 'to think Europe, Islam must appreciate its connection with Christendom' (95), Meddeb recounts three examples to the contrary: Ibn Arabi's attribution of Islamic notions of charity and leniency to the influence of Christianity; the 1357 construction of a synagogue in Toledo; and the appearance of a 'turban-wearing messiah presenting his illuminated body under the new name of Sabbatai Tsevi, alias Mehemed Kapici Bachi, preaching Islam in a synagogue, praying now as Jew, then as Muslim' (102–3). Deploring the displacement of Andalusia's *Convivencia* as the codeword for an ecumenical Mediterranean by a post-Lepanto dichotomy, Meddeb makes a point of emphasising these contrasting dispositions, which propelled the *Reconquista* of Al-Andalus, as well as the defeat of the last remains of the Byzantine Empire and subsequent Ottoman expansion into the Balkans, by showcasing the different dynamics exhibited in the conversion of the *mesquita*, the Grand Mosque of Cordoba, into a cathedral and the inverse changing of the Aya Sophia into a mosque. Where the Spanish monarchs and Catholic clergy made every effort to efface any signs of Moorishness from the church, the Ottomans altered neither the Aya Sophia's overall exterior nor its interior appearance. When Spain first unleashed a campaign of forced conversion, followed by the expulsion of the remaining Muslims and Jews from the Iberian Peninsula, many of these refugees found refuge in the Ottoman Empire.

Meddeb's advocacy of religious plurality, and his criticism of the repression of women and the feminine, are further pursued in Chapters 7 and 8, where he reflects on attitudes towards death, tombs and funerary rites in different religions. These concern not only Christian and Muslim burials, but also those of the ancient Egyptians and the Japanese, the purpose being to establish that there are no fundamental differences in the ways in which humankind treats its dead.[47] In defining his own relationship with Islam, Meddeb admits that, although he does 'not reside in the house of dogma' (156), he remains of Muslim ancestry, and that even in exile he was 'redoing the itinerary of *Talismano*' (168):

> I have learned that I was thus conforming to the tradition of which I was reminded by the mendicant of Herat during my Afghan peregrinations: 'Islam was born a stranger and it will return to being a stranger, so blessed are the strangers.' (158)

From this survey it follows that, aside from the narrator's wanderings, recurring themes and tropes in the novels include the cityscapes of leading sites of traditional Islamic learning around the Mediterranean, as well as the visual culture associated with calligraphy and religious imagery.

Cityscapes and Wanderings: The Double Genealogy of a Literary Nomad

Aside from Tunis, *Talismano* also features other cities in North Africa and the Eastern Mediterranean: Turkey's Konya and Karaman are mentioned when contemplating the relationship of the thirteenth-century Sufi poets Rumi and Yunus Emre with the art of writing.[48] North African centres of traditional Islamic learning receive a less positive mention and treatment. Morocco's famous mosque university of al-Qarawīn (al-*Qarawiyyīn*, also written al-Karaouine) in Fes is first described as a 'pedantic gem, archaic presence, gangrene of the just' (106), and then roundly condemned for lending itself to become

> [t]he protective western boundary for a set of decadent ideas – namely, that of a hegemonic Islam, a reductive monotheism, bordering on Christendom, both masters of a civilisation claiming to be unique and universal, believing in progress and taking comfort wherever natural instinct is suppressed. (157)

Located further east, its Egyptian counterpart in Cairo found itself treated no more kindlily a few pages earlier:

> Al-Azhar, its two halls clumsily open one to the other, two separate epochs separated by levels of unequal height, functionally similar and complementary. Mercenary penchant among those who teach, centuries-old submission to the Word, perfection of reading methods, backed by a plethora of powers: Fātimid, Ayyūbid, Circassian, Bahri, Mamlūks on parade, Khedives, a people surveyed and mapped by the benediction of doctors of the faith, totalitarian sheikhs, sects paralyzing the true fire, man's faith perpetually consumed in a hearth that quells any ardour or rebellious flame, bellows at hand to check disruptive urges, to contain faith's harshness, to eradicate its chaos, quicksilver and gold. (105)

Halfway between these two lies the third of 'this erudite triad of the death throes' (106): the Zaytūna of Tunis, where Meddeb's forebears had received their education and found employment, and where later

> [a] certain boy's father taught him in this eminent mosque: hear the words of a consummate scholar of the hadith, the law reverberating among the polytheistic columns and capitals [...] the hard-and-fast formulation of law, to be handed down exactly as it was received. (107)

Earlier in the novel, Meddeb contrasted urban decay and the repressive orthodoxy emanating from the pillared halls of Egypt's Al-Azhar, Tunisia's Zaytuna and Morocco's Al-Qarawīn with the North African countryside, where another strand of Islam dominated:

> Different vision of bodies for sale, the Middle Atlas Mountains, desert's edge, mausim, harvest festival time, ritual prostitution at rural shrines, Moulay Idris and elsewhere, outside the city, beyond the constraints of urbanity, theology, business, and all the various trades that organise the history of a city like Fez that extends its influence well beyond its borders, tending to centralise and cancel out all difference. (47)

In all the cited instances, the guardians of Sunni orthodoxy are criticised as repressive institutions demanding unquestioned adherence to both law and dogma, imposing discipline designed to crush human passion and desire, and promoting unimaginative literalism at the expense of creative thinking, artistic freedom and popular ways of giving expression to piety.

More positive associations are accorded to worldly localities, such as *souk al-ʿattarine*. This spice and perfume market in Tunis, 'where a famed creator of talismans reads the stars via dusty translations of extracts from the Enneads of Plotinus' (85), serves to allude to the autodiegetic author's predilection for Neoplatonic emanation theories, which exercised considerable influence on the theosophy of Ibn Arabi. Also located in Tunis is the now largely abandoned Jewish ghetto (*hāra*). Set apart from the capital proper, its site triggers a lamentation over the torn identities of Middle Eastern Jews, split between 'being Arab in body, in celebration, in sex, in food, in song, in dance, in their secret lore and eloquence, in their feelings and their reason', on the one hand, and loyalty towards 'the body that corrupts the Arab world, Israel' (88), on the other. As a result of the community's Europeanisation, most Arab Jews have become 'enemies of their own past [...] fascinated by the prodigious success of the occidental machine beneath the torrid oriental sun' (89). The same fate befell the largely Jewish Moroccan port city of Essaouira. Known until the 1960s by its Portuguese name Mogador, with its 'spotless rooftop terraces, all outward signs proclaiming harmony, stars of Islam, of David, reconcile each other, Kufic square of prophetic fortune, Baraka. Solomons seal, the green of conquest splashed onto doors' (94). Its community may have dwindled to a few dozen and its one hundred synagogues been turned into attics and warehouses, but it nonetheless remains a 'city of asserted Jewishness, walls permeated by a Hebraic atmosphere despite desertion and dispersion' (95).

Across the Strait of Gibraltar, the scene is no different: 'What remains of the souk of Grenada, rushing to find the final footsteps of the Moor, sighs and tears; discovering nothing left of consolation' (236).[49] A visit to the Alhambra, palace of the last Muslim dynasty to rule over the Iberian Peninsula, leads Meddeb to contemplate the findings of his fellow Tunisian Ibn Khaldun (1332–1406). The way this fourteenth-century spin doctor-cum-political pundit formulated the laws of history, capturing the 'premonitions of decadence, theorizing repetition, determining its cycles and phases' (236), demonstrate not just that 'esprit the corps and tribalism are still the engines of Arab power', but also that the only historians worth their salt are those capable of thinking in terms of systems: 'But alas! and as ever, the politicians do not follow suit' (237).

In terms of civilisation and cultural achievements, medieval cities of Islam, such as Fes, rivalled the likes of Renaissance Florence. However, unlike in Italy's centres of mercantilism, 'the investment of its wealth is turned in upon itself, into dens of pleasure-seeking' (156). Extrapolating this tendency to the modern era, the narrator concludes that as today's Moroccan 'moves to Casablanca to sell his soul in hopes of living the perfectly conventional synthesis between skill sets assimilated from the West and refinements preserved from the East', his dormant potential remains unrealised, because, just as had been the case in the past, 'any reasonable attempt to claim power after having acquired a fortune' came to naught (156). This stagnant state of affairs is again taken up in the final pages of the third section, where the narrative of *Talismano* ends with a hallucinatory vision. In the face of Turkish and Spanish invasions, interventions from French Algeria, as well as internal pressures from rural uprisings, 'the first to hide, then to give away the keys to the city, are the learning men' (255). Political history is then left to 'serve to further the notion of nation as the guarantor of legitimacy, an unimaginative political logic in thrall to so-called universal standards of power' (256).

Although *Phantasia* is almost exclusively set in Paris, in both novels the narrator's wanderings through the urban spaces of the Mediterranean's southern – North African, oriental – and northern – European, occidental – shores challenge the implied binary of a dichotomous view of the Mediterranean as a geographical and cultural divide, a maritime space separating two continents, projecting instead an alternative cultural contact zone. These meandering accounts of Mediterranean cityscapes turn urbanity into a literary vignette, suggesting that place and space, or geography, are as much a consideration in postcolonial theorising as time, or history. So aside from Stuart Hall's question 'When was "The Post-Colonial"?', it is just as important to ask where the postcolonial is.[50] As Dabashi and Vattimo have shown in their critiques of Levinas and Rorty, there is no unequivocal answer to their 'where' question, nor to Hall's 'when' question for that matter, because human realities, also on a global scale, are ambiguous.[51]

Effigy and Idol

A central feature in *Talismano*'s storyline is an idol in the form of an effigy, which fulfils multiple functions in the novel's narrative: first and foremost, it is introduced to articulate the power dimensions involved in the relationship between religious officialdom and popular expressions of religiosity. This is illustrated by the employment of such opposites as femininity versus the patriarchy of Islamic authority figures, as well as the eros–thanatos nexus representing the tension between life-affirming sexuality and the death drive. The main producer of the effigy is the sorceress Saïda. After she has directed what amounts to a grave-robbing expedition, the effigy – stitched together from body parts scavenged at a cemetery – is described in horrifying and disgusting detail:

> The organs sutured thus send the odd odor of symbolism wafting through the air: head of a woman; long, weightless hair stirred by the bubbles that appear in the formaldehyde wherein it bathes; [...] Three-eyed: one green, the other blue, and the one in the middle of the forehead dusky and plaintive as a gazelle's. Large ears, wrinkled and hairy. A mouthful of gold teeth gleaming behind lips stiff and fleshy. Round-tipped nose, but with hints of the freed African slave. The neck long, slit once in a passion that's now anyone's guess, deadly quarrel now on public display. Narrow shoulders, long limbs, elegant bearing. The chest: four mothering breasts, Artemis of Ephesus or some unlikely incarnation of Ceres. Navel, fountain amid taut skin over slightly rounded belly, culminating in narrow hips. Overpowering rawness of a vagina now enlarged into flower or wound, scattering of hairs between two legs; thin, disjointed stems, knees missing, fine ankles, bony toes, inordinately long.[52]

Ronnie Scharfman has interpreted these features and references to female deities as a 'positive valorization of the feminine pole'.[53] Commenting on the effigy's public display in 'Otherworld Procession',

Scharfman's second article on *Talismano* considers the carnival and subsequent revolt in the novel's final section 'the climax of the text's theoretical preoccupations'.[54] In a section entitled 'Meddeb's battle of the sexes: Eros and Thanatos', the focus is again on the feminine. As erotic desire triumphs over death, 'roles are reversed, power structures inverted, joyous blasphemy and sacrilege substituted for institutionalized religion' (93), thus turning *Talismano*'s narrative into a discourse of open possibilities. Returning to the same theme again in another intervention published ten years later, Scharfman interprets Meddeb's 'dosage of fantasy and reality, poetry and prose, Eros and Thanatos' as an attempt to 'dilate the limits of being, of knowing, of inventing'.[55] Rather than succumbing to the Freudian death drive, Meddeb's alternative is a defiant thanatography: 'If the institution (of justice, religion, writing) threatens the body with death, then the only life-affirming response consists in pre-empting that threat, rewriting the sentence in as many ways as possible' (98).

For a further analysis of the crucial figure of the effigy/idol, I suggest supplementing the secondary literature on *Talismano* with another body of literature: that of teratology. Originally a medical term for the field that studies abnormalities of physiological development in organisms during their lifespan, teratological imaginaries have been adopted by, among others, Rosi Braidotti and Patricia MacCormack, to accommodate the fascination with the grotesque and monstrous in recent postmodern thinking.[56] An uncanny creature, such as an effigy composed of dead human body parts, therefore qualifies for a reading through this teratological lens. In this case, I will rely on Richard Kearney's *Strangers, Gods and Monsters: Interpreting Otherness* (2002). The third title in a triptych that also includes *The God that May Be* and *On Stories*, the three books together form a 'philosophy of the limit' designed to take readers beyond the entanglements of postmodernity.[57] I have two reasons for selecting this particular study of alterity. First of all, elements of the postmodern theorising of monsters selected by Kearney dovetail with the depictions of *Talismano*'s effigy. Secondly, instead of stopping at the inherently nihilist interpretations of postmodern deconstructionists, as a long-time follower of Paul Ricoeur, Kearney uses the latter's 'hermeneutical model of narrative comprehension' in an effort to achieve a more (re-)constructive alternative understanding of the monstrous to help us accept 'ourselves-as-others'.[58]

The grotesque effigy can indeed be captured in deconstructionist idioms of horror and evil explored by Julia Kristeva, Jean-François Lyotard and Slavoj Žižek, which Kearney characterises as a '*teratology of the sublime*'.[59] However, this association of evil with 'horror, unspeakability, abjection and nothingness' carries with it the risk of a questionable version of the sublime, whereby

> [t]he upwardly transcendent finds its mirror image in the downwardly monstrous [...] By this account, horror is just as 'ineffable' as the vertical transcendence of God (invoked by Levinas and the negative theologians). There is, in short, an apophasis of the monstrous analogous to an apophasis of the divine. (88)

If Kearney's contention that 'abjection is intrinsically related to *perversion* and *digression*' (89) is accepted, then the idol episodes in *Talismano* can be read as instances of an inevitable 'crossing over of the dichotomous categories of Pure and Impure, Prohibition and Sin, Morality and Immorality' (90). The same applies to Lyotard's aesthetic approach to the sublime conceived as 'a category for dealing with experiences which are beyond categories'. Consequently, 'the postmodern artist, by extension, is one who bears witness to the indeterminable, operating at the limit of the imagination's own dissolution, where all one's senses are subverted' (92). On the other hand, however, rather than subscribing to the post-structuralist dispersal of the subject and the reduction of the human self as 'dumb, immobilized, as good as dead', Meddeb would reinterpret Kearney's characterisation of Lyotard's nihilist version of sublimity along the lines of the Sufi notion of *fana'*, or extinction of the ego, which will be taken up in more detail later on. Similarly, Slavoj Žižek's sense of the sublime as embodied by the cyborg, 'whose very robotic impersonality marks the victory of the death instinct (thanatos) over the life instinct (eros)' (97), stands in diametrical opposition to Meddeb's life-affirming thanatography. It is in this sense that, instead of 'lapsing into apocalyptic dualism' (99), Meddeb's employment of the idol in *Talismano* fits better with an interpretation by means of a diacritical hermeneutics grounded in a philosophy of action like Ricoeur's, one that does not shy away from practical judgements:

> It is not enough to be open to radical alterity – though this too is essential to ethics. One must also be careful to discern, in some provisional fashion at least, between good and evil. Without such discernment, it seems nigh impossible to take considered ethical action. (100)

Adopting Ricoeur's use of the Aristotelian notions of *phronesis* and *catharsis*, Kearney proposes a hermeneutics of action 'as a way of learning to live with the monsters in our midst so that by revisiting and renaming them we might outlive them' (103). Transposed to *Talismano*, this means that also the transformation of the sacrality of the religious world through creative blasphemy, like the people's fashioning of an idolatrous effigy, 'will be in the final analysis, life-affirming'.[60]

With the effigy finished, the perpetrators of this atrocity are at a loss for words and gestures of veneration. Not quite knowing what to do with the puppet idol, they decide to seek guidance from the alchemist Ya'qūb because of his familiarity with mummies and the sciences of the ancient Egyptians. Here Meddeb inserts an impressionist picture ringing with Islamic references: 'The master pilgrim enthroned at his shop, gum Arabic to sweeten the mouth, cleansing waters from the sacred well, zemzem, rebirth and purification to resume life's blank page, reunion with his fitra'.[61] Unable to locate Ya'qūb, the crowd sets out for Saïda's other key co-conspirator, Master Mahmūd, whose religious credentials are even more indisputable than those of his Jewish counterpart:

> [He] respects Jewish customs and holidays, learned their poetry, recites Genesis in Aramaic, has uncovered the secrets of cabalistic [*sic*] interpretation, settles disputes regarding peripateticism of the Toledano and Hispanically Judeo-Arab sort, contests Avicenna's theory of emanation. (84)

The narrative continues with more descriptions of downtown Tunis, interspersed with further digression into philosophy and North African history. Fanning out into discursive excursions to the earlier-mentioned centres of traditional Islamic learning, the narrative turns more overtly political:

> Signaling allegiance to the idol, a simulacrum that shall rid us forever of the archaic resonance, and celebrate our outmaneuvering of the powerful. [...] The idol produced in such a way is nothing in itself, does not feed a new fiction to furbish faith and belief; rather it puts an end to a kind of power, a cult of submission. (112)

Whereas Meddeb's earlier-mentioned negative descriptions of al-Azhar, al-Qarawiyyīn and al-Zaytuna serve to criticise the dominant discourses emanating from these three North African mosque-universities, a trio from the margins of society, consisting of a sorceress, a Jewish alchemist and a Muslim alchemist, provides a vehicle for introducing alternative expressions of piety that stand in stark contrast to those of a religious establishment claiming to be the custodians of truly Islamic religious beliefs. The three protagonists' subsequent instigation of what constitutes a violation of what is deemed acceptable Islamic religious practice on the part of the crowd illustrates the repressed sentiments simmering under the surface of Muslim societies. These frustrations extend also to the patronising attitudes of nineteenth- and twentieth-century proponents of modernisation in the Muslim world featuring towards the end of *Talismano*, such as the 'sheikh of the Nahda', the Egyptian Islamic reformer Muhammad 'Abduh (1849–1905) and the Tunisian trade unionist and advocate for women rights, Tahar Haddad (1899–1935):

> This is unacceptable, Tahar finally exclaims: in my day, I defended women, I sought scrupulously to integrate them, I called for their liberation, but when I see what is happening in this lawless city, I am staggered by the scandal. (245)

> We called for a cultural rebirth by returning to our pure origins, to the fundamentals of our religion, to a more righteous age; we provided, through a series of concordances, that our Book already contained all the technical miracles that transformed this century! We advocated for the unification of all the juridical schools, for an end to meaningless rhetoric, for an effort to make the acquisition of modern science a pious duty, to assimilate the boldest of inventions so that we may rekindle our golden age [...] And what do I see here? The worst debauchery, the most disgraceful disarray, the mortifying spectacle of Arabs in an all-out attack on civil reason. (246–7)

These harangues are met with defiance, dismissing "Abduh's babble' and mocking the Moroccan independence activist 'Allāl al-Fassi's 'pedantic collar, fez worn at a tilt' (248). A more welcoming reception is prepared for 'the venerable blind man Taha [Husayn]' (1889–1973). In contrast to political figures, modern Egypt's man of letters is depicted as

> sarcastic, caustic humanist, whose words are recognizable among a thousand others, whether spoken or written, if only because he can be likened to the blind man of Ma'arra, master wordsmith and writer of fictions. (253)[62]

Although in Hoda El Shakry's estimation the religious symbolism attached to the effigy operates as an 'anthropomorphic reconstitution of myth' rather than the substitution of one institutionalised form of religious authority for another, this does not take anything away from the political objectives of the mob led by the sorceress and the two alchemists.[63] Quite the contrary: for El Shakry, noting how Meddeb drew inspiration from the scandalous *mujūn* and *maqāma* poetry, as well as the derisive writings of the polymath al-Jāḥiẓ (d. 868), the novel's anti-hegemonic intentions are evident as the rebellious mob is cast in the role of revolutionaries. Referring in the same breath to the 'aesthetics of vulgarity' (68) developed in Achille Mbembe's *On the Postcolony*, El Shakry draws parallels between *Talismano*'s idol, Meddeb's mobilisation of the Qur'an and Sufism, and his criticism of Islamic modernisers and independence activists. Describing the voice of *Talismano*'s autodiegetic narrator as 'self-consciously neurotic and blatantly antitheological' and the novel itself as polyphonic, El Shakry concludes that the novel is conceived as a tool of resistance:

> *Talismano*'s transference between fiction and revealed scripture materializes in the text drafted by the revolutionaries as a substitute for the hegemony of the Qur'an. Much like the idol, the revolutionary text is an assemblage of various textual and religious traditions. (70)

The broadening of textual and visual references to other religious traditions is pursued further in Meddeb's second novel *Phantasia*, where the focus shifts to the Christian tradition and its accommodation of imagery and visual arts.[64] Here Meddeb also relates the Christian notion of the incarnation to blasphemous statements of ecstatic Sufis, such as Bistami's rapturous exclamation 'glory be to me, how great is my majesty' or al-Hallaj's 'I am the Truth'.[65] This last reference suggests that Meddeb was influenced by the unrivalled al-Hallaj expert and devoted Catholic Louis Massignon, who had characterised the martyr of Baghdad as a 'Qur'anic Christ' – an inversion of Pope Pius XI's reference to Massignon himself as a 'Muslim Catholic'.[66] Meddeb goes on to argue that, because Islam did not cultivate this notion of incarnation by providing its own theorisation, there is the risk of taking the Christian interpretation as universally valid. It also debars Muslims from appreciating the subtle distinction made by the doctors of the church between the icon as the positive and the idol as the negative image.[67]

Illustrative of this blind spot on the part of Muslim theologians is that for the theoretical underpinnings of his article on the place of icons and idols in the novels of Meddeb, Ziad Elmarsafy had to rely on Catholic thinkers, such as the French philosopher Jean-Luc Marion.[68] This is an interesting choice because in both his philosophical and his theological work, Marion only deals with Christianity, without making reference to other religious traditions.[69] That does not mean that Marion's phenomenology cannot be profitably employed in analysing the work of writers like Meddeb. Theorising icon and idol as two separate categories of what Marion calls 'saturated phenomena' offers a useful conceptual framing for capturing Meddeb's religious virtuosity in comparison to a largely unmusical Islamic tradition when it comes to imagery.[70] Together with such assertions by the literary scholar and art historian W. J. T. Mitchell that 'the opposition between pictorial and linguistic representation favors the image', and that 'seeing is believing and vice versa', Marion's differentiation between saturated phenomena is reflected in the distinction made by Meddeb between icon and idol as positive and negative images of the sacred respectively.[71]

For Thomas Connolly, this was an invitation to further explore *Phantasia* as 'an extensive engagement with Christian – specifically Roman Catholic – culture, theology, and aesthetics'.[72] He illustrates the way in which Meddeb allowed the incarnation 'to infiltrate the modern Muslim imaginary' (140), with the latter's description of *The Deposition from the Cross*, an altarpiece from 1528 by the Italian Jacopo Pontormo (1494–1557). Delicately navigating between a willingness to accept divine incarnation while simultaneously denying the crucifixion of Jesus, Meddeb's ambiguous delight in the visual economy of Catholic religious art would 'probably set him alongside the so-called heretics named in *Phantasia*' (147). Like Elmarsafy, who invokes Mitchell's observation that 'ekphrastic hope and fear expresses our anxieties about merging with others', Connolly interprets Meddeb's exposure of his readers to 'numerous *ekphraseis*' as a way of demonstrating the Muslim's ability to reconcile 'the aniconism of Judaism and iconolatry of Christianity'.[73] It is for the sake of this reconciliation of the monotheisms that came before Islam that Meddeb appropriates incarnation to fashion an Islamic aesthetic grounded in Arabic calligraphy on a par with representations of divine incarnation in Christian art. In *Phantasia*, this shift to calligraphy takes place in Chapter 9 (not 8, as Connolly erroneously wrote), where the narrator leaves through 'an unnamed book containing color reproductions of Arabic calligraphy'.[74] This turn is already foreshadowed by the narrator's observation in Chapter 2: 'When the image is banned, the letter is exalted'.[75]

The Enigma of Writing

Phantasia replicates the trajectory in *Talismano*, where the autodiegetic narrator announces that he is 'moving toward the calligraphers now', heralding the shift from the fabrication of the effigy to the writing of charms. In comparison with the effigy, which the Muslim mainstream evidently rejects as idolatrous, as a sacred object bearing a transitory figuration of image and text, the novel's eponymous talisman is a less controversial but nonetheless ambiguous trope. Notwithstanding the ambivalence of Islamic orthodoxy towards the use of amulets and charms, there is a growing body of scholarship demonstrating the enduring significance of magic and occult sciences across many regions of the Muslim world and throughout time.[76] In *Talismano*, the autodiegetic author-narrator draws and writes a charm that hints again at a wider spectrum of cultural references beyond the bilingualism of the Francophone Maghrebian milieu from which Meddeb operates:

> I set about repeating, calm but bruised: *The sword that severs/the crescent that shimmers/No sword like truth/No succor like sincerity*. Elsewhere, male

> circles and crescents doubled female, assembled, eye gazing upon floating sword, measure of history, qalam reed pen reassuring the will to write in emulation of the fiat, equivalence of the huwa, itselfness of the Sūfi and the Tao ideogram.[77]

This description of the talisman is packed with religious symbols and linguistic hints: to begin with, 'the sword that severs'. This points to *Dhu'l-Fiqar*, the magical sword with the spliced tip, allegedly taken as booty at the Battle of Badr and then bequeathed by the Prophet Muhammad to his cousin and son-in-law Ali, whom the Sunni Muslims recognise as their fourth and last rightly-guided Caliph and Shiʿa claim as their first Imam. Sincerity (*ikhlās*) and *qalam* (reed pen) refer to the titles of the 112th and 68th chapters of the Qur'an respectively. *Huwa*, the Arabic word for 'he', is part of Sufi incantations during séances, called *dhikr* in Arabic. Exclaimed in a state of ecstasy, it indicates the Sufi's abandonment of the self. In this last case, the religious referencing is not confined to Islam alone, but expanded with a comparable Chinese ideogram to Taoism. This extension of the charm's religious symbolism beyond Islam is pursued further in the third part of *Talismano*, in another passage laden with religious referents:

> prophylactic sign, warding off the evil eye by a simple fish icon, by Lilla Fatma's hand, Lady who some – Louis Massignon and his disciples, for instance – fearlessly insist on associating with the Virgin, Fātima az-Zahra, declared mother to her father, source of wisdom, tabernacle where plays of light and oil and wax gravitate.[78]

The juxtaposition of the fish, as a very early symbol for Christianity, and the Virgin Mary alongside Fatima, the Prophet's daughter and Ali's wife, and the latter's association with the protective charm of the five-fingered hand called *Khamsa*, suggests more than just a generic linking-up between the Judaeo-Christian and Islamic traditions.[79] This connection is further evinced by the inclusion of the name of Louis Massignon. Both in his writings and his engagement with the Badaliyya Sodality he co-founded, Massignon frequently turned to the Catholic and Muslim devotion to Mary and Fatima respectively.[80] Massignon's conflation of Mary and Fatima is captured by the designation 'mother to her father'. It suggests an identification of Mary as Our Lady of Sorrows – the mother of Jesus grieving over her dead son – with the deep state of mourning of Muhammad's faithful daughter following the Prophet's passing and her subsequent maltreatment by the first Caliphs, leading to an untimely death just six months later. The closing phrase mentioning light, oil and wax conjures up associations between the so-called Light Verse in the Qur'an, which features a lamp lit by oil from a 'blessed olive that is neither from the East or the West', and candles burning in front of a church's tabernacle in which the Eucharist is stored.

A further dissection of the charm is provided in Hoda El Shakry's *The Literary Qur'an*, where the talisman is characterised as 'a pastiche that combines stock praises of God and Qur'anic invocations with more unorthodox elements such as the inclusion of the Taoist compound ideogram 道'.[81] It brings together the religious symbols of sword, crescent and circle with the names of God (Allah) and Adam at the top, and those of Jesus, Jonah and Isaac, as well as Ali Abu Talib, at the bottom. El Shakry further adds that the talisman also calls to mind the connection between the Qur'an chapter entitled 'The Germ' (or 'Blood Clot', *Sura al-'Alaq*), containing the first revealed verse, and the chapter 'The Pen' (*Sura al-Qalam*). For this El Shakry takes her cue from Muhammad Asad's annotated translation published as *The Message of the Quran*. In his commentary, Asad links the divine creation of humankind out of a germ-cell or clot of blood with the pen as the implement for spreading knowledge of the divinely revealed word.[82]

A jumping-off point for Meddeb's meditations on the role of language in connecting humanity to the divine, and more specifically what happens when trying to articulate or capture God in written form, is provided by a passage from al-Hallaj's *Kitāb al-Tawāsīn*, a text that was first published in a critical edition with detailed comments by Louis Massignon:[83]

> They have written these words from Hallāj, purged of their theocentrism: *The point is the principle of any line, and the line is but an assemblage of points. And all lines, straight or curved, spring from this same point. And anything that falls under our gaze is a point between two others. Here is the evidence that* [the void] *is apparent through each act of contemplation. This is why I declare: there is nothing in which I do not see nothingness* [the void]![84]

Struggling with the paradox that while writing is supposedly meant 'to help the word break free from its reduction', it actually appears to result in a 'monumental loss of meaning', Meddeb suggests that 'we do not write with the intention of giving idea a body, of generating a theory, of formulating a truth, of preparing minds to receive a message, but rather we write to make real the possibility of an act whereby in the One, we might endure' (114). So instead of conceiving of writing as 'a process of designation that would unify word and image' (114), it is more accurate to recognise 'that Islam is governed by a reverse dynamic: the One is affirmed by the violence of the word' (116). Muslims are not alone in this: when fashioning the talisman, we have already seen that the narrator also included the Chinese ideogram for the *Tao* (*Dao*), usually translated as 'The Way', introduced into Chinese thought through the *Tao Tê Ching* of the sage Lao Tzu (sixth century BCE).[85] Further on in *Talismano*, the narrator exhorts the calligraphers to

> [g]o write on the catafalque of the saint in your finest archaic kūfi script – a frieze against the green covering – the following precept that has come from the land from which we have so much to learn, blurred proximity of China: *Defiling rough wood to make out of it utensils, such is the crime of the carpenter.*[86]

This final phrase comes from a story narrated by the other master of Taoism, Chuang Tzu or Zhuangzi (c. 369–286 BCE), entitled 'Horses' Hoofs'.[87] It affirms what the narrator had suspected all along and what he wanted to put to the test; that while calligraphy is both key and threshold to grasping and experiencing the universe, it is also the 'orphan of meaning' on account of the separation between writing and image effectuated by the introduction of the alphabet, something which the Chinese managed to avoid by retaining a writing system consisting in ideograms:

> To test our conjectures, one need only single out the behavior of an atheist in the following places: here he is in China, where we find he is a calligrapher, Taoist, in harmony with the world, untouched by crisis, in Europe, we discover he is a painter, Christian [...] finally he can be found in the Islamic, either Christianly contaminated, or regressively pantheistic, brainless, lost, Sūfi, vernacular, all complaint and compassion, imitating jubilance, crushingly archaic, revivifying the reliquary of the ancient – always preaching, able to remain ante-Islamic, pagan by body.[88]

A similar point is made in *Phantasia*, where the narrator asserts that for a self-confessed Muslim atheist also it is possible to appreciate Islamic calligraphy in Arabic without residing 'in the house of dogma'.[89]

In their close readings of Meddeb's theory of writing, which he calls allography (a generic term used to denote different ways of writing letters), Dina al-Kassim and Hoda El Shakry characterise the emerging new epistemologies as 'networks of travel' and 'nomadic cartographies of resistance'.[90] Far from referring to frivolous wanderings, both notions are consciously conceived to escape fixed meanings. With a nod to Deleuze, they form rhizomatic networks of writing (El Shakry) designed to re-imagine alternative futures (Al-Kassim). There are differences between their respective interpretations of the function of calligraphy in Abdelwahab Meddeb's novels. While both engage in hermeneutical readings, they do so in different registers: where the language of al-Kassim seems to echo Paul Ricoeur's *Figuring the Sacred*, El Shakry's appears to resonate more with Gianni Vattimo's advocacy of a grammar and syntax.[91] I suggest that both these interpretations of Meddeb's attempt to escape standardised identities and avoid rigid interpretations and fixed meanings by imagining alternative futures actually reflect a hope for open possibilities as advocated by Hamid Dabashi's hermeneutics of alterity and expressed through its concomitant new rhetoric.

The enigma of writing is not confined to Meddeb's reflections on calligraphy alone, but is closely tied up with the bilingualism that shaped his double genealogy. It is important to guard against too narrow an understanding of these twin terms as referring only to the Arabic and French languages. Instead they are better taken as references to the wider cultural legacies of Europe and the Muslim world. In *Talismano* this is evinced by the juxtaposition of thinkers and writers, past and present, from both East and West, from the world of Islam and Europe, who have grappled with such questions as what it means to trade one language for another, what happens with the invention of a new literary genre or when one episteme is replaced by another, and how language is affected by the transformation from speech into writing. Thus, Herman Hesse's oeuvre exemplifies what Meddeb calls 'the concordance between Western and Eastern gnosis, pitting Muslim talisman against a Romanesque sculpture'.[92] An estimation of the writings of Miguel de Cervantes deserves to be cited at length. Interrogating the author of *Don Quixote*, whose early modern picaresque of a knight-errant deploring the disappearance of a world of chivalric romance not only was, ironically, the starting point for a new genre of novels, but also heralded the advent of post-*Reconquista* Spain, Meddeb writes:

> Question him, make his parable easy, his low-down sarcasm, fabled vehemence owed to the masochistic abuses of Iberian tradition, which so fiercely endeavors to obliterate its Arab, Berber, and Jewish centuries, [...] The text, he says in mime, faithfully records the hand that undertook to transcribe it by referencing misplaced documents, unknown to the official archives, taking advantage of chance encounters, talkative Bohemian woman, Shahrazād in tatters, Arabic manuscript ending up as wrapping paper, [...] erudite masters of recited commentary, polyglot pleasure, of Ximénes de Cisneros, along with the severity of Ignatius Loyola's exercises. (232)

The same is true of Meddeb's references to both Muhammad ibn Idris al-Shafiʿi (767–820 CE), the great systematiser of Islamic law, and to Abu Hamid al-Ghazali (1056–1111 CE), Sunni theologian and fierce critic of Avicenna, who after an enigmatic absence of more than a decade returned as a more mystically-inclined figure to become the most frequently cited Muslim after the Prophet Muhammad himself:

> Praying before the tomb of Imām Shāfiʿī, monumental splendour in wood, gigantic ribbon of calligraphy as if to strengthen the base of the dome, I awaken Ghazālī, who says to me: I only just fell asleep. But, in patience and love, I shall respond: writing is a matter of temperament, a gift. I retreated from the world, fled society, did not write for ten years, wringing dry my solitude; but some force called me to write, to refute, to illustrate, to comment to counsel, to rectify, to conciliate, to reproduce, to prescribe. But one more thing: how will you understand what I mean if you yourself do not write? I had a friend, who was impotent; one day he asked me what an orgasm felt like; I told him: I thought you were merely impotent, but now I see you're an idiot. There is knowledge that is incommunicable, there is a knowing-how that requires experience, a bodily initiation. (234)

These references to a doctor of law and sober Sufi stand in marked contrast to the ecstatic Sufism of al-Bistami and al-Hallaj and may seem odd in view of Meddeb's misgivings about Sunni orthodoxy, unless one rereads the above passage, as Hoda El Shakry suggests, through the lens of Ebrahim Moosa's *Ghazālī and the Poetics of Imagination*, where he

> employed the very materials used by his predecessors, such as verses of the Qur'ān; prophetic report (*aḥādīth*); philosophical, legal, and theological discourses; and the narratives of mystics ... so that they constituted an organic unity. Not only was the whole of the new narrative very different from the sum of its parts, but the narrative also transformed the whole. (38)[93]

The novels *Talismano* and *Phantasia* point at an early preoccupation with the visual aspects of religious traditions, as well as with the mystical purport of the act of writing. That does not mean Meddeb was deaf to the aural aspects of language. Far from it: aside from referring to calligraphy as a corrosive art, and drawing parallels between calligraphy and storytelling, Meddeb has also noted that every young Muslim is already exposed to hearing Qur'an recitations long before being introduced to reading and writing.[94] Moreover, Meddeb's very concern with allography lies precisely in exploring these connections between the written sign and the phoneme. It would also have been out of step with Meddeb's attentive attitude towards the multilayered richness of Islam as a religious tradition and the multifaceted aspects of its cultural heritage. These explorations of the relationship between spoken and written language depend heavily on historical figures who made a name as both literary writers and Sufis. When visiting Rumi's tomb in Konya, the autodiegetic narrator is reminded of the poet's words: 'When writing, I am in my place. I wrong no one. But I prefer speech. I enjoy teaching, disclosing, to disciples unto themselves.'[95] This leads to another recollection of Ibn Arabi's remark that 'writing is neither vomiting nor pleasure nor giving birth, it is the death of the self' (230).

Muhammad's Ladder and Dante's *Divine Comedy*

This kind of Sufi wisdom also informs Meddeb's engagement with Muhammad's Night Journey (*isrāʿ*) and his ascension (*mirāj*) into the Heavens. A central theme in the seventh sura of the Qur'an, it is the only event in the Prophet's life story that can be considered a miracle in what otherwise is an all-too-human account of his life. While the Qur'an only alludes to this episode, the hadiths relate this nocturnal journey in greater detail. According to the story, Muhammad is carried on the back of a mythical winged steed named Burāq from what the Qur'an calls 'the Holy Mosque' to 'the Furthest Mosque' – generally taken to be references to Mecca and Jerusalem respectively. Not all reports agree on whether Muhammad's subsequent ascension, in the course of which he traverses the various heavens and meets a number of biblical prophets, was part of that same journey, or whether it must be considered a singular event.[96] Aside from its inclusion in Ibn Ishaq's authoritative biography of Muhammad, *The Life of the Messenger of God* (*Sīrat Rasūl Allāh*), later Islamic learning uses the episode to interpret the journey of the deceased soul to the Divine Judge, while in Sufi literature it symbolises the release of the human soul from the bonds of the world of senses towards knowledge of the Transcendent.[97] This is, for example, the case with the earlier-mentioned *Kitāb al-Tawāsin* of al-Hallaj and Ibn Arabi's *Book of the Night Journey to the Most Noble Place* (*Kitāb al-isrāʾ ilā maqam al-asrā*), or an extract from his massive *Meccan Openings* (*Futūḥāt Makkiyya*) entitled 'The Alchemy of Happiness'.[98] This last text Meddeb used for 'La palimpseste du Bilingue: Ibn ʿArabi et Dante', his contribution to Abdelkébir Khatibi's study of bilingualism.[99] This essay latches on to speculations about Islamic influences on Dante's *Divine Comedy* by such leading scholars of Islam as the Spanish Jesuit and Orientalist Miguel Asín Palacios, the Italian linguist Giorgio Levi della Vida and Maxime Rodinson, a French Marxist sociologist and expert on Semitic languages.[100]

Meddeb continues his exploration in *Phantasia*, where the parallels between the Night Journey and the *Divine Comedy* are illustrated with references to *Livre d'Eschiele Mahomet*, or the *Book of Muhammad's Ladder*, an early French rendition of an Arabic treatise that is now considered lost.[101] It was probably first made available to European audiences in the second half of the thirteenth century by courtiers of King Alfonso X of Castille (1221–84): first in Castilian by his Jewish physician Abraham al-Faquim (a corruption of the Arabic *al-ḥakīm*: wise man, physician), then in Latin, into which it was translated by the king's secretary Bonaventura of Siena.[102] When manuscripts of these translations were rediscovered in 1949, it further fuelled the polemical debates about the influence that Islam has exercised on Dante. More importantly, the dynamics leading to these translations into a variety of European languages evince a Mediterranean ecumenism of lively cultural interactions between Jews, Christians and Muslims.[103]

Instances of Sufism

Abdelwahab Meddeb's writing life ended where it had begun: with reflections on Sufism. In 2014, a final volume of his poems appeared under the title *Portrait du poète en soufi*, while one year after his death, the publisher Albin Michel released a collation of radio talks, in which Meddeb presented vignettes of figures from the history of Sufism under the title *Instants Soufis*. As the preceding pages have shown, Meddeb's novels already contained many Sufi references. These early allusions were followed by translations from the rapturous poems of al-Bistami and from Suhrawardi's Illuminationism. In the 1990s, Meddeb also published several poetry collections of his own that featured Sufi themes. These include *Aya dans les Villes*, *Les 99 Stations de Yale*, *Matière des Oiseaux* and *Tombeau d'Ibn 'Arabi*, as well as a prose meditation, entitled *Blanches Traverses du Passé*. Only these last two have been translated into English, appearing in a single volume with Fordham University Press under the title *Tombeau of Ibn Arabi and White Traverses*, with an afterword by the philosopher Jean-Luc Nancy that was not included in the French original.[104] This engagement with Sufism was motivated by Meddeb's opposition to Islamism, and his particular interest in ecstatic Sufis formed an important component in his wider challenge to hegemonic religious discourses, political and intellectual, Islamic and otherwise. In that sense his double genealogy has another double meaning: it refers not only to his bilingualism as an expatriate Tunisian Muslim residing in France, but also to his intellectual navigations between his urban '*ulamā*' pedigree and North Africa's *zawiya* culture – the popular veneration of saintly figures, usually revolving around their tombs or shrines in the countryside. Moreover, his juxtaposition of mystics and literary figures from both the Islamic world and Christendom points up yet another non-binary way of thinking about different religious traditions, rejecting dichotomies that posit Islam and Christianity, or Orient and Occident, as each other's opposites. Aside from the frequent references to both Muslim and European writers in his novels, this is also the case with *Les 99 Stations de Yale*. The title of this 'Islamo-Christian meditation' refers to both the so-called ninety-nine beautiful names of Allah (*al-asmāʾ al-husnā*) and the Stations of the Cross. It offers a reflection on Meddeb's own liminality as a poet, illustrating his moving back and forth 'between two dwellings' with references to the Sufi poet al-Niffārī (d. 965) as the counterpoint to Friedrich Hölderlin and other German Romantics.[105]

Like Navid Kermani's *Forty Lives* and *Love Writ Large*, the posthumous volume *Instants Soufis* offers the most comprehensive overview of Meddeb's interest in the historical significance of Sufi masters from the past. It comes with a preface by Christian Jambet. A frequent collaborator of Meddeb, this erstwhile Maoist activist and former member of the *nouveaux philosophes* who ended up as an expert on Shiʿa Islam writes that, with *Instants Soufis*, Meddeb had returned to a biographical genre adopted by many Muslim authors from the past.[106] Where Navid Kermani took his scholarly cues concerning Sufism from Annemarie Schimmel, Meddeb's engagement with ecstatic Sufism was very much indebted to France's foremost Al-Hallaj expert, Louis Massignon, while the lectures of Jambet's teacher, Henry Corbin, were instrumental in unlocking Ibn Arabi's theosophy and the Illuminationism of Suhrawardi. Abdelwahab Meddeb's oeuvre affirms Ziad Elmarsafy's claim in his book *Esoteric Islam in Modern French Thought* that 'the version of Islam shaped by 'Shīʿism, Sufism and Illuminationism, and those thinkers who devoted their lives and careers to them [...] now holds a central place in modern French intellectual life'.[107] With regard to Abdelwahab Meddeb this must come with a caveat. Given he is a literary writer, and in keeping with his self-description as an errant prolific writer, Meddeb's treatment of religious questions remained unsystematic and unstructured. In contrast to the three academics, Meddeb was not concerned with developing a scholarly interpretative scheme. Unlike Massignon – notwithstanding the latter's own disavowal of being a theologian in the academic sense of the word – Meddeb never wrote the kind of sophisticated mystical theology or theory of substitution developed by this piously Catholic intellectual. The family resemblance between Meddeb and these three scholars actually consists in their shared lack of objective, neutral, 'scientific' distance from the subject of study, which has been an irritant for other academics.[108] It could be argued that this makes them intellectually more honest, not just in the sense of being transparent about their personal religious investment, but also in demonstrating an implicit awareness of what Smith and Whistler call the Christian theological and Western philosophical contaminations that continue to affect and shape post-secular and postmodern thinking about religion.[109]

Instants Soufis too reflects Meddeb's resistance to the false binary of an imaginary, embellished and intelligent Islam versus a supposedly real, bloodthirsty and stupid variant. In response to his own rhetorical question as to whether 'the Islamist utopia is not an imaginary Islam as well', Meddeb answered that a day-to-day religion oriented towards death would not have survived for fifteen centuries.[110] His conclusion, that the schizophrenia looming behind such dichotomous depictions can only be avoided by carefully distinguishing between what must be considered contingent and what belongs to the essential in a religious tradition, echoes what the Lebanese-Syrian poet Adonis argued in his writings about Arabic literature and Sufism.[111] This is very much in line with Meddeb's earlier observation in *Talismano* that as a historical model and alternative to present-day nihilism and despair, 'Sūfism prevails over politics'.[112]

Another striking aspect of *Instants Soufis* is the prominence accorded to women: more than a quarter of entries feature female Sufis or women from the entourages of famous Sufi masters. Several chapters mention Umm Ali al-Balkhi and Fatima of Nishapur, married to members of al-Bistami's entourage, but also acknowledged as Sufi teachers in their own right. According to Meddeb, Umm Ali possessed a quality usually associated with men: *futuwwa*, or chivalry, which is in turn a precondition for '*firāsa*; the ability to interpret signs hidden for others' (60). Her remark that 'it is better to deny yourself what you need than to humiliate yourself by getting it' Meddeb interprets as an example of the 'flourishing of morality by remaining master of the sovereignty of the self' (75). Meanwhile, Fatima is given credit for expounding on other aspects of that supposedly masculine *futuwwa*, namely *al-ithār*, or privileging the other, and *al-sidq*, sincerity (136). While the modest disposition of women like Umm Ali and Fatima may explain the lack of attention given to female Sufis in traditional Islamic learning, for Meddeb, it establishes that 'anonymity is one of the signs of high spirituality, the exemplarity of feminine sanctity' (70). Recalling al-Sulami's *Dhikr al-Niswa al-Muta'abbidāt al-Sūfiyyāt* as one of those rare historical works foregrounding the role of women in Sufism, Meddeb's conclusion that 'it bears witness of the feminine participation in universal wisdom' sounds rather Perennialist (74). That the significance of female Sufis from the past is not just historical is illustrated by the attack by Salafi fanatics on the mausoleum of Tunisia's Sayyida Manoubia (d. 1267) in 2012. This sacrilegious event incited Meddeb to write a reflection on the idea of the gift: 'Perhaps the state of disorder in which the world finds itself is due to the withholding of the gift by today's humankind, which finds it so hard to open its hand'.[113] This attention to Sufi women also invites a comparison with the feminine pole in Louis Massignon's interpretations of hospitality. Although not exactly known as a feminist, and primarily concerned with the figures of the Virgin Mary and another Fatima, the Prophet's daughter, Elmarsafy rightly notes that in Massignon's interpretative scheme 'femininity names the capacity for receiving the divine guest'.[114]

Throughout *Instants Soufis*, Meddeb speaks of the sovereignty of the subject or individual autonomy as a necessary precondition for recognising humans as moral beings. As a gesture towards an open society, Sufi claims to universalism as an 'antidote to exclusivist identitarian ideologies' (38), and their lack of fear of 'transgressing the boundaries of the community' (41), connect Meddeb with Jambet's interest in antinomian Sufis. In his studies of the ninth-century Malamatiyya movement in Khorasan and the Ismailis of Alamut ('the Maoists of the Middle Ages'), Jambet depicts their resistance to state power as both a soteriology and a quest for justice. Although this projection of a 'continuum between esoteric thought and political efficacy' differs from that of Jambet's teacher Corbin, it shows how the scholar of Islam specialising in Muslim communities that are depicted as heretical sects by the self-proclaimed Islamic mainstream still mirrors the radical student activist of the sixties and seventies. It also points at Foucault's assertion 'that all philosophy is liberation and self-transformation; that philosophy is the care of the self and the art of existence', which not only influenced the young Jambet, but suffused Meddeb's writings as well.[115]

Meddeb's introduction to *Instants Soufis* ends with a quotation from Hölderlin: 'Where danger looms, salvation grows as well'.[116] This observation by Kermani's 'Sufi of German literature' concerning the need of risk-taking also applies to an internal opposition affecting Sufism itself: the divide between what Meddeb called 'men of excess and of sobriety'.[117] By now it is manifestly clear that Meddeb was especially attracted to the former. In a chapter on *shaṭḥ*, the exclamations made in a state of rapture that characterises the likes of al-Bistami and al-Hallaj, Meddeb draws on the definitions of these often controversial statements given by France's two leading French scholars of Sufism: *locutions theopatiques* (Massignon) and *paradoxes inspirés* (Corbin). Meddeb interprets these paradoxical and scandalous formulas as verbal manifestations of inspiration by the Divine (*lāhūt*) in human form (*nāsūt*).[118] Notwithstanding the fact that these take place in a mental state 'where the subject is absent to itself, while God speaks through its lips', Meddeb maintains that this separates the resulting 'sudden, violent linguistic act' from the enunciating individual, thereby in effect 'affirming the sovereignty of the subject' (87).

Similar paradoxical understandings of selfhood by ecstatic Sufis are already found in *Talismano* and *Phantasia*, such as Attar's reference to al-Hallaj's call that 'the prayer of the passion must be preceded by ablutions with blood'.[119] In *Phantasia*, this reference follows immediately after a passage in which al-Bistami speaks of Iblis, an Arabic term for Satan or the devil:

> At Eden's Gate, Bistami professed his inspiration: 'God made Iblis a dog among dogs; he made the world carrion. He made Iblis sit at the end of the road of the world, where the road to the underworld commences; and he said to him: I put you in charge of whoever leans toward carrion'.[120]

Although Meddeb's oeuvre does not provide any citations or direct references, in the earlier-mentioned *Kitāb al-Tawāsīn*, al-Hallāj too enters into dialogue with the devil. In his critical edition from 1913 and in his magnum opus from 1922, *The Passion of al-Hallāj*, Massignon explains that 'al-Ḥallāj considered Satan to be the most devout of the monotheists, one whose preaching is equal to that of Muhammad'.[121] Although his Catholic piety stimulated Massignon to draw a parallel between the crucifixions of Christ and al-Hallāj, he was nonetheless acutely aware that the martyred Sufi was first and foremost a Muslim. In Ziad Elmarsafy's estimation, 'the jarring coexistence of these two seemingly irreconcilable identities is symptomatic of Massignon's method and thought', and as such, an integral part of his understanding of hospitality, capable of accommodating the intercultural and intersubjective realities of the other as both stranger and guest.[122] Massignon's exegetical efforts must have inspired the – in Muslim eyes – equally scandalous association with the Christian doctrine of incarnation found in Meddeb's novels:

> How could I fail to recall the Sūfi experience, in thought and practice, devoted to the glory of extinguishing the I, rendered wholly material and only very secondary ascetic: Hallāj sobbed, lost in laughter: *Kill me, loyal friends, for in death I shall regain life*; cosmic offering of the body to shatter the screen that separates man from his nature, far from martyrdom's redemption in death.[123]

From the very first mention of al-Hallaj in *Talismano*, Meddeb appears to also follow Massignon in his complex understanding of al-Hallaj as not only a 'Qur'anic Christ', but a 'man of desire' as well:[124]

> Pigeons recall a tribe come up from the Comoros beneath the Magellanic Clouds one moonlit night to keep vigil over the Mesopotamian tomb of Hallaj, perpetuating his memory by endless rounds of prayer, ceaseless billing and cooing, discretely erotic affection.[125]

A poem written a few years later begins with a nearly identical opening phrase, 'ashen doves of the Comoros', whose 'cooing tells of sobs, funereal voices', after which Meddeb switched to a female beloved who 'proclaimed her avowal of faith, lips against lips, the fires of our bodies lured a bestiary'.[126] In both instances this refers to the so-called Haqqi doves, nesting in a minaret of the mosque in Baghdad's Suq al-Ghazl, from where al-Hallāj's ashes had been dispersed. Popular legend has it that the cooing of these doves sounds like '"haqq", in memory of this dying man's cry "Ana'l Haqq"'.[127] Although Massignon has repeatedly asserted that al-Hallāj equated *'ishq*, the Arabic for desire, with God's Being or the essence of the Divine, like *al-haqq* (Truth), such words are only approximations of what al-Hallāj was trying to convey. Massignon characterised such messages by the term '*psychagogie*', which Elmarsafy compares to 'a process not unlike Socrates' maieutics'.[128] Elmarsafy's understanding of Massignon's fascination with the languages of love and desire form the nodal points where religion and art are joined, linking the self and the other, the lover and beloved in an 'act of literary creation' that can be said to apply to Abdelwahab Meddeb as well.[129]

Creative Imagination: Appropriating Ibn 'Arabi's Ardent Desires

What Massignon did for Meddeb's understanding of al-Hallāj Henry Corbin did for his engagement with the poetry and thinking of Ibn Arabi. Describing Corbin's interpretations of the Andalusian sage as a therapeutics in the search for existential certainties, Elmarsafy suggests reading this hermeneutics in Cartesian terms:

> Which is to say that the locus of certainty for Corbin is necessarily individual (as opposed to collective), internal (as opposed to social), personal (as opposed to institutional), and spiritual (as opposed to historical and material). The source of the truth cannot come from outside oneself: it can only be a personally and spiritually ascertained and enacted reality.[130]

Although she frames it in Islamic rather than Western philosophical jargon, Hoda El Shakry shares Elmarsafy's take on Corbin in relation to Meddeb. Drawing from Corbin's seminal *Creative Imagination in the Sūfism of Ibn Arabī*, she contends that for Corbin, metaphorical exegesis, or *ta'wīl*, must not be understood allegorically, but symbolically: 'a transfiguration of the literal texts, referring not to abstract truths, but to persons'.[131] As an esoteric hermeneutics most profoundly articulated in Sufi philosophy, this provides a helpful instrument in interpreting Meddeb's literary writings:

> [aligning] not only with the narrative strategies employed in the novels themselves but also with the intertextual figures and texts cited therein. Sufism

> functions as one of the many modalities through which I read the expression of Islam as a polyvalent set of practices, beliefs, and doctrinal as well as hermeneutical approaches.[132]

After their first introduction in the novels *Talismano* and *Phantasia*, allusions to Ibn Arabi's poetry and theorising of the doctrine of 'the Unity of Being', or *waḥdat al-wujūd* in Arabic, are further pursued in *Tombeau of Ibn Arabi* and in *Instants Soufis*. In this last publication Ibn Arabi is first mentioned in connection with the earlier-noted importance of the feminine pole in Sufism. Several entries refer to his account in the treatise *Holy Spirit* (*Rūḥ al-Quds*) of four women who influenced his spiritual attainments.[133] According to Meddeb, it was Ibn Arabi's interaction with these women and their refined spirituality that convinced him that 'every human being has in itself a feminine and masculine part'.[134] This dovetails with this earlier passage in *Phantasia*:

> I dedicate this sequence to Ibn Arabi, for whom the coitus is a spiritual realization incarnating the most accomplished of prophets, Muhammad, whose wisdom is enunciated in the love of women, exalted between perfume and prayer. Why are the two sexes attracted to each other? Just like Eve came from Adam, man goes to woman, in whom he recognizes something of himself. [...] On this inherited hierarchy, Ibn Arabi builds the scene of experience. I love women because *they are the location of the effect*.[135]

In *Instants Soufis*, Meddeb describes Ibn Arabi's famous collection of odes, entitled *Interpreter of Ardent Desires* (*Tarjumān al-Ashwāq*), as a 'sublime theatre peopled by personages of high civility, care of self, submitting to a code of chivalrous spirit'.[136] In another account about Sufi salons where men and women intermingled freely, Ibn ʿArabi mentions yet another female Sufi, the sister of Abū Shujā Zāhir of Isfahan, named Fakhr al-Nisā, who gave him *ijaza* – permission to teach the religious insights he had learned from her. At the Isfahan court, he also learned of a girl named Nizam, which he translated as 'symbol of cosmic harmony' (80). According to Meddeb, it was his love for this 'most perfect incarnation of the divine theophany' that led Ibn ʿArabi to ponder the different words in Arabic for woman – *marʾa*, which has no plural, and *nisāʾ*, women, which is without a singular – and contemplate the 'problematic of the One and the Multiple' (81). Thus, reflections on femininity also contributed to the formulation of his doctrine of the Unity of Being. These narrations in *Instants Soufis* mirror the first reference to Ibn ʿArabi in *Talismano*, where Meddeb already alluded to the Neoplatonic emanation theories that chime through in Ibn Arabi's theosophy:

> And they discuss contemporary Asiatic thinkers and classically heretical oriental writings, checking their Ibn 'Arabi and their Ikhwān as-Safā' (Brothers of Purity): *The One is divided into two*; yes, but there is always a return to unity, itself the origin of number.[137]

Such instances of intertextuality can be found throughout Meddeb's writings, for example in passages on Ibn 'Arabi's thinking about Sufi language or in relation to the ninety-nine beautiful names of God. In a text from *Instants Soufis* about fasting and the Divine Name *al-Fātir*, Meddeb explained that Ibn 'Arabi used the name as a metaphor for the distinction between the sacred and the profane. Therefore, when the term *al-Fātir* is used for God it means 'Creator', but when applied to humans it refers to 'breaking the fast'.[138] When writing about the adoption of the fast, Ibn 'Arabi pointed at the parallels between the first revelation to Muhammad, which occurred during the month of Ramadan, and the abstention practised by biblical figures, such as King David, the Virgin Mary and Jesus (145). In a reflection from *Talismano* on his own first name, Abdelwahab (Servant of the Most Generous Bestower), which is also a composite of one of these ninety-nine Divine Names, Meddeb writes:

> He is said to have paraphrased Ibn 'Arabī: *It is a gift as Seth is a gift for Adam ... the son is the secret reality of the progenitor ... Every gift in the entire universe is made manifest according to this law: ... no one shall receive anything that does not issue from himself*. And I still carry that native utterance in my body, for it was the origin of my name: am I not persistently called the servant of He who gives? To find I am sealed by my name into the act of giving, here is what leads to excess in debauchery, to squandering of fortune.[139]

Another imagined conversation from *Talismano*, in which Ibn 'Arabi characterises the act of writing as 'the death of the self', can be read alongside a passage from *Phantasia* about Ibn Arabi's wanderings from his native Murcia to places as far away as Isfahan, Tashkent and Herat and what these taught him about the law of hospitality. This lesson 'confirmed the principle that invites you to be the *hyle* [Greek for matter, substance] *so that you can take the form of any of the religions*' – a phrase from what is probably the most quoted passage from the *Interpreter of Ardent Desires*:[140]

> My heart has become capable of every form:
> It is a pasture for gazelles and a convent for Christian Monks.
> And a temple for idols and the pilgrim's Ka'ba
> and the tables of the Tora and the book of the Koran
> I follow the religion of Love: whatever way my Love's camels take,
> that is my religion and my faith.[141]

Matching the format of sixty-one poems in *Interpreter of Ardent Desires* in his own poetry collection *Tombeau of Ibn Arabi*, Meddeb explained:

> These LXI stanzas were written between Paris and Tunis, from spring to fall 1984, with a passionate energy, at that time in which revelations, previously attributed to living gods, change into unconditional epiphanies, Aya inscribes her name on the note-books of the betrothed who lead the song, in her actuality, she revives the medieval Nidam [or Nizam], the young Persian, elder sister of Beatrice, with whom Ibn 'Arabi fell in love, in Mecca, in the year 598 of the Hegira, and who was the woman who inspired his *Tarjuman al-Ashwaq*, 'The Interpreter of Ardent Desires,' the divan in which certain motifs travel from one shore to the other, crossing centuries and languages, as if to accept the celebration of love, the source of movement, without which the universe would be void.[142]

In the title of the English translation, the French word for tomb or shrine – *tombeau* – is left untranslated. That this was for a good reason the philosopher Jean-Luc Nancy has explained in his 'Afterword: Three Questions about *Tombeau of Ibn Arabi*':

> A *tombeau* is a poetic genre invented in the Renaissance to celebrate a dead person [...] Among the Moderns, Mallarmé gave a unique touch to the genre with the 'Tombeau d'Edgar Poe' [...] It stands in the immortal presence of death. The dead person's death is not forgotten [...] Poe, through his 'Tombeau,' becomes the *Poète*. Ibn Arabi, by the *Tombeau* that Meddeb raises, becomes the lover who eternally *enters into enjoyment* [*jouissance*].[143]

When pursuing the question of whose voice we actually hear in *Tombeau of Ibn Arabi*, Meddeb responds to Nancy that 'it is Ibn 'Arabi speaking. It is he who speaks with the voice of Meddeb', but without implying either reincarnation or a case of schizophrenia. Instead, it is the single worldly voice of '*the beautiful Arab with the Latin voice* [...] *neither from the east, nor from the west*' (112–13, original italics). In contrast to Jean-Luc Marion, the other Jean-Luc of postmodern French philosophy demonstrates a vivid interest in Islam. In this regard, Nancy's relationship with Meddeb can even be compared to that of a seeker or novice (*murīd*) with his master (*shaykh*). It also evinces Meddeb's assertiveness as a member of Khatibi's Maghrebian intellectuals, whose radical bilingualism pushes back against the 'literary inequality and relations of dominance' signalled by Pascale Casanova, leading another commentator to conclude:[144]

> With *Tombeau d'Ibn Arabi*, Meddeb swiftly turns his back on the hegemony of postcolonial literary prose, emerging as a writer uniquely poised to generate a new francophone lyric infused with the Sufi traditions of al-Andalus, North Africa, and the Near and Middle East.[145]

Although *Tombeau of Ibn Arabi* is not a translation of the *Tarjuman*, as Meddeb progresses it becomes increasingly difficult to tell his voice apart from that of Ibn Arabi, or to distinguish between their respective objects of desire – until the closing lines of Meddeb's final stanza: the phrase 'my palms are two paper lanterns, which gleam in the muted air of Mecca' forms the most explicit textual merger with Ibn Arabi's own commentary on the corresponding sixty-first poem in *Interpreter of Ardent Desires*:

> That I am passionately in love with Salmá who dwells at Ajyād [...] 'Ajyād' (plural of جيد, neck), a place at Mecca. Here it refers to the place in the throat through which the breath passes.[146]

In *Instants Soufis*, Meddeb characterised this final poem from *Interpreter of Ardent Desires* as an illustrative example of the perennial trans-historicity of the Arabic language, which enables a literate Arab from the twenty-first century to appreciate and comprehend a text written in the twelfth century.[147] That for Meddeb himself this cultural framework extends beyond the Islamic world becomes clear from his preface to the English translation of *Tombeau d'Ibn Arabi*, where he recalls his earlier essay on Dante and Ibn Arabi (vii–viii), and his visits to pilgrimage sites between Paris and Carthage, in Italy and Andalusia, as well as the homage paid at 'the actual tomb of Ibn Arabi' in Damascus (viii, x). He ends these introductory remarks with the observation that 'the climate where I was born and grew up, on the African coast that looks toward Europe while being lapped by the waves of the Mediterranean', makes Tunisians of his generation 'anthropologically the contemporaries of Euripides, of Raymond Lull' (x–xi).

Trans-historicity having just been mentioned, this is an opportune point to return to the contrast between the archaic and postmodern addressed in the earlier discussion of the Francophone Maghrebian milieu and make a brief excursion into the influence of George Bataille's writings about early Islam on the development of Deleuze and Guattari's notion of deterritorialisation in *A Thousand Plateaus*.[148] Although Abdelwahab Meddeb alluded to Bataille's *The Accursed Share* in a collection of political essays, published under the title *Sortir de la Malédiction*, and even made explicit reference to Deleuze's notion of deterritorialisation, this has received little attention in the secondary literature.[149] While giving a nod to Bataille's notions of the 'accursed share' (*part maudite*) and of community as 'an experience of unselving', Anna Levett does not say anything concerning his writings about early Islam. Her discussion of Meddeb's suggestion that Sufism offers a possibility for opposing the hegemonic identity politics of the Arabisation and Islamism of the

Maghreb with the formation of 'ecstatic communities' contrasts with Hédi Abdel-Jaouad's emphasis on individuality in his writings about Meddeb and the archaic thirty years earlier.[150] In contrast to this relative neglect on the part of most students of Meddeb's work, Andrea Khalil is one of the few to draw on Bataille in her analysis of *Tombeau of Ibn Arabi*. According to her, the movement between different worlds, and the constant puncturing of the temporal veil between past and present, that characterise Meddeb's writing 'resist sublimation or an identity-building process' along standard Freudian or Marxist lines.[151] Instead they enable a form of what she calls sacred writing that remains in a constant flux and bears an affinity with Deleuze and Guattari's challenge to the 'symbolic constructions of psychoanalysis' (180). Instead of sublimating erotic desire, the sacred word directs the libidinal impulse towards a 'loss of the self (*extase*)', as well as a vacillation between spaces and meanings (180–1). Opposed to producing an architecture of meaning, the ecstasy of the sacred word transgresses, moves, or vacillates between spaces, meanings, states of being. A further examination of Bataille's writings on the sacred leads Khalil to conclude that, although he does not possess the intimacy of Meddeb's double genealogy or share his bi-cultural religious heritage, Bataille can nevertheless be considered a precursor of Meddeb, where it concerns the latter's rewriting of the poetry of Ibn Arabi.

The Western Exiles of Suhrawardi and Abdelwahab Meddeb

Henry Corbin is instrumental not only for Meddeb's understanding of Ibn Arabi, but also for his engagement with Suhrawardi. A poetic translation of Suhrawardi's *Tale of Western Exile* (*Qiṣṣa al-ghurba al-gharbiyyah*), which Meddeb prepared in 1993, was heavily indebted to an earlier scholarly version by Corbin, included in *Shihaboddin Yahya Sohravardi, Shaykh al-Ishraq: L'Archange empourpré*.[152] This was just one of many studies Corbin had dedicated to this twelfth-century Persian Sufi and his Doctrine of Illumination since the late 1930s. In fact, the preface to another book, *The Man of Light in Iranian Philosophy*, tells how 'as a young man Corbin was introduced to Sohravardi by his teacher Louis Massignon, who presented him with a lithograph of the martyred shaykh's Arabic masterpiece Hikmat al-Ishraq'.[153] In this last book, Corbin dealt not only with Suhrawardi, but also with other interlocutors, such as Ruzbihan al-Baqli, Najm al-Din al-Kubra and 'Ala' al-Din al-Simnani. Meddeb's own interest in Suhrawardi goes back to his first novel, where he had already alluded to the Doctrine of Light (*hikmat al-ishrāq*) and to the shaykh's violent death:

> *Nothing can defeat me. I triumph over darkness with my Light, and triumph over light with my Enlightenment. I repent for nothing I have done. I have not awakened as if from a dream. I am not of those who would change.* Maqtūl, slain, and not shahīd, martyr. Blood spilled to water the earth, to spite political blindness and regenerate, sacrifice to pantheistic waves, liquid infiltrating into rock, expansion of being into something that escapes man, but is not God.[154]

This passage came immediately after Meddeb's introduction of al-Hallāj, thus setting a context in which both are presented not as docile martyrs of the faith, but rather as defiantly dying in order to return to a truth that transcends our reality. More references to Suhrawardi are found towards the end of the novel, where they form part of a broader interrogation of knowledge and the senses, of embodiment and immanence:

> There is knowledge that is incommunicable, there is a knowing-how that requires experience, a bodily initiation.
>
> The teachings of Plato gave us the Idea. He perceived the meaning of love, but perverted its rule by abasing bodily contact. From India to China the matter was more effectively dealt with: the wise men conjured up the spark that flares within us, we beings of clay, kindling us, either masculine of feminine: rendering sacred the principle of love, the upwelling of the soul.
>
> The Christians obsessed with deadly transgression, gathered the corrupting clay from out of the Platonic text. Then, they denied the body. Out of that neutering error was born a second front of compartmentalized thought: Aristotle seeks to reflect the real through accidental flaw, from the pug nose to the cleft foot. You will therefore understand my criticism of the Arab Peripatetics and especially those who obscure the light of vision with the veil of thought! How can one be confined to speaking the body [*sic*] in isolation when everything calls out to think it, to live it to perfection? The same goes for the written word: I contest any writing restricted to describing things as they are observed, as nothing but fixedness without grasping the implications that transfigure them.[155]

Here, Suhrawardi's Illuminationism is contrasted with the legacies of Platonic, Aristotelian and Christian thought, and more positively compared with the Asian traditions to the east of Persia.[156]

In the epilogue of *Talismano*, Meddeb engages in a play of words with the Arabic title of Suhrawardi's treatise, *Qiṣṣa al-ghurba al-gharbiyyah*: 'I join those bound westward, taghrīb and not ghurba, to gather the scattered forces of nomads, Sahrāwis and Touāregs'.[157] The phrase '*taghrīb* and not *ghurba*' – 'going west, not into exile' – implies, therefore, not an alienation or estrangement, but purposeful westward migration. In the same passage, where the narrator speaks of a 'reorganization of space', as well as a cultural reorientation, 'cutting ourselves off from Mediterranean habits', as opposed to withdrawal into the desert 'to revive the pagan spirit of the Bani Murra' (260), leads the narrator to experience[158]

> [a] curious emergence of my former life, Laure in Paris, comfort and decorum, winter remedy for Venetian flu, Adda Francesca, colors of Rome fleeing then rushing back into my arms, encounter with dogs, wandering hunted, France, Europe [...] then digest the rectitude of a history off-center [...]. (261)

Further cross-references to Suhrawardi can be established between *Phantasia* and *L'Exil Occidental*, the collection of autobiographical essays named after Meddeb's essay on Suhrawardi's treatise. Just five pages long in its Arabic version, it begins with a preface, in which Suhrawardi recalls what the 79th sura of the Qur'an refers to as *al-ṭāmma al-kubra*. Variously translated as 'overwhelming event' (Ali) and 'the great catastrophe' (Arberry), it refers to the apocalyptical chaos on Judgement Day when human souls are separated from their bodies.[159] In the 'Tale of Western Exile' this is symbolised by a traveller held captive by the unjust inhabitants of the Tunisian city of Kairouan, and eventually released after what must be presumed to be a ransom payment by his family. Interpreting this as an allegory of the 'angelic selves and higher intellects that the seeker finds during his spiritual itinerary', Elmarsafy qualifies this as a story of divination:[160]

> In line with much theurgic literature where the lesson imparted during the initiation is really that of inducing the soul's departure from the body before the death of the latter. This injunction translates a saying of the Prophet Muhammad that is much beloved by the Sufis and, needless to say, by Meddeb himself: 'Die before you die' (*Mūtū qabl an tamūtū*) – die, that is, to your material self, that your spiritual self may live and grow. (109)[161]

Compared to Corbin's erudite and faithful rendition of both the Arabic and Persian versions of Suhrawardi's text, in his own inexhaustible visionary quest Meddeb used a fair degree of poetic licence. His dissection of the Arabic root *gh-r-b*, which carries the meaning of both 'west' and 'strange', and his invocation of its partial cognate *h-j-r*, suggest associations not only with exile and migration, but also with exclusion and alienation (72–4). While retaining copious Qur'anic and other relevant references, Meddeb framed the recital with other texts as well, examining the pre-Islamic poetry of Arabs and the arid milieu of the deserts from which it arose (19–53).

Elhariry has situated Meddeb's translation in a broader discussion of the poetic use of what he calls 'ornithological imagery', not only in

Meddeb's own earlier collection of poems, *Matière des Oiseaux*, but expanding it with Attar's *Conference of the Birds* and Baudelaire's *Les Fleurs du Mal*.[162] Admitting that any assumptions regarding the latter's familiarity with Sufism is speculative, Elhariry nevertheless insists that Baudelaire's and Meddeb's attraction to the same poetic images is too specific to be dismissed as coincidental. In fact, Elhariry is convinced that placing Sufi poetry in such a wider perspective shows that celestial birds and dragons 'are an integral component of the sensorial deregulation that renders poetic mediation possible' (70). To prove his point, he compares Corbin's and Meddeb's translations of the stanzas from Suhrawardi's 'Tale of Western Exile' that refer to the Light Verse in the Qur'an:

> I placed the lamp in the mouth of a Dragon, who dwelt in the waterwheel castle; underneath was a certain Red Sea; overhead were celestial bodies of which no one knows from where came their rays of light except their Creator and 'those who have a firm experience in the knowledge'.[163]

> I put the lamp in the mouth of the dragon living in the waterwheel tower. There was a Red Sea below; above, stars of which no one knows the origins of its rays of light except for their creator and *those who are very learned*.[164]

Meddeb's translations of early and classical Sufi masters are not translations in the conventional sense of the word. Rather than faithful renditions of the actual wordings of the original texts, they are better understood as meditations on the underlying doctrines and ideas, or – put differently – poetic rewritings in the target language of what Walter Benjamin called the meaning and sense of the historical source texts.[165] Together with his own collections of poems, Meddeb's reflections on the annihilation of the self in the *shataḥāt* of al-Bistami and al-Hallaj, or the theosophies of Ibn Arabi and Suhrawardi, can also be related to Paul Ricoeur's *Oneself as Another*. In these studies of identity, person and selfhood, Ricoeur takes as his point of departure the tension between Descartes' sceptical *cogito ergo sum* argument and the latter's confident demonstration of the existence of God as the only ultimate foundation of certainty. However, in the Third Cartesian Meditation this order is reversed, 'placing the certainty of the cogito in a subordinate position in relation to divine veracity'.[166] The hermeneutics of the self at which Ricoeur eventually arrives via his characteristic detours into Nietzsche and careful unpacking of the notions of personal and narrative identities provides an illuminating refraction of Meddeb's Sufi translations and poems, but also of his reflective prose and essays, as well as the meandering narratives of his novels.

This esoteric dimension in Meddeb's writings also begs the question of how it can be squared with his stance towards the political use of religion. Whereas it is quite easy to see how Ibn Arabi's hermeticism or Suhrawardi's Illuminationism are considered heretical from the viewpoint of traditional Sunni Islam, let alone the literalism of reactionary Muslims, it seems more difficult to reconcile these with that other heresy: the anti-hegemonic, open-ended and democratic hermeneutics of postcolonial Maghrebian writings. *Instants Soufis* ends precisely with a consideration of what Sufism has to offer for Muslims in the present. Aside from being 'an aide in living through the problems with which we are confronted on a daily basis', it also provides guidance for confronting the two big global challenges facing humankind today: war, and the ecological crisis.[167] In order to deal with these maladies of society and nature, Meddeb expounds on the aesthetic and ethical aspects of Sufism. Inspired by the aesthetics underlying Islam's architectural heritage and celebration of decorative geometrics, he draws a parallel between the guilds of artisans and Sufi brotherhoods, comparing their relationship to sets of 'communicating vessels' (174). For a Sufi-inspired ethos that is suited for the world of today, Meddeb turned to the *Book of Nuances and the Impossibility of Synonymity* (*Kitāb al-furūq wa manʿ al-tarāduf*) of the ninth-century Sufi al-Hakim al-Tirmidhi (not be confused with the hadith collector Imam al-Tirmidhi). Making the first explicit articulation of an Islamic *apocatastasis*, or restoration of perfection in all humankind, grounded in a notion of Adamic equality that is also found in the works of al-Kindi, al-Farabi, the Brethren of Purity (*Ikhwān al-Ṣafāʾ*) and Ibn Arabi, Meddeb concluded that 'they are the ones we need to rediscover today in order to respond to the fanatics among us' (178).

A Muslim Atheist against Islamism

After the 9/11 terrorist attacks in the USA and subsequent atrocities perpetrated by radicalised Islamists throughout Europe and elsewhere in the world, Meddeb's writings take a more pronounced political turn. But there was more to it than that. This is how Christian Jambet formulated it in his preface to *Instants Soufis*:

> The fracture in the consciences provoked by 11 September 2001 has had devastating effects on both bodies and spirits. For Abdelwahab, it was the great turning point in his 'life curve', as the expression which Massignon used for the subject of Hallaj has it.[168]

Aside from monograph-length critiques of political Islam, the transcripts of Meddeb's radio talks were also bundled into edited volumes.[169] In fact, these three collections of brief vignettes mixing opinion and literary prose not only resemble the format of *Instants Soufis*, their titles too reflect distinct religious connotations. The first and last ones, *Contre-Prêches: Chroniques* (2006) and *Les temps des inconciliables: Contre-Prêches 2* (2017), are exactly what their French titles want to imply: sermon-like counter-narratives to Islamism and highbrow discourses on religious orthodoxy. The other volume, *Sortir de la malediction: L'Islam entre civilisation et barbarie*, appears to gesture towards the 'accursed fields' in Friedrich Hölderlin's study of Empedocles and Greek tragedy.[170] That these meditations contain the same religious themes and Islamic references already found in Meddeb's literary writings should therefore come as no surprise. In his radio programmes, Meddeb also talked about cosmopolitanism, cultural hybridity, the *entre-deux*, and his double genealogy.[171] Recurring themes include reflections on the Mediterranean as a contact zone between Islam and Christendom, illustrated by the *Convivencia* of the three Abrahamic religions when Spain was still called Al-Andalus, and its subsequent transformation into a contested space, separating its northern and southern shores after the Battle of Lepanto between the Holy League and the Ottomans in 1571 (111).[172]

In her book *The Politics of Muslim Intellectual Discourse in the West*, Dilyana Mincheva presents Abdelwahab Meddeb as an exponent of critical Islam.[173] Emphatically not aiming at the annihilation or elimination of religion or theology, such a critique must be understood as a hermeneutical device for interpreting religion as a human intellectual product and interrogating the grounding of eternally valid truth claims in appeals to a transcendent God. In the case of Abdelwahab Meddeb, this consisted in the production of artistic, aesthetic, creative, poetic contributions to the articulation of religion, or what Ricoeur would call 'figuring the sacred'.[174] Although it privileges both rational and esoteric knowledge, critical Islam is not to be taken 'for a rigorous and systematic theory' (25). Instead, it is better understood as a 'poetic and imaginative process [that] does not aspire to affirm unalterable and incontestable truths' (28). Meddeb being a literary writer from the Francophone Maghrebian milieu, his double genealogy does not confine him to either one of these poles, those of the former coloniser and those of the former colonised. Instead, he finds himself in a 'complex in-between, which is multilingual, hybrid, autonomous, and fluid, and which can be described with neither of the two terms' (83). The liminality of Meddeb's approach also shines through in his self-identification as a 'Muslim atheist'.[175] While he embraces the institutional secularity of the French Fifth Republic, in the case of Meddeb this does not translate into the complete dismissal of Islam's scriptural heritage, but rather into a 'dialectic of the archaic and post-modern', already signalled by Abdel-Jaouad in 1991, and revisited more recently by David Fieni as part of his examination of Meddeb's 'radical and critical secularization'.[176]

Other commentators, however, have serious misgivings about Meddeb's interpretation of Islam. Sura Qadiri's evaluation of Meddeb's 'literary path towards an Islamic atheism' consists in a two-pronged critique of his argument that post-Islamist atheism is a logical or natural development from within Islam itself, but one which is also situated within a broader development that encompasses post-theological ways of thinking evolving from the Judaeo-Christian traditions.[177] Examining both Meddeb's literary and his politically engaged writings, Qadiri detects a tendency both to highlight Islam's historical susceptibility to a fragmentation of its doctrinal universalism into localised traditions and to advocate the 'severing of the strong link between the notion of God and the understanding of sacred scripture' (53). Meddeb's post-foundational reading of Islam fits into a manner of reassessing sacred scriptures that has emerged as a third stage in the development of atheism since the Enlightenment, and that Christophet Watkin has identified as 'post-theological' in his *Difficult Atheism* (2011).[178] It is also manifested in what Hent de Vries has called the 'turn to religion' in contemporary philosophy (1999). To illustrate this point, Qadiri refers to Meddeb's frequent collaborations with Jean-Luc Nancy. Singling out the latter's argument that secularisation is not a deviation '*from* the path of Christianity', but rather 'a progression *within* Christian thinking' (60), Qadiri contends that this is also Meddeb's preferred road map for plotting the future of Islam.[179] While Qadiri may be right in suggesting that he does not command the same degree of influence among Francophone European Muslims as – until his recent fall from grace – Tariq Ramadan, the posthumous publication of no fewer than three volumes of writings shows that there is still an audience for Meddeb's work. Moreover, outlandish writings by idiosyncratic authors, such as Abdelwahab Meddeb, affirm that Ibn 'Arabi's 'creative imagination' is very much alive among present-day Muslim writers.

Concluding Remark

It appears that my take on Meddeb's literary writings gels with that of Hoda El Shakry. This concerns not just her cautioning against the 'false binary between "secular" Francophone and '"religious" Arabophone literary traditions', or her attentiveness to the Islamic referents used by Meddeb and the ways in which he has explored the possibilities of the narrative in writing theology.[180] There is also a shared deeper methodological and theoretical affinity with the charitable interpretations afforded by the hermeneutics of Paul Ricoeur, as evinced by a remark in the introduction to *The Literary Qur'an*, where she characterises her approach as a bridge between critical hermeneutics and hermeneutic phenomenology 'that accounts for semiotic ambiguity and multivocality' (2). Such a generous organic interpretation amounts to a rhizomatic understanding of Meddeb's double cultural and intellectual heritage as a kind of rooted cosmopolitanism along the lines of the nomadic thinking theorised by Deleuze, Guattari and Shayegan.[181] This facilitates an understanding of how his double genealogy enabled Meddeb to transcend the limitations of European literary criticism and history writing by replacing the dichotomy of secular and religious discourses with a dialogical reading in order to tease out the inherent polyvalence of Islamic textual practice, thus allowing us to appreciate Meddeb's own assertion that religious texts are not immutable, but remain open to constant interpretation, inviting heterodox or heretical, even subversive, readings of the Islamic tradition.

Castilian in Catalonia, Frenchified in Spain, Spanish in France, a Latin in North America, nesrani *in Morocco, and Moor everywhere, as a result of my wanderings, I would soon become that rare species of writer not claimed by anybody, alien and opposed to groupings and categories.*

Juan Goytisolo, *Forbidden Territory*, 23.

We believe in a world without borders
wandering Jews
heirs to Juan the Landless
we shall encamp there where instinct leads us
the Mohammedan brotherhood attracts us and within it we shall find refuge

Juan Goytisolo, *Juan the Landless*, 74.

Chapter 3

Andalusian-Islamic Footprints

In the same year as Abdelwahab Meddeb's native Tunisia gained independence, the twenty-five-year-old Spanish author Juan Goytisolo decided to make Paris his new home. This move to what Pascale Casanova had dubbed the 'Greenwich Meridian of Literature' was not just motivated by his desire to follow in the footsteps of his favourite North and Latin American writers.[1] By 1956, Goytisolo had already gained fame and notoriety as a literary *enfant terrible* in Francoist Spain. Finding a new home in exile was actually made necessary by the suffocating censorship under the general's fascist dictatorship, and also by his need to free himself from the social and moral restraints of his conservative Catholic bourgeoisie milieu. However, even after the *caudillo*'s death in 1975 and Spain's subsequent transition from ultra-nationalist authoritarianism to a constitutional monarchy with a functioning parliamentary democracy, Goytisolo chose to remain an expatriate writer. Staying in France until the late 1990s, he then moved to Morocco, alternately living in Tangier and Marrakesh for the rest of his life. In spite of this self-imposed lifelong exile, and notwithstanding a self-admitted relatively late exposure to Spain's own literary legacy, Juan Goytisolo became one of the most important Spanish writers of the late twentieth century, and a frequently mentioned candidate for the Nobel Prize. Although these laurels eluded him, he did receive the 2014 Cervantes Prize, which is regarded as the equivalent award for the Spanish-speaking world.

Juan Goytisolo (1931–2017) was born in Barcelona into an upper-class family of Basque origin that had made its fortune in the Cuban sugar industry. However, by the 1930s, the family's wealth was already dwindling, a downward trend further aggravated by the Spanish Civil War (1936–9), as well as by his father's financial ineptitude and lack of business acumen. Originally a staunch monarchist, José Maria Goytisolo remained a devout Catholic and loyal supporter of the Franco regime, notwithstanding the fact that the Nationalists' air force was responsible for the untimely death of his wife in 1938. Growing up motherless, young Goytisolo had inherited his mother's literary interests and developed his initial taste by reading voraciously from her library, which consisted primarily of French novels. Despite its linguistic proximity, Catalan was largely ignored by the Spanish-speaking milieu in which Juan and his siblings were raised.[2] Adding North American authors such as Faulkner, Hemingway and Dos Passos to his reading diet, Goytisolo ironically only became acquainted with the great medieval Castilian poets and Spanish Renaissance writers after moving to France.[3]

The Greenwich Meridian of Literature

The first ten years of living in Paris were a crucial period in Juan Goytisolo's further development as a writer.[4] This was not just because he consolidated his reputation as a promising young author who was not afraid of challenging and provoking the Franco regime. At least as important were the new intellectual influences to which he became exposed after his arrival. Although it had been a voluntary move, Goytisolo's connections in the communist milieu (his brother Luis was a party member and for that reason was briefly imprisoned under the Franco dictatorship) and his struggles with his sexual identity were sufficient reason for him to seek out a less constrictive society than that of Spain, opting for self-imposed exile in the more hospitable cultural milieu of 1950s Paris. While his growing reputation as a writer certainly eased his entry into the literary circles described in Casanova's *World Republic of Letters*, it was through his relationship with Monique Lange (1926–96) that he gained access to the wider intellectual milieu gravitating around the *Quartier Latin*.[5] A distant relative of the philosopher Henri Bergson, Lange came from a family of Parisian intellectuals, but grew up in French Indochina. Aside from being a writer in her own right, she worked as an editor for the Gallimard publishing house and was friends with many of the French and expatriate author and thinkers of the day.[6] In spite of Goytisolo's – eventually open – homosexual relationships, Monique and Juan remained together for forty years, even concluding what must be considered a marriage of convenience of sorts in 1978.[7]

In his memoirs, Goytisolo wrote how taking up a position with Gallimard as a reader enabled him to make his own connections with the leading existentialist philosophers of the time, noting how he became close to the 'fellow traveling' Jean-Paul Sartre, whereas the 'moralizing'

Albert Camus kept a reserved distance.[8] Referring to himself as a 'provincial greenhorn' from Catalonia, Goytisolo also mentions trips to Spain in the company of Simone de Beauvoir, and meeting such people as Roland Barthes, Georges Bataille and Marguerite Duras.[9] Name-dropping aside, the most important person in setting Goytisolo on a new course as a writer was the vagabond poet and writer Jean Genet (1910–86). It is worth noting that, when recounting their first meeting some thirty years later, Goytisolo employed an Islamic referent:

> My Lailat-ul-Qadr fell on 8 October [1955], perhaps in the sacred month of Ramadan, on the night I first went to the place where I now write these lines and met both Monique and Genet, two people who in different ways decisively influenced my life, an encounter like a new dawn.[10]

Lailat-ul-Qadr, or 'Night of Power', refers to the night in which the Prophet Muhammad was visited by the Archangel Gabriel to receive the first divine revelation of what would become the Qur'an.[11] When assessing the impact of this 'only adult influence on the strictly moral plane', Goytisolo describes his friendship with Genet as 'an adventure from which no one can emerge unharmed' (297). It was Genet who, stripping Goytisolo of all vanity and opportunism, directed him towards the subjective authenticity that has informed all his writing since penning the novel *Count Julian*. On a personal level, Genet also gave Goytisolo the courage to admit his attraction to working-class – often illiterate – men of southern Mediterranean extraction and to come to terms with his loss of interest in Europe and his being 'at ease only among Arabs' (298). These references to Islam and the Arab world in connection with Jean Genet are already indicative of a wider cultural and intellectual reorientation affecting Goytisolo since the late 1950s. The Sufi terms used in that description are reflective of the mystical turn in Goytisolo's later literary writings. On two occasions, Jean Genet would make a direct appearance in Juan Goytisolo's writings: in the 1983 novel *Landscapes after-the Battle*, and in an essay from 1997 entitled 'The Poet Buried at Larache'.

Aside from realising the extent of the cultural and intellectual isolation he had suffered in Spain, for Goytisolo, the first decade in France was also a time of growing disillusionment with communism after the full extent of the atrocities under Stalin had come to light. The events of 1956 in Hungary, followed by disenchanting visits to Cuba and the USSR in the early 1960s, did the rest to free Goytisolo from the Marxist realism theorised by the Hungarian literary critic György (Georg) Lukács and lead him to develop an appreciation for the alternative literary theory of the Spanish philosopher José Ortega y Gasset instead. It was, especially, the introduction to the avant-garde writings of the likes of Artaud, Bataille and Breton that definitively stripped Goyitsolo of his 'ideological blinkers'.[12] However, new impulses came not only from the world of the arts, but also from more academically inclined trailblazers. Realising that he was hindered by the weight of Spanish history and that his knowledge was further restricted by his own linguistic limitations, the drop-out law and humanities student became an autodidact in the fields of philosophy and literary theories that would shape his own idiosyncratic interpretations of literature and religion. Beginning with a serious study of the Russian formalists and of structural linguistics, Goytisolo's new educational trajectory took him towards what Paul Ricoeur called 'the narrow gate through which hermeneutic philosophy must pass if it does not want to cut itself off from those disciplines which, in their method, turn to interpretation, exegesis, history and psychoanalysis'.[13] Thus Juan Goytisolo morphed into a 'Spanish man of the world', whose ability to assimilate elements from Europe's non-Hispanic culture enabled him to observe his country of origin from a more cosmopolitan perspective.[14]

While structuralism and intertextuality were crucial in shaping Goytisolo's creative literary output and critical essays from the late 1960s and the 1970s, an expansion of his theoretical and philosophical interests becomes detectable in the 1980s. Aside from an appreciation for the parallels drawn by Mikhail Bakhtin between medieval popular culture and modern avant-garde literature in terms of their anarchic celebration of heterogeneity and openness, the British Goytisolo expert Stanley Black also registers 'a slight disdain for the followers of Derrida, Lacan and the *Tel Quel* school' on the part of Goytisolo.[15] Instead he showed a growing interest in the critiques of modern society by philosophers associated with the Frankfurt School, and in the rejection of modernity's 'repressive scientific rationality' by the likes of Jean Baudrillard, Michel Foucault and Jean-François Lyotard. Increasingly concerned with questions of cultural hybridity and postcoloniality, Goytisolo's writings also exhibit an affinity with the new epistemology laid out by Gilles Deleuze and Félix Guattari in *A Thousand Plateaus*, in particular their concept of nomad thought.[16] Also, I intend to show how Goytisolo's writings from the 1980s can be read through the lens of Daryush Shayegan. Aside from the latter's own employment of nomad thinking, there is another parallel between, on the one hand, Deleuze and Guattari's deterritorialisation and Shayegan's adoption of Suhrawardi's *nâ kojâ âbâd* – or 'nowhere land' – and, on the other, the utopian landscapes sketched by Goytisolo.[17]

Mudejarismo: An Instance of Ibero-Islamic Creolisation

Goytisolo achieved a further widening of his cultural horizon through his familiarisation with the notion of *mudejarismo*. The term was coined by the philologist and linguist Américo Castro (1885–1972) to describe the Hispano-Arabic culture, or – in Goytisolo's words – 'Islamic-Occidental crossbreeding' between Christian, Muslim and Jewish cultures in the Iberian territories which once fell under Muslim rule, and which were collectively known as Al-Andalus.[18] *Mudejarismo* was conceived in opposition to the competing notion of the *Reconquista*, the Christian recapture of the Iberian Peninsula advocated by proponents of Spanish nationalism since the nineteenth century. Before studying Castro's work in earnest, Goytisolo had only a vague notion of this former Muslim or Moorish (from the Spanish *moro*) presence in Spain. Recalling his childhood in Catalonia, he noted:

> As for many Spaniards of my generation, the term 'Moor' was associated, from an early age, with vague disturbing images of violence and terror. It would be necessary for twenty years to pass before I overcame the imprints of that period and succeeded in establishing a fruitful personal relationship with the Arab world in its triple dimension of space, body, and culture, a relationship that would soon be transformed into the central axis of my life.[19]

Castro first used the term 'literary Mudejarism' in 1948, applying it in a comparative study of the Andalusian Islamic scholar Ibn Hazm (994–1064) and the Castilian poet Juan Ruiz, nicknamed the Archpriest of Hita.[20] In Castro's later work, Mudejarism features alongside another central concept: *morada vital*. Translating the latter as 'the collective consciousness of a society or cultural group', the American Hispanist Michael Ugarte adds the nuance that this must not be regarded as the outcome of some sort of social-political determinism. On the contrary, historical actors are not passive recipients, but active agents: 'Human beings invent themselves and construct their own style of life and identity.'[21] Given the broader significance of this idea of Mudejarism for the development of a revisionist historiography of Spain and for navigating the debates surrounding the equally controversial ideas of *Reconquista* and *Convivencia* (living together), it is worthwhile unpacking the term a bit further before examining Goytisolo's own take on the concept and its deployment in his creative writing and contemplative prose.

The term *mudejarsimo* is derived from the Castilian *mudéjar* (*mudèixar* in Catalan), which in turn is a corruption of the Arabic *mudajjan* (مدجن), carrying the double meaning of 'one who remains behind' and of someone who is subject to the payment of a tribute in return for protection.[22] Originally it was used for Muslims who had chosen not to emigrate following Christian advances in the Peninsula and ultimately accepted subjugation to non-Muslim jurisdiction and political authority. As a cultural reference, *mudéjar* was first applied to an architectural style that had begun to emerge in the twelfth century, eventually becoming one of the defining features of the great Gothic cathedrals north of the Pyrenees. Pedro Chalmeta notes that as a legal instrument it constitutes an inverse imitation of *dhimma*: the protection conferred on Christian and Jews in Muslim territories in return for the payment of a special tax (*jizya*). Another difference between *dhimma* and *mudéjar* is that the statute of the *mudéjar* 'was covered only by a diplomatic accord' and therefore lacked the divine guarantee of the original pact extended to non-Muslims by God and the Prophet.[23] Chalmeta goes on to observe that the term *mudéjar* only first appeared in Spanish in 1462, as an alternative to the more conventional *moro* or *saraceni*. That is just a few decades before its effective abolition following a decree of compulsory conversion issued by the Catholic monarchs Isabella of Castille and Ferdinand of Aragon in the wake of the fall of Granada.

In the opening chapter of the four-volume *The Conversos and Morisco in Late Medieval Spain and Beyond*, Francisco Márquez Villanueva offers a balanced treatment of the concept's development amid the polemics triggered by the controversial thesis concerning the cultural-historical influence of Islam on European literature posited by Américo Castro and – before him – by Miguel Asín Palacios. That these debates have still not subsided and continue into the twenty-first century is evinced by reactions to such works of history as María Rosa Menocal's *Ornament the World*. Her suggestion that the Iberian *Convivencia* of Muslims, Jews and Christians represented a 'culture of tolerance' is rejected in counter-narratives such as Dario Férnandez Morera's *The Myth of the Andalusian Paradise*.[24] The merit of Márquez Villanueva's measured assessment lies in his repeated cautioning against comparing this *Convivencia* to current standards of religious tolerance informed by liberal thinking. Central to Márquez Villanueva's argumentation is that rather than a binary opposition of Islamic *Jihād* versus Christian *Reconquista*, the history of the Iberian Peninsula between the eighth and the sixteenth centuries is best conceived in terms of a 'subtle and not very well known processes of acculturation', whereby the living and mixing together of Christians, Jews and Muslims 'occurred by osmosis', without the adherents of the three religions losing their individuality.[25] According to Márquez Villanueva, the origins of the institution can be traced to eleventh-century Toledo, where the then-ruling Castilian monarchs understood they had no other option than to tolerate the presence of non-Christians, because 'their kingdoms lacked the demographics, and economic and cultural resources, to get any benefit from their conquest [of Muslim territories]' (37). Consequently, the city became a translation capital comparable to ninth-century Baghdad, replacing Cordoba as the Peninsula's cultural centre and itself becoming the 'focus for Western intellectual progress over the next few centuries' (38). Also important to note is that Mudejarism was a political instrument for regulating the socio-economic functions of three religious groups. Operating on a communal level, it was not concerned with the rights of individual believers. Márquez Villanueva further notes that, despite being formally interdicted on both sides, 'intercultural contacts occurred constantly and through many channels' (34), including frequent side swapping and sexual relations. Márquez Villanueva concludes therefore that the concept's significance lies in the fact that 'Mudejarism has made [it] possible to access historical facts that were either invisible or had been sidelined by purist (castizo) ideologies' (42). The same is true for Márquez Villanueva's final estimation of what happened at the advent of the modern era:

> The die was cast. Mudejarism, the creative 'solution' of the low-medieval political conscience, was turned, at that moment, into the Morisco 'problem' of modern times. The breakdown in the policy of mutual respect and cooperation between the three communities, unequivocally marked by the establishment of the Inquisition in 1480 and the expulsion of the Jews in 1492, was determined by an extremely small and supreme circle. These senior members of the Christian community (not the people at large) felt sufficiently strong to become convinced that they no longer needed the other two groups, who from then on were considered an obstacle or burden that needed to be shaken off. (46)

Juan Goytisolo being an 'unruly disciple of Américo Castro', it is through his idiosyncratic application of Mudejarism in his creative writing that it gained value on a personal level.[26] In two essays packed with hermeneutical hints, Goytisolo explicitly characterised the texts he had published since the 1970s as instances of Mudejarism, adopting it as a term of reference for the creative use of cultural difference, in contradistinction to the academic study of the phenomenon.[27] Contrasting the ways in which the *Mudéjar* artists engage the Arabo-Islamic heritage with the 'aseptic, deconditioned, "scientific" approach' of Arabists and other scholars studying non-Western cultures, Goytisolo variously described his own introduction to Arab culture as somatic, vital, seminal and genesiac.[28] It was grounded in a sense of human solidarity emerging from his personal witnessing of the constant discrimination North Africans had suffered since settling in Paris at the time of the Algerian war of independence. Although he acknowledged the significant impact of Castro's scholarly work, he felt a greater personal affinity with figures like Richard Burton and T. E. Lawrence. Moreover, as a creative writer venturing beyond the confines of Spanish language and literature, Goytisolo further asserted that all good literature

> is situated at an infinite crossroads – a veritable wind rose – of paths, influences, readings, tendencies and so on, commingled or amalgamated in a heterogeneous melting pot. The literary work is always impure, a hybrid fertilized by its contacts and encounters with the universal patrimony. There are thus no univocal influences or exclusive sources or single geneses; only polygenesis, bastardization, mixture, promiscuity. (94)

Consequently, Juan Goytisolo's engagement with the Spanish classics and the way in which he later integrated these readings with text material from the Muslim world, from which he then forged his own postmodern contributions to contemporary Spanish literature, was very much coloured by a 'fecund Mudejarismo' (9).

In combination with his idiosyncratic readings of the Spanish classics and moderns, the influences of Mudejarism and the *Rive Gauche* milieu on Goytisolo have shaped an outlook that can be considered an instance of rooted cosmopolitanism. On account of his increasingly frequent and extensive references to the cultural heritage and social mores of the Islamic world, his 'wavering between two cultures and languages', the resulting 'clash of which implies crossbreeding, bastardy and contingency', resonates with both Abdelwahab Meddeb's double genealogy and the West-Eastern affinities of Navid Kermani.[29]

Shifting Gaze: Postmodern and Postcolonial Concerns in the Writings of Goytisolo

The so-called Álvaro Mendiola trilogy is generally regarded as the watershed publication separating Goytisolo's early novels written in a realist Marxist vein from the postmodern experimentations characterising his writings from the mid-1960s onwards.[30] And indeed, with *Marks of Identity* (1966), *Count Julian* (1970) and *Juan the Landless* (1975), the contours of Goytisolo's literary experimentations with intertextuality and Mudejarism become increasingly discernible.[31] While their formal qualities reflect an awareness of the role played by language in changing the relationship between text and reality, with each volume, Goytisolo's blending of different viewpoints into a literary theory of his own becomes increasingly clear. The resulting cultural limbo is further articulated in subsequent fiction and non-fiction prose writings, where Goytisolo continues to deal with the perennial concerns of conflict and displacement, death and violence, as well as the relation between writing and sexuality. Apart from the Mendiola trilogy, the work that has received most attention from anglophone Hispanists is *Makbara* (1980). Together with the trilogy's second and third volumes, this novel may also be considered as forming an alternative trilogy, a point that Goytisolo seems to have implied himself in an essay from 1981 entitled 'From *Count Julian* to *Makbara*: A Possible Orientalist Reading'.[32] However, the secondary literature on all four of these novels has paid preciously little attention to his references to Islam and the Muslim world. As a scholar of religion, I take this as a prompt to redress that situation. I will use existing critical studies of Goytisolo's work to the extent that they serve my objective of providing a comprehensive treatment of these Islamic referents, and how Goytisolo deploys them for his own literary purposes. For that reason, I will deviate from grouping Goytisolo's novels into trilogies, and concentrate first on *Marks of Identity* and *Count Julian* as initial postmodern experimentations with texts and a reorientation vis-à-vis Spanish history-writing. Next, I will discuss *Juan the Landless* together with a later novel, *Landscapes after the Battle* (1983), as exponents of Goytisolo's first nomadic excursions and engagement with postcoloniality. After that I move on to an interrogation of the dynamic between eros and thanatos, which I see at work in *Makbara* and in a later, slimmer volume, *Quarantine* (1991), as well as in Goytisolo's increasing interest in mysticism.

That these alternative groupings do not constitute ruptures of the same radicality as the Mendiola trilogy I intend to show by reading all these texts alongside meditations found in Goytisolo's two-volume autobiography *Forbidden Territories* and *Realms of Strife*, as well as in the literary criticism contained in the English-language essay collections *Saracen Chronicles* and *Cinema Eden*.[33] I continue my diversion from a strictly chronological treatment of Goytisolo with examinations of the religious turn in Goytisolo's writings and subsequent *re*-turn to more explicit social-political concerns and concomitant, distinctly realist representations of developments and events affecting the Muslim world. The key to disclosing these seemingly contradictory aspects of Goytisolo's later writings can be found in *The Blind Rider* (2003).[34] Although classified as a novel that received praise from fellow writers Mario Vargas Llosa and Carlos Fuentes, parts of it can also be considered a third instalment of his memoirs. Goytisolo notes how his mystical preoccupations in *The Virtues of the Solitary Bird* (1988) were triggered by anguish over the death of many friends as a result of the AIDS epidemic and by the fear of having caught the virus himself because of the symptoms of another infectious disease contracted during a visit to Egypt. He then goes on to explain how his return to political writings and travelogues describing visits to conflict zones in the Muslim world must be attributed to the theological disenchantment he felt after Monique's death in 1996.[35]

Aside from marking the end of Goytisolo's Marxist ideological leanings and involvement with the Spanish Communist party, the Álvaro Mendiola trilogy also involves a shift from the classic humanist outlook of a society's cultural elite to that of the *marginado*, or marginal intellectual on the social periphery: the nonconformist individual and anarchist rebel committed to provocative gesturing.[36] Reflective of this intellectual liminality, from then on Goytisolo's continuing concern for the marginalisation of 'the downtrodden' is pursued from a transcultural angle, characterised by an increasing use of Islamic referents and employment of religious language. With regard to the latter, it will become clear that Goytisolo's vehement anti-clericalism – stimulated by the Catholic church's complicity with the repressive Franco regime – does not constitute a rejection of religion or theological thinking as such, something the previous chapter has also demonstrated with regard to Abdelwahab Meddeb. Equally important to note is that Goytisolo's use of religious rhetoric 'pokes fun at the ideal of perfection that sees sanctity in the denial of the body and such natural functions as sex and excretion'.[37] This particular preoccupation with the false dichotomy between body and spirit also turns the sex/writing nexus into a recurring feature, first detectable in Goytisolo's writings from the early 1970s and culminating at the turn of the millennium in *A Cock-Eyed Comedy* (2000).

This shifting gaze is actually already prefigured in an essay published in 1962 under the title 'Spain and Europe', which Goytisolo discussed at some length and detail in *Realms of Strife*. Written during 'a period of literary fame that bore no relation to the real merits and stature of your work' (Goytisolo often addresses himself in the second person), and which therefore was also a time of personal dissatisfaction and unhappiness, Goytisolo began to look differently at Spain and its place in Europe.[38] The relationship of his native land with the rest of the continent is just as fraught with 'tensions, turmoil, sublimated instincts, and opposing demands' (232) as those tormenting his inner self. Putting Spain's ill-fitting political history alongside the decolonisation process of the 1950s and early 1960s, he concludes that, since 'Europe represented the dead past and the third world, a luxuriant, brilliant future', Spain should be looking in another direction: towards 'a human and cultural landscape that would soon fascinate you' (233). Spain having failed to integrate with Europe north of the Pyrenees, Goytisolo ponders whether it is not time to take seriously the words of an intellectual with whom he often found himself at odds: 'It is now perhaps time to Africanize, as Unamuno would say, and turn the stale irony of that phrase "Africa begins at the Pyrenees" into a slogan for our banner' (234).

A Different Take on Spain

Marks of Identity (1966) and *Count Julian* (1970) herald such a crucial transformation in Goytisolo's oeuvre that they led even to the outright dismissal of the early novels and travelogues of the young Juan by the maturing author himself.[39] This shift away from traditional literary representations on a purely constative plane (mimesis) towards experimentations with autodiegetic narration and self-referentiality, intertextuality and the use of language on a performative plane, whereby the reader is made aware of writing as a process, is not unlike Abdelwahab Meddeb's preoccupations with the question of *écriture*.[40]

Aline Schulman has characterised the first volume of the Álvaro Mendiola trilogy as both a picaresque novel and a *Bildungsroman*. The work is set in 1963, it's time-frame coinciding with the twenty-fifth anniversary of Franco's delusional project of Spanish self-aggrandisement, giving Goytisolo an opportunity for a sarcastic evaluation of Spain's so-called 'years of peace'.[41] Politics aside, however, *Marks of Identity* is first and foremost about the existential crisis experienced by Goytisolo himself, but told through the novel's main character Álvaro. Connecting memories from his youth of reading Oswald Spengler's *The Decline of the West* and *The Twilight of the White Races* by Maurice Muret with recollections of documents and papers from the family archive, he tries to reconstruct a sense of self by synthesising elements from his biography with

> certain obscure and revealing facets of life in Spain (the personal and the collective, the public and the private, joined together harmoniously both the inner search and the outside evidence, the intimate understanding of yourself and the growth of civic awareness in the Taifa Kingdoms)[42] [...] uprooted from your native soil (the cradle of heroes and *conquistadores*, saints and visionaries, madmen and inquisitors: the whole Iberian fauna), your own adventures and those of your country had taken divergent directions: you went one way, the bonds that had once linked you to your tribe having been broken, drunk and astonished at that new and incredible freedom of yours; along the other way, your country and that group of friends who were persevering in their noble efforts to change it, paying with their persons the costs that from indifference or cowardice you had refused to pay, coming to

> their maturity at the price of indispensable mistakes, they were adults, with the concise tempering that you did not have: the harsh experience of jail that you had never known; a strict awareness of the limits of the alienated dignity, that you all had. With an empty memory after ten years of exile, how could you reconstruct that lost unity without doing it mischief?'[43]

Further on in the story, by the time Goytisolo's alter ego Álvaro has settled in Paris, he 'had reached the final conclusion that the real danger was not to come from the distant, remote, and invisible Asians': the 'yellow peril' as conjured up by the culture pessimists and Catholic personalists associated with the French periodical *L'Esprit*.[44] Although identifying himself with the Spanish political and intellectual exiles in France, Álvaro now witnessed a new 'wave of pioneers and *conquistadores* who were emulating Magellan, Cortés, and Pizarro' crossing the Pyrenees and 'infiltrating the developed nations of the Common Market' (198–9). It caused the evaporation of any remaining sense of nostalgia, which was replaced by an appreciation for an errant and vagabond Spain. Instilling a desire to travel further south, the following scene from a hospital visit narrated at the end of the novel affirms this growing fascination on the part of Álvaro/Goytisolo with what lies beyond the European continent, and also prefigures the second volume of the trilogy:

> The old men who were dying without families, the workers maimed by their own tools, the Arabs and Negroes who, *allah yaouddi*, moaned in a language you did not understand, had shown you the path along which, some day or another, you would have to pass if you wanted to give back clean to the earth what in purity belonged to it. You should look for your salvation there. (285)

For that reason, *Count Julian* must be considered the true watershed publication within Goytisolo's oeuvre. Although Álvaro Mendiola continues as the trilogy's protagonist, it is in the antagonist of this second story, Count Julian of Septa (the present-day Spanish enclave of Ceuta in North Africa), that Goytisolo finds a voice for the unruly individual as a transcultural hero moving back and forth between Europe and the world of Islam, both past and present. That this figure is very much modelled on Jean Genet is shown by an epigraph inscribed at the beginning of the first part of the novel, which was taken from Genet's *The Thief's Journal*: 'I dreamed of Tangier, whose proximity fascinated me, and the prestige of this city that is more or less a favorite haunt of traitors.'[45] This quotation fits seamlessly with the reputation of the semi-legendary figure in the accounts of the conquest of the Iberian Peninsula in the name of Islam: Don Julian, Count of Ceuta, who is usually depicted as a treacherous vassal who turned on his king and enabled the

Muslim invasion of 711 CE.[46] At the time, the Kingdom of Hispania was under the political control of the Visigoths, a people of Germanic origin who had been Romanised in Late Antiquity and converted from their initial allegiance to Arianism to Nicene Christianity in the final decades of the sixth century. Goytisolo takes this controversial aristocrat to compose an alternative historiography of Iberia in the early Middle Ages, challenging the hegemonic Castilian depictions of Spain's past as the eventual triumph of Catholicism over Islam that gloss over or flatly deny the cultural hybridity of Spanish identity.

And yet *Count Julian* remains a very Spanish book. Few other writers are able to capture what, on account of its cultural and political history, remains one of the European Union's more enigmatic member states.[47] The English title is an abbreviation of the original Spanish version: *Reinvindicación del Conde Don Julian* – 'The vindication of the Count Don Julian'. The book is indeed a diatribe against everything that Spain – or, more accurately, official Spanish history-writing – stands for, and what Goytisolo hates about the country: the denial of its Moorish past; the Catholic Inquisition and genocidal conquest of the Americas; the Church's complicity with autocratic monarchism and its condonement of fascism; the country's social conservatism and its concomitant sexual repression. Goytisolo refused to subscribe to such official accounts, and repackaged the story of the Muslim occupation of the Iberian Peninsula as a fantasy of an expatriate Spaniard in Tangier about a new invasion of Spain from North Africa led by a contemporary incarnation of the figure whom official Spanish historiography has cast as one of the greatest villains of the Iberian past. Embracing the liminality of this literary persona, Goytisolo projects a contemporary alter ego with the same name, whose pronouncement that 'tomorrow will be another day, the invasion will begin all over again' turns him into an almost messianic figure bent on rectifying the course of Spain's post-*Reconquista* history.[48] However, before exploring the literary function of Julian and appreciating Goytisolo's reinterpretation of his character, a brief sketch of the historical context and scant facts concerning Julian's role in the invasion from North Africa is in order.[49]

Most of what we know of this late seventh- and early eighth-century Visigoth initially came from historical accounts in Arabic where the name Julian – assuming this was indeed his Christian name! – is rendered as Ulyan.[50] On the basis of what can be pieced together from these sources, Julian was one of four key players in the story of the 711 invasion of southern Spain, the other three being Musa ibn Nusair (640–714), the de facto Arab ruler of North Africa governing from Kairouan in present-day Tunisia on behalf of the Umayyad Caliphs; the latter's army commander based at Tangier, a Berber by the name of Tariq ibn Ziyad (670–720); and Roderic (Rodrigo in Spanish, 688–711), the last King of Hispania. Julian is thought to have been a nobleman or at least a prominent merchant appointed by the Visigoth rulers to coordinate trade between the southern Iberian and North African coasts. It is likely that this aristocrat acting as governor of Ceuta was also in charge of Algeciras on the other side of the Gibraltar Straits.[51] The Arabic sources mention that Julian was not only in direct contact with Musa ibn Nusair, but had also maintained relations with one of the latter's predecessors, Uqba ibn Nafi (d. 683), the conqueror of Ifriqiyya, the Arabic rendition of the former Roman province of Africa, which had encompassed present-day Libya, Tunisia and Algeria. This means that Julian had been visiting and residing in North Africa for more than three decades prior to Tariq's invasion. From this it can be inferred that the first reconnaissance missions sent into southern Spain by Tariq were shipped across with boats belonging to Julian. The motivations for Julian's decision to become an accomplice in the actual military campaign, with which the eventual Muslim occupation of most of the Iberian Peninsula had begun, are diffuse. This is where the fourth key player in the drama takes the stage.

King Roderic/Rodrigo too is vilified in later Spanish sources, where he is depicted as an usurper who snatched away the throne of Hispania from the sons of the penultimate Visigoth King Wittiza (687–710). In his *Muslim Spain Reconsidered*, the British historian Richard Hitchcock questions this account because of evidence that Roderic had been rightfully elected king by the Visigoth nobility. Despite the legitimacy of this succession practice, it seems he nevertheless faced opposition from proponents of dynastic rule. There is indeed mention in Arabic sources of overtures to Tariq ibn Ziyad on the part of Wittiza's sons, and that they came to an agreement to make common cause against the elected monarch, which eventually was ratified by Musa ibn Nusair and the Caliph al-Walid I in Damascus.[52] The exact role of Julian in all this remains speculative. He may have sided with the sons of Wittiza out of a sense of loyalty to the previous ruler he had served as governor of Ceuta, but this conflicts with Julian's own agreement with Musa to help Tariq establish a foothold in Iberia. More pragmatic, or opportunistic, reasons include considerations that Visigoth infighting and civil war was bad for business, or would create a power vacuum Julian could exploit to strengthen his own position. Several Arabic sources further suggest a personal grudge of Julian against Roderic. According to these accounts, the king had violated the honour of one of Julian's daughters during her stay at his court.[53] Although Hitchcock dismisses this as 'the stuff of a later legend', an alternative designation is furnished by Denise Filios.[54] On the basis of Hayden White's argument that medieval chronicles are not dry recordings of facts ('what really happened'), but totalising explanations of events, she suggests reading such texts as 'belief tales' intended to construct realities for both narrators and audiences.[55]

This supposed incident eventually became material for medieval chivalric romances in which Julian's daughter, eventually named as Florinda la Cava, is recast as a seductress. The resulting transformation of Julian's daughter into a woman of ill repute is even mentioned in *Don Quixote*, where Cervantes claimed that a promontory on the North African coast referred to in Spanish as La Cava Rumia is actually a corruption of the Arabic *Qabr ar-rūmiyyah*, tomb of the Byzantine or Christian woman, which in local pronunciation sounds like *qăḥba ṛūmiyya*, or Christian prostitute.[56] This would also account for Cervantes' characterisation of La Cava as *la mala mujer christiana* or 'bad Christian woman'. Such refashioning of the incident – whether it truly transpired or not no longer matters – plays an important role in Goytisolo's portrayal of Julian. With a nod to the *Arabian Nights*, Stanley Black characterises the novel's narration as cast in a 'Scheherezadian mould', because it too employs a narrator whose life depends on storytelling through the manipulation of life and art.[57] The result is a story in which reality and fantasy become increasingly, yet purposefully, confused. A very critical reading that takes Goytisolo's treatment of the story of Rodrigo and Florinda la Cava in an entirely different direction is provided by Brad Epps, whose five-hundred-page study of the novels written between 1970 and 1990 offers a very detailed dissection of Goytisolo's complicated relationship with sexuality and gender questions. Using theorists of feminism such as Simone de Beauvoir, Judith Butler and Luce Irigaray, Epps claims that, notwithstanding Goytisolo's reputation as 'an unconventional and independent thinker, a staunch defender of marginal positions and unpopular opinions, and a fervent critic of dominant ideology', in this instance he remains beholden to a tradition of masculinity which silences the voices of women in history.[58] In line with this interpretation, Epps further suggests that 'Goytisolo's sardonic commentary on the West's phantasmatic fear of Islam provides another commentary, an unwittingly disturbing commentary on men's fear of women, in the West and in the Islamic world' (58). Moreover, the punishments meted out to Rodrigo in *Count Julian* reflect an aggressively liberating homosexuality that remains inextricably tied up with misogyny. On account of what Irigaray refers to as a coercive sexual symmetry, this type of masculinist homosexuality amounts to a denial of difference and thus 'becomes synonymous with fear of female genitalia, gynophobia' (90–1). Whether one considers such deep readings persuasive or not, the uncertainties surrounding the very historicity of Julian enabled Goytisolo to experiment further with the dispersal of identity and narrative form.

I suggest reading *Count Julian* as Juan Goytisolo's postmodern retelling of the history of North African–Iberian relations. An important hint in this regard is *Count Julian*'s opening epigraph, which is taken from Luis García Valdeavellano's *Historia de España* (1952). In this passage, a 'mysterious person whom Moslem historians almost always refer to as Ulyan, though his real name was probably Julian, or perhaps Urban, Ulbán or Bulian' is introduced as 'a Berber, a Visigoth, or a Byzantine', who as early as 682 already made contact with Uqba bin Nafi, the conqueror of North Africa.[59] Goytisolo exploits these ambiguities not just to blur distinctions between fiction and fact, history and myth, language and reality, or in order to creatively interrogate the distinction between history and discourse in the structural linguistics of Ferdinand de Saussure, Roman Jakobson and Émile Benveniste. By joining together a cultural-historical identification with the Muslim narrative and literary associations with the Baroque poetry of Góngora, Goytisolo turns *Count Julian* into a parody of both Spain's official historiography and the country's literary canon cherished by apologists for the Franco Regime and traditional critics alike.[60]

Goytisolo's intention of challenging the hegemonic discourses on Spain's medieval past projected by official Spanish historiography is also evidenced by another epigraph attributed to Américo Castro, which is inserted before the second part of *Count Julian*: '*flatus voci* and gesticulation'.[61] The importance of this invocation becomes clear when we recall Castro's view of humans as active agents in shaping their own history.[62] In this part of the novel, Goytisolo elaborates the contemporary alter ego of Julian and the motivations behind his agenda for a new Muslim invasion of Spain from North Africa. The realisation that 'one's true homeland is not the country of one's birth', to which one is only bound by language, undergirds Goytisolo's experimentations with the discursive formations of history-writing.[63] In this instance, this is achieved by disrupting the levels of narrative through the contemporary doubling of the historical pair of Julian and Tariq ibn Ziyad and their fantasies about a second North African invasion of Spain. Thus the stage is set for a definitive break with Spain and the rectification of the historical error marring its modern past:

> Flee them, Julian, take refuge in the Moorish café: safe from your own people, in your African land of adoption [...] but wait: there is no hurry:

> you will carry out your treasonous deed: your stubborn serpent is patiently awaiting the revenge it has planned for centuries. (105–6)

This menacing prospect of a new Muslim invasion is taken up again in Part Three with another reference to a passage from Alfonso the Wise's *Crónica General* with vivid depictions of threatening Moorish warriors with faces 'dark as pitch', cruel and dangerous horsemen mounted on horses that 'were as swift as leopards' (108). What follows is a hallucinatory tale of the modern-day Julian's increasing identification with Islam and the Muslim world:

> Oh prophets of Baghdad, Córdoba, Damascus! Oh my beautiful, noble language, the weapon of treason: a gleaming, sharp-honed scimitar, an army of cruel, burnished blades, rally round me, ye pure-blooded Bedouins [...] gaze upon the tempting straits [...], the burning sands of Tarifa, the eagerly awaiting rock of Gibraltar! Your lexicon must be rescued: the age-old linguistic fortress must be dismantled. (165–6)

Trading the hoods of Catholic penitents still worn today during Andalusia's Holy Week processions for a Muslim turban, Julian becomes 'the lord and master of the wa-l-lah' (107), as Goytisolo's intertextual experimentations reach their culmination in the novel's finale. Conflating an orgy of violence with Spaniards congregating at a doll's shrine after a 'Moorish necromancer and little sorcerer's apprentices from the mosque of the Aisauas' had paid homage to the effigy, in a scene reminiscent of the idol parade in Abdelwahab Meddeb's *Talismano*, 'the worshipers line up in Indian file, and with the doll on a stretcher, begin marching smartly down the street', until in the end – after being miraculously revived – the doll 'in an immaculate djellaba, a snow-white turban atop its head, [...] invokes the name of Allah in faultless Arabic, and manifests its ardent desire to become a convert to Islam' (202).[64]

This would-be conversion story at the very end of *Count Julian* hints at a shift from Juan Goytisolo's exploration of the creative possibilities furnished by post-structuralist intertextuality towards new avenues afforded by what Hamid Dabashi calls the liberation geography of the postcolonial world of the late twentieth century. As part of the narrative's manipulations of space and topography, *Count Julian* also reprises Álvaro's preoccupation with atlases and maps already found in *Marks of Identity*. Now a map of Morocco triggers spectres of 'warriors with kinky hair, pureblooded Bedouins [who] will one day occupy the entire length and breadth of Spain' and of fantasies about 'another Count Julian hatching dark and treacherous plots' (7). Goytisolo's depiction of Tangerine landmarks brings together images from today's Middle

East and memories of the Arab past: posters of Egyptian singers Umm Kalsúm and Farid-el-Atrach in the city's cafés merge with attempts to emulate the medieval poet Al-Mutanabbi, conflating formulations like 'waves galloping like stud stallions toward the opposite shore' with recollections of 'the victorious armies of Tariq' (49) crossing the Straits towards 'the enemy coast: less than three hours by boat to the vaguely outlined looming bulk of Gebal-Tariq' (55).[65] Stanley Black characterises Goytisolo's description of these wanderings through Tangier's labyrinthine streets as a 'texto-medina' – a trope equally applicable to *Juan the Landless* and *Landscapes after the Battle*.[66] For this 'meandering through the ghettos and banlieues of New York, Barcelona and Paris – the "medinas of the West", as he called them', Juan Goytisolo coined the Spanish neologism *medinear*, which evidently has its French equivalent in Abdelwahab Meddeb's *médiner*.[67]

Rereading these now more than fifty-year-old passages of Julian's fantasies about a new Muslim invasion of Europe from North Africa with today's disturbing images of migrants and refugees congregating in the Spanish enclaves of northern Morocco in mind, it is difficult not to attribute a degree of clairvoyance to Goytisolo. In an article published ten years before the 2015 migrant crisis, Andrea Albrecht used *Count Julian* to critically interrogate the collective identity formations dominating the post-Cold War political discourses since the turn of the last century. Goytisolo's writings offer a counter-narrative to essentialising or homogenising conceptualisations of culture as manifestations of a worrying boom in identity-related buzzwords. As such must also be counted the celebratory references to a rebirth of Europe in the wake of its expanding unification process by otherwise critical thinkers such as Jürgen Habermas and Jacques Derrida. Texts like Goytisolo's *Count Julian* maintain that the inviolability of particular collective identities within a multicultural or hybrid context depends on respect for their individual integrity grounded in an unconditional recognition of difference. Within the framework of *Count Julian*'s remythologisation, failure to acknowledge this principle would vindicate the actions of such unruly individuals or 'dissidents' as Julian.[68] Transposed from the literary-discursive to the political-historical plane, if the fictitious modern-day Julian's conspiratorial second invasion of Europe is interpreted as prefiguring the very real human waves from North Africa flooding into 'Fortress Europe' today, then the atrocities pervading the novel's narrative constitute a serious warning of political violence as a realistic prospect when defining international relations in terms of culture wars or projecting the post-Cold War world order as a clash of civilisations.[69] Already in 1970, Goytisolo appears to write with a sense of foreboding of what is to come; except that, instead of the protectionist propaganda talk of the rightwing populists at the beginning of twenty-first century, the defiant and uncompromising rhetoric comes from those on the other side of the fence.

Cultural Border-crossing and Linguistic Code-switching

Whereas the first two volumes of the Álvaro Mendiola trilogy revolved around the post-structuralist dispersal of man, *Juan the Landless* inaugurated a growing preoccupation with the questions of postcoloniality, which are explored further in *Landscapes after the Battle*. In both instances Goytisolo's concern with socio-economic and cultural-political issues are articulated artistically through aesthetic experimentations with literary texts, combining the centrifugal forces of epistemic and geographical decentring with linguistic code-switching. I consider *Landscapes after the Battle*, written in 1983, to be Juan Goytisolo's key postcolonial text. Recalling his disenchantment with the Soviet Union and leftist regimes elsewhere, it establishes him as an ideological trailblazer heralding the end of the dichotomous Cold War world-view and a prophetic figure projecting an alternative world order for the next century. In this latter regard, *Landscapes after the Battle* can be considered a precursor of Michel Houllebecq's visionary novels – albeit with a twist. Goytisolo's triumphant and weirdly utopian account of the presence of the formerly colonised in the metropole stands in marked contrast to Houllebecq's dystopian interrogation of the populist and Islamophobic fall-out from the new millennial culture wars.[70]

In fact, Goytisolo's interest in the postcolonial was already prefigured by the author's earlier-mentioned fascination with the seedy neighbourhoods of Barcelona and disenfranchised peasants of southern Spain. After his move to Paris and first visits to Tangier, it would grow into an increasingly consummate preoccupation. The gestation of the first two volumes of the Mendiola Trilogy took place in the early 1960s, when the decolonisation of Africa was still in full swing and the Cold War was at its height. That particular global situation accounts for the binary opposites still projected in *Marks of Identity* and *Count Julian*, where Goytisolo pitches reactionary Spanish nationalism and conservative Roman Catholicism – or even Christian Europe as whole – against Communists, social renegades and North African Muslims. The idea of an opposition between East and West – or, more accurately and importantly, the North–South divide in prosperity – may have made sense during the age of imperialism and ensuing independence struggle, but it no longer represents the state of affairs in the postcolonial world. Goytisolo's memoirs from the mid-1980s already betray his changing world-view:

> My subsequent obsessive movements whether in Paris, Istanbul, New York or Marrakesh – the instinctive seer's guesses guiding my steps toward territories neither sterilized nor subject to rigorous planning or control [...] the present metropolitan centers threatened by the subtle, avenging infiltration of the formerly colonized, the marginalized, and the victims.[71]

In an article written a few years earlier, Goytisolo had even coined a verb for it: 'Paris is thirdworldifying.'[72] This idea that, currently, the colony is as much in the metropole as the metropole used to be in the colony has been an important element in the transformation of Hamid Dabashi's Islamic liberation theology into a hermeneutics of alterity that challenges the false binaries imposed by obsolete dichotomous world-views. The way postcoloniality features in Juan Goytisolo's creative writing reflects the ideas of other philosophers and postcolonial theorists I have used in my earlier work on Islamic intellectual history. Keeping in mind Deleuze and Guattari's notions of deterritorialisation and nomadology, as well as the postcolonial theorising of Homi Bhabha and Daryush Shayegan, my analysis of *Juan the Landless* and *Landscapes after the Battle* will show how they can be read as instances of what Vattimo calls the 'fictionalized experience of reality'.[73]

Like *Count Julian*, the third volume of the Mendiola trilogy is also named after a historical figure: King John of England (1167–1216). The son of Henry II and Eleanor of Aquitaine, he was nicknamed *Jean sans terre*, or John Lackland, because as the youngest child he was not bequeathed any territories on the European continent. According to Michael Ugarte, Goytisolo took the original Spanish title *Juan sin tierra* from *Jean sans Terre*, a collection of poems published in 1936 by the bilingual Alsatian poet Ivan Goll (1891–1950), in which the historical character stands for the condition of modern man as increasingly disconnected from his cultural roots.[74] Goytisolo too uses *Juan sin tierra / John the Landless* to illustrate the uprootedness of the novel's principal figures and of himself. Brad Epps notes the additional relevance of the lemma on King John in the *Encyclopedia Britannica*, which depicts him as 'disgraced and disgraceful, detested and detestable' – making the similarity with the flawed character of Count Julian of Ceuta fairly obvious.[75]

Juan the Landless is divided into seven untitled chapters referred to only by Roman numbers, but of particular interest for the present purposes is also a lengthy intermezzo wedged between Chapters III and IV, which also consists of seven vignettes. It features three further individuals of historical significance, who can be considered as cultural border crossers between Europe and the Muslim world, and who were already briefly introduced in the second chapter where the scene shifts from what is in fact an excursion into the Cuban connections of Goytisolo's own family to alternating descriptions of Paris and the Moroccan city of Marrakesh, until 'you will reach the next oasis thanks to subtle instinct of the Meharis: Anselm Turmeda, Father Foucauld, Lawrence of Arabia?: amid those of your kind at last'.[76] Inspired by the trio's exploits, the narrator concludes the passage with the lines:

> We believe in a world without borders
> wandering Jews
> heirs to Juan the Landless
> we shall encamp there where instinct leads us
> the Mohammedan brotherhood attracts us and within it we shall find refuge.[77]

The most prominently present of these three is T. E. Lawrence (1888–1935), the British archaeologist and military intelligence officer who became famous through his memoir of the Arab Revolt (1916–18), published as *The Seven Pillars of Wisdom* and adapted into a blockbuster film by David Lean. Roughly a generation older, also the French aristocrat and army officer-turned-priest Charles Eugène Viscount of Foucauld (1858–1916) was a renowned desert explorer, attaining additional fame as a martyred missionary who was eventually canonised in 2022 by Pope Francis. As Goytisolo's near-contemporaries, these two individuals receive more attention in the secondary literature than the third historical figure: Anselm Turmeda (Fray Anselmo Turmeda, 1355–1423).[78] This renegade Franciscan Friar can be considered a photo negative of his fellow Mallorcan Ramon Llull (1232–1315), who is briefly mentioned in Abdelwahab Meddeb's *Tombeau of Ibn Arabi*.[79] Whereas the latter had set out missionising among the Muslims of North Africa and writing important works of Christian apologetics, Anselm eventually embraced Islam and became a courtier of the Hafsid Sultan in Tunis, adopting the Arabic name Abdallah al-Tarjuman al-Mayurqi al-Muhtadi.[80] From the perspective of hegemonic Spanish historiography, this made Turmeda as treacherous an individual as Julian of Ceuta, while his controversial poetry in Catalan did not endear him to Castilian Catholic officialdom either.

Instead of discussing the seven intermezzos in the sequence in which they appear in *Juan the Landless*, I will reorganise them chronologically in accordance with the historical appearance of the three historical figures-turned-literary characters. The first, entitled 'hairottomaniacs' (86–101), consisting primarily of a tour around the landmarks of Istanbul and references to the classical poets Ovid and Homer, introduces Turmeda as follows:

> The ancient, centuries-old author of the *Offering of a Learned Man*: the visionary Ibn Turmeda in person, come from his distant and delightful retreat to offer witness of his apostasy, accompanied by his son Mohammed: their venerable beards rival those of the sage patriarchs, and their eyes, like those of a falconer, observe the gregarious hordes of tourists flocking through the Orta Kapu, sheltered beneath the broody hen's wing of an officious shepherd: a dragoman with a diploma, a polyglot, who, after taking their tickets, will guide them to the sultan's reception rooms. (86–7)

Offering of a Learned Man is short for *Offering of a Learned Man, against the Followers of the Cross*: the English title of *Tuḥfat al-Adīb fī al-Radd ʿalā Ahl al-Ṣalīb*, a treatise by Turmeda in Arabic. It is a refutation of Christianity penned when he was working in Tunis as 'the chief customs officer of the kingdom and the majordomo of the palace of Abu Faris Abd al-Aziz' (129) – the Hafsid ruler of North Africa at the time. In the final intermezzo, entitled 'With Ibn Turmeda back to the open sewer', the protagonist of *Juan the Landless* visits the Mallorcan convert's tomb in Tunis where he contemplates, together with Turmeda, what is bound to be history's verdict of the latter's 'apostacy and proselytism in favor of Islam' (144). While the imaginary duo find themselves 'fraternally united in the accursed abjuration of the Spanish convert to Islam' by their compatriots, they are certain that Abdallah al-Tarjuman's new co-religionists will accord him 'his rightful, eternal inclusion on the list of Mohammedan anchorites' (144). The picture of this late medieval cultural and religious border crosser that arises from these description bears a close affinity with the figure of the traitor in *Count Julian*, and the context in which he makes a final appearance in *Juan the Landless* does nothing to correct that image. With an evident nod to Turmeda's most renowned treatise *Disputation with a Donkey*, the fifth chapter relates how 'following the precepts of the venerable Ibn Turmeda, we have democratised the animal hierarchy and no longer take ourselves to be, as we once did, the lords and masters of anyone'. Quite the contrary: while adding a reference to the movie classic *King Kong*, 'on the ruins of churches and ideologies we shall give ourselves over to the intoxicating pleasures of clandestine, nocturnal worship of the mighty gorilla of the film and of his paradigmatico-explicit categorical-imperial COCK'.[81]

The intermezzos about Foucauld and Lawrence also contain such provocative sexual associations. The first intermezzo featuring the hermit of the Sahara desert bears the title 'The phallus of Ghardaïa' (123), while one of the vignettes about Lawrence, called 'the eighth pillar of wisdom', refers to the rape suffered by Lawrence when he was held captive by Ottoman soldiers in Syria with the phrase 'on the road to Damascus and the naked humiliation of Deráa' (104). While Ugarte remains silent on the subject, another American Hispanist, Randolph Pope, notes that 'Goytisolo appropriates the Lawrence myth and reinterprets him, choosing to stress the thrill of action, the power of assimilation, and the homosexual camaraderie in his life, over the evident pain, distrust, and separation voiced by Lawrence himself'.[82]

Meanwhile, the desert is presented as an ascetic and purifying space, offering an opportunity 'to pass beyond the limits of your narrow, petty destiny by following the example of hermits like Simeon Stylites (388–459) [who] disdaining worldly glory, retired to the inaccessible heights in search of superior perfection' (105). That also goes for another intermezzo, concerning Père de Foucauld's mission among the Berbers living along the Algerian–Moroccan borderlands and among the Tuareg tribes of the Southern Sahara, which relates the French priest's 'longed-for martyrdom at Tamanrasset, the dazzling apotheosis of your career', and Álvaro's reading of de Foucauld's *Oeuvres Spirituelles*, which stimulated his own desire to seek out 'the bare expanses of the Sahara' (138).[83] Having thus set up the writing–sexuality nexus that will remain a constant in *Juan the Landless* and throughout Goytisolo's subsequent writings, the same intermezzo also links the alteration between languages to (homo)sexual liberation: 'erasing insofar as possible the traces of your previous paltry existence: having finally rid yourself of your irksome English personality thanks to the clever use of a highly colloquial Arabic'.[84] Conflating postmodern self-referentiality with an exhortation addressed to Lawrence, the narrator continues:

> Put your own adventitious model before the reader as an exemplar of the battle against clichés: henceforth making no effort to disguise the unavoidable ambiguity of language recreating your world on the blank page: the liberation of Damascus is not pressing, and ascending at the head of the *Islamic body*, you will tarry once again in the luxuriant foliage of the hanging gardens of Babylon.[85]

This linguistic connection between Arabic and Islam and its relevance to religious border-crossing also appears in another intermezzo, unrelated to either Foucauld or Lawrence: 'Excursion into Nubian territory'. Citing the Qur'an chapter 'The Infidels' (*Sura al-Kafirun*), in which the Prophet calls for religious tolerance, the passage in question also emphasises the auditory aspects of the Qur'an:

> [...] the African subsoil is satisfaction enough for you as you follow the ritual of the suras absorbed from the lips of the dragoman and abandon yourself to its sonorous spell with crude and cruel joy
> oh infidels
> I do not worship the one whom you worship
> nor do you worship the one whom I worship
> I shall not adore the one whom you adore
> Nor shall you adore the one whom I adore
> Keep your religion, I've got my own! (112)

The importance of hearing the Qur'an being recited – a point already encountered before in the chapter on Navid Kermani – is taken up again towards the end of this excursion, where 'the voice of the almocri[86] chanting his chaplet of suras from the Koran' acts as an incentive to further engage with a new language and culture (and religion) The same passage also calls on the protagonist to wage 'holy war until it embraces the entire country', but then shifts to invoke 'the omnipotent powers of writing' (115). At the end of the novel, Goytisolo gestures again to *Sura al-Kafirun* with a final instance of linguistic code-switching, when the original Arabic wording is transliterated phonetically using Latin script, followed by a handwritten invocation in colloquial Arabic:

> People who do not understand me, stop following me
> our connection has ended
> without a doubt, I am on the other side
> always with the pariahs
> knives ready. (268–9)

Such evident resonances with Abdelwahab Meddeb's *écriture* are present in *Landscapes after the Battle* as well. This is a more fragmented novel composed of seventy-eight mini-chapters, and language alternation and calligraphic code-switching are present right from the very start. The book opens with an eerie depiction of the Parisian neighbourhood of Le Sentier (where Goytisolo lived at the time) as it falls victim to what is described as a 'gradual penetration' by 'foreign elements'.[87] This 'unmistakable invasion' is reflected by the appearance of graffiti and street signs in an alphabet unknown to an elderly resident witnessing these changes. Adding to the menace is the suggestion that these are the work of a furtively moving silhouette belonging to a 'person with kinky black hair' (2). Convinced that the multiplication of these writings has everything to do with the increasing presence of foreigners in his neighbourhood, the novel's central character opines that 'somebody ought to look into what those scribbles meant, maybe those people were up to something' (3). Once the language in which these mysterious writings are written is identified as Arabic, it is evident that 'some petroleum emirate had bought up the entire quarter' (5).[88] When even the name of the Communist newspaper *L'Humanity* is Arabised into *Al-Insāniya* (الانسانية), the narrator concludes that Paris is being 'colonized by those barbarians' (5). Such instances of global relocation and re-inscription can be read as Muslim manifestations of what Homi Bhabha calls the articulation of subaltern agency.[89] Shifting the scene away from Le Sentier, Goytisolo introduces yet another handwritten slogan in Arabic, reading 'Death to France, long live the revolution'. It turns out that the main character has wandered into Barbès; a run-down and crime-infested quarter at the foot of Montmartre with 'Arabs, blacks, Pakistanis, West Indians climbing up the stairs and down' (37).[90] In a vignette nearly halfway through the novel, entitled 'Split personalities', the self-confessed patriot and 'presumed aborigine of Le Sentier' decides to respond in kind, 'scrawling his stubborn countersigns: THE ARAB LEAGUE GOVERNS FRANCE, PARIS IS FOR THE FRENCH' (60, original capitals).

However, as the novel progresses, the main figure, now alternately referred to as the 'bizarre hermit of Le Sentier' (67), 'silent introvert' and 'misanthropic subject' (84), appears to have had a change of heart. Not only has he become a copyist of Sufi texts, but now, 'the gradual de-Europeanisation of the city, the appearance of Oriental souks and hammams, peddlers of African necklaces, graffiti in Arabic and Turkish – fills him with rejoicing' (86). While these newly found sympathies make him look more and more like the author, Goytisolo is not averse to self-mockery. Dismissing the wandering urban hermit as culturally illiterate, he finds it obvious that 'by no stretch of the imagination would you find him in those cafés of the Latin Quarter, Montparnasse, or Saint-Germain-des-Prés full of Latin American and native-born graduates' (84–6). Instead, in another instance of cultural border-crossing and confusing play with identities reminiscent of Meddeb's *Talismano*, Goytisolo introduces a 'great Moslem hermit-saint, seer and medium' (39), an expatriate Sufi shaykh going by the name of L'Sa Monammu, who provides his Parisian disciples with talismans.[91] The following passage is illustrative of the mystical power accorded to written charms in certain forms of popular Sufism, which was also mobilised by Abdelwahab Meddeb in his criticisms of the arrogance of Islamic officialdom:

> Those who have just had a consultation emerge from the room, silent and self-absorbed, clutching a triangle of paper: on returning home, they are to immerse one corner of it in a glass of water which they are then to drink down in one gulp, throw the second in the fire, and sew the third inside their clothes in such a way that it will be in constant contact with their skin; or secure a lock of hair of the person loved or hated, plus a recent photograph

> of that person, whereupon he will write out a potent formula, guaranteed to bring results. (39)

The earlier-noted interrelatedness of eroticism with such linguistic metamorphoses and the fluidity of cultural identities as a recurrent theme throughout *Juan the Landless* and *Landscapes after the Battle* is further evinced by explicit and repeated identification of sexuality with the act of writing. Thus, the earlier-mentioned intermezzo in *Juan the Landless*, entitled 'The phallus or Ghardaïa', also contains the line 'looking forward to the clandestine pleasure that the flow of the pen (of the sex organ) will create in the space of the text' (127), while another passage about Lawrence of Arabia reads:

> The mighty subterranean stream that feeds both sexuality and writing: your obdurate gesture of grabbing the pen and allowing its filiform liquor to flow, prolonging the climax indefinitely: leafing, for inspiration through the pages of your copy of *The Seven Pillars*. (210)

In the penultimate chapter of *Juan the Landless*, Goytisolo returned yet again to the association of penmanship with sexual gratification, whereby the wielding of the pen 'guides your footsteps in their festive Sunday afternoon wanderings: through Ghardaïa, Istanbul, or Fez: Belleville, Barbès, or the Gare du Nord' (249).

The centrality of this writing–sexuality nexus is evident not only from the variations on this theme in *Juan the Landless* and *Landscapes after the Battle*, but also from Goytisolo's essays of literary criticism and from academic scholarship on his work as well. Both bodies of work acknowledge the importance of the Mexican diplomat and writer Octavio Paz (1914–98) in helping Goytisolo to overcome the exaggerated body–soul duality of Christendom and the way this has been carried over to other binaries (reason–irrationality, spiritual–sensual, cerebral–sexual) that continue to dominate modern Western thought. In particular, Paz's *Conjunctions and Disjunctions* can be accorded the same significance in developing Goytisolo's appreciation for the acceptance of corporeality and sensual pleasure in the Muslim world as Castro's Mudejarism can be for a new conceptualisation of Iberian-Islamic history.[92] In applying the closing of such schizophrenic disjunction between sex and its repression to his attempts to come to terms with his own homosexual proclivities, Goytisolo employed the term 'the sotadic zone'.[93] It is borrowed from *The Sotadic Zone: Social and Sexual Relations of the Mohammedan Empire*, a controversial book by the British explorer and Orientalist Sir Richard Francis Burton (1821–90). Originally published as an appendix to Burton's equally notorious translation of the *Arabian*

Nights, it is based on two ethnographic reports he wrote about his undercover investigations into male prostitution in Karachi.[94]

Goytisolo has continued to explore Europe's fraught relationship with corporeality and bodily functions in literary essays on the Spanish classics, comparing and contrasting those works with Islamic culture. Illustrative is a passage from the essay 'Quevedo: the Excremental Obsession', where the Spanish Renaissance writer's coprophilia is used to examine differences between Christian and Muslim world-views, including their attitudes towards the afterlife: 'Whereas the picture of the Koranic Eden captivates the Muslim's mind with the colours and sensuality of its palette, Christianity has failed lamentably in its attempt to depict heaven for us' (59). This leads Goytisolo to conclude that 'religion and eroticism are not antonymous terms for the Muslim; his law does not bar him from the satisfactions of physical pleasure and his paradise is a portentous condensation of all the fantasies and chimeras of the desert-dweller' (60). The same essay also notes how the writings of Ibn Hazm (994–1064) and Juan Ruiz's ribaldry are permeated by the 'joyous exultation of carnal pleasure' (59). While the 'fecund Mudejarismo' (9) suffusing the Archpriest of Hita's *Book of Good Love* explains the poem's lecherous tone, the inclusion of Ibn Hazm seems less obvious and warrants a further explanation. Ibn Hazm was a religious scholar from Cordoba and belonged to the now defunct Zahiri School of Islamic Law. The name refers to its strict adherence to the literal or outward (*zāhir*) meaning of both the Qur'an and Ḥadith (the corpus embodying the Traditions of the Prophet or Sunna) texts. For that reason the school is considered to have represented a very strict form of Sunni Islam. However, Ibn Hazm was also the author of a treatise on love called *Tawq al-Ḥamāma*, which translates as *The Ring of the Dove*. The significance of Ibn Hazm for Goytisolo personally becomes clear from a statement attributed to this Arab-Andalusian poet cited in his memoir *Forbidden Territory*. The passage where Ibn Hazm refers to an inevitable law that 'destroys the toughest, unleashes the most consistent, demolishes the sturdiest, dislocates the stoutest, settles in the recesses of the hearth and makes the forbidden legitimate' made Goytisolo acutely aware that the repression of his own homosexual desires was a direct result of his having been born in 'an unsuitable cultural and social environment'.[95] Buried underneath these creative dealings with cultural-religious diversity and different attitudes towards corporeality in Goytisolo's novels and literary criticism lie some fundamental epistemological questions that are inextricably linked to the postmodern and postcolonial era.

Epistemic and Spatial Aspects of Goytisolo's Writings about Postcoloniality

As for these epistemic aspects of Goytisolo's creative work, I believe that regimes of knowledge advocating intellectual humility, such as Vattimo's weak thought and the nomadologies of Deleuze, Guattari and Shayegan, can fruitfully be employed in reading novels like *Juan the Landless* and *Landscapes after the Battle*, as well as literary criticism that addresses Cartesian dualism and European schizophrenia vis-à-vis corporeality. In contrast to Brad Epps's distinction between Vattimo and Deleuze, which fails to recognise the affinities between these two anti-foundationalist philosophers of difference, I propose that a merger of the two also helps us to look beyond Goytisolo's writings as a 'post-structuralist critique of a repressive Western rationality'.[96] Instead of applying them separately, as Brad Epps has done, merging these two alternative regimes of knowledge will enable an approach that is not only closer to Hamid Dabashi's hermeneutics of alterity but also reflective of a disposition of worldly cosmopolitanism which he saw flourish in the literary humanism of the classical Persian poets, and which I see at work in contemporary postmodern and postcolonial artistic experimentations by the likes of Juan Goytisolo.

The collective schizophrenia with which Goytisolo diagnosed the West echoes Deleuze and Guattari's Capitalism and Schizophrenia project, first expounded in their *Anti-Oedipus* and further elaborated in *A Thousand Plateaus*. Goytisolo too rebelled against overly neat dichotomous divisions dictated by a logic of binary oppositions that denies the ambivalent heterogeneity of worldly realities in the name of ideological stability.[97] In Goytisolo's view, the urban societies of North Africa and elsewhere in the Muslim Mediterranean have retained religiously inspired epistemes concomitant with their earlier-mentioned appreciation for a corporeal–spiritual integrity, which Christendom had lost towards the end of the Middle Ages as described by Bakhtin in his study of Rabelais. Goytisolo expands on this in an essay from 1984. 'Medievalism and Modernity: the Archpriest of Hita and Ourselves' argues that avant-gardist writers like himself are in the business of restoring what he sees as the characteristics of Europe's medieval popular culture: an anarchic mixture of styles and registers accommodative of openness and heterogeneity.[98] Like Deleuze and Guattari's nomadology, Gianni Vattimo's weak thought too lacks the metaphysical ground for absolute truth claims. This weakening of metaphysical thinking results then in its replacement by an 'ontology of decline', in which epistemology revolves around ethics and in which 'final authority is attributed to *beings* rather than "metaphysical Being"'.[99]

To break the terminological and conceptual ties with the language of modern European philosophy, these postmodern regimes of knowledge require a new grammar and vocabulary, replacing the propositional, demonstrative and logical language of traditional philosophy with an edifying rhetorical language, using metaphors (like the 'Death of God') and symbols (hence the interest in semiotics and aesthetics). In the case of Goytisolo, his interest in the intersections of postmodernity and postcoloniality found its academic-intellectual expression in what he called his 'tardy vocation as [a] linguist and ethnologist'.[100] Stimulated by the already briefly mentioned 'auditory enjoyment inherent in the first stages' of hearing a new language (145), he began studying the Arabic dialect of Morocco and then Turkish so as 'to draw nearer to a physical and cultural bodily ideal' (148). These initiatives too correspond to Hamid Dabashi's argument for the need for a new rhetoric as part of his hermeneutics of alterity. Most vignettes in *Landscapes after the Battle* gesture towards an undermining of the strong assertions emanating from modern Western rationality. However, Goytisolo also included nativist pushbacks. Aside from the verbal exchange of the earlier-mentioned graffiti war, the novel also features an ultra-nationalist terrorist organisation, calling itself 'The patriotic militia of Charles Martel' – named after the grandfather of Charlemagne who stopped the Arab-Islamic expansion across the Pyrenees at Poitiers.[101] Goytisolo is concerned not so much with the risk of failure to restore harmony as with the inability to accept disharmony. It is here that Goytisolo's invention of 'labyrinthine itineraries to disorient yourself' merges with Vattimo's equation of emancipation with disorientation, and the expression of the latter's ontology of decline through a 'fictionalized experience of reality which is our only possibility of freedom'.[102]

The anti-teleologies of Vattimo's weak thought or the nomadology of Deleuze and Guattari are not only translated artistically into the open possibility of fictionalised experiences of reality or utopian parodies long the lines of what Abigail Lee Six has called an epistemic 'no-place of utopia' – echoing the *nâ kojâ âbâd* ('imaginal space' or 'nowhere land') identified by Daryush Shayegan in Suhrawardi's Illuminationism.[103] What also needs to be articulated in readings of *Landscapes after the Battle* are the spatial transformations brought about by postcoloniality as unpacked in 'Hermeneutics and Anthropology', Vattimo's critique of Richard Rorty's Eurocentrism, and Dabashi's 'liberation geography'.[104] By adding such geographical mappings to the epistemological mix, a spatial dimension is added to Epps's paraphrasing of Vattimo's assertion that 'there is no great Other absolutely beyond the West'.[105] Similarly, Deleuze and Guattari's distinction between, on the one hand, the sedentary, 'striated' and closed spaces of empire and the 'smooth' and open spaces of the nomadic habitat on the other can be applied metaphorically to Goytisolo's literary imaginations of hegemonic Spanish culture dominated by suffocating orthodox Catholicism and the more permissive urban societies on the Islamic side of the Mediterranean respectively.[106] In *Landscapes after the Battle* they also find concrete expression in the oppositions drawn between Baron Hausmann's redesign of nineteenth-century Paris and the migrant quarters escaping that imperial re-organisation of the French capital's public spaces:

> The Paris of the Bourbons and Bonapartes, planned by its architects in such a way as to dampen the potential of social explosions, leaves him unimpressed. [...] What appeals to him – and suits his lamentable vulgar tastes – is the allogenic, postcolonial barbarized Paris of Belleville and Barbès, a Paris that has nothing cosmopolitan or cultivated about it, but on the contrary is uncouthly foreign and illiterate.[107]

Markedly absent from Goytisolo's topography in *Landscapes after the Battle* are the *banlieux* on the outskirts of Paris where the vast majority of the second- or third-generation descendants of immigrants, as well as more recent arrivals, are accommodated. In that sense the imagined labyrinthine itineraries through Paris and Turko-Berlin Kreuzberg, Cairo's City of the Dead, Istanbul and other 'medina-cities' featured in some of Goytisolo's other writings bear a greater resemblance to the urban peregrinations of similar characters modelled after Baudelaire and Benjamin's figure of the flâneur found in Abdelwahab Meddeb's novels *Talismano* and *Phantasia*.

Earlier in this chapter, I credited Goytisolo with a degree of clairvoyance concerning the migratory pressures on Europe's southern borders, postcolonial cultural penetration and ultra-chauvinist counter-currents. His prophecies are not restricted to such prospects of new culture wars alone. While the exclusively urban peripateticism in *Landscapes after the Battle* is used to explain the wanderer from Le Sentier's 'profound aversion [...] to nature and rural landscape', at the same time, the 'inveterate urban dweller' makes an exception for public parks, because 'as Green movements and ecological groups never cease to point out, the tangled jungle in which he lives lacks those open communal spaces which, in their jargon, are the lungs, the breath of oxygen of the great city'.[108] Remember that this was written in 1983, so well before the establishment of the Green parties in Germany, France and elsewhere in Europe. However, a few pages further down it reads:

> The increasing amounts of carbon dioxide accumulating in the atmosphere since the beginning of the industrial revolution are absorbing more and more of the Earth's heat radiation, thereby producing a greenhouse effect, by virtue of which its heat is retained rather than being dissipated in space, thereby causing a gradual increasing in the overall temperature of the terrestrial globe. (64)

Already in the early 1980s, before organisations such as Greenpeace obtained a seat at the table of international fora dealing with environmental issues, and decades before notions such as the greenhouse effect or global warming gained worldwide currency, a Spanish writer whose main preoccupations appeared so far to have been confined to revisionist interpretations of the national history of his home country and a concomitant fascination with the Orient (which also contained an unmistakable vein of eroticisation) shows himself also to be a perceptive observer of the dire consequences of the excessive exploitation of the planet's resources for the future of humankind in the post-industrial era.

As postmodern experimentations with difference and intertextuality, the Islamic referents in *Count Julian* were primarily contrasted with the hegemonic Spanish *Reconquista* discourse, projecting a triumphant Catholic Spain over and against the Muslim world. From *Juan the Landless* onwards, Juan Goytisolo appears to have further internalised Américo Castro's Mudejarism in his political-cultural thinking, enabling him to think beyond dichotomous world-views of an Islamic East over and against the West. I therefore disagree with Abigail Lee Six's conclusion, in which she projects a 'radical divergence between East and West' onto texts such as *Landscapes after the Battle*.[109] Although opposing pairs, such as order–chaos are helpful in terms of analysis, the 'attack on duality' (39) that distinguishes Goytisiolo's writings since the Mendiola trilogy belies the persistence of dichotomous world-views. Instead, they demonstrate an ambition to transcend what in our 'post-everything' world amounts to an obsolete and therefore false binary.[110] Epistemically and spatially, Goytisolo's creative expression of this new world-view resembles Hamid Dabashi's hermeneutics of alterity in terms of its condensation of the latter's 'liberation geography', and its borrowings from the nomadology of Deleuze and Guattari, and from Vattimo's weak thought and advocacy of fictionalised experience.

'Eros and Thanatos Intermingled': Orientalising Desire

From *Juan the Landless* onwards, Goytisolo's writings have disrupted dualities and dichotomies based on binary oppositions between the spiritual and cerebral on one side, and the corporeal and sensual on the other, by replacing these with the play of desire. Drawing simultaneously on Bataille and Baudrillard, Brad Epps characterises this as '*always ambivalent*, love and death simultaneously'.[111] That Goytisolo shares this view he shows in the first novel to have appeared after the Mendiola trilogy, *Makbara* (1980), where he writes about 'a dead city with a few breaths of life left, Eros and Thanatos intermingled'.[112] This connection between death and desire is aptly captured in a book by the American philosopher and scholar of religion Mark C. Taylor, entitled *Grave Matters*. With an evident bow to Jacques Derrida's *The Gift of Death*, Taylor writes: 'Contrary to expectation, the deadly openness of the future creates the space of desire. [...] Without the remote proximity of death there would be no desire.'[113]

One reason for postponing my discussion of *Makbara* until now and grouping it together with *Quarantine* (1991) is the references in their titles to Islamic burial practices and funerary lore.[114] *Makbara* is taken from the Arabic word *maqbara*, meaning cemetery, graveyard and tomb. In his introductory remarks to the English translation of *Quarantine*, Peter Bush also draws attention to Goytisolo's use of an old Spanish word for burial grounds: *macabro*. Bush goes on to note that Goytisolo was 'reintroducing into modern Spanish a word' – evidently derived from the Arabic – 'that was used by medieval writers like the Archpriest of Hita whose language reflected the coexistence of Jewish, Arab, and Christian cultures in Spain before Ferdinand and Isabel'.[115] As for *Quarantine*, that title refers an Islamic belief that for a period of forty days after death the human soul stays in the vicinity of the grave, remaining in a state of limbo.[116] Certainly, when compared to *Quarantine*, *Makbara* has received a great deal more attention from literary critics. Aside from the monographs I have cited so far, the novel also featured in special issues of the *Review of Contemporary Fiction* (1984) and of *Horizons Maghrébins* (1995). Primarily focused on Goytisolo's continuing experimentations with intertextuality and postmodern narration, the attention paid to Islamic references has been limited.

Largely set in Morocco, *Makbara* mirrors Goytisolo's own physical move – in a double sense of the word – to the other side of the Mediterranean so as to be in close proximity to his male lovers. It also prefigures the widening geographical scope of Goytisolo's subsequent writings. Although *Landscapes after the Battle* takes place primarily in Paris, its final pages describe the City of the Dead on the outskirts of the Egyptian capital Cairo.[117] Another indication of the expansion of Goytisolo's interest from the Maghreb to the eastern parts of the

Mediterranean is a number of essays he wrote about Egypt and Turkey – originally published in Spanish in 1990 and later included in *Cinema Eden*.[118] Finally, although one of the central figures in *Quarantine*, Ibn Arabi, was born in Murcia, he spent much time in the holy cities of Mecca and Medina, before ending his days in Damascus. Moreover, *Quarantine*'s narrative also plays out against the background of the 1990–1 war in the Persian Gulf. This widening geographical ambit of the Muslim world, paralleled by an expanding and deepening interest on the part of Goytisolo in things Islamic, is reflected in a growing prominence of religious themes and places related to the Muslim world.

Aside from their references to cemeteries and the liminal state of the soul after death, both *Makbara* and *Quarantine* are mudejar texts through and through. In his essay 'Mudejarism Today' from 1985, Goytisolo admits as much himself: 'A novel such as *Makbara*, written to be read aloud, according to the medieval Andalusian and Castilian tradition still observed today among the storytellers of the public square of the Xemáa-el-Fna, is thus an essentially Mudéjar text.'[119] Writing some six years later, in the opening page of *Quarantine* Goytisolo notes how the novel condensates his 'skimming and gleaning in the *Divine Comedy*, works by Ibn Arabi, books by Asín, different versions of the Prophet's nighttime ascent, Sufi anthologies, Miguel de Molinos's *Spiritual Guide*'.[120] 'Mudejarism Today' also explains how *Makbara* actually grew out of an essay provisionally called 'Reading of the Archpriest in Xemaá-el-Fná'. It still constitutes the novel's final chapter, but under a different title: 'A Reading of the Space in Xemaá-el-Fná'.[121] The space taking the place of the Archpriest of Hita is the central square in the southern Moroccan city of Marrakesh. The substitution of this centuries-old home of Arab storytellers thus expands the originally conceived public reading of Juan Ruiz's ribald poem *Book of Good Love* to the Muslim world's wider oral tradition, which occasionally was also recorded in written form, for example in the world-famous *Arabian Nights*, as well as in the less well-known (at least in the West) *Tales of the Marvellous and News of the Strange*.[122] The significance of Goytisolo's interest in this subject is further corroborated by the fact that he returns to it again seventeen years later in another essay entitled 'The Oral Patrimony of Humanity'.[123] Opening with references to Bakhtin's study of Rabelais and to Juan Ruiz, it illustrates that – for Europe – the late Middle Ages heralded the end of the 'time when the real and imaginary mingled'. However, Marrakesh, by contrast, is the one city that 'upholds the privilege of sheltering the extinct oral patrimony of humanity, labelled contemptuously as "Third World" by many'.[124]

Dedicated to 'those who inspired it and will not read it', *Makbara* is in effect an attempt to salvage what Goytisolo regards as a vital aspect of humankind's cultural heritage. I will illustrate this with two elements lifted out of the story: Marrakesh's central square, and the pariah-like aspects of the various composite characters populating the story. The first of these to be introduced is an angelic figure with evidently religious connotations. A 'Self-titled Intercessoress and Mediatrix of All Graces', she metamorphoses in the course of the narrative into a troubled European transgender 'androlatress', who, after suffering sexual abuse, ends up prostituting herself, 'joining the horde of camp followers and harlots trailing in the wake of the Moroccan infantrymen and soldiers of the Legion'.[125] The next person to step onto the stage is another vagabond-like individual, a returning expatriate Moroccan storyteller – called in colloquial Moroccan *halaiquí* (someone sitting at the head of a circle [*halqa*] of listeners):

> escorted by the mute respect of his admirers: happy to have him among us once again, to realise that neither distance nor the years have taken him away from us forever, still our brother, as in the good old days when he performed here in these very streets: exhibitions of strength and skill, an incomparable command of the spoken word, recitations from the Koran: laughing till tears came to our eyes at his bawdy stories. (45)

This *halaiquí* makes his first proper appearance in the chapter from which *Makbara* takes its title: 'Seaside Cemetery'. This also constitutes the novel's core chapter laying out its other themes: Morocco as the setting for the onslaught of modernity and its concomitant economic and cultural transformations, but located also in a supposedly lecherous Orient, a background against which to paint pictures of sexual proclivities that yet again carry with them an autobiographical charge:

> their day off on Friday, a picnic on the beach; a dead city with a few breaths of life left, Eros and Thanatos intermingled; nocturnal forays of soldiers and epheboi, wild transvestites on the prowl: panting, whispering, furtive caresses: the slow spasms of coupled bodies: images, memories that suddenly surface at various forks in the path:[126] here I love, he loved, you loved, long-vanished faces of young boys and girls, the rough ground cushioned by the folds of a heavy Saharaui burnoose: spying again the vast panorama of the ocean [...] an area walled off by the thousands of gravestones aligned in roughly symmetrical rows all along the steep cliffside. (50–1)

The space where this Moroccan storytelling is kept alive is Marrakesh's central square. Goytisolo describes it as 'an agora, a theatrical performance, a point of convergence: an open plural space, a vast common of ideas' (242), where audiences can witness the 'fierce rivalry of the halca: multiple, simultaneous attractions' (250). In its efforts to modernise itself, today's Muslim world is torn between religious experiences and practices that have been socially embedded for centuries and 'official' Islamic orthodoxy upheld by often-uneasy alliances of a religious officialdom with the postcolonial state. In *Makbara* this is illustrated by contrasting sketches of oral and written expressions of religiosity unfolding on the central plaza of this southern Moroccan frontier city between the western reaches of Islamic civilisation and the Sahara desert. Public scribes, expounders of the Law of the Qur'an, and other students of the Qur'an are pitched against gnaua dancers, clowns, mimes, flute players, collectors of snakes, and a giant with a strong and bald-shaven skill, who 'surpasses in both eloquence and height all halaquís staging their acts in the square' and whose 'fabrications of a Rabelais redivivus at once extol and make a mockery of the perils of sexual pleasure' (257). The contrast between *Makbara*'s creative literary imaginations inspired by Qur'anic and other religious tropes and the kind of logocentrism embodied in the orthodoxy dogmatism of Islamic officialdom run parallel with Abdelwahab Meddeb's challenge to the nomocratic (rather than theocratic!) interpretations of Islamic scriptures disseminated by establishment *'ulamā'*.[127]

Towards the end of the novel, as the Angel has made her way to the city of Uxda (Oujda) on the Morocco–Algeria border, a European incarnation of the *halaiquí* ties the various storylines together:

> from this point on the explanations vary appreciably: some say they saw her land in the cemetery of Bab Dukkala, full of energy, in high spirits, youthful, optimistic despite her years and the difficulties of a long, exhausting journey: the story has it that she made her home base there till her death, hanging about the entrances to military bases, offering her services, devoutly, fruitfully, tirelessly fulfilling her apostolic mission
>
> others say she resides in Sidi Yusuf Ben Alí, dresses like a Moslem woman, and walks along the wall each day, headed for the tannery of Bab Debbagh in the hope of meeting her old flame
>
> still others claim that she lives or lived happily with the latter till death overtook them, but I, the European halaiquí who have told you this story, assuming different voices and roles in turn, making characters fly from one continent to another without having moved for an instant from the fraternal group that we form, am not able to confirm the truth of any of the versions. (238–9)[128]

Like the historical actors vilified in official historiography, custodians of oral traditions or fallen angels also find themselves on the margins of modern-day societies. Bearing in mind Abigail Lee Six's observation that, although traitor and redeemer stand in sharp contrast to each other, 'they can both be subsumed under the concept of pariah', Goytisolo's dedication of *Makbara* to these outcasts can be read as a kind of redemption.[129] Also, the European storyteller's interstitial position between two cultures underscores the utopianism of Goytisolo's envisaged rescue of this vital but dying part of humankind's literary heritage; collateral damage from the collective schizophrenia with which Goytisolo has diagnosed all modernising societies. These two elements, liminality and utopia as a 'nowhere land', have been signalled by several Goytisolo experts.[130] However, aside from their refraction through the lens of literary criticism, this utopian *entre-deux* also affords a hermeneutical reading informed by Daryush Shayegan's *Cultural Schizophrenia* and by his adoption of Suhrawardi's notion of *Nâ kojâ âbâd* – the imaginal space between the intelligible and sensible which also translates as 'nowhere land'.

As with *Juan the Landless*, *Makbara* too orientalises and eroticises the Arab world and Islam.[131] However, in both cases this falls under poetic licence. In a self-reflective essay published under the title 'From *Count Julian* to *Makbara*: A Possible Orientalist Reading', Goytisolo begins by acknowledging the relevance of Edward Said's Orientalism critique.[132] Also worth mentioning in this regard is that, in turn, Edward Said wrote approvingly of Goytisolo in his article 'Orientalism Reconsidered', and again in his book *Culture and Imperialism*, where he includes Goytisolo, together with Jean Genet, the Tunisian writer Albert Memmi and the British Africanist Basil Davidson, among those who have 'crossed to the other side'.[133] Of particular significance with regard to Goytisolo's own fictional and non-fictional writings is the observation regarding an author's responsibility towards his material. He goes on to explain how, in other essays about Morocco and its relationship with Spain, it was the work of the Moroccan philosopher Abdallah Laroui, but also Marx and Bakunin, that enabled him to approach the 'historical, geographical and humanity entity called Morocco [from] a clearly anti-colonial, democratic and emancipatory perspective'.[134]

Goytisolo's literary writings featuring Morocco and Moroccans – and by extension the world of Islam and Muslims – are the product of a mental world in which empirical reality is relegated to a secondary role for the sake of accommodating the opaque instinctive drives shaping the contradictions and ambiguities that are also part and parcel of the human condition. While deviating from rational discourse in order to accommodate these 'areas of shadow, its obscure motivations, its secret vibrations', he insists that 'being contradictory is in no sense synonymous with being incoherent' (215).[135]

Equally relevant is to recall Goytisolo's assertion that as a creative writer of mudejar texts he distinguishes himself '*from Arabists properly speaking*' (2, original italics). It is with this vital distinction between 'the Orient as a theatrical performance [...] and empirical reality' in mind that Goytisolo underwrites the conclusion that in literature, 'the East and Islam are represented according to a totality of concepts and images that are not related to reality or to concrete experience but to a vast concatenation of desires, repressions, fears, spectres, rivalries, prejudices' (213).[136] With a veiled reference to his own dedication of *Makbara*, Goytisolo acknowledges that the novel may not be of great interest to Moroccans themselves because it is 'still a novel for Europeans', but with the explicit purpose of making what he emphatically calls a Christian West aware of the fact that this supposedly oppositional other called the Islamic East is inhabited by people 'whose differences from ourselves are not greater but lesser in number than the myriad points of contact' (227). I am therefore not persuaded by Brad Epps's estimation that Goytisolo depicts an 'idealized and totalized Islam (based more on Morocco and Turkey, both bordering Europe, than on Iran and Yemen)'.[137] It seems to me that Juan Goytisolo's stance resembles that of Abdelwahab Meddeb in terms of their respective creative provocations and combatively engaged writings about Islam: all the more so because – as Epps himself wrote earlier – Goytisolo is 'no stranger to strong assertions' (290). Most compelling in this regard is a passage from *Makbara* itself, occurring a few pages after the European storyteller weaves together the various storylines. Situating this 'traveler in a constant moving, vagabond world: attuned now to the rhythm of all the others: in graceful and fruitful nomadism', Goytisolo's digression into politics and economics reads:[138]

> Survival of the nomad idea as a utopia: a universe without a government or a leader, the free circulation of persons and goods, land owned and used in common, the tending of flocks, sheer centrifugal force, the abolition of private property and hierarchy, of rigid spatial boundaries, of domination based on sex and age, of the ugly accumulation of wealth: emulating the fruitful freedom of the gypsy who respects no frontiers: encamping in a vast present of quests and adventure: [...] creating structures to welcome the world-wanderer, free ports of trading and talking together, marketplaces, little bazaars for the exchange of ideas. (244–5)

This passage not only echoes Bataille's critique of capitalism in *The Accursed Share* or *The Treatise on Nomadology* by Deleuze and Guattari; it also contrasts with the dystopian atmosphere in Goytisolo's subsequent novel *Landscapes after the Battle*, or the mood dominating in the one after that, *The Virtues of the Solitary Bird*. My reason for disrupting the chronological sequence of Goytisolo's novels is that the theme of liminality or in-betweenness emphatically recurs in *Quarantine*: in this instance, however, not so much in an intercultural sense as in relation to human mortality.

Graves Matter: Idioms of the Islamic Macabre

Although a slimmer volume than *Makbara*, or the three volumes of the Mendiola trilogy for that matter, *Quarantine* is richer in direct and explicit Islamic and other religious references pertaining to death and burial.[139] The novel creatively unpacks the state of limbo in which the human soul finds itself after death and which Muslims refer to as *barzakh* – a word thought to be Persian in origin.[140] According to this Islamic belief, for a period of forty days the soul remains in the vicinity of the grave, where it is interrogated and punished by two angelic beings named Munkar and Nakīr. While the word *barzakh* occurs a few times in the Qur'an, the names Munkar and Nakīr are nowhere mentioned. According to the Scottish historian of Islam Montgomery Watt, in the Qur'an chapter 'The Believers' (*Sura al-Mu'minin*) the term *barzakh* retains its original meaning of barrier or obstacle (Q. 23:100).[141] In another instance, it is presented as an isthmus between two seas (Q. 55:20). Some Qur'an commentators and exegetes have interpreted this in a physical sense as the grave being a location between earthly life and the hereafter, or as the separation between hell and paradise. Others have opted for a moral reading, interpreting *barzakh* as a prohibition by God. Eschatological readings by, for example, Ibn Arabi present *barzakh* as separating the domain of human existence from the realm of pure spirits, or as the distinction between the material and spiritual world.[142] Lacking scriptural foundation, because authentic early Ḥadiths too are silent on the matter, the origins of Munkar and Nakīr as Islamic equivalents of the 'angel of death', or what S. R. Burge calls 'Tempters of the Grave', remain unclear.[143] Their role as interrogators and punishers of the souls of the dead is extrapolated from other Qur'anic passages mentioning angels without specifically naming them. In his article for the *Encyclopaedia of Islam*, the Dutch scholar of Islam Arent Jan Wensinck maintains that the earliest explicit mention of Munkar and Nakīr can be traced to a ninth-century Islamic legal text:

> The interrogation of the dead in the tomb by Munkar and Nakīr is a reality and the reunion of the body with the spirit in the tomb is a reality. The pressure and the punishment in the tomb are a reality that will take place in the case of all the infidels, and a reality that may take place in the case of some sinners belonging to the faithful.[144]

The resulting theological ambiguities surrounding the precise meaning of *barzakh* and the origins of Munkar and Nakīr leave all the more room for an author's imagination and creative application.

Given the meaning of its title name, it will come as no surprise that *Quarantine* is composed of forty episodes. Undoubtedly relying on his readings of Asín Palacios, but also paralleling Nasr Hamid Abu Zayd's research, throughout *Quarantine* Goytisolo's literary treatment of *barzakh* is primarily refracted through the lens of Ibn Arabi's sepulchral philosophy:

> After flying to the in-between world of *barzakh*, spirits continue in possession of their bodies and the latter adapt the subtle form, the way you see yourself in dreams. For the other universe is a resting place where appearances change continually, like fleeting thoughts in the inner dimension of this world.[145]

Ibn Arabi unpacked his interpretations of *barzakh* in several books of his encyclopaedical *Meccan Openings* (*Futūḥāt al-Makkiyya*) and in a smaller, lesser-known work, *The Epistle of the Human Tree and Four Birds* – which Goytisolo mentions by name in the fifth episode.[146] In his magisterial annotated translations from Ibn Arabi's main work, William Chittick explains how *barzakh* is first presented in Ibn Arabi's writings on ontology, where it appears under the heading 'Imagination', called *khayāl* or *mithāl* in Ibn Arabi's vocabulary.[147] While imagination is used to underscore the dependence of all existing things on the Divine as Manifest Being, the term *barzakh* is employed to illustrate that imagination is to be understood as an intermediate reality and therefore inherently ambiguous, but nonetheless intelligible to the human faculty of reason:

> The *barzakh* is something that separates a known form from an unknown, an existent from a nonexistent, a negated from an affirmed, an intelligible from an non-intelligible. It is called *barzakh* as a technical term (*iṣṭilāḥ*) and in itself it is intelligible, but it is only imagination. For when you perceive it and are intelligent, you will know that you have perceived an ontological thing (*shay' wujūdī*) upon which your eyes have fallen. But you will know for certain by proofs that there is nothing there in origin and root.[148]

This can also be inferred from the Qur'anic comparison of the *barzakh* to an isthmus separating two seas (Q. 55.20), which implies that the waters of the two cannot mix. And yet, despite this radical ontic divide, epistemically the imaginal world mediates between the two because both the spiritual and corporeal worlds are intelligible. Goytisolo's citation of Ibn Arabi's words shows how seriously he has studied 'the Greatest Master and Seal of the Saints' (11), because Chittick too notes how Ibn

Arabi often refers to dreams as 'the most common human experience of the nature of imaginal things' (119). It also invites Goytisolo to further speculate on the nature of *barzakh* or the imaginal world as an intermediate reality:

> Did the manifest permeability between the two worlds obey the arbitrary nature of the laws ruling dreams or was it the effect of the metamorphosing powers of the spirits that lie inactive during quarantine because of the barzakh? (67)

From other references it becomes clear that in *Quarantine* the focus remains vested in the association of the *barzakh* with the grave as a location between a human's earthly life and its continued existence in the hereafter: 'Are you in the subterranean Gehenna [Arabic for hell], a dwelling that exudes shadows, or the barzakh or intermediate world where, in the words of the Seal of Saints spirits don a subtle form?' (48). At the end of the novel Goytisolo connects his reflections on human mortality with his lifelong preoccupation with the act of writing:

> We are at the end of the quarantine. One more day, one more chapter and I'll leave you, far from the barzakh [...] Write, keep writing about me, you heard. Only your interest and the interest of those who read you can continue to keep me alive! (120–1)

With regard to Munkar and Nakīr, *Quarantine* reverses the order in which they are usually mentioned in the Islamic tradition. In his introduction of the duo, Goytisolo touches on their obscure origins:

> Contrary to legend they weren't repulsive, sinister looking blacks, with disfigured faces and voices resounding like thunder, nor did their eyes flash in the darkness [...] Their voices! Nakir's resounded grave and diaphanous, no blurred edges, despite the rather defective quality of the amplification. Munkar's revealed a playful tone as if nourished by subterranean irony or consummate knowledge of human weakness. (26–7)[149]

In other instances, the Tempters of the Grave feature separately, for example in episode seven, where the nameless narrator-protagonist thinks he 'can hear Munkar's mocking laugh in the pitch-dark' (33), or in episode twelve, where Nakīr appears when he contemplates the connection between his own desires and Ibn Arabi's visions of an attractive young man:[150]

> You alone enjoy the sight of him and though you are momentarily deprived of speech and can't greet him, you guess that it is Nakir himself. [...] Stretched out on the freshly polished floor you will let him wash you and knead you, inert beneath his hard, supple hands, as passive as a corpse in the act of

> purification [...] Although he keeps your face pushed against the floor blind to all sight, you will register the unimaginable scene as if your spirit had been released and could contemplate itself from the outside. (49–50)

The wider significance of the Murcian mystic for experiencing the liminality of imaginal worlds described is indicated by *Quarantine*'s references to Ibn Arabi's *Book of the Ascent*, or what Meddeb called *Muhammad's Ladder*, and Dante's *Divine Comedy*, as well as Goytisolo's pointers to the engravings made by Gustave Doré and to Hieronymus Bosch's painting *The Garden of Earthly Delights*.[151]

That Goytisolo continued his postmodern experimentations with intertextuality in his post-Mendiola novels becomes manifestly clear when we compare the following two passages taken from *Quarantine*'s episode twenty-nine and the final lines from *The Virtues of the Solitary Bird* respectively:

> Who told you Nakir and Munkar work here? Bellows the female functionary. [...] Better catch a direct flight to Cairo. At their airport they'll find you a pen-pusher to sort through the red tape. Get yourself a taxi and go to the southern macabre: they'll be there at night in one of the mausoleums or Sufi lodges in the City of the Dead. (97)[152]

> Free at last of his tortures on the threshold of the solitary night, awaiting Naquir and Muncar in the shadows of the underground chamber, pressures, confined spaces, anxieties, interrogation confrontation, subtle vagabondage of his double or ka alongside the tomb of Ibn Al Farid within the walls of the City of the Dead. (150)[153]

These geographical references to Cairo's necropolis recur several times in *Quarantine* and point back also to the penultimate vignette in *Landscapes after the Battle*, where the earlier-mentioned wanderings of Goytisolo's flâneur through the medina-cities 'are all summed up now in a single place: the Cairo cemetery of the Mamlukes [*sic*] miserable and proud City of the Dead'.[154]

Published a decade apart, *Makbara* and *Quarantine* show how Juan Goytisolo's interest in Islam and his engagement with its heritage had deepened. In *Makbara*, his concern for a disappearing world of oral literature is expressed through descriptions and contemplations of cemeteries on the outskirts of cities; in *Quarantine* the focus narrows to a single grave, that of a beloved who has passed away. Although turning inward to meditations on the fate of the individual human soul, the story nonetheless unfolds against a background of world events, in this case the Gulf War of 1991. While *Makbara* and *Quarantine*'s concern with death and desire, decay and mortality points towards the eros–thanatos nexus, the death drive's connotations of extinction and self-erasure also reflect a mystical element, witness this observation in *Quarantine* on the precariousness of human existence – 'life not yet annihilation, ifná or fana' (35) – and a reference to al-Hasan al-Basri's admonition to '*Gently walk the earth, it will soon be your grave*' (38).

Goytisolo's Mysticism: Jean Genet, St John of the Cross and Sufism

Despite the anti-clerical streak in Goytisolo's religious (and political) views, the novels written during the 1980s evince a growing fascination with the mystical dimensions of Christianity and Islam. That this was initially still very much tied up with sexual desire becomes clear from a passage in *Landscapes of the Battle* called 'The rendezvous', where the fiasco of an encounter with a female sex-worker morphs into a fantasy about a séance of the whirling dervishes, in which the main character's imagined sodomisation is conflated with mystical ecstasy: 'The way of love leads to this Unity', which then brings about 'a total experience, the feeling of truth hidden behind seventy-seven veils'.[155] This conflation of the corporeal and spiritual implies a rejection of the body–soul dualism discussed above, and reveals a longing for a kind of transcendence that does not require the intervention of any God.

Before further discussing concrete references to Sufism in Goytisolo's literary work, I first want to show the debt Goytisolo owes to Jean Genet for articulating this kind of spirituality. For this I will juxtapose a vignette from *Landscapes after the Battle* with another passage about Genet from Goytisolo's memoirs, and read these together with the essays he wrote about Genet and Sufism in the 1990s. Appearing under the heading 'Vain reflections of a condemned man', in *Landscapes after the Battle* it reads:

> My literary ideal: the wandering Sufi dervish. A man who shuns vanity, scorns the rules of decorum and social convention, seeks no disciples, tolerates no praise. His virtues are kept modestly hidden, and to further conceal them he delights in practices that are contemptuous and base: he therefore not only brings upon himself the reprobation of his fellows, but provokes them into ostracizing and condemning him. (249)

Three years later, Goytisolo wrote in *Realms of Strife* about the archetypical unruly but morally upright individual:

> Set oneself the *Genetian ethic of the* malamatí *as a difficult literary and human ideal: openly practice what laws and customs reproved, infringe norms of prudence and respect, brazenly accept the insults and pinpricks of gossip:*

> *renounce the prestige of behaviour based on conformism or the exercise of official bounty: on the contrary, protect oneself behind a shield of disdain in order to preserve secret virtue, sacrifice advantage and honour to scrupulous fidelity to oneself: live in a world without difference in the burnishing and perfection of purity.*
>
> *When you scandalize family or tribal morality [...] the decision not to respect consensual norms and zealously preserve your deviation from the priase [sic] or reproval of others delivers you the opportunity to transmute into a source of energy the disorder in your emotional life, the solar gravity of its fire.* (275, original italics)

The term *malamatí* in the above passage refers to the *malāmatīyya*, a word derived from the Arabic verb *lāma*, 'to blame'. According to the lemmas in the authoritative *Encyclopaedia of Islam* written by the scholars of Islam Fred de Jong and Hamid Algar, the term was originally used to describe an Islamic tradition centring around the 'doctrine that all outward appearance of piety or religiosity, including good deeds, is ostentation'.[156] However, the designation was soon 'usurped by antinomians who actively sought the blame of others', and came to be used interchangeably with *Qalandar*, a 'vagabond of scandalously offensive behaviour'.[157] At face value, Goytisolo's association of the term with Jean Genet seems to affirm this last false – if widespread – usage. However, a comparison of the above passages with a more detailed reading of de Jong and Algar reveals a deeper and more genuine connection on account of a shared moral sincerity and purity not motivated by either the expectation of divine reward or the approval of fellow humans. Most likely first emerging in ninth-century Nishapur, at that time the most important city of Khorasan province in what is now north-eastern Iran, the *malāmatīyya* are thought to have posited an inward and hidden spirituality over and against effusive and public expressions of devotion. Whereas de Jong noted that the origins of their contrarian disposition can be traced to non-Muslim sources, such as the Cynics of ancient Greece and early Syrian Christians, Algar emphasised the *malāmatīyya*'s own claim of following the example of the Prophet and his Companions as corroborated by the Qur'anic verse 'They struggle in the path of God and fear not the blame of any blamer' (224). The fact that the *malāmatīyya* are included in the writings of al-Hujwiri, al-Suhrawardi and al-Sulami also seems to confirm Algar's contention that they were considered contrapuntal to Sufism.

Goytisolo makes a similar point in an essay about the veneration of saints in Morocco (referred to as *marabouts* or *walis*), and in another about the disciples of Jalal al-Din Rumi, the Mevlevis, popularly also known as the 'whirling dervishes'. In the first case, he refers to Ibn Arabi, who 'very significantly places the *malamatis* in the higher category of the servants of Allah'.[158] In the other, Goytisolo suggests that the eccentric behaviour of Rumi's spiritual guide (*murshid*) Shams al-Din al-Tabrizi was 'perhaps influenced by the concealed ethics of the transgressors or *malamatiya*' (99), to whom he ascribes a 'singular conception of the many paths to perfection' (105).[159] In 'The Poet Buried in Larache', an article about a visit to Jean Genet's tomb (another grave that matters), Goytisolo not only invokes the above passage from *Landscapes of the Battle*, but also reaffirms Genet's antinomial malāmatī connection:

> Scornful rejection of the sympathy or admiration of others, the indifference to reputation of the 'lone man in the crowd', as Ibn Arabi defined the *malamati* gives us one of the essential keys to the last decades of Genet's life. (27)[160]

With regard to Genet's grave and its association with the veneration of saints, there is also the following passage from *Quarantine* to consider: 'And your pilgrimage to the tomb of the Poet buried in Larache, serene in spirit like a visitor to a wali, knowing full well you would come across other devotees attracted by his grace and sanctity' (55). Juan Goytisolo's sustained interest in the *malāmatīyya* and his lasting preoccupation with Jean Genet do not only capture a strong drive to lead a virtuous life in the face of adversity by emulating the latter's example. This is already manifested in earlier forms of pitiless self-examinations that have characterised Goytisolo's writings since the Mendiola Trilogy. Although his next novel, *Makbara*, was already predominantly set in Marrakesh – otherwise known as 'the medina of the seven men', a reference to the city's seven Sufi patrons – Juan Goytisolo's engagement with and growing personal investment in the spiritual dimensions of religion were definitively shaped by developments occurring in the 1980s.[161] For *The Virtues of the Solitary Bird*, a novel revolving around the discalced Spanish Carmelite friar and mystic Juan de la Cruz (Saint John of the Cross, 1542–91), this concerned first and foremost the outbreak of the AIDS pandemic in the early 1980s. Also important was Goytisolo's introduction to the research of the Puerto Rican Hispanist Luce López Baralt, whose advocacy of Mudejarism make her a successor to Américo Castro and Miguel Asín de Palacios.[162] For the present purposes I lift two elements out of the story of Saint John of the Cross for further discussion: the spiritual cross-pollination between Christianity and Islam traceable in the latter's writings, and the parallels that can be drawn between the persecution of the Carmelite reformer by his calced detractors and the tensions between Sufism and nomocentric Islamic orthodoxy.

As indicated by its title, *The Virtues of a Solitary Bird* singles out a particular symbol from the different tropes identified by López Baralt in her writings about Islamic influences on Spanish literature since medieval times.[163] What sets Saint John's solitary bird apart from other avians featuring in European literature since Homer and Virgil is its 'total lack of Western antecedents'.[164] A precise identification of sources or mapping of its lines of transmission is complicated by the disappearance of John of the Cross's own tract on mystical bird symbolism, called *The Properties of the Solitary Bird*. In Goytisolo's novel, one of the characters sets out to reconstruct the missing document, which appears under the slightly different title of *Treatise on the Qualities of the Solitary Bird*.

López-Baralt explains how from this last text, which left only sporadic traces in Juan de la Cruz's main surviving work, *The Spiritual Canticle*, it can be inferred that the Saint took the notion of the solitary bird from David's Psalm 101:8, and that its characteristics point towards a bird in flight as an allegory for the human soul in ecstasy. She also draws attention to two literary oddities in this description that suggest the alleged non-Western origin of this symbolism: the bird has no determined colour, and its beak is always turned in the direction of the wind. Building on the work of Asín Palacios, López Baralt's own research has rendered 'very significant clues as to St John's "ornithosophy" in the literary tradition of Islamic mysticism' (74). The starting point is the bird-soul image found in the Qur'an chapter 'The Ant' (*Sura al-Naml*), which mentions King Solomon being taught '*manṭiq al-tayr*'. While this can be translated as language or speech of the birds, it should be remembered that this Arabic phrase is also the title of the earlier-mentioned allegory by Attar, *The Conference of the Birds*. Attar, however, was certainly not the only one to adopt and adapt this phrase. As other examples, López-Baralt further mentions the Sufis Bistami and Najm al-Din al-Kubra, the philosopher Avicenna, the theologian al-Ghazali, and yet another Persian poet, Sanā'ī. The wide use of this bird symbolism was the reason for Henry Corbin to speak of a '*cycle de l'oiseau*' (75). Even though this 'bird cycle' features an avian multitude rather than a solitary bird, López-Baralt insists that

> the concrete particulars which the Muslim mystics and St John of the Cross employ in their formulations of the symbol are often the same. More than once, we will see, the coincidence is so startling that it forces us to consider the possibility of filiation. (77)

On the basis of a close reading of the peculiar and enigmatic characteristics of *The Spiritual Canticle*, López-Baralt ventures to speculate that the most profound influence on Saint John may have been exercised by a Persian text of Shihab al-Din Suhrawardi, 'The Note of the Simurg' (*Safir-i-Simurg*). The parallels between the respective bird-soul symbolisms of the Muslim and the Christian martyr encompass not only its solitary stillness (alone and static in its highest stage of contemplation), but also the indeterminate colour, the connection between the position of the bird's beak as a manifestation of the soul's unification with God and the breathing of the Divine breath, and – finally – its soft song reaching all but heard by only a few (78–85). That Goytisolo has been an attentive student of López-Baralt's research is evinced by the following – of course apocryphal – citation from the lost *Treatise on the Qualities of the Solitary Bird*:

> I was alone, she vanished,
> Serene, fleet of wing, inclined to fly to the heights, subtle, colorless, perfect,
> I plunged into profound contemplation of the virtues of the solitary birds.[165]

What admittedly remains 'one more enigma in a long list of enigmas surrounding the work of the saint' is the question of transmission.[166] While, at the time of Juan de la Cruz, Iberia's Muslim heritage was still in the very recent past, there is certainly no indication that the Carmelite friar could read Arabic, nor is there any further information available as to how texts and symbols predominantly originating in the Persianate parts of the Muslim world had made their way to its western parts.

Aside from a coda about Attar's *The Conference of the Birds*, in *The Virtues of the Solitary Bird* the discalced Carmelite's *Spiritual Canticle* is juxtaposed alongside excerpts from the wine poetry of 'Umar Ibn al-Farid (1181–1235), Ibn Arabi's *Interpreter of Ardent Desires* and *Odes to Shams-Tabrizi* written by his disciple Rumi. The novel's opening epigraph already points up evident parallels between a verse from Ibn al-Farid's *Praise of Wine* or *Al-Khamriyya* (spelled *Al Jamriya* by Goytisolo) and the 'inner wine cellar' mentioned in *The Spiritual Canticle*.[167] Merging them later into a single verse, 'we drank in memory of the Beloved a wine that intoxicated us before the creation of the vineyard!' (113), Goytisolo turns to Muslim exegetes of this trope of drinking wine:

> One saying wine really means that there is no other God but God and saliva is Mohammed the prophet of God, and another that if you mix true existence (wine) with the forms of perishable things, you must not abandon the One you love, for the Beloved's vital sap (saliva) comes directly from that. (139)

There are also the instructive parallels between the persecution of Juan de la Cruz and the tensions within the Islamic tradition between logocentric-nomocentric orthodoxy and the spiritually focused Sufi discourses, a polarity that also informs Goytisolo's Sufi references in his other novels and that points back to the connections he made between the ethics of Jean Genet and Muslim exponents of Islamic antinomianism. With regard to *The Virtues of the Solitary Bird*, this parallel extends further to the novel's contextualisation in relation to the AIDS pandemic: as its global impact became increasingly discernible, so did the conflicting rhetoric of empathy and compassion for the victims on the part of some, and self-righteous moral condemnation by others. This last point is communicated through the introduction of a character who goes by the name Ben Aïds. Unfortunately, this English translation does not quite capture the originally intended wordplay. As in other Romance languages, the disease caused by HIV is called SIDA in Spanish, and the character in question is therefore called Ben Sida, featuring in the novel as a mysterious Sufi who provides Juan de la Cruz and his present-day alter ego with glosses from Ibn al-Farid's *Praise of Wine*. Both Goytisolo himself and the Hispanist Manuel Ruiz Lagos have recorded that there actually was a historical figure of that name, also known as the Blind Man of Murcia. These were aliases of a scholar and anthologist named Abu'l-Hasan Ali ibn Isma'il al-Mursi al-Andalusi (1007–66).[168] It is also this Ben Sida who warns the novel's protagonists of the 'obtuse bloodthirstiness of the unreformed Carmelite Friars' (139), the key adversaries of both Juan de la Cruz and his ally Teresa of Avila, as well as the stratagems of the Holy Office of the Inquisition. Thus the novel narrates how eager the Church authorities were to know whether there was indeed a connection 'between the effect of the "from the inner wine cellar of my Beloved I drank" and the glosses that instead of shedding light on its sense following an orthodox interpretation envelop it in a complex hermeneutical net at once redundant and contradictory' (139). Of the Church authorities, suspecting that the Carmelite was indeed familiar with Ibn al-Farid, Ibn Arabi and Rumi, Goytisolo writes:

> The most recent comparative studies that had come into their hands did not allow them to harbor the slightest doubt on the subject, they established with complete clarity the complicity existing between my doctrine and that of the sectarians of Islam. (86)

For a work of fiction, *The Virtues of the Solitary Bird* provides a high level of detail regarding the Church's investigations against the future Saint John of the Cross and intimate knowledge of López-Baralt's historical research into the genesis of de la Cruz's version of the Solitary Bird:

> We were looking for your *Treatise on the Qualities of the Solitary Bird* and have not found it, did you swallow it whole as witnesses state? Have you put it in a safe place in some monastery of the Reformed Carmelites?, thanks to our missions in lands of the infidels and incursions into higher Ottoman schools

> of learning we know that the image of the mystic bird appears frequently in their poetry of the Saracen sect, a number of heretic books, printed outside our domains, mention its presence in Kubra, Algazel and Avicenna. (88)[169]

That this kind of intertextuality is also at work within Goytisolo's own literary output, and that his concerns over the persecution of alleged heretics extend to both the Christian and Islamic traditions, becomes clear from the following passages from *The Virtues of the Solitary Bird* and from his next novel *Quarantine* respectively:

> They had sent emissaries to the principal higher schools of learning of the Orient to request information about the Shadilis, they are convinced that there exist secret points of convergence between your poems and those of the visionaries and mystics of the poisonous Mohammed sect. (77)

> Ibn Taymiyya, Torquemada, and Menéndez Pelayo [...] their narrowmindedness condemned as heretics, zendiks, Kaffirs, and other abominable deviations: noble Ibn Arabi, Greatest Master and Seal of the Saints; Al Hallajj, Al-Bisthami, and Suhravardi; Shadili, the illumed, and the quietists, the sublime Miguel de Molinos, Don José Maria Blanco. What a wonderful lesson they're being given! They conceived of paradise or xanna as the exclusive club of a small clique and ignored Rahma, the Unique One's limitless mercy. (45–6)[170]

Cross-references between spiritual preoccupations and literary publications also remain part of the books Goytisolo wrote during the final decade of his writing life. In *The Blind Rider* from 2003, we read how 'he remembered the time when he'd been inspired by the idea of a chimerical transcendence. Reading Saint John of the Cross had consoled him during another period of anguish.'[171] He goes on to explain that instead of facing a possible death sentence in the form of a positive HIV test, he turned to mysticism and poetry, in particular *The Spiritual Canticle*. While reading such texts appealed to Goytisolo's 'propensity to hermeticism', it was Monique Lange's observation that living with him was 'like serving an apprenticeship in solitude' that shook Goytisolo out of his introspections: 'Gradually he put aside his reading and immersed himself in the brutality of the real' (23).

Return to Realism: Full Circle?

Goytisolo's return to writing about current affairs and political events is already prefigured in his novels from the first half of the 1990s, *Quarantine* and *State of Siege*, which are set against the background of actual conflicts not just affecting local Muslims but involving the Islamic world at large. In *Quarantine*, the narrative is interspersed with references to the 1991 Gulf War, which broke out in response to the invasion and occupation of the Persian Gulf Emirate of Kuwait by neighbouring Iraq. Code-named Operation Desert Storm, as the first armed conflict to receive 24/7 televised coverage it also provided other intellectuals with material for writing about this first fully mediatised war. The dynamics of Operation Desert Storm spoke to the imaginations of philosophers like Jean Baudrillard and Paul Virilio.[172] The conclusion of Baudrillard's provocative *The gulf war did not take place* (1991) could easily have been written by Goytisolo:

> Our wars thus have less to do with the confrontation of warriors than with the domestication of the refractory forces on the planet, those uncontrollable elements as the police would say, to which belong not only Islam in its entirety but wild ethnic groups, minority languages.[173]

In Virilio's *Desert Screen*, total technological warfare usurps attributes traditionally associated with the Divine: omnipresence and omnivoyance. The contrast Virilio sketched between what he calls the mystical fundamentalism of holy war and the technological fundamentalism of pure war, enabling a 'deterrence of the strong by the weak', is something that is indeed also at work in Goytisolo's fiction.[174]

State of Siege is set in the city of Sarajevo during the Bosnian war (1992–5), during which its population was exposed to constant sniper fire, while their Serbian adversaries were also involved in wiping out the city's multicultural heritage by targeting the National Library with its invaluable archives and unique collections of manuscripts from Ottoman times. Like *Quarantine*, *State of Siege* was written and published at the very time when the hostilities were still unfolding. In both novels, Goytisolo's literary treatment of events that were actually transpiring can be considered examples of magic realism in the same vein as found in the novels by the Latin American 'boom' writers. When the first images of casualties beamed from TV screens, *Quarantine* describes how, on 17 January 1991, the main character 'gave up grazing among the rings of people, his distinctive, fertile nomadism', in order to withdraw to his house near Marrakesh's central square.[175] As the narrative continues to merge rioting demonstrators in Algeria, Egypt and the West Bank with the carnage of bombings in Beirut, the 1982 massacres in the Palestinian refugee camps Sabra and Shatila and the 1988 poison attack on Kurds in the Iraqi town of Halabja, the nameless protagonist cannot help but wonder whether what he is watching on television is not 'simply the beds of the Tigris and Euphrates gushing into the Medina of the Seven Holy Men' (37). Situated in a concretely identifiable theatre of military operations and offering a more coherent storyline than the other books discussed so far, *State of Siege* revolves around a macabre switch of corpses (the death theme yet again) orchestrated by a local historian specialised in Sufism. It is certainly also no coincidence that this subterfuge is primarily directed against a representative of Spanish officialdom: a strait-laced major serving with the 'International Mediation Force', which obviously stands for UNPROFOR, the United Nations Protection Force that was operational in the former Yugoslavia during the conflict. Here the creative imaginary aspect of magic realism is represented by an alleged descendant of one of the Seven Saints of Marrakesh by the name of Sidi Abu al-Makârim, whose body needs to be taken away from the war zone and repatriated. In *State of Siege*, the Malamatiyya, Ibn Arabi and Rumi all make reappearances. There are also references to Saint John's *Spiritual Canticle* and *La Celestina* of Fernando de Rojas. Further allusions to mysticism are found in an appendix that is attached to the novel proper, reproducing the collections of poems entitled *The Sotadic Zone* and *Astrolabe* attributed to a enigmatic author with the initials 'J. G.', which are at the centre of the intrigues playing out in *State of Siege*.[176]

Looking back at Juan Goytisolo's oeuvre, we see that reality was actually never absent from his work, nor from the Álvaro Mendiola trilogy. Even in his postmodern experimentations and interrogations of postcoloniality, Goytisolo creatively employed historical actors with relations to the Muslim world; complex figures operating as cultural border crossers, whose ambiguous roles Goytisolo interrogated through the prism of treason (the Visigoth Julian of Ceuta; the Mallorcan convert to Islam Anselm Turmeda; St John of the Cross), or by connecting cultural brokerage to questions of sexual orientation, when it concerns individuals caught up in the imperialist designs of Britain (Richard Francis Burton and T. E. Lawrence). Hovering in the background as the constant link between these themes is Jean Genet. The same applies with regard to historical events and developments. In *Count Julian*, an envisaged new invasion of the Iberian Peninsula from North Africa can be read as an allegory for the migratory pressures resulting from the disparity in economic prosperity and prospects between Europe and the Global South in the postcolonial era, beginning with the recruitment of labourers from North Africa (and elsewhere around the Mediterranean) in the 1950s and 1960s, to repeated full-blown crises since the beginning of the twentieth century that were exacerbated by the refugee streams as a result of political violence. I also refer to the passage in *Landscapes after the Battle* concerning climate change.

Juan Goytisolo has kept up this interplay between reality and imagination through the manipulation of texts until the very end of his active writing life. A final example of this intertextuality is illustrated by comparing the novella *The Blind Rider* from 2003 with Goytisolo's earlier essays about Chechnya and other conflict zones in the Muslim world in the 1996 travelogue *Landscapes of War* (obviously a title pointing back at *Landscapes after the Battle*), which combines war reportage with literary criticism.[177] In both books, Goytisolo meditates on *Hadji Murad*, Leo Tolstoy's posthumously published novel inspired by his own involvement as a young soldier in the Russian military campaigns in the Caucasus during the 1850s.[178] Drawing a parallel between the octogenarian Russian count's ill-fated final journey ending with his lonely death at a desolate Russian railway station and his own forays in Chechnya, an equally ageing Juan Goytisolo reaches the conclusion that 'oblivion was the only true God'.[179]

No one knows what it means to be born and to live on the brink, between two worlds, knowing and understanding both of them, and to be unable to help explain them to each other and bring them closer. To love and hate both, to hesitate and waver all one's life. To have two homelands, and yet have none. To be everywhere at home and to remain forever a stranger. In short, to live torn on a rack, but as both victim and torturer at once.

Ivo Andrić, *Bosnian Chronicle*, 313.

But we belong to no one, we're always on the frontier, always someone's dowry. [...] The saddest land in the world, the most unhappy people in the world. We're losing our identity, but we cannot assume another, foreign one. We've been severed from our roots, but we haven't become part of anything else; [...] we live at a crossroads, at a border between peoples, in everyone's way.

Meša Selimovic, *Death and the Dervish*, 330.

Allah, I have been so tired for over six hundred years now, a Moslem monarch all alone in the middle of the vast Christian expanses [...] I beg you: Finally grant me oblivion, My Lord! Make them remove my blood from these cold plains.

Ismail Kadare, *Three Elegies for Kosovo*, 87.

Chapter 4

Europe's Ottoman Past

For most of his writing life, Juan Goytisolo's literary occupation was primarily concerned with the far west of the Muslim world, but the previous chapter has also shown that his later interests shifted eastward and that he became concerned also with events in Bosnia and Chechnya. When it comes to Islam and the Muslim world, the authors in this chapter have concentrated on the political history of South-Eastern Europe – this in contrast to Goytisolo, Kermani and Meddeb's interest in Sufism. Most attention will therefore be given to the dominance of the most western of what Marshall Hodgson called the Islamic 'gunpowder empires' of late medieval and early modern times: that of the Ottoman Turks.[1] The expansion of their empire into Europe turned the region they referred to as the Balkans into a double – or even triple – periphery: a cultural and religious crossroads between the north-western frontier of the Muslim world, the western edge of Eastern Orthodox Christianity and the Catholic Adriatic.[2] This Ottoman penetration into the Balkans coincided with a waning of Islamic influence on the south-western edge of the continent: the Iberian Peninsula, or Al-Andalus in Arabic. Thus, the analogy of communicating vessels presents itself again: less than half a century after the surrender of Constantinople to the Ottoman Sultan Mehmet II in 1453, the last Moorish ruler in Spain handed over Granada to the Catholic monarchs Ferdinand and Isabelle of Castille. In the century that followed, Spain and Portugal were eventually almost completely emptied of any Muslim (and Jewish!) presence. Many of these refugees found a new home in these Ottoman domains, leaving only Europe's south-east with a sizeable Muslim presence.

This chapter's selection of authors, who have used the Balkans' Ottoman past as a tableau for their storytelling and psychological portrayals, includes Yugoslavia's only Nobel Prize laureate, and two nominees for that prize, from the same country and Albania respectively. When, in the wake of the collapse of Albania's autocratic Communist regime, Ismail Kadare (1935–2024) decided to leave the country because he feared a backlash against him personally amid the ensuing political chaos, his move to Paris only solidified his reputation as an internationally renowned writer. Meanwhile, the excessive identity politics following the break-up of the former Yugoslavia during the 1990s gave a second lease of life to the writings of Ivo Andrić (1892–1975) and Meša Selimović (1910–82). Although often regarded as historical novels, the storytelling of Andrić, Kadare and Selimović certainly does not meet the criteria set by the main theorist of Marxist literary realism, George Lukács.[3] Instead, the trio's writings bear a closer resemblance to the realism of nineteenth-century French novelists, such as Balzac, Flaubert and Stendhal. This choice of genre requires a more detailed and extensive excursion into political history than has been necessary in the preceding chapters.

The Balkans' Ottoman Past: Between Historiography and Mythmaking

The Ottoman presence in South-Eastern Europe lasted nearly half a millennium and was heralded by the conquest of the one-time capital of Thrace, Adrianople, in the early 1360s.[4] Renamed Edirne, it became the new Ottoman capital until the fall of Constantinople, while also serving as springboard for further expansion into the Balkans at the expense of the Byzantine Empire and the regional kingdoms of Bulgaria, Hungary and Serbia. Another major confrontation between the Ottoman invaders and Serbian-led defenders near Pristina in present-day Kosovo, some twenty-five years later, that became known as the Battle of the Blackbird Field of June 1389, was elevated by nineteenth-century Serbian nationalists as the defining landmark event of Ottoman expansion.[5] While its military outcome was indecisive, the battle left both the Turkish Sultan Murad I and the Serbian autocrator Prince Lazar dead, reducing the latter's feudal lieges to Ottoman vassals and opening the way for the annexation of Bulgaria. At the beginning of the fifteenth century, further penetration of South-Eastern Europe's interior was temporarily halted as a result of a challenge of Ottoman rule in Asia Minor (now western Anatolia) by a rival Turkic warlord from Central Asia: Timur Lenk (1336–1405) – in English also referred to as Tamerlane. His invasion not only disrupted the Ottoman expansion but also triggered an eleven-year-long succession war. However, after the conquest of Constantinople by Mehmet II in 1453, Ottoman expansion in the Black Sea area and the Balkans got under way seriously, reducing Moldova and Wallachia (in present-day Romania) to tribute-paying dependencies. After another – more decisive – battle at Kosovo in 1448, Serbia and Bosnia were incorporated into the Ottoman Empire. From the sixteenth century onwards, the Sultans used the Balkans for launching invasions into central Europe. Further south, the Peloponnese had fallen in 1460 and Albania followed in 1468 after the death of the warrior-hero Gjergj Kastrioti, better known by his sobriquet Skanderbeg. Most of the territories inhabited by ethnic Albanians remained within the Ottoman Empire until its collapse, sending delegates to the Grand Assembly in Istanbul until 1912.

Despite this long occupation, the Turks never really assimilated with the peoples they subjugated. In part this can be explained by what motivated their conquests in the first place. Before anything else, the Ottoman Empire was a military enterprise; a war machine bent on territorial expansion in order to obtain access to supply markets of 'men to fight wars, and money to pay for them'.[6] In this respect, the dynamics of Ottoman expansion can be considered a rerun of the Arab conquests under the early Caliphs in Medina and the Umayyad dynasty of Damascus. Consequently, religion, and – with that – conversion to Islam, did not feature prominently in Ottoman political designs for the lands they were bringing under their control. When it did take place, Islamisation was largely confined to urban centres, or *kasaba* as they were called in both Ottoman Albania and Bosnia.[7] Most of these, including the current Bosnian capital Sarajevo, were new settlements established by the Turkish invaders.[8] More important than the difference between Muslims and non-Muslims was therefore the distinction between the Ottoman ruling class and what in Turkish were called the *rayah*. This originally Arabic term, which also occurs in the Qur'an, means 'flock', and was later used generically for subjected peoples, both non-Muslim and Muslim. Within the Ottoman Empire's European domains, Albania and Bosnia, together with Kosovo, form exceptions in terms of their comparatively high percentage of conversions to Islam among their indigenous populations. This stands in contrast to the Ottoman possessions in Thrace and Bulgaria. Located closer to Asia, these areas were exposed to large-scale settlement by Turkic Muslims from Anatolia. In the Empire's contested frontier with what are now Hungary, Romania and Serbia, the local population remained predominantly Christian.

Literary writings featuring Islamic referents by contemporary authors from the former Yugoslavia and Albania continue to be an integral part of what Noel Malcolm calls the myth-making about the Balkan's Ottoman past, in the sense that the individuals in question have been implicated in that process in two ways.[9] First of all, by actively contributing to this myth-making through their own literary productions; and secondly, through the exploitation and manipulation of their writings by others to suit theír respective political agendas, thus perpetuating the mystification of the history of South-Eastern Europe in that way as well.

The Bosnia Trilogy of Ivo Andrić

Since Ivo Andric's main literary output was produced between the 1920s and 1960s, it could be argued that he should be considered a precursor of more contemporary authors. However, in view of the exploitation of his writings by warring parties in the former Yugoslavia during the 1990s, I will treat him here as an author with continuing present-day relevance.[10] Also intriguing is that, before turning to full-time writing, Ivo Andrić had a diplomatic career that took him all over Europe and into the highest echelons of foreign policymaking in inter-war Yugoslavia. And yet, his literary oeuvre is almost entirely dedicated to the parochial settings of his native Bosnia, eventually earning him the highest possible accolade, the 1961 Nobel Prize for literature. Moreover, Ivo Andrić is not just the only Yugoslav to ever win that award; he also is the only person known to have met the two individuals who fired the most fateful gunshots in twentieth-century European history: Gavrilo Princip, whose assassination of the Habsburg heir apparent on 28 June 1914 triggered the First World War, and Adolf Hitler, whose suicide in April 1945 spelled the end of the Second. All this warrants a more detailed biographical account than the profiling of the two other authors in this chapter, or those discussed in the preceding chapters.

Of Catholic Croat origin, Ivo Andrić was born in the same year as Yugoslavia's future autocratic ruler Marshal Tito.[11] Allegedly he first saw the day of light in the central Bosnian town of Travnik, which had served as the administrative centre of Ottoman Bosnia between 1699 and 1833, and again from 1840 until 1851. It is not clear why he was born there, because his family was originally from Sarajevo. Because of these obscurities, it was rumoured that the man registered as his mother's husband was not Ivo's biological father and that he was actually sired by a Catholic priest. Perhaps this was also the reason why, by the age of two, Ivo had already been put in the care of an aunt and her Polish husband, who worked for the Habsburg Empire in the eastern Bosnian town of Višegrad. Although Austria-Hungary had occupied Bosnia-Herzegovina since 1878 and had taken effective control of its governance, legally, sovereignty rested still with the Ottoman Empire. Until the Austrians' formal annexation of the territory in 1910, this made young Ivo Andrić technically a subject of the Sultan. It was in Višegrad that Andrić received his primary school education and first heard tales about earlier Ottoman times that would later inspire his novels and short stories. Aside from Turkish-Islamic, Croat-Catholic and Serbian-Orthodox influences, Bosnia was also home to a popular culture with a rich folklorist component featuring witches, goblins and fairies. In fact, Andrić's very first publication, a poem entitled 'In the Twilight', was published in 1911 in a periodical called *Bosanska Vila*, which translates as *Forest Fairy*. Throughout his life, Andrić continued to express his admiration for the Bosnian Muslim way of speaking Serbo-Croat.[12]

During his high-school years in Sarajevo, Ivo Andrić became acquainted with a fellow member of the Mlada Bosna or Young Bosnia Movement, by the name of Gavrilo Princip. As a university student in Zagreb, Vienna and Krakow (1912–14), Andrić went on to play a leading role in the nationalist Serbo-Croat Yugoslav Progressive Youth Movement, but was not involved in the assassination plot against the Austrian Archduke Franz Ferdinand. However, on account of his association with these anti-Austrian movements, Andrić too was arrested. After brief detention in Slovenia, he was sent into internal exile until 1917. It was here that, sequestered at a vicarage in the central Bosnian village of Ovčarevo, Andrić was first introduced to ageing Franciscan friars who had still lived under Ottoman rule. According to his biographer Michael Martens, this not only kindled an interest in the monastic archives that would become an important source for his later writings about Bosnia's past: what Andrić's learned about the monks' caution and cunning towards the Ottoman authorities (an attitude characterised in Turkish as *muzevvir*) he would put to good use during his later diplomatic career (99).[13] Moreover, these war times also shaped Andrić's recurring concerns as a literary writer; especially his skepsis regarding 'the value of victory and victors' (112) in armed conflicts.

At the beginning of the interbellum Ivo Andrić's life took a turn for the better. As the protégé of his former teacher Tugomir Alaupović, who was now the Minister of Religion of the newly-founded independent Yugoslavia, Andrić was given a position at the ministry in Belgrade. Soon, however, he asked for a transfer to the foreign service, because it offered better career prospects. This was the beginning of a meteoric rise through the ranks of Yugoslavia's diplomatic corps. First representing what was officially called the Kingdom of Serbs, Croats and Slovenes at the Holy See in Rome, Andrić was appointed in quick succession to increasingly senior consular posts in Trieste, Bucharest, Graz, Marseilles and Paris, then Madrid and finally Brussels. After serving as his country's representative at the League of Nations in Geneva (1930–3), he returned to the Foreign Office in Belgrade, where he held the senior posts of director of political affairs (1935–7) and deputy minister (1937–41). Eventually he was appointed Yugoslavia's envoy to Berlin (1939–41), where his main government contact was the ministry's state secretary Ernst von Weizsäcker, but where on occasion Andrić would also meet Hitler in person.[14] According to Martens, 'there has rarely been a diplomat as suitable for the profession as the always silent, reserved and careful Andrić, who as it were tiptoed through life' (131). These qualities not only served him well in his government career; they were also instrumental in his surviving the war in German-occupied Belgrade and in adapting to Yugoslavia's Communist era. In fact, the only consistent political conviction that can be attributed to Andrić is an unwavering support for a united Yugoslavia; in every other respect, he was like 'political flotsam' (461) floating along on the main current. It was thanks to a rare instance of personal courage shown at the beginning of the war that Andrić managed to retain his good name and integrity: to his credit, he declined a German offer of enabling a comfortable exile in Switzerland after the invasion of Yugoslavia in 1941. Instead, he chose to be detained and then sent back to Belgrade to sit out the three-year occupation, keeping his head down and writing frantically. Diplomatic dexterity also helped Andrić avoid imprisonment or worse following the Communist takeover in 1944.

Deftly walking the tightrope between political quietism and ingratiating himself sufficiently with the Tito regime, Comrade Ivo Andrić succeeded in becoming post-War Yugoslavia's main man of letters.[15] While his joining the Communist Party worked to their mutual benefit, it was greeted with dismay and even open revulsion by many former friends and acquaintances in what were now considered the bourgeois circles of Yugoslavia's pre-war incarnation. All considered, Ivo Andrić's working life was divided in two, but in both the diplomatic and literary fields he managed to reach the very top of these professions.

In relation to the subject matter of this book, and this chapter in particular, one text dating back to the early days of Andrić's diplomatic career needs to be included in the present excursion: his doctoral thesis on religion in Bosnia during Ottoman times from 1924. This was in response to a new government rule introduced a year earlier, which required civil servants of a certain rank to hold a university degree. As Andrić had never graduated, his budding diplomatic career was under threat of being cut short before it had even properly begun. Fortunately, the young consul's superiors enabled him to study for a degree at the University of Graz during his posting there and thus secure a continuation of his employment. Within a year, Andrić had submitted a thesis in German, which was translated into English and published, under the title *The Development of Spiritual Life in Bosnia under the*

Influence of Turkish Rule, seventy-five years later. The probable incentive was the appearance of a Serbo-Croatian version a few years earlier, which had triggered polemical debates about Andrić's views of Islam. After lying dormant for decades, this all but forgotten dissertation had been unearthed by Muslim intellectual activists from Bosnia, who used it to accuse Andrić of being an 'Islamophobic hater of Turks' (149). Surprising, even the respected British Balkan historian Noel Malcolm appeared to jump on this bandwagon, accusing Andrić of caricaturing Muslims and 'willful blindness'.[16] In this instance, it seems as if this acknowledged expert has fallen victim to the very myth-making and misinterpretations of the Balkans' Ottoman past he so rightly criticises in his historical studies of Bosnia, Kosovo and Albania. This is all the more remarkable because a careful reading of the dissertation shows that Malcolm and Andrić are actually often in agreement when it comes to interpretating the dynamics of Bosnian history.

While the dissertation is certainly not a work of brilliance even by the standards of the time, and is marred by the tendency to speak of peoples and cultures in terms of 'advanced' and 'backward', it is nonetheless important to bear a few things in mind.[17] First of all, the dissertation should be read as an effort on the part of a young diplomat trying to rescue his career. Secondly, it was presented as part of a course in Slavic philology, not in Ottoman history or the study of religion, let alone Islamic studies. The underlying research had also been conducted not so much for academic reasons per se as with future literary purposes in mind. The material collected in Graz and – before that – in archives and libraries in Italy, France and his native Bosnia would continue to inform Andrić's future stories and novels. This was also recognised by two prominent scholars of Islam from the former Yugoslavia. Both Smail Balić, a Bosniak academic who spent the better part of his career as a librarian in Austria and Germany, and Alexandre Popovic, an expert on Sufism working in Paris, have given more measured and even appreciative assessments of Andrić's research than the politically motivated activists. While finding him seriously wanting in terms of his academic knowledge of Islam, both Balić and Popovic acknowledge Andrić's talent as a creative writer and praise the quality of his literary oeuvre. His archival investigations into Bosnia's Ottoman past must therefore be judged in that particular light.[18] Unfortunately, this was not the only time Andrić's writings were abused for political purposes. An even worse case of opportunistic exploitation was the way in which a short story, entitled 'A Letter from 1920', was cynically manipulated by Radovan Karadžić, former leader of the Bosnian Serbs and now a convicted war criminal responsible for the ethnic cleansings in Bosnia during the 1990s.[19] A telling illustration of the conflicting interpretations of Andrić's work and the diverging opinions about his person is the following wry joke recorded by his biographer Martens:

> The Serbs hate Ivo Andrić because although he died a Serb, he was born as a Croat. The Croats hate him because he was born a Croat but died a Serb. The Bosnian Muslims hate Andrić because he was born. (455)

Almost simultaneously with the completion of his thesis, Andrić published a first collection of short stories. Two more volumes followed as his diplomatic career progressed during the 1930s. These early literary writings were read with appreciation by the controversial German jurist and political philosopher Carl Schmitt, who, in turn, brought them to the attention of the author Ernst Jünger, then already a literary celebrity – albeit a notorious one – on account of his provocative novels inspired by his own harrowing battlefield experiences during the First World War. During his time in Berlin, Andrić and Schmitt even became friends on account of their shared admiration for the French Catholic writer Léon Bloy (1846–1917). When Andrić became *persona non grata* as a result of the German invasion of Yugoslavia, Schmitt sent him a copy of Martin Luther's German translation of the Bible by way of consolation. Because of his appointment to increasingly weighty professional positions and the subsequent war years, between 1936 and 1945 Ivo Andrić published no new literary work.

The three novels that together form the so-called Bosnian trilogy were written between April 1942 and October 1944, when the former diplomat lived in virtual seclusion in Belgrade. *The Bridge on the Drina*, *Bosnian Chronicle* and *The Woman from Sarajevo* were all published at the same time in 1945. Set in the Bosnian-Serbian frontier town of Višegrad where Andrić had spent his childhood, *The Bridge on the Drina* offers a parochial impression of the history of Bosnia from the viewpoint of the rayah. Although concrete Islamic referents are relatively few, the story revolves around milestone events transpiring in Ottoman Bosnia between the 1560s and 1910s. The second volume, *Bosnian Chronicle*, takes place during the Napoleonic era (1807–14), when French troops occupied the Dalmatian coast along the Eastern Adriatic. The scene is moved from Višegrad to Travnik (the author's alleged birthplace), the provincial capital from which the novel also takes its original title in Serbo-Croatian: *The Travnik Chronicle*. The final volume, *A Woman of Sarajevo*, about a female war-profiteer in early twentieth-century Sarajevo, is less relevant for the purposes of this chapter, other than that it is set in a similar poisoned political atmosphere as Juan Goytisolo's *State of Siege*, written half a century later.[20] *The Bridge on the Drina* narrates the Ottoman past as a mixture of history and legend in a similar vein to Andrić's earlier short stories. The various chapters can therefore also be read as short stories in their own right. In fact, one story from 1931, 'The Bridge on the Žepa', can be considered a pre-study for the novel.[21] The narrative of *The Bridge on the Drina* skims relatively quickly over the three centuries following the construction of the bridge to concentrate on the period when Bosnia was under Austrian rule (1878–1918). It was this novel that the Nobel Prize Committee explicitly mentioned in its motivation for awarding Andrić the 1961 Nobel Prize for literature. On the occasion of the one-hundredth anniversary of the author's birth, Stanford University hosted a conference on Ivo Andrić led by the veteran Balkan historian Wayne S. Vucinich.[22] When the conference proceedings appeared in 1995 under the title *Ivo Andrić Revisited: The Bridge Still Stands*, Yugoslavia had already disintegrated and descended into civil war. *The Bosnian Chronicle* not only covers a more compressed period of time; it also deals much more explicitly with hard historical facts, developing both the novel's narrative and its main characters along the lines of the literary realism adopted by the great French novelists of the nineteenth century, whom Andrić greatly admired. While *The Bridge on the Drina* focuses on local events with political realities featuring faintly in the background, *Bosnian Chronicle* magnifies the rivalries among Europe's great powers. Coinciding with the Napoleonic elsewhere in Europe, and the nearby Serbian uprising (1803–14) led by Đorđe Petrović (better known by the sobriquet Karađorđe and ancestor of the three Yugoslav kings whom Andrić had represented as a diplomat), the story revolves around the machinations of the French and Austrian consuls stationed in Travnik vis-à-vis the Ottoman authorities and each other. This is also reflected in the original title of the English translation, *The Days of the Consuls* (1992). This was also a subject matter on which, as a former diplomat, Andrić could write with authority.

One characteristic marking all of Andrić's writings about Ottoman Bosnia, including his dissertation, is the cavalier use of certain terminology: in particular his use of the word 'Turk'. Aside from reflecting the political-historical vocabulary employed in early modern Europe in relation to the Ottoman Empire – according to which the Sultan is often referred to as the 'Grand Turk' – the choice may have been influenced by the circumstance that the writing of the thesis coincided with the formation of a Turkish Republic by Mustafa Kemal Atatürk on the remains of the Ottoman state. However, throughout *The Bridge on the Drina* and *Bosnian Chronicle*, Andrić also refers to the Muslim population of Bosnia as local or Bosnian Turks, Višegrad or Travnik Turks, or even simply as Turks. The accurate and politically more correct alternatives to these misnomers would be Bosniaks.

The Ottoman Bosnia of Mehmed (Meša) Selimovic

Meša Selimovic always remained in Ivo Andrić's shadow. Born Mehmed Selimović into a leading Muslim family from Tuzla, a salt-mining town in Bosnia's north-east, from his own genealogical research he learned that he descends from an originally Orthodox Christian – part Serbian, part Montenegrin – family, some of whom converted to Islam for pragmatic reasons. A trained philologist, he worked as a teacher and in the cultural sector in Sarajevo, before moving to Belgrade in 1971. Initially, Selimović had little success as a literary writer; his breakthrough only came in 1966, with the novel *Death and the Dervish*, earning him most of Yugoslavia's literary prizes and a nomination for the Nobel Prize.[23] Although it lacks a specified time frame or location, references to uprisings in the Karjina and Posavina areas and to the Sinan Tekke and Mount Igman suggest mid-seventeenth-century Sarajevo as the main place of action. The novel's story, which revolves around the dervish Ahmed Nuruddin's culpability for the death of his brother Harun while in Ottoman captivity, is thought to have been informed by the murky circumstances surrounding the wartime execution of Selimović's own brother Šefkija by the Communists.[24] As a result *Death and the Dervish* has been widely read as an allegory seeking to indict the Communist regime for the death of the author's brother. The US-based Slavist Marina Antić finds such universalising interpretations too closed and reductive. They do not do justice to the open-ended possibilities offered by multi-layered literary texts in general and the particular ambiguities of *Death and the Dervish* itself.[25] Moreover, her research has also demonstrated that key characters in the novel are actually based on historical figures mentioned in chronicles about seventeenth-century Sarajevo.[26] Selimović's reputation as a writer was solidified by another novel from 1970, *The Fortress*. It tells the story of Ahmet Shabo, a war veteran returning home to Sarajevo at the end of the eighteenth century to marry a Christian girl and becoming involved in a raid to break a friend out of jail. Filling the time gap between Andrić narrations of sixteenth- and nineteenth-century Bosnia, together with *Death and the Dervish*, these are the only works of Selimović to have been translated into English. Although he emphatically self-identified as a Serbian writer, in both novels, Selimović very much engages with the ethno-religious diversity of his native Bosnia, comprising Serb, Croat and Serbo-Croat-speaking

Muslim communities. His historicised interrogations feed into such rhetorical questions as those of the American Slavist Henry R. Cooper:

> Which set of national myths will an individual choose to celebrate as his or her own? Which group of people will he or she celebrate them with? Despite contemporary appearances, movements among these groups have been appreciable over time, and the boundaries until recently have remained porous.[27]

Ismail Kadare's Ottoman Cycle

Born roughly a generation later than Andrić and Selimović, Albania's most widely translated and internationally most renowned author hails from the southern Albanian town of Gjirokastër. Whereas Andrić was born in the same year as Tito, Kadare shares his birthplace with Albania's future dictator, Enver Hoxha (1908–85), who ruled Albania with an iron fist for more than forty years. At that time, Albania was still a monarchy under King Zog, but Kadare's formative years and half of his professional life were spent in a republic first guided by Stalinism, and later modelled on Mao's ideology.[28] As indicated by his given name, Ismail Kadare's family was of Muslim origin, and one of his maternal great-grandfathers had been a bard associated with the Bektashi Sufi order. Winning his first literary price at age seventeen, Kadare went on to study languages and literature at the University of Tirana, and at the Gorki Institute in Moscow (1958–60). These postgraduate studies were cut short as a result of Hoxha's break with the Soviet Union. Already a published author, for the next thirty years Kadare would live in the Albanian capital Tirana – except for the two years (1967–9) he was forced to spent in rural Berat as a result of Hoxha's own 'Cultural Revolution'. Not long after that he had his international breakthrough thanks to a French translation of his 1963 novel *The General of the Dead Army*. As a result of the literary successes he began to enjoy abroad, and despite joining the Communist party in 1971, from then on Kadare's relations with both the older Albanian literary establishment and regime dogmatists remained turbulent. Following decades of censorship, banning of books and disappointment with the lack of reforms, Kadare left Albania for France in 1990. Also, after the fall of Hoxha's successor Ramiz Alia in 1991, and despite repeated calls from Albania to run for the country's presidency, Kadare continued to live for most of the time in Paris; only in his final years he decided to return to Albania, where he passed away on 1 July 2024. Kadare is the recipient of many international literary prizes, honorary doctorates and memberships of academies and learned societies, as well as other honours and accolades, but the Nobel Prize for Literature has always eluded him, despite his being nominated more than a dozen times.

Like Ivo Andrić, Ismail Kadare has been no stranger to controversy, although this was more due to his political stances than has been the case with the quietist Yugoslav. In all fairness, though, Albania's idiosyncratic Communist Regime was more unpredictable and repressive than Titoist Yugoslavia at its worst. It required political savviness and crafty – '*muzevvir*' as the Ottomans would have called it – acumen to mentally and physically survive under the mercurial Enver Hoxha.[29] The resulting opaqueness of Kadare's relationship with the regime divides both literary critics and political observers.[30] A comparison of Andrić and Kadare's literary output points up similarities as well, whereby the differences are a matter of degree rather than of kind. Instead of engaging in formal experimentations like Kermani, Meddeb or Goytisolo, as authors of novels with epic dimensions, Andrić and Kadare remained traditional storytellers. Andrić has explicitly invoked Stendhal and Thomas Mann as the key inspirers of his writing style: but his notebooks also mention other great novelists of the nineteenth century, as well as the poetry of Ovid, Petrarch and Goethe, and philosophers as different as Avicenna, Rousseau and Renan, alongside readings of the Qur'an and of the work of the historian Leopold von Ranke. Although Kadare considers his obedience to the European 'laws of literature' to be infused by a Homerian, instead of a Socratic-Platonic, spirit, his loyalty to the epic genre is based on the same kind of documentary material and historical factuality as Andrić's novels, thus bearing the same imprint of the literary realism of Gustave Flaubert.[31] In this respect, Ismail Kadare too can be said to match Ivo Andrić's literary profile of adding 'the talent of a novelist to the exactitude of a chronicler'.[32] However, underneath this affinity with the realism of the nineteenth-century novelists lies also an image of the Ottoman Turks that can be traced back to the Renaissance Humanists, whose depictions are an admixture of medieval crusader rhetoric and the Greek-Roman topos of the barbarian.[33]

Six of Ismail Kadare's nearly forty novels and novellas deal with Albania's Ottoman past. Written over a period of three decades (1968–97), like all his books, this 'Ottoman cycle' too has been subject to Kadare's habit of repeatedly revising his own published work. Definitive versions were only produced after Kadare's self-imposed exile in France and take as their point of departure the French translations of his complete works published by Librairie Arthème-Fayard in Paris since 1993. Also, many of the translations into English draw on these revised French rather than the original Albanian versions.

Although not written or published in accordance with the chronological order in which the events they describe have unfolded over time, three of the Ottoman cycle's titles deal with the period before Albania's eventual subjugation and incorporation into the Ottoman Empire. In spite of the fact that they were written over a period of almost thirty years, there is a remarkable degree of intertextuality. First published in 1970, *The Siege* tells the story of a failed Ottoman campaign against an Albanian stronghold as it is repelled by Albania's national hero George Castrioti Skanderbeg. Appearing eleven years later, *The Three-Arched Bridge* is set almost a century earlier, at the time of the first Turkish incursions into South-Eastern Europe. The publication of *Three Elegies for Kosovo* (1997) coincided with the political crisis erupting in exactly that part of the former Yugoslavia. In this novella, Kadare revisits the (alleged) landmark battle of 1389 between the Serbian King Lazar and Ottoman Sultan Murad I. The fact that the Battle of the Blackbird Field was fought in what is now the Republic of Kosovo and that Ismail Kadare makes it into an Albanian story is in itself already indicative of the political-historical complexities surrounding the Ottoman past in this part of the Balkans. The over-simplifications that are so characteristic of the modern ethno-religious identity politics dominating the political scene in the republics that once were part of the multi-ethnic and multi-religious Ottoman Empire is further demonstrated by such facts as Kosovo being the home of the Serbian Orthodox Patriarchate of Peć (Peja) since 1346, but also harbouring a population that is not just majority ethnic Albanian, but 95 per cent Muslim as well.

The intertextualities between the historical accounts from late fourteenth-century Albania actually also extend to the other titles in the cycle dealing with much later periods in history, while also largely moving the scene away from the Albanian periphery to the Ottoman metropole, Istanbul. With titles referring to cruel punitive measures meted out by an increasingly paranoid and authoritarian state, *The Traitor's Niche* (written 1974–6, first published 1978) and *The Blinding Order* (written 1984, but not released until 1991) take place during the reign of Sultan Mahmud II (1808–39). On the one hand, this period saw the introduction of a series of reforms known as the *Tanzimat* (1839–76) that propelled the Ottoman Empire into the modern age. On the other, there also was a tendency towards greater centralisation and Ottomanisation in the domain of culture: in *The Traitor's Niche*, Kadare highlights Ottoman attempts to obliterate the Albanian language and its cultural heritage. Cross-references also continue in *The Palace of Dreams* from 1981. Although lacking any mention of explicit dates, from the narrative it can nonetheless be inferred that this story about a state surveillance agency called *Tabir Sarrail* unfolds in the late 1870s.[34]

As novels set in the Ottoman Empire of the nineteenth century, *The Traitor's Niche*, *The Palace of Dreams* and *The Blinding Order* are united by a Kafkaesque atmosphere of menace radiating from a totalitarian state apparatus into which the crumbling realm was transformed in the final decades of its existence. This has stimulated a reading of these texts by Kadare scholars as *romans à clef* covertly criticising Albania's Communist regime. Indeed, there are parallels with the increasing authoritarianism of the Ottomans as their empire weakened. In most instances, Kadare's wilful anachronistic treatment of the Ottoman past has therefore been interpreted as transpositions of that period onto Albania's Communist era. Such readings seems to overlook the fact that totalitarian repression only took hold once the Ottoman Empire's slow decline reached its final decadent stage, exemplified by the reign of Sultan Abdulhamid II (r. 1876–1908), a veritable psychopath overseeing a regime of terror that lasted almost thirty years. Even when accepting Rebecca Gould's suggestion that allegory is indeed the hallmark of Kadare's authorship, in this case too its political-historical purport must still be further problematised. Can a pre-modern and – to an extent – early modern hegemonic warrior state that was nonetheless accommodative of ethno-religious diversity be cast in the same role as a twentieth-century regime subscribing to a totalising political ideology like Communism? A reverse projection of Hoxha's Albania onto the nineteenth-century Ottoman state terror described in *The Traitor's Niche*, *The Palace of Dreams* and *The Blinding Order* is actually a more accurate reading of the literary employment of anachronism than taking the whole Ottoman past as representative of Oriental despotism *tout court* and treating that as an allegory of modern-day totalitarian ideologies, all of which – Stalinist, Fascist, even Maoist – ultimately have European genealogies. Such questions indeed sit very uncomfortably with Ismail Kadare's agenda for Albania's reintegration into the community of European nations.

Enemy at the Gates: The Early Ottoman Incursions

In the 1350s, some two generations after a Turkmen warlord of the Oghuz tribal federation by the name of Uthman Ghazi (Osman the Raider) had carved out a *beylik* (principality) of his own in Asia Minor, thus becoming the eponymous founder of the Ottoman dynasty, his forces crossed over into the European continent for the first time. Illustrative of the Ottomans' future designs was the transfer of their capital in 1369 from Bursa in western Anatolia to Adrianople, an erstwhile Byzantine city located on present-day Turkey's borders with Greece and Bulgaria. Renamed Edirne, it became the Ottomans' springboard for their further penetration into South-Eastern Europe's interior. In one of his novels set in Ottoman times, Ismail Kadare has concerned himself specifically with these earliest Turkish invasions of the Balkans.

The Three-Arched Bridge is set in the aftermath of the Ottoman victory in the Battle of Maritsa, which was fought in 1371 near the village of Chernomen. Now called Ormenio and located on today's Bulgarian–Greek border, it became the Ottomans' gateway into Macedonia and Southern Serbia. The narrator is the monk Gjon, son of Gjorg Ukcana. From another one of Kadare's novels, *The Palace of Dreams*, which was written earlier but published in the same year as *The Three-Arched Bridge* (1981), it becomes clear that he is also an ancestor of the Köprülü family. In the late seventeenth and early eighteenth centuries, this Albanian clan produced no fewer than six Ottoman Grand Viziers. The novel tells the story of the construction of a bridge at the so-called 'Wicked Waters' (*Ujana e Keqe* in Albanian). This created an extension of the old Roman *Via Egnatia*, now redubbed 'the Road of the Balkans', after the name the Turks had given to the entire peninsula.[35] Connecting Thrace and Illyria, an ancient name for Albania and the rest of the areas along the Eastern Adriatic, in the less distant past the road had already played its part in Christian Europe's relations with the Muslim East:

> In the past three hundred years or so, all the holy crusades had passed along it. They said that two of the leaders of the First Crusade, Robert Giscard, Count of Normandy, and Robert, Count of Flanders, had slept a night at the inn a mile down the road from us, which since then had been called 'The Inn of the Two Roberts'. (26)[36]

This idea of Albania as a frontier between Christian Europe and the Abode of Islam returns several times in the course of the narrative, for example, in a conversation between Gjon and a fellow monk from somewhere else in Europe, named Brockhart. Discussing the decline of Byzantium, the dialogue between the two clerics, in which they agree that the Ottomans are an imminent danger to Christendom, reads:

> 'These Turks are an imminent danger for you too, aren't they?'
> 'Yes, they are on our doorstep.'
> 'Ah yes, you are where Europe begins'. (65)

The same conversation is also used to insert an exposé of the origins of the Albanian people. Gjon explains to Brockhardt how, as descendants of the Illyrians, 'we Albanians, together with the Greeks, are the oldest people in the Balkans' (65). And while in Latin their lands are referred to as Arbanum or Albanum, the Albanians themselves have started calling it Shqipëria, from *shqiponjë* meaning 'eagle' (65). After a rather dismissive remark about the Slavs as relatively new arrivals from the steppes in the East, Gjon considers the more recent arrivals from Asia as a much greater menace: 'Now, the Ottoman language is casting its shadow over both our languages, Greek and Albanian, like a black cloud' (66). Elsewhere in the novel, Gjon reports that he 'saw dervishes everywhere. It struck me that these horrible vagabonds could only be the scouts of the great Asiatic state that destiny had made our neighbour' (58). With the completion of the bridge, the monk concludes that 'another evil appeared on the horizon – the Turkish state. The shadows of its minarets are slowly stealing towards us' (4), giving him a 'premonition that the destiny of Arberia [yet another name for Albania] will soon change' (5), and that future bloodshed will also involve Asians. In this respect, the three arches of the bridge can be read as symbolising Albania's position on the crossroads between the Catholic Adriatic, Greek-Slavic Orthodox Christendom and the Ottoman *Dar al-Islam*.

Like other novelists writing in the great nineteenth-century tradition of realism, Ismail Kadare too provides documentable data, using historical figures as characters and actual events to structure the narrative and make the story more compelling. Thus, before letting the chronicler Gjon observe that relations with their Muslim neighbours had not always been acrimonious, Kadare introduces the House of Kastrioti, which provided the Albanian coat of arms with the double-headed eagle and to which also belonged the national hero Skanderbeg; the Muzakas, counts of Myzege; and the Duke of Gjin; as well as the North Albanian princely Balsha family; their originally Byzantine southern counterparts from Vlora; and the Topia family, which claimed the throne of all Albania. All these 'Albanian princes, like those everywhere in the Balkans and the Byzantine emperors themselves, have for some years been calling on Turkish units for use in their internecine squabbles' (45). This phrase expresses an estimation very similar to Noel Malcolm's historically contextualised interpretation of medieval alliance and allegiance:

> Modern Balkan writers tend to view anyone who cooperated willingly with the Turks, or invited them as allies into the area, as guilty of the most heinous treachery against their nation and their identity. But this way of looking at the past is highly anachronistic. Every medieval ruler made use, when possible, of other people's armies; and drawing in a potentially threatening power to divert it against one's enemies was also normal practice.[37]

However, by the time of Gjon's writing the tables have turned. 'Turks have been appearing increasingly often all over the Balkans' (44), and the monk regards them with suspicion: 'What is to be expected from a people who hide their very origins: their women?' (45). Ominous signs are also witnessed in the immediate vicinity of the bridge, where Gjon noticed yet another dervish, who 'paused at the first arch of the bridge, fell on his face in front of the victim, and intoned an Islamic prayer in a deep and mournful voice' (124). When eventually the Byzantine naval base in the strategically important bay of Vlora is ceded to the Ottomans by a joint decree from Bursa and Constantinople, 'the hunger of the great Ottoman state could be felt in the wind' (148). As 'more than half of the Balkan Peninsula was now under the Ottoman crescent' (150), the tide was clearly turning against the noble families of Albania. Although some continued to hold out, others gave in: aside from Bosnian and Croat rulers, 'three of the eleven lords of Arveria had also accepted vassalage' (153). In one of the final chapters, Kadare turns to a particular aspect of traditional Turkic warfare: the need for ritually cursing the enemy before going into battle. In this instance, the announcement of a 'Commination Against Europe' was exceptional in the sense that, while 'their chronicles told of the cursing of castles and the domains of rebellious pashas, and even whole states, before an attack began [...] there was no case of an entire continent being cursed' (160). Gjon speculates that given the magnitude of this task, the empire's chief curse-maker or caster of spells must have been summoned from the capital to ensure a successful Ottoman military subjugation of Europe.

The Battle of Kosovo and its Aftermath

Although the earlier-mentioned Battle of Maritsa was of greater strategic significance, in Serbia, Kosovo and Albania, but also elsewhere in South-Eastern Europe, the 1389 Battle of Kosovo Polje (which translates as Blackbird Field) is considered the watershed event inaugurating the Ottoman era in the Balkans. In his histories of Bosnia and Kosovo, Noel Malcolm pays ample attention to the mythologisation of this event by later Christian, especially Serbian, nationalists. His critical assessments in this regard have repeatedly earned him the ire of nationalist Serbian historians, who appear to be susceptible to a particular kind of touchiness when it comes to challenges of their depictions and interpretations of their own and the wider Balkans' past. However, the mythical proportions this battle has acquired in Balkan historiography are not just confined to Serbs, but extend to Albanians and Kosovars as well. It remains a defining element in connecting the Muslim presence in this part of the Balkans to its Ottoman past. The literary significance of the legendary battle is evinced by the fact that Ismail Kadare returns to it no fewer than three times in his six-volume Ottoman cycle. Aside from his 1997 novella *Three Elegies for Kosovo*, it had already featured in *The Siege*, Kadare's first novel set in Ottoman times written almost three decades earlier, and the event is mentioned yet again in *The Palace of Dreams*.

Questioning the historicity of the ways in which the Battle of Kosovo has been depicted in nationalist Serbian narratives in a chapter in his history of Kosovo entitled 'The Battle and the Myth', Noel Malcolm dissects in great detail the uncertainties surrounding what actually transpired on the Blackbird Field in June 1389.[38] First dismissed are false claims that the battle destroyed the medieval Serbians' empire and put them immediately under Ottoman rule. Although its demise had already set in more than three decades earlier, Serbian statehood actually survived until the middle of the fifteenth century. In their history of Albania, Fischer and Schmitt describe how since the 1370s, the Kosovo area had been disputed territory between Serbia's leading prince, Lazar Hrebeljanović, and the region's most powerful monarch, King Tvrtko of Bosnia, while the North Albanian Balsha family continued to hold on to Montenegro after having had to relinquish Peć and Prizren to Kosovo's local strongman and Lazar's son-in-law, Vuk Branković. By 1385, Gjergj II Balsha (also known as Đurađ II Balšić or George II Stracimirović) had agreed to become an Ottoman vassal.[39] Amid this Serbian and Albanian infighting, the Ottomans were already eyeing the lucrative silver mines of Bosnia and Serbia as they prepared for the confrontation north of the capital of today's Kosovo, Pristina. Aside from the Balshas, other Albanians who joined forces with Sultan Murad I were the Catholic warrior tribes of the Malësi, the Mirdita and the Këlmendi. Also included in the Ottoman ranks were units of Bulgarians and Greeks.

There is disagreement as to whether the battle rendered an Ottoman victory or whether its outcome should be adjudged a draw, the only factual certainties being that in its aftermath both the Ottoman Sultan and the Serbian leader Lazar were dead. Most of what is known about the battle is orally transmitted through both Serbian and Albanian ballads and epics, many of which were only put into writing centuries later. It was therefore not until 1601 that a monk from Ragusa (present-day Dubrovnik) blamed treachery on the part of Vuk Branković for his father-in-law's death, treachery which eventually also reduced Lazar's son and successor Stefan Lazarević to Ottoman vassalage. At the beginning of this chapter, I already pointed to the parallel between the Ottoman expansion into Europe and the Arab conquests of the seventh and eighth centuries. This parallel can be further extended to the question of Christian collaborations. It appears to me that the role of Christian turncoats and vassals in the Ottoman ranks described in the epic ballad tradition of the Balkans is not so different from the literary use of the alleged Visigoth traitor Count Julian's involvement in the invasions of the Iberian Peninsula discussed in the previous chapter.

The exact circumstances of Lazar's demise have remained obscure. The only contemporaneous – and prosaic – source, from a Catalan and written before 1402, has the Serbian prince die in a confrontation with Ayna Bey, an Anatolian cavalry commander of the Ottoman army's left wing.[40] According to Turkish historians, however, Lazar was captured and then executed on the orders of Sultan Murad's son and successor Bayezid. While early Serbian sources give a similar reading, there arose an Orthodox Christian cult of religious texts proclaiming Lazar a martyr. While this 'liturgical celebration of Lazar's death' can be traced to such early church accounts, Malcolm emphasises that 'the whole idea of a national-religious celebration of this day is, in fact, a nineteenth-century invention' (78). As for the death of the Ottoman Sultan Murad, while the Catalan account identifies a Hungarian knight as the killer, literary folk traditions in Serbian claim that Murad had already been assassinated before the battle by Miloš Kobilić (or Óbilić), a warrior fighting in the ranks of Lazar, whereas domestic Ottoman chronicles only mention a solitary Christian soldier as the sultan's murderer. In his own literary treatment of this subject matter, Ismail Kadare has latched on to these historical obscurities, using them to call the official Ottoman accounts into question. Already in *The Siege*, one of the story's main protagonists, the Ottoman army's quartermaster general, interrogates the campaign chronicler Mevla Çelebi about the mystifications surrounding Sultan Murad's death. Although *The Siege* is loosely modelled on the 1450 sacking of Krujë in Central Albania, and therefore takes place some seventy years after the Battle of the Blackbird Field, rumours concerning the dubious circumstances under which the sultan met his end continued to persist over the following decades. In response to the quartermaster general's questioning, Mevla Çelebi recounts what he has learned from the Ottoman chronicles: that a lone Balkan soldier reportedly stabbed the sultan to death. Pressed further, the chronicler admits that the Sultan's eldest son Jakup was also killed the moment he arrived at the tent of the murdered monarch, allegedly on the order of the council of viziers, so as to avoid a power struggle for the throne, and that the younger son, Bayezid, was proclaimed sultan. The quartermaster then reveals that 'the murder of the Sultan himself ... wasn't perpetrated by a Balkan assassin at all' (152). This storyline is picked up again almost a hundred pages further on in the novel, where the quartermaster initiates Mevla Çelebi into what really transpired in the Ottoman camp at the time. After learning that the killing of Sultan Murad was an inside job, the chronicler contemplates casting these conflicting accounts of the course of events into a single tale. This passage deserves to be quoted at length as an illustration of how different version of a single event can come into circulation:

> First canto: Sultan Murad Han on his white horse, when the battle is done, [...] a ragged Balkan with running sores rises up from the ground [...] an even barer blade [...] plunges it straight into the Sultan's heart. That's the story you read in all the chronicles. [...]
>
> First counter-canto: a murder really did take place, a strange one indeed. The man on the horse wasn't Murad Han but his body double. And the man who knifed him wasn't a Balkan but a dervish who had been specially trained for the job [...]
>
> Second canto: the Sultan's tent. [...] The Sultan laughs but the viziers frown [...] the Grand Vizier declares, 'When the shadow falls, its owner must fall too.' At which point they set upon him and stab him to death.
>
> Second counter canto: They wanted us to believe that the Sultan had perished at the hand of a Christian. [...]
>
> Third canto: at the other end of the camp, a message reaches the heir to the throne, Jakup Çelebi [...] Jakup nonetheless feels a sinister foreboding.
>
> Third counter-canto: when they set off for Kosovo they had already laid plans to kill the monarch, whatever the outcome of the battle. The aim was to put on the throne not the elder son, in proper order of succession, but the younger son, Bayezit [*sic*], for it was he who had the viziers' preference. [...]
>
> Canto the last: Prince Jakup enters his father's tent [...] 'But that's my father [...] They told me only his shadow had been slain!' [...] Whereupon they slay Jakup as they had slain the father.
>
> Counter-canto the last: The younger brother, Prince Bayezit, [...] had actually known all about it for some time [...] the new monarch covers his tear-streaked face with his hands, but nobody will ever know what the tears were really made of and why they were shed. (241–3)

This was written in 1968 or 1969. More than twenty-seven years later, Kadare returned to the battle and its aftermath in his *Three Elegies for Kosovo*. After rehearsing some of the details already mentioned in *The Siege*, Kadare pursues the question of why the legitimate heir Yakub was killed together with his father. The argument put forward is that his younger brother Bayezid was on the side of a group of conspirators favouring the empire's westward expansion in Europe, whereas Sultan Murad and Prince Jakup wanted to focus on Asia. These courtiers and military commanders were disappointed that the Sultan had not been convinced of the merits of the long-term strategy put forward by his *kapudan pasha* (admiral of the fleet):

> Europe is like a bad-tempered mule, Grand Sovereign, and these three peninsulas dangling down there are like three little bells. Once we have silenced the first, the Balkan lands, we shall attack the second, Italy, land of the Cross and the Infidel. And then we shall strike the third bell, the land of the Spaniards, where Islam once reigned but was driven out. (15)

Viewed from the Albanian standpoint, the first elegy concludes that 'the assassination of the Sultan and the heir apparent has been to our disadvantage, because it has opened the way for Ottoman aggression against us' (31). It not only recounts the political machinations behind Murad and Jakup's murder, but also situates the battle itself in the wider political context of the time. Earlier in the chapter, Kadare had used the trope of tavern gossip to set the scene for speculations about the Ottoman ruler's motivations for moving the capital from Bursa to Adrianople, whether it was his intention 'to shift his empire to Europe' (6), or just 'to keep an eye on the quarrels of the peninsula's princes' (7). A further thickening of the plot is suggested by the story of the collusion of another son of Murad, Cuntuz, with Andronicus, the son of the Byzantine Emperor John V, to turn against their own fathers and seize power for themselves. Upon discovery of this plot, the monarchs 'had their sons punished in Byzantine fashion by blinding' (8).[41]

Again, in the fashion of the nineteenth-century realist novel tradition, the first elegy also introduces the historical *dramatis personae* on the European side: Kings Tvrko (or Tvrtko) of Bosnia and Mircea of Romania were expected to fight with Serbia's Prince Lazar, whereas another Serb, Marko Krajlević, was siding with the Ottomans. As a result of such internal divisions, 'the discussions about the quarrels of the native princes turned spontaneously to their secret alliances, in particular to their bondage to the Turk' (7). Expanding the scope to the wider Adriatic, the first elegy continues:

> It was said that the Albanian princes had allied themselves with Lazar of the Serbs and Tvrko of the Bosnians. Emperor John V was wavering, and there was still no word from Prince Constantine [of Bulgaria]. Nor from Mircea of Rumania [*sic*]. As for the other Serb, Marko Krajlević, all the omens showed that he was preparing for a new betrayal. (13)

Thus Kadare's first elegy confirms the ambiguities governing early interactions between the Ottomans and Balkan potentates also noted by Malcolm. It shows the fluidity of the regional state of affairs in the late fourteenth century, and that therefore any projection of a clear-cut dichotomy between Christendom on the one hand and an Islamic realm on the other does not reflect the complex realities appertaining at the time.

The political fallout from these shifting loyalties and rivalries is the subject matter of the second elegy, where Kadare turns to those Albanian and Serbian literary traditions of epic ballads which Malcolm also identifies as the source material for the mythmaking around the Battle of Kosovo. As composing bards and minstrels join the stream of refugees leaving the Balkans for the safe zones of central Europe, their new audiences are surprised by the persistent internal divisions among 'the Serbs with their *guslas*, the Walachians [*sic*] and Bosnians with their flutes, and the players of the one-string *lahuta* from the Cursed Peaks' (35).[42] Invited to sing at the court of an unidentified European lord, his guests become annoyed with the bards, whose songs are directed more against each other than against the common enemy that had overrun their lands. The only one speaking in their defence is an elderly noblewoman. When the other courtiers dismiss the hatred radiating from these Balkan battle songs as comparing poorly with earlier performances of the *Chanson de Roland* or the *Siegfried Saga* by their French and German counterparts, 'the Great Lady' – from which the second elegy takes its title – chastises the critics: 'These tales bring to mind the Greek tragedies [...] perhaps the greatest wealth of mankind' (70–1). However, when she asks them to recompose their wondrous tales of cruelty and sorrow, the Balkan bards insist that they were 'minstrels of war' and that they were not able to 'break out of the mould' (73).[43] Disappointed, the ageing noblewoman deplores how the legacy of ancient Greece has been lost as a result of 'the negligence of erudite men, the monastic librarians, the scribes and abbots' (71). The longevity of these native song traditions, as well as the persistent preoccupation with the Battle of Kosovo, are borne out further in *The Palace of Dreams*, which is set in the 1870s. It contains a scene in which descendants from the originally Albanian Köprülü dynasty invite both Bosnian and Albanian rhapsodists to sing the praise of their hosts and perform the 'Ballad of the Bridge of the Three Arches'. In another episode, the novel's main character, Mark-Alem, uses his position in the state archives to access the secret files on the Battle of Kosovo: 'Although the language was ancient, and many of the words were incomprehensible' (131), as he reads about warfare on the battlefield, as well as the subsequent assassination of the Sultan and the crown prince, 'his imagination was filled with a vision of the plain of Kosovo in northern Albania' (135).

Kadare's third elegy too is dedicated to the murdered sultan. The first elegy having closed with a kind of postscript about the burial of Murad's intestines and blood on the battlefield, the final episode is a surreal lament by Murad's soul as he contemplates the centuries that have gone by since the battle: the temporary fall of the Ottoman dynasty when the central Asian warlord Tamerlane defeats and captures the treacherous

Bayezid; new warfare on the Blackbird Plains, but now between Catholic Albanians and Orthodox Serbs. Although the Balkans remains divided, after 170 years the following becomes clear:

> The Christian Cross turned out to be more powerful than it seemed. Our Crescent withdrew from Vienna, the Hungarian flatlands, sombre Poland, Ukraine, Crimea, and finally the Balkan lands, which I believe we had loved the most. (86)

When a full six centuries have passed, with shreds of newspaper twirling around the dead sultan's grave bearing the names of the Serbian President Milosević and American and British foreign ministers Albright and Cook, as well as snippets of news about atrocities in the area and NATO interventions, Murad's despondent soul calls out to Allah: 'Finally grant me oblivion, My Lord! Make them remove my blood from these cold plains' (87).

The stories of *The Three-Arched Bridge* and *Three Elegies for Kosovo* are about threat perception. Both are concerned with the first territorial losses of the European dominion to a new Islamic power coming from Asia. Unfolding almost a century later, *The Siege* is set at the time when the Ottomans establish a presence in South-Eastern Europe that would last almost half a millennium, but it also already contains hints of an emerging intellectual revival elsewhere in Europe that would eventually lead to the political turning of the tables in the centuries to come, narrated in that third elegy.

Occupation: Ottoman Provincial and Military Administration in the Balkans

The occupied territories in the Balkans needed to be administered and integrated into the Ottoman state structures. In the beginning, the territories of the Ottoman Empire were divided into two large domains: the *Rumelia Eyalet*, encompassing all European territories, and the *beylerbeylik* of Anatolia (in 1593 also renamed *eyalet*), covering the Asia part of the realm. The chief authority in each of these eyalets was called *beylerbey*, governor-general. Emphasising the martial orientation of the Ottomans, each domain also fell within the jurisdiction of a so-called *kadiasker* or 'military judge', who was answerable to the Grand Vizier in Istanbul, and later to the highest religious office-holder, known as the *Şeihülislam* (from the Arabic *Shaykh al-Islam*).[44] With the Empire's exponential growth in the fifteenth and sixteenth centuries, the number of governorates was also expanded. These provinces were divided into *sancaks* (also spelled *sanjak*) or districts, led by a *sancakbey* or *mutasarrif*. Thus, in 1580, the *sancaks* of Bosnia and Hercegovina, together with parts of Slavonia, Croatia, Dalmatia and Serbia, were integrated into an *eyalet* of their own.[45] The Albanian possessions, in Ottoman Turkish collectively referred to as *Arnavutluk*, were organised into several *sancaks* within the overarching Rumelia Eyalet.[46] Below the district level came the rural fiefdoms known as *timar* (led by a *timariot*), sometimes brought together into an overarching *zeamet* under a *za'im*. Over time, this *timar* system morphed into hereditary land ownership. In the novels of Andrić and Selimović, these landed gentry of the Ottoman Balkans are referred to by their Ottoman-Turkish titles bey or beg. The earlier-mentioned *kasaba*, or towns, fell under the jurisdiction of a judge or kadi, forming a *kadilik*.[47] These urban centres served not only as imperial hubs for administrative and military control, but also for the dissemination of Islamic culture. Larger towns were subdivided into *mahalle* – neighbourhoods or quarters grouped around a mosque, church, or synagogue. Under the Ottomans' so-called *millet* system, these different religious communities were largely self-governing in terms of their internal affairs.[48]

Ottoman successes in expanding their territories into South-Eastern Europe and elsewhere must be attributed to their military prowess and the particular organisation of their army. With the passing of time, the erstwhile nomadic Ottomans transformed their fast-moving cavalry geared towards lightning attacks into a sophisticated military machine consisting of a number of specialised units. In line with the tradition of literary realism, Kadare's first Ottoman novel, *The Siege*, provides a great many details about the composition of the forces involved in beleaguering the Albanian castle and of their operational functions. Adding to the novel's realism are descriptions of the more mundane aspects of military campaigning and an army in the field that are seldom mentioned in historical accounts. On his rounds through the camp, Kadare lets his designated campaign chronicler take note of the hustle and bustle of an army camp, the squalor, the fatigued soldiers, the burying of fallen soldiers, and the care for those wounded in battle. There is even a description of what nowadays would be referred to as PTSD:

> During his long saunter through the camp Mevla Çelebi had heard about a special unit in the army, consisting of priestly men who were part healers and part sorcerers, and whose task it was to calm soldiers afflicted with mental disturbances after battle. In the old days they were killed, like any man who could not hold back his tears, but in the course of the last year the rules had been made less harsh. (100)

Kadare's – but also Andrić's – descriptions of Ottoman warfare also include some gruesome practices that have persisted through the ages. *The Siege* mentions collectors of body parts searching the battle fields 'for teeth, fingers, locks of hair, ears, nails and eyelashes' (55), while *Bosnian Chronicle* contains an almost identical episode, in which the consuls are shown the spoils of war collected by an Ottoman army during the First Serbian Uprising (1804–14): 'Onto the mat poured a huge quantity of severed human ears and noses, an indescribable mass of pathetic human flesh', leading the shocked French consul to conclude that 'this is what these people were like. This was their life. This was how the best of them behaved' (226). There is something disingenuous about this last passage, because if history has taught anything, it is that such atrocities have been perpetrated worldwide and that, unfortunately, they continue today.

In *The Siege*, Kadare has also highlighted the role of technological innovations in the military successes of the Ottomans, such as the use of gunpowder and the casting of cannon, as well as other military stratagems (tunnelling, biological warfare by spreading disease). One of the novel's central themes is the opposition to the ideas of military innovators – often of non-Turkic descent – on the part of the traditional Turkish military commanders and religious establishment (the army's mufti, his astrologers and spell-casters, as well as the warrior dervishes). Within the Ottoman military the main division was between irregular and regular troops.[49] The elite forces were formed by the *sipahi*, a heavy cavalry drafted from feudal lords with landholdings (called *timar*) in the Ottoman territories, and a special infantry corps known as the janissaries. The latter occupied a special place in the empire's armed forces. They were founded in 1365 by Murad I – the sultan who was later killed at Kosovo. The word 'janissary' derives from *yeŋi çeri*, meaning 'new soldier'. This is a kind of euphemism for the way in which these men had been recruited, namely through a special tax imposed on the populations in the conquered territories. It was known as the *devşirme*, which can be translated as boy levy or boy tribute.

The Boy Levy (*devşirme*) as Human Resources Pool and Conversion Tool

In *The Bridge on the Drina* and *The Three-Arched Bridge*, Ivo Andrić and Ismail Kadare connect the construction of the bridge with this institution of the *devşirme*. Its mechanics effectively consisted of the abduction by Ottoman tax collectors, specifically designated for this task, of boys from the age of ten upwards – although their ages could actually range from eight to twenty.[50] Thought to have been introduced first in the Balkans in 1380s, the system was predominantly applicable to non-Muslims, hence the institution can be considered as both a human resources pool for staffing the Ottoman state apparatus and as an instrument for converting these soldiers and bureaucrats to Islam. These child recruits were not only trained for the military (as so-called janissary novices or *acemi oğlans*); the most talented boys were groomed for positions in the state bureaucracy, which could even include the highest offices in the land. In the case of Albania, Noel Malcolm has noted that no fewer than forty-two grand viziers originated from there.[51] The writings of both Andrić and Kadare feature such products of what, in itself, remains an inhumane practice even by the standards of the time. And yet, while certainly Andrić has vividly described the harrowing scene of children being taken away from their families, and has delved into the psychological effects on the boys involved, it is also true that poorer people regarded the *devşirme* as a chance for a better life or an opportunity for upward social mobility. Gábor Ágoston also notes that, as an exception, 'the Muslims of Bosnia were subject to the *devşirme* because they requested and were granted this favor during their initial mass conversion to Islam after the conquest of the region in 1463'.[52]

Whereas in the case of Kadare's novels the link with the boy levy is somewhat tenuous, Andrić is on sounder historical ground in relating the building of bridges over the Drina and the Žepa to an instruction by one of the most successful exponents of the *devşirme*: Sokollu Mehmed Pasha (c. 1505–79), the then Grand Vizier of the Ottoman Empire. His name is a Turkish corruption of the Serbian Sokolović, a village in the Višegrad district, where he was born as Bayo son of Dimitriye. In the novel, the boy is taken away at the age of ten, but the French historian and Ottomanist Gilles Veinstein places it at the relatively advanced age of sixteen or even eighteen, simultaneously suggesting further that, as a scion of a Serbian family of minor rural nobility educated at the Mileševa monastery in south-west Serbia, the late recruit was from the outset earmarked for special assignments. Taken first to the sultan's palace at Edirne (not straight to Istanbul as the novel seems to suggest), Bayo Sokolović converted to Islam and took the name Mehmed.[53] After a brief stint in the Janissary Corps, in 1535, Mehmed was transferred for duties at the Topkapi Palace (also known by its *pars pro toto*, 'The Sublime Porte'). Serving in ever closer proximity to Sultan Suleyman the Magnificent (r. 1520–66), by the early 1540s Mehmed had already risen to the rank of imperial chamberlain, before being appointed *kapudan pasha* following the death of the legendary admiral Hayreddin Barbarossa in 1546. Having thus reached the apex of the military apparatus, in 1549 Mehmed Pasha was promoted to *beylerbey* of Rumelia. It is said that in that capacity he revisited his birthplace for the first time since being pressed into Ottoman service, and that he began using his newly acquired power to manoeuvre relatives into important positions. Thus he arranged for his father to be appointed administrator of a religious endowment (*vakuf*, *waqf*) in Bosnia, after the latter's conversion to Islam and adoption of the name Jamal al-Din Sinan Beg. He also lobbied for his brother Makarije – who remained Christian – to be appointed head of the reinstated Serbian Orthodox Patriarchate of Peć. Noel Malcolm has challenged the reduction of such actions to mere instances of nepotism:

> We need not suppose that Mehmed Sokolović's primary motive was either nepotism or secret Christian sentiment: there were good political reasons for this move. It was clearly in the interests of the Ottoman state to enjoy better relations with its Orthodox subjects, now that the main enemy powers ranged against the Empire in the West were all Roman Catholic.[54]

In 1554, Mehmed Pasha was recalled to accompany the Sultan on his campaign against his arch-rivals in the East: the Safavid dynasty of Persia. When the war ended, he was appointed to the Imperial Council (*Diwan*) as third and second vizier before becoming Suleyman the Magnificent's last Grand Vizier in 1565, a position he would also continue to hold under the next two sultans until his own death in 1579.[55] Having married one of the sultan's granddaughters, he had now also become a member of the imperial family. Sokollu Mehmed Pasha was also present when Suleyman died unexpectedly during another military campaign against the Habsburgs. In a failed attempt to avoid a mutiny in the military ranks, the Pasha had all witnesses to the Sultan's demise executed. Accompanying Suleyman's corpse back to Istanbul, he managed to quell opposition against the appointment of his father-in-law as the new Sultan Selim II by bribing both the janissaries and the Sipahi cavalry. As Grand Vizier, Sokollu Pasha performed one of his most extraordinary feats: organising a naval expedition across the Indian Ocean to Aceh, a Muslim sultanate located on the northernmost tip of the island of Sumatra in present-day Indonesia. Another one of his 'Pan-Islamic projects' concerned efforts to garnish support for the rebellious Moriscos of Granada against the Spanish throne.[56] However, it was also during his term in office that the Ottoman navy suffered a memorable defeat at Lepanto in 1571, causing a turnaround in the Mediterranean's balance of power and heralding the empire's gradual decline.

In *The Bridge on the Drina*, Andrić situates the construction works between 1566 and 1571, the crucial transition period between the heyday of Ottoman rule under Suleyman the Magnificent and its downturn in the wake of the Battle of Lepanto. He also mentions how the Grand Vizier, who served no fewer than three consecutive Ottoman sultans, ended up being stabbed to death by a 'half-demented dervish' (21). Although judgmental and lacking in nuance, Andrić's phrasing indicates he was conversant with scholarly findings from the 1930s and 1950s that challenged earlier sources from the seventeenth century blaming a disaffected Bosnian *timariot* (landholder) for the murder. Veinstein refers to the research work of Bosnian historians Safvet-Beg Başagić and Muhamed Tajib Okić, which points at disgruntled followers of Shaykh Hamza Bali, the Bosnian-born leader of an offshoot of the Melami-Bayrami Sufi order, who had been executed in Istanbul in 1573.[57]

The importance of Andrić's biographical sketch of Mehmed Sokolović in *The Bridge on the Drina* lies not so much in its historical accuracy as in its illustration of the ambiguity of the institution of the *devşirme*.[58] Andrić interprets Mehmed Sokolović's decision to build a bridge at Višegrad as an attempt to alleviate the sense of homesickness that even continued to plague the ageing Grand Vizier when he was at the height of his power: 'that physical discomfort that the boy had felt on that November day [in 1516] and which never completely left him, though he changed his way of life, his faith, his name and his country' (20). Accordingly, through Sokolović having the ferry across the Drina replaced by a firm, physical link between his Bosnian homeland and the Ottoman possessions to its east, and adding the construction of a *han* or carsavanserai to the project as well, 'there disappeared also the strange pain which the Vezir in his childhood had brought from Bosnia' (75).[59] Equally telling is the observation added to Andrić's recounting of the circumstances of Sokollu Mehmed Pasha's assassination in 1579, where he writes that 'he looked more like an ageing and battered peasant from Sokolovići than the dignitary who until [a] short time before had administered the Turkish Empire' (76). Aside from shifting the attention from the political significance to the humanity of such towering figures from the Ottoman past, it also signals the precarious nature of such high office. In a later chapter, he lets one of his characters, the Višegrad schoolmaster Hussein Effendi, draw a parallel between the murder of Sokollu Mehmed Pasha and the assassination of the Austrian Empress Elizabeth (Sisi) in 1898 by an anarchist:

> Despite all his power and wisdom he was unable to escape his appointed hour. Those whom the Grand Vizier hindered in their plans, and they were a great and powerful party, found a way to arm and suborn a mad dervish to kill him. (244–5)

In *Bosnian Chronicle*, Andrić would return to the uncertainties attached to Ottoman officialdom where he describes how two disgraced grand viziers, already demoted to the governorship of Bosnia, continue to be exposed to the whims of the Sublime Porte as they eventually lost even that degraded office as well.[60]

In contrast to the direct connection of the bridges across the Drina and Žepa which Ottoman grand viziers establish in both Andrić's novel and his short story, Ismail Kadare's linking of the three-arched bridge to the mighty grand vizier dynasty of Albanian origin known as the Köprülü (alternatively spelled Quprili or Qyprili by Kadare) is based on an imaginary projection back in time, because the building of the bridge at the Wicked Waters pre-dates the actual Ottoman occupation of Albania, and with that also the introduction of the *devşirme*. In several of his novels, Kadare lets his literary characters connect the Köprülü family name with the Albanian and Turkish words for bridge, *ura* and *köprü* respectively. I have called this connection tenuous, because the real link of the Köprülü family with a bridge concerns an entirely different location, namely the town of Vezirköprü in the Black Sea region of northern Anatolia. What is not disputed, however, is that the founder of the family, the later Köprülü Mehmed Pasha (1578–1661), was indeed born in Rudnik, near the town of Berat in south-central Albania, from where he was taken to Istanbul for service at the Ottoman court.[61] In the first pages of *The Palace of Dreams* (1981), the main character, Mark-Alem, reads the following passage in a chronicle kept in the family library:

> Our patronymic is a translation of the Albanian word Ura [*qypriya* or *kurpija*]; it refers to a bridge with three arches in central Albania, constructed in the days when the Albanians were still Christians and built with a man walled up in its foundations. After the bridge, which he helped to build, was finished, one of our ancestors, whose first name was Gjon, followed an old custom and adopted the name Ura, together with the stigma of murder attached to it. (7)

The interrelations between the bridge, the Köprülü viziers and their nineteenth-century descendants recur with further cross-references in the novella *The Blinding Order*:

> The house she was going to join was related – distantly, it is true, but related nonetheless – to the famous Köprülü clan. To the degree that its name, Ura, was none other than the former and original patronymic of the Quprilis – translated, for reasons of state, from Albanian into the Ottoman Köprülü. (135)

A few lines further down, Mark-Alem makes a reappearance too, now as a ten- or twelve-year-old nephew sitting with a grand uncle named Aleks Ura who, 'eager to explain the origin of the family's name to the boy, had drawn a sketch of a three-arched bridge for him – a bridge located somewhere in central Albania where some kind of sacrifice had occurred in the dim distant past' (135). Pre-dating these two direct references to the Köprülü bridge connection is an episode in *The Traitor's Niche*, featuring one Lala Shahini, an early nineteenth-century Ottoman official charged with obliterating any traces of Albanian culture and national memory as part of a cultural homogenisation campaign that fits with the late Ottoman Empire's Pan-Islamic political agenda:

> Whenever Lala Shahini remembered the Qyprili family, he would smile and shake his head in admiration. The sultan wears the crown, but the Qyprilis steer the helm of state, everybody said of them, the only family in the world to inherit the post of grand vizier like a dynasty. (146)

This passage affirms that among the dozens of Albanians who have held the office of grand vizier of the Ottoman Empire throughout the ages, the Köprülü clan was exceptional in retaining control of the office between 1656 and 1711, providing no fewer than seven grand viziers – either through the bloodline or through in-laws – and remaining part of the Ottoman aristocracy until the empire's very end.[62]

By showcasing such success stories as those of Sokollu Mehmed Pasha and the Köprülü family, along with descriptions of their psychological traumas as victims of an inhumane institution, literary depictions by novelists like Ivo Andrić and Ismail Kadare offer more multi-layered and richly textured accounts of the Ottoman past than those rendered by academic historians. The emerging image is further completed with other ambiguities inherent in the cultural hybridity shaped by different religious influences that also forms part of this Balkan mosaic.

From Adhesion to Conversion: The Islamisation Process in the Ottoman Balkans

As was also the case with the early Arab conquests of the seventh century, the Ottoman conquerors had no explicit intention of converting subjugated peoples to Islam; their campaigns were about territorial expansion in order to get access to resources for their military apparatus: human, monetary, and in kind. Equally important is to view the eventual Islamisation of South-Eastern Europe from a *longue durée* perspective and to recognise the fluidity of its dynamics.[63] Echoing an earlier-mentioned observation by Noel Malcolm, fellow historians Fischer and Schmitt note that, already before the arrival of the Ottomans, 'to change religious allegiance as a function of political loyalty was not uncommon, nor was it unusual for Albanian noblemen to switch between confessions several times' (36). That remained true also during the Ottoman period, when again 'conversion was less a religious act than a demonstration of political allegiance and loyalty to the ruling dynasty' (62). In this regard, it may be more accurate to adopt Arthur Nock's terminology and speak of religious adhesion rather than conversion.[64] Religious syncretism – the admixture of practices from pagan origin with Christian and later also Islamic rituals and beliefs – remained widespread among the rural populations in the Ottoman Balkans. With regard to the Albanian territories, Clayer, Fischer and Schmitt, and Malcolm all point at the presence of crypto-Christians (more specifically, crypto-Catholics).[65] Perpetuated over generations and lasting until the twentieth century, this was not, Malcolm notes, an urban but rather a rural phenomenon confined to 'cohesive villages' (133) in central Albania and in the mountain range between Macedonia and Kosovo.[66]

In the same context, I have also already briefly signalled the fact that – in comparison to other parts of South-Eastern Europe – Bosnia, Albania and Kosovo are exceptional in terms of their comparatively high percentage of conversions to Islam among their indigenous populations. Aside from a later influx of Muslims from other Balkan areas that were gradually lost to the Ottoman empire, in the case of Bosnia, the rivalling presence of Roman Catholicism and Eastern Orthodoxy may have pressed adherents of the local Bosnian church into embracing Islam. In his doctoral dissertation, Ivo Andrić still subscribed to a theory that has since been discredited: that the Bosnian church was an offshoot of the Bogomils, a heretical movement originating in tenth-century Bulgaria subscribing to a Manichaean theology of dualism.[67] In his dissertation, Andrić refers to the Bogomils as 'Patarins' (3–13). The use of this particular term suggests the use of source material from Ragusa and from Italy proper, because the term 'Patarin' was not used in Bosnia itself. Moreover, there is actually no indication of either Bosnian or other Catholic sources identifying the Bosnian church as Bogomil. The Bosnian Church identified itself simply as 'Christian', with a monastic tradition grounded in the rules of St Basil (330–79) and possibly also influenced by the ninth-century missionaries Cyril and Methodius. While none of this precludes the presence of Bogomil or other dualist influences per se in the region, there is firm evidence dating back to the twelfth century of the Bosnian Church acknowledging the supremacy of the Pope in Rome. Moreover, by the time of the arrival of the Ottomans, Franciscan monks (Andrić's prime historical source) were in full competition with the Eastern Orthodox Church over ecclesiastical control in Bosnia.[68]

This complex picture seems to support Noel Malcolm's estimation that 'many factors were involved in the spread of Islam in Bosnia, and that if the special attitude of the Bosnian Church was a factor at all, it was not one of the most important' (29). Malcolm goes on to qualify the connection between the Bosnian church and the Islamisation process in early Ottoman times as 'indirect and rather negative', triggered by the church's own 'weak and fractured ecclesiastical history' (57), and a parallel Catholic–Orthodox rivalry.[69] Equally untenable – although still widely believed, despite proof to the contrary – is another theory claiming an immediate mass conversion to Islam on the part of the Christian land-owning elite after the Turkish conquest of Bosnia. Supposedly motivated by a desire on their part to keep possession of their estates, such economic motivations too are insufficiently compelling, because 'it is not true one had to be a Muslim in order to become rich in the Ottoman Empire' (65). All in all, there is every reason to believe the suggestion that 'the process by which Bosnia gained a majority population of Muslims thus took the best part of 150 years' (54).

In Albania too, the Islamisation of the local Albanian-speaking populace was a long-term process. Until his death in 1385, Balsha II had been one of very few remaining Albanian noblemen opposing the Ottomans, while four years later, his brother George II Stracimirović (Gjergj II Balsha) sided with the Ottomans against Bosnian King Tvrtko in the Battle of Kosovo.[70] When, in the course of the fifteenth century, Ottoman incursions became increasingly intense, noble families, such as the Muzakas, Dukagjin and the Kastriotis, turned to Islam. Illustrative in this regard is the journey of Albania's national hero Skanderbeg. A son of the devoutly Orthodox Ivan Kastrioti and a Serbian noblewoman of the Branković clan, young Gjergj or George had been surrendered as a hostage to placate what Fischer and Schmitt call 'the marcher lords, Albanian noblemen who had converted to Islam' (52), and who served as commanders guarding the Ottoman Empire's frontiers. In Istanbul, he converted to Islam and was eventually appointed governor of the fortress of Krüje in Central Albania, which stood as a model for the castle in Ismail Kadare's *The Siege*:

> He displayed extraordinary talents as a warrior and as a military leader participating in numerous Ottoman campaigns in Serbia, Wallachia and Transylvania. His exploits earned him the surname Iskenderbey (or Skanderbeg), lord Alexander, a reference to Alexander the Great that was intended as a symbol of military prowess. (50)

It was only after the assassination of his father that George Kastrioti abjured his allegiance to the Ottomans and renounced his affiliation with Islam. His former stronghold of Krüje went back and forth between Ottomans and the Albanian rebels until his death in 1468. A decade later, Venetian-controlled Shkodër had fallen to the Ottomans as well, and its population was given the choice to leave for Venice or convert to Islam. Fischer and Schmitt agree with Malcolm that with regard to the Islamisation of the Balkans, instead of a sudden embrace of Islam en masse, adhesion developed gradually and in pace with the expansion of Ottoman control:

> The conquest was a protracted process that began in the 1380s, lasted for more than 120 years and came to an end only ca. 1500. It was also not a simple case of Asian invaders and regional resistance. Actors and agencies were much more complex and usually interwoven. (44)

As elsewhere in the Balkans, among Albanians too, Islamisation was very much a urban phenomenon, with Turkish influence being more pronounced in the towns (*kasaba*) of Kosovo and Macedonia, such as Prizren, Skopje and Bitola (then known as Monastir), than on the plains west of the Albanian highlands. Losing the towns, 'Catholic culture had lost its urban base and retreated into the mountains' (56). From the middle of the seventeenth century, however, it appears the Ottomans began to pursue a more active Islamisation policy in Albania than elsewhere. Most likely, this was motivated by the Ottoman desire to garner support from local warlords as well as in an effort to quell local resistance to their protracted war with Venice between 1645 and 1675:

> Albanians, who had offered the Ottomans determined resistance, became the most Islamized people in the Balkans. Indeed, particularly from the mid-seventeenth century on, a majority of Albanians converted to Sunni Islam, and Albanians can be considered, along with Muslim Bosnians, the pillar of Ottoman rule in the imperial peripheries on the Adriatic and in central Europe. Albanian and Bosnian Muslims kept the Christian majority population in the Ottoman Balkans in check and filled the ranks of those Ottoman armies that for centuries attempted to conquer east central Europe. (57)

Compared to their modest share in the overall demographics of the Ottoman Empire, an extraordinary large number of Albanian Muslims ended up occupying leading positions in the Ottoman military and administration. In the nineteenth century, Albanian warlords established themselves as renegade regional potentates, like Ali Pasha Tepelena (1740–1822) of Ioannina, or succeeded in establishing a lineage of viceroys and kings that were independent in all but name, as was the case in Egypt with Mehmet Ali (1769–1849), whose descendants remained on the throne until 1952.

Cultural Hybridity: Traces of Religious Syncretism and Crypto-Christianity

Ismail Kadare and Ivo Andrić have also used their novels *The Three-Arched Bridge* and *The Bridge on the Drina* to write about cultural hybridity of the eventual Ottomanisation and Islamisation of Albania and Bosnia, including manifestations of religious syncretism and the phenomenon of crypto-Christianity. Both authors inserted aspects from religious practices and traditions of non-Christian and non-Islamic origin, such as pre-existing beliefs in naiads or water nymphs (Kadare) and *vilas* or fairies (Andrić), as well as legends of immurement. In both instances, these transmitted stories about human sacrifice are presented in the context of their literary accounts of attempts to sabotage the building of the bridges. In the case of Kadare, this is done by ferrymen opposed to the construction of a bridge across the Wicked Waters. When the works are constantly delayed, supposedly because of 'the wrath of the naiads and water spirits' (95), the bridge builders turn to the local lord of the liege, who only offers them a piece of cryptic advice: 'If it is true, as you say, that your enemies have hit upon the idea of destroying the bridge with the help of myth, then you should devise some way of punishing the culprits in kind' (75). Taking inspiration from a legend told by wandering bards about three masons and the immurement of one of their wives, the building crew decide to find a scapegoat of their own. The end of the matter is that a destitute local man agrees to be walled in, in return for financial compensation to his family. The Monk Gjon leaves no doubt as to what he thinks of this practice: 'We were dealing with a crime pure and simple, Murrash Zenebisha had been murdered' (111). In fact, already in the opening pages of *The Three-Arched Bridge*, Kadare lets Gjon explain that the first reason for writing his chronicle is to provide a corrective for 'the truths and untruths about this bridge in the eleven languages of the peninsula' (4) that had been circulating about a human sacrifice said to have taken place during the building works. He does not regard it as a ritual 'dedicated to the naiads of the waters, but just a straightforward crime' (4). While the builders thus emerge victorious from their conflict with the ferrymen, it is clear that the chronicler holds both sides morally responsible for using an 'ancient legend in their savage contest' (114). By establishing an intertextual link between *The Three-Arched Bridge* and *The Palace of Dreams*, Kadare wants to show how the atrocity continued to haunt the chronicler's descendants centuries later, when he lets Mark-Alem contemplate his so-called 'Quprilian sadness':

> He thought of his distant ancestor called Gjon who on a winter's day several centuries before had built a bridge and at the same time edified his name. [...] And so that the bridge might endure, a man was sacrificed in its building, walled up in its foundations. [...] perhaps that was why the Quprilis had changed their name to Köprülü: to avoid being identified with the bridge. (89)

As mentioned above, Kadare's bridge over the Wicked Waters was already built before the actual Ottoman occupation of Albania, but a comparable immurement story in Ivo Andrić's *The Bridge on the Drina* shows that such practices endured well into the sixteenth century. By that time Bosnia had already been firmly integrated into the Ottoman Empire, and also its population had been brought firmly into the fold of Sunni Islam. But in Višegrad too, the building works are marred by delays as a result of sabotage by workers pressed into corvée labour on the bridge. And again, given that 'the common people easily make up fables and spread them quickly, wherein reality is strangely and inextricably mixed and interwoven with legend' (31), the culprits, bent on frustrating the construction works, try to hide their actions by having recourse to a ruse, spreading 'the rumour that it is a *vila*, a fairy, who is destroying the works at the bridge' (32). And just as in the Albanian version, 'tales blended and spread quickly': according to one ballad transmitted by a Montenegrin *gusla* player, the *vila* had intimated that 'she would not cease her work of destruction until twin children, Stoja and Ostjoja by name, should be walled into the foundation' (32). According to local adaptations of this storyline, it was the Turks who had walled the still-born children of a local madwoman into the bridge. In both novels these practices of immurement are said to have gone on since time immemorial to ensure successful completion of any important building, not just bridges, but also castles, city walls and so on. Rebecca Gould has linked the sanctification of such stories of violence to Christian notions of sacrifice and René Girard's theorising of the scapegoat, but given the context of sabotage in which these parallel legends from Albania and Bosnia are presented, I suggest reading Andrić and Kadare's accounts as prefiguring the suspicions of the local populace towards outside interferences that were perpetuated in the anti-state sentiments among both local converts to Islam and those remaining Christian and Jewish throughout the Ottoman period.[71]

The Bridge on the Drina also contains other instances of cultural hybridity reflecting divergent interpretations of local legends and monuments on the part of the Christian and Muslim inhabitants of Višegrad. Already in the novel's opening pages, Andrić relates how indentations into the chalky banks of the river are imagined to be 'the hoofprints of some horse of supernatural size' (8). While the Christians attribute these to Šarac, steed of Marko Kraljević (King of the Serbs until his death in

1395), the Muslims are convinced they belong to 'Djerzelez Alija on his winged charger' (9). Also known as Gjergj Elez Alia in Albania or Gürz Ilyas in Turkish, this legendary heroic figure is thought to have been inspired by Ali Bey Mihaloglu (1425–1507), a fifteenth-century Ottoman military commander who had served as the first *sancakbey* of Smederevo (later the *pashalik* of Belgrade) and was given a landholding (*timar*) near Višegrad. This Djerzelez Alija had already been the subject of the very first short story published by Ivo Andrić in 1920.[72] Similarly, depending on whether you are a Christian or a Muslim, a tomb located in the vicinity of the Višegrad bridge is considered to be either the final resting place of Radisav of Unište, leader of an uprising by indentured bridge builders, or of Sheik Turhanija, a martyred dervish or Sufi, who 'wanted to be buried without mark or sign, so that no one would know who was there. For, if ever again some infidel army should invade by this route, then he would arise and hold them in check' (9–10).

Ismail Kadare too gives further examples of religious syncretism. Confronted by the prospect of a Turkish invasion, the chronicler of the bridge concludes that 'Ottoman pressure involved a kind of seduction. It struck me as no accident that they had chosen the moon as their symbol. Under its light, the world could be caressed and lulled to sleep more easily' (149). References to the moon as a religious symbol are already found in the first novel of the Ottoman cycle. In the opening page of *The Siege* it is embedded in an ominous threat by the invaders, ensuring the beleaguered Albanians that 'the only seeded field you'll see will be the sky, and your only sickle the moon' (3), while a few pages further it recurs in an observation by the puzzled pasha commanding the Ottoman forces:

> It struck him as rather odd that the Christians, having seen Islam take possession of the moon, had not promptly made their own emblem the sun, but had taken instead a mere instrument of torture, the cross. (7)

In *Three Elegies for Kosovo*, Kadare returns to this symbolism yet again: 'The Turks, before they ground the world under their heel, would conquer the skies. They had put the crescent moon on their banners' (58). Although the crescent moon is now regarded as the quintessential symbol of Islam, its origins are much older. Aside from its occurrence in ancient Middle Eastern iconography, a connection with the pre-Islamic sky deities of the peoples of the Central Asian Steppes should not be discounted either, especially since it is the Ottomans who are credited with firmly embedding the symbol of the crescent moon into the Islamic tradition. *Three Elegies for Kosovo* also contains a passage where the partial interment of Sultan Murad's remains on the Blackbird Plains is connected to ancient beliefs of the peoples of South-Eastern Europe itself:

> That his blood and intestines should be buried in the Christian soil of Kosovo, had a clear significance. As is commonly known, the ancient Balkan people believed that everything linked with blood is eternal, imperishable, and guarded by faith. The Turks, who had at that point interacted with the Balkan people for over half a century had, it seems, assimilated some of this symbolism. By pouring the monarch's blood on the Plains of Kosovo they wanted to give those plains, just as they had done with their invasion, a direction, a fatality, both a curse and a blessing at the same time, in other words, a 'programme', as one would call it today. (31–2)

Nearer to modern times are the effects of the long durée and fluidity that characterised the dynamics of the Islamisation process in the Balkans on the ways in which influences of competing religious traditions continued to colour the region's cultural hybridity. Earlier in this chapter, I signalled the complex situation in Bosnia with regard to the existence of an indigenous Bosnian church alongside Roman Catholicism and an Eastern Orthodox presence that was made only more diffuse by the suggestions of Bogomil or other dualist influences. With respect to Albania, various historians highlight the phenomenon of crypto-Christianity. Fischer and Schmitt mention it in their discussion of claims of a 'specific Albanian version of European Islam' by nineteenth-century nationalist activists, which rests on the combined influence of religious indifference, and a preference for Sufism over adherence to mainstream Sunni Islam, as well as the existence of 'so-called Crypto-Christians, or people who embraced Islam because of fiscal and government pressure, behaved as Muslims in public spaces and were treated as such by government officials but continued to be Christians in the privacy of family life' (59).[73] While nationalists may have exaggerated its prevalence, crypto-Christians do indeed feature prominently in visitation reports of Catholic clergy, who also had a tendency to 'put considerable pressure on Catholic Christians to openly confess their beliefs' (92). In the case of Kosovo, Noel Malcolm reports that it 'eventually involved whole communities behaving outwardly as Muslims, while retaining a secret adherence to Catholicism' (132), adding that Albanians even coined a specific term for them: *laraman*, which translates as parti-coloured or piebald.[74]

Hints as to the persistence of this crypto-Christianity over many generations – which can be partly explained by the condoned practice of Christian women married to Muslim men of raising their daughters as Christian – are found in Kadare's *The Traitor's Niche* and *The Blinding Order*. Set in the early nineteenth century, the Ottoman courier charged with carrying severed heads to Istanbul observes that 'churches that were turned into mosques came back as soon as they could in a shadowy form' (61). Similarly, in *The Blinding Order*, situated in the 1850s, it is stated that the protagonist Xheladin's family,

> like many households of Albanian descent, had maintained over the generations the custom of including within its bosom members of different, that is to say opposite, faiths. Her father-in-law, Aleks Ura, was Christian, but one of his sons, who had gone into the navy, had been brought up a Muslim, whereas the other, her future husband, remained a Christian. Maybe the father would have done the same with daughters had he had two of them, but since Marie was the only one, he had tried, in a sense, to split her in two. As he could not raise her in two faiths at the same time (though such cases were not unheard of), he had given her two first names, each from a different religion. So for her first family and close friends, her name was Marie, for the rest of the world, including her fiancé, it was Miriam. (133–4)

In *The Palace of Dreams* too, the protagonist's frustration with his own name suggests a similar religious ambiguity:

> Mark-Alem suddenly felt an almost irresistible desire to discard 'Alem', the Asian half of his first name, and appear with a new one, one used by the people of his native land: Gjon, Gjergj, Gjorg. Mark-Gjon, Mark-Gjergj Ura, Mark-Gjorg Ura. (152)

The same point is taken up again in adapted form on the novel's penultimate page, when Mark-Alem 'remembered how on the fateful night he had longed to throw off the protective mask, the Islamic half-shield of 'Alem', and adopt one of those ancient names which attracted danger and were marked by fate' (189). Read together with invocations of the legacy of Homer, such references to other aspects of Albania's antiquity as well as the Christian substrata preceding the arrival of Islam fit with Ismail Kadare's agenda for re-embedding Albania more firmly as an integral part of Europe.

Transgressive Piety: the Sufi Factor

Turkologists and Balkan historians all emphasise the prominent role of Sufism, especially that of the Sufi or Dervish orders (*tariqa*, *turuq*), in the formation of the Ottoman Balkans, making it yet another component in the dynamic mix of its Islamisation process.[75] The writings of Andrić and Kadare, however, show only a passing interest in the topic; even in the case of Selimović's *Death and the Dervish*, Sufism is not a central theme in the novel. This stands in marked contrast to the extensive and intensive engagement with Sufism on the part of the authors discussed in the previous chapters. Where Andrić limits himself to the occasional undifferentiated reference to dervishes, accompanied even by judgmental characterisations like 'mad' (76) and 'ragged and half-demented' (245), in the cases of Kadare and Selimović there are at least also concrete identifications of Rifa'i, Mevlevi and Bayrami dervishes.

Of greater significance is the attention Kadare and Selimović pay to active dervish participation in the Ottoman conquests and their continuing involvement in later-day warfare. These form valuable contributions to a more comprehensive and, with that, nuanced understanding of the place and role of Sufis in the Islamic tradition. Most – also academic – writings about Sufism tend to focus exclusively on its spiritual dimension, which is generally taken as assurance of religious toleration or even ecumenism. That Sufism can also have a martial component is not mentioned very often. Both *The Siege* and *Death and the Dervish* contain episodes describing the involvement of militant dervishes in warfare. In several scenes, Ismail Kadare writes about the role of dervishes in preparing Ottoman troops for an assault on the Albanian castle, at one point singling out the Rifa'i, an order known for the highly-charged nature of their *dhikr* or séances, which can include controversial practices, such as piercing parts of the body with sharp objects:

> Drums were being sounded in every quarter. Dervishes whirled and fell, prayed and screamed without respite. 'We shall teach the Sacred Koran to these accursed rebels', a *sheh* [shaykh] was proclaiming. 'On their lands which are as humped as a demon's back, we shall raise minarets blessed by Allah! [...] We shall ensure that these infidels learn how to bow towards Mecca five times a day. We shall wrap their sick and troubled skulls in the balmy turban of Islam.' (54)

> The Rufais [Rifa'i] had started their dance. Soldiers jostled to get a better view of them jumping up and down to the beat of the drum. It was a sinister, monotonous dance. They would squat on their heels, then rise up with a fast-paced, obsessive swaying movement, uttering loud screams that made your blood run cold. In a trance, their faces were pale and their eyes half-closed. (55)

Describing the burial of fallen soldiers in mass graves, Kadare goes on to write how 'shirtless dervishes with bloodstained forearms grasped corpses by their hands and feet and swung them energetically over the edge' (101). In other instances, they are depicted taking part in the actual hostilities, even performing daring feats, such as capturing an enemy soldier alive so that the Ottoman army physician could examine him physically in order to determine the condition of the castle's defenders at the end of a prolonged siege:

> A dervish really did appear on the top of the wall with a body over his shoulder. With feline agility, the dervish grasped the top of a ladder and without dropping his load began to climb down. He must surely have been shouting out that he was carrying a prisoner on orders from the Pasha, because the janissaries on their way up swung to the side to let him pass. (252)

That Sufi militancy was not something confined to these early conquests alone is demonstrated in *Death and the Dervish*. In the second part of the novel, Meša Selimović shifts the scene some twenty years back in time to Ahmed Nuruddin as a 'young dervish-warrior' (243), fighting the Austrians in what must have been the 1630s. In his initial contemplations of that period in his life, the now forty-year-old shaykh dwells on the difficulties he experienced in adjusting to military life:

> I limited myself to saying the prayers that were part to military duties, such as marches and sentry watches. At that time I was struck by the strange, discouraging thought of how a man who is spiritually more developed than others is in a difficult situation, unless he is protected by his position and the fear that position instills. Such a man becomes a loner. (245)

Eventually Nuruddin adjusted to his new role, because in one of the final chapters, when things come to a head as a result of some morally very questionable actions on the part of the now mature Sufi, his mind returned to those days of fighting on the Austrian–Bosnian border:

> I was the only one who knew that this new Sheikh Nuruddin was very similar to the young dervish who had swum across the river with a bare saber in his teeth, to attack the enemies of the faith. He was very similar to that crazy dervish who had been different from today's because he had not had the cunning or wisdom. (360–1)

Such acts of what can be called 'transgressive piety' are not unique to the Balkans or to the Ottomans.[76] In the nineteenth century, Sufi militancy also played an important role in resistance to Russian expansion into the Caucasus and parts of Central Asia, and to British incursions into the Sudan. The example of Imam Shamil (1797–1871), the rebellious Avar from Dagestan who mobilised the Naqshbandi and Qadiri Sufis of the North Caucasus, continued to inspire the insurgency against Moscow in twentieth-century Chechnya, while descendants of Muhammad Ahmad ibn Abdullah (1844–85), who ignited the Mahdi uprising (1881–99), still play a prominent role in Sudanese politics.[77]

The first Sufi orders to operate in the Balkans were the Halveti and Rifaʿi. They formed part of trans-regional networks stretching across the wider Muslim world. While the latter was founded by Ahmad al-Rifaʿi (d. 1183) in southern Iraq, the former is thought to have originated in

Eastern Iran, from where it quickly spread via Azerbaijan to Anatolia.[78] Thanks to the sultan's personal patronage, the Halveti thrived, especially, during the reign of Bayezid II (r. 1481–1511). This motivated the order's leader in Anatolia, Çelebi Khalifa, to move its centre from provincial Amasya to the capital Istanbul. The integration of Sufism into the social structures of the Ottoman Empire was aided by the so-called *tekke* (elsewhere in the Muslim world known as *khanqah* or *ribat*). Sometimes mistranslated as monasteries, these were prayer houses or retreats led by a local Sufi master, called shaykh or pir. Located in towns throughout the Ottoman empire, they were open not only to local residents but also to wandering dervishes. Tekkes often maintained relations with professional guilds (*esnāf*) for financial reasons, connecting the Sufi orders to the traditional bazaar economy. Provided they remained loyal to Sunni orthodoxy, the Halveti and Rifaʿi orders, as well as other large transnational *tariqa*s arriving later in the Ottoman empire, such as the Naqshbandi and Qadiri, would also continue to flourish after the Ottomans began emphasising their own credentials as upholders of Sunni Islam.[79] However, there were also heterodox exponents of Sufism, like the earlier-mentioned Hamzevi, who became targets of repression by the central government. Although there is no explicit attention to this heightened doctrinal rectitude in Ottoman Islam to be found in the literary writings of Andrić, Kadare or Selimović, the earlier-mentioned assassination of Sokollu Mehmed Pasha by a Hamzevi dervish in revenge for the execution of their shaykh could be taken as 'circumstantial evidence' of a Sunni clampdown on what were regarded as manifestations of heresy. Another implicit indication is Selimović's use of Qur'an verses as epigraphs in each of the chapters of *Death and the Dervish*, and the frequent occurrence of references to suras from the Qur'an in sermons or religious discussions throughout the novel.

With respect to Albania and Kosovo, a special place was occupied by another controversial dervish order: the Bektashi (also spelled Bektaşi),[80] founded in central Anatolia, in the middle of the thirteenth century, by Hajji Bektash. Their veneration of Ali ibn Abi Talib, the Prophet Muhammad's cousin and son-in-law, suggests Shiʿa influences. Together with the inclusive role accorded to women, this was already sufficient reason for Sunni Muslims to situate the Bektashi dervishes on the very periphery of what they consider appropriate Islamic orthodoxy. But there is even more to it than that. Writing about the significance of the Bektashi in Kosovo, Noel Malcolm adds:

> The most heterodox order of all was the Bektashi, which became the official order of the Janissaries: no doubt it had a special appeal to soldiers who had been brought up as Christian children, given that the Bektashi adherents

> would drink wine and ignore the fast of Ramadan, and that their version of Muslim theology included a quasi-Trinitarian doctrine. (134)

While even the perception of theological affinity to Christianity would be sufficient reason for Sunni condemnation, it may also serve as an explanatory factor for the Bektashis' relative openness towards Orthodox Christians. According to Fischer and Schmitt, Bektashi influence was strongest in the southern parts of Albania, 'where major *tekkes* were founded in Tetovo in 1569 and Gjirokastër in 1780' (84). However, by the nineteenth century their connection with the janissaries began to backfire: when Sultan Mahmud II disbanded the janissary corps in 1826 as part of his reform programme (*Tanzimat*), the Bektashi were persecuted too. This chequered history may also help to explain why a remarkable number of Albanian nationalists involved in the so-called League of Prizren (located in Kosovo, not Albania proper!) came from Bektashi backgrounds.[81] Pursuing a political agenda of *Rilindja*, which translates as Albanian Awakening or Albanianism, these nationalists advocated an Albanian version of a non-Turkish – European – Islam diametrically opposed to the Sunni narrative which the Ottoman Empire had been disseminating since the sixteenth century.[82]

Conservative Dogmatists versus Open-minded Humanists

After the conquest of Egypt in 1517, the Ottoman Empire became the most significant political representative of Sunni Islam among the three so-called 'gunpowder empires' dominating the Muslim world from the sixteenth through the nineteenth centuries – the other two being the Shiʿa Safavids in Persia and the Mughals of India, who were accommodative towards both Sunni and Shiʿa Islam. With the capture of Cairo, Sultan Selim I had not just ousted the ruling Mamluk dynasty; this also put an end to the puppet Caliphate of descendants of the Abbasid dynasty who had continued as nominal heads of Sunni Islam after their relocation to Cairo following the fall of Baghdad to the Mongols in 1258.[83] With Egypt came also the overlordship of the Hijaz region in Western Arabia, turning the Ottoman sultans into the Custodians of the Two Holy Mosques of Mecca and Medina, a sobriquet traditionally accorded to the caliphs.[84] From the sixteenth century onwards, emphasising this Sunni identity formed an integral element in the Ottomans' rivalry with the Shiʿa Safavid dynasty to the east. As part of this transformation, the Sunni *ʿulamāʾ*, the religious scholars who traditionally regard themselves as the heirs to the prophet in terms of Islamic doctrine and learning, began to form the core of the empire's religious officialdom led by a *Şeihülislam*.

It is important to realise that also this 'Sunnitization' did not completely end the religious ambiguity of the Ottoman Empire. Further evidence of the persistent hybridity of its system of governance can be found in Ottoman legal practice, whereby Islamic law (usually, but not entirely accurately, referred to in Ottoman Turkish as *şeriat*) functioned alongside a continuing accommodation of customary – often orally transmitted – law (*őrf*) and a system of secular legislation known as *kanun*, consisting of the issuing of imperial decree (*firman*).[85] In *The Bridge on the Drina*, Ivo Andrić illustrates how, also in modern times, such injunctions from worldly authorities continued to receive divinely-guided underpinnings:

> In those twenty-five years in the middle of the nineteenth century the plague raged twice at Sarajevo and the cholera once. When this happened the town kept regulations which, according to tradition, had been given by Mohammed himself: 'While the Pestilence rages in some place do not go there, for you may become infected, and if you are already in the place where it rages then do not depart from that place lest you infect others.' But since men do not observe the most salutary of regulations, even when they derive from the Apostle of God himself, if not forced to do so by 'the power of the authorities', then authorities on the occasion of every 'plague' limited or stopped completely all travel and postal communications. (112–13)

The financial instrument holding the whole edifice of the Ottoman religious establishment together was a kind of charitable endowment, known as *waqf* (*vakif* in Turkish and Albanian; *vakuf* in Serbian), which stands outside the state administration. Both Andrić and Selimović's novels repeatedly mention such legal bequests of property and money. For example, in *The Bridge on the Drina*, the construction of the bridge and the establishment of a *han* or caranvanserai was not only important for the Ottoman empire's physical communications; it also, Andrić writes, constituted an act of piety: 'the expenses for maintaining the caravanserai came from the *vakuf*, the religious endowment, which Mehmed Pasha had founded from the rich properties seized in the newly-conquered territories of Hungary' (75). Similarly, in the opening pages of *Death and the Dervish*, the head of the Tekke explains how 'this building was formerly the harem of the ancestor of the wealthy Ali-aga Janich, who donated it to the order to serve as a meeting place for dervishes and a shelter for the poor' (6). There are also more opportunistic reasons for establishing a *vakuf*, because it also enables the ring-fencing of private wealth from taxation or outright confiscation by secular authorities, not an unusual practice in the case of an autocratic feudal regime such as that of the Ottoman Empire. In *Death and the Dervish*, Hassan, the erstwhile estranged son of Ali-aga Janich, eventually 'made an agreement with his father to turn both of their portions of the estate into a wakf, for the salvation of their souls and for their memory, for the benefit of poor people and the homeless' (255). Aside from providing money for the property's upkeep, the initiators would often appoint family members and their descendants as administrators of these endowments, effectively turning them into family trusts. Such functionaries were called *muteveli* in Turkish, a term derived from the Arabic *mutawalli* (trustee). In *The Bridge on the Drina*, the family of the first *mutevelia* continue to bear that name even long after the *vakuf* funds have been depleted. One of its descendants even becomes a lead character in the chapters dealing with the time Bosnia came under Austrian rule.

The cultural hybridity of the multi-faceted religious diversity sketched so far also forms the background for the encounters between different fictive characters that all three authors have staged in their literary writings, pitching those susceptible to superstition, religious dogmatism or stubborn traditionalism against the more open-minded inquisitiveness of their intellectual opposites, who seem more capable of exercising that faculty of critical thinking shared by all humankind, and who exhibit confidence in the ability for sound moral judgement and for acting in a spirit of toleration.

Such diverging dispositions are already prefigured in Ismail Kadare's intentionally anachronistic treatment of the Ottoman Past in *The Siege*. Throughout its narrative, the portents of the army mufti and his astrologers, the casters of curses and spells, as well as the dervishes as exponents of Ottoman conservatism and fatalism are set against the calculations and innovations presented by the technocrats: the quartermaster general, the physician, the military and civil engineers. Charged with developing an artillery to bombard the castle walls and finding ways to subvert the defensive structures in other ways, both engineers are also presented as eccentrics. A 'famous caster of cannon', Engineer Saruxha had an 'aura of mystery surrounding his work' (22), and quite a temper to boot. Even more enigmatic is the architect Giaour: 'nobody rightly knew the origins or the nationality of the man who was acquainted with every secret of the structures of fortresses' (23). He speaks broken Turkish, his name being actually an Ottoman slur meaning an infidel. He also has an unnatural gait and a strange physical appearance: 'many suspected he was really a woman, or at least half-man and half-woman – a hermaphrodite, as people say' (23). Absorbed in their technical trades, the duo execute their tasks with single-minded, almost autistic, dedication; Saruxha and Giaour are what we would nowadays call nerds. Much of what they proposed was lost on the old-fashioned army commanders, who relied on the strength and courage of their battle-hardened cavalry and infantry. Stuck in between was the army commander, Uslun Pasha. Realising 'that two opposing groups had now constituted themselves among his council' (45), he appreciated the quartermaster general and Engineer Saruxha's way of thinking, 'but for all the confidence he had in their intelligence, he was not sure of their hearts. As for the captains, it was the other way around, he trusted their courage more than their wisdom' (45). The physician Sirri Selim, meanwhile, has a more worldly attitude. Aside from his expertise in medicine and in the application of his scientific understanding (by the standards of the fifteenth century) of disease and contamination in what in today's language would be biological warfare, Sirri Selim also has knowledge of ancient Greek civilisation.[86] On one occasion, he describes to the chronicler Mevla Çelebi how the Greeks tricked the Trojans with a wooden horse in order to enter and conquer their city (215). On another, he uses his knowledge to console the campaign poet Sadedin, who has been blinded in one of the attacks:

> 'Many centuries ago, in Ancient Greece,' Sirri Selim said, 'there was a blind poet just like you.' [...] 'His name was Homer and he wrote a great epic about a garrison called Troy, which the Greeks destroyed,' Sirri Selim went on. 'Two months ago, Prince Mehmet, our future Sultan, said in a speech that God had designated the Turks as the avengers of Troy.' (193–4)

All this is anathema to the mufti and his entourage. On the one hand, Kadare has this religious office-holder rage against the soldiers' lack of dedication to the tenets of Islam – 'Our religious spirit is being weakened! Atheism is spreading' – and the mufti insists 'that reading of the Koran be made obligatory, that alcoholic beverages be banned, and that the sale of captive women and the presence of prostitutes be similarly forbidden' (273). These last points do not sit well with the professional soldiers: 'They all knew that of all possible conflicts within a war council, outright hostility between the military and the religious commanders was the one that could have the direst effect' (274). On the other hand, the mufti is also described as being under the influence of astrologers, dream interpreters, spell casters and other magicians. With this, Kadare appears to suggest that religion and superstition are not far apart, or, for a self-confessed atheist like himself, perhaps even one and the same thing.

Similar opposing dispositions and outlooks are sketched in *Death and the Dervish*, where Selimović amplifies the differences between Shaykh Ahmed Nuruddin and his childhood friend Hassan.[87] The dervish being of peasant stock and unable to throw off his persistent provincialism, his attitude and background are contrasted with those of the rich landowner's son:

> He had finished school in Constantinople, wandered the East, he had taught as a muderris in a madrasah, worked as an official at the Porte and as a military officer, but he left all that behind. He went to Dubrovnik for some reason, and returned to the kasaba with a Dubrovnik merchant and his wife. People said that he was in love with the fair-skinned Catholic woman. (99)[88]

This was not his only digression from religious morality, or violation of social mores: 'Too talkative for service at the Porte, too tempestuous for a muderris' (100), he had become a cattle drover and caravaneer operating between Wallachia and Serbia and Dalmatia and Austria, while also maintaining an adulterous liaison with the wife of his stable hand. Nuruddin's challenging of Hassan over this matter is then developed at length in a contentious exchange between the two friends. As Nuruddin expresses his preference for 'the strict order of a dervish', Hassan's paraphrased response reads: 'Order is finality, a firm law, a reduction of possible ways of life, the false conviction that we can keep life under control. But life keeps slipping away, and the more we try to keep hold of it, the more it eludes us' (121). When Nuruddin has recourse to the Qur'an as the determinant of 'all relations between people' (122), offering the necessary principles that can be applied to any individual case, Hassan first provokes Nuruddin by declaring the stoning of an adulteress 'rather old-fashioned', but then develops a lengthy argument leading him to conclude that 'life is larger than any principle, morality is an idea, but life is what we live' (122–3). With his insistence on religious prohibitions to avoid sinful living, Hassan warns Nuruddin that this 'only creates hypocrisy and spiritual cripples' (124). A similar humanist attitude is displayed in Hassan's discussions with another resident of the tekke, the taciturn and bookish Hafiz-Muhammad. Stimulated by Hassan's Socratic prodding, Nuruddin notices how

> Hafiz-Muhammad, who for three months had either kept quiet or only talked about ordinary things, continued his exposition on the origin of the world, which was strange and inexact, and unsupported by the Koran. But the picture that he developed was interesting. Taken from one of the many books he had read (God only knows which one) and enlivened by his imagination, it glittered with the fire of his lonesome fevers, when in delirious visions he saw the beginning and the end of the world. It seemed like blasphemy. (98–9)

Recognising that Hafiz-Muhammad's ideas were derived from the ancient Greek philosophers whose works Avicenna had disseminated throughout the wider Muslim world, Nuruddin continues to reject any ideas that 'truly denied the role of God in the creation of the world'

(101). Although, in the novel's opening pages, Nuruddin himself throws around quotations from Ibn Sina and the latter's nemesis al-Ghazali, as well as the poets Abu Faraj and Rumi, and notwithstanding the fact that at one point he challenges the rigid scripturalism of his brother-in-law the Kadi Aini-effendi, it turns out that Nuruddin remains what he has always been, '[t]he dervish of a distinguished order, the sheikh of a tekke, a confirmed defender of the faith' (141), sharing the same closed world-view as the local beys. Initially he is still impressed by the self-confident independence of the likes of Ali-aga Janich, who in response to Nuruddin's question as to whether he really did not fear anybody, responded 'God a little bit, the sultan not at all, the vizier about as much as my bay horse' (413). As his plans to exact his revenge on those he holds responsible for his brother Harun's death take shape, Nuruddin too begins to display the same hostility as the local elites against the interferences by officials appointed by the central government. By manipulating both the bazaar shopkeepers and '*kasaba* scum' (479), he manages to orchestrate an uprising against the local authorities and use its outcome to carve out a power base for himself, eventually securing his own appointment as kadi, once that position had become vacant after the rioting mob had killed the incumbent, his own brother-in-law Aini-effendi.

When reading such episodes, it is important to guard against measuring them by today's epistemological and moral yardsticks. In this regard, Marina Antić's challenge, in her interpretation of *Death and the Dervish*, to both the political and the existential aspects of what Fredric Jameson has called ethical criticism must be extended to the writings of Andrić and Kadare as well; otherwise, one 'projects as permanent features of human experience' and thus as a kind of 'wisdom about personal life and interpersonal relations, what are in reality the historical and institutional specifics of a determinate type of group solidarity or class cohesion'.[89]

'Interfaith Relations' in the Ottoman Balkans

Under the Ottoman *millet* system, the various religious communities had always been living alongside – not with! – each other, because if and when they did reside in close proximity to each other, as was the case in the provincial towns, Muslims, Christians and Jews kept to themselves in their respective quarters or neighbourhoods. This is how Ivo Andrić describes their interactions in *The Bridge on the Drina*:

> Turks and Serbs went out to work and met one another with dull and expressionless faces, greeted one another and talked together with those hundred or so commonplace words of provincial courtesy which had for times circulated

> in the town and passed from one to another like counterfeit coin which none the less makes communication both possible and easy. (93)

Only when faced with circumstances affecting them all, for example when Višegrad was hit by floods, would the leaders of the different communities explore ways to cope with the situation or co-operate to provide relief:

> There were the *mukhtars* (the Moslem leaders) and the *kmets* (the Christian headmen) of all quarters, exhausted and wet to the skin, after having wakened and moved to safe quarters all their fellow citizens, Turks, Christians and Jews mingled together. The force of the elements and the weight of common misfortune brought all these men together and bridged, at least for this one evening, the gulf that divided one faith from the other and, especially, the *rayah* from the Turks. (83–4)

In a later chapter on the Austrian occupation of Bosnia, Andrić narrates an episode in which senior figures from the respective religious communities are summoned to communicate the instructions of the new authorities to the population. On the Muslim side this involved Višegrad's schoolmaster Hussein Effendi and Mula Ibrahim; for the Orthodox Christians Pop Nikola; and on behalf of the Jewish community Rabbi David Levi. Of Mulla Ibrahim and Pop Nikola, Andrić writes that they 'had been close acquaintances since youth and good friends, insofar as one could speak of friendship between a Turk and a Serb' (150). Mula Ibrahim 'seemed with his clear blue childlike eyes more like some hermit or some poor and pious pilgrim than the *hodja* of Višegrad, descendant of many *hodjas*' (147); he was also known to be a generous individual who 'never refused anyone and never handed out expensive charms or amulets as other *hodjas* did' (148).[90] Already past seventy, Pop Nikola was the son of a priest executed by the Ottomans; in his youth he had been a firebrand forced to spent time in exile in Serbia. After settling down he had now administered his parish for over fifty years, and no one else 'enjoyed such general respect and such a reputation among all the townspeople without distinction of faith, sex or year' (146).

However, along with growing government repression against their local populations, the territorial losses in the Balkans and the resulting influx of displaced Muslims into the remaining Ottoman areas, such as Bosnia, had also led to increasing tensions and a sharpening of divisions among the different religious communities themselves. In the wake of the Serbian uprising of the early 1800s, Višegrad became both a destination for Muslims fleeing from Serbia and a base of operations for volunteers fighting the rebellious forces of Karađorđe. Andrić describes how it was these refugees, having had to give up their lands, who 'spread hatred and called for revenge' (95)' and how 'drunk with bitterness, from desire for vengeance', it was the Muslim irregulars who 'longed to punish and to kill' (97). After the revolt had been quelled it remained 'difficult to say what were the true feelings of either side': the Muslims, 'gratified that the revolt was now far away from them', and the Serbs, who 'as was natural, remained disillusioned and disappointed' (93). Seen from the Muslim perspective, however, things did not improve in the course of the nineteenth century. When, by the 1850s, the frontier between the Eyalet of Bosnia and what the Serbians alternatively called the Sanjak of Smederevo or Pashaluk of Belgrade effectively became a state border, and a new Serbian strongman, Miloš Obvrenović (1783–1860), began administering the territory in the Sultan's name in 1858, this too 'influenced trade and communications, and the mutual relations of Turks and Serbs' (106). In narrating this episode, Andrić demonstrates sensitivity to the Muslim plight: as 'the Turks had now to abandon even the last towns in Serbia', he writes with compassion about 'a pitiable procession of refugees from Užice' (108). His atmospheric description of the unfolding human tragedy involving over a hundred families extends over several pages: 'Some of the townsmen looked compassionately at the refugees and remained silent, while others greeted them with "*merhaba*", tried to stop them and offer them something' (111), as they made their way to Sarajevo.

With renewed warfare erupting between the Ottomans and the Serbs in the late 1870s, 'heads of decapitated Serbs again appeared on the *kapia*' (130).[91] However, when, after the hostilities had ceased, the Austrian army sent in an occupational force, Andrić notes a difference: in contrast to the harsh repression under the Ottomans, 'there was no killing or cutting of heads' (185). This, however, did not end Muslim mistrust of foreign Christian powers, whether Orthodox Serbian or Catholic Austrian. By way of illustration, Andrić tells the life story of Mujaga Mutapdžić, who had come from Užice as a five-year-old, only to leave again ten years later on account of the arrival of the Austrians and settle in Nova Varoš in the Sanjak.[92] There he remained until the Balkan Wars of 1912, during which he joined the Ottoman army in order to fight against the Serbs and Montenegrins, only to end up again in Bosnia after the Turks had given up the Sanjak. The impact of more than a century of intermittent warfare on the relations between Muslims and Christians in Bosnia becomes clear from their reactions when the river at Višegrad floods again:

> Only this time men of different faiths were not mingling together or bound by the feeling of solidarity and common misfortune, and did not sit together to find help and consolation in talk as at those times. The Turks went to Turkish houses and the Serbs, as if plague-stricken, only to Serbian homes. (357)

The Sick Man of Europe and the Onslaught of Modernity

Even if the naval battle at Lepanto of 1571 and the failed siege of Vienna in 1683 were not decisive defeats, both events can nonetheless be considered as having ended Ottoman dominance in the Mediterranean and halted its territorial expansion in Central Europe, setting in motion its very gradual but nevertheless irreversible decline. In the wake of the Austrian–Ottoman Treaties of Karlowitz (1699) and Passarowitz (1718), in the course of the eighteenth century, Russia became the Sublime Porte's main nemesis in South-Eastern Europe. At the turn of the eighteenth to the nineteenth century, as the Ottoman Empire became exposed to additional threats from France and England, Selim III initiated a reform programme known as *Nizam-e Cedid* or 'New Order', which came to naught again in 1807, when the sultan was deposed by internal reactionary forces opposed to these innovations. Coinciding with the Industrial Revolution, it became clear that the 1800s belonged to the Great Powers from post-Napoleonic northern and western Europe: Britain, France and Prussia. It was against this background that the Ottoman Empire came to be referred to as the 'sick man of Europe'. The first person thought to have used this label was Tsar Nicholas I in a meeting with Austrian Chancellor Klemens von Metternich in 1833. From then on the designation was also used in the great narrative of rivalries and concomitant diplomatic manoeuvrings around the so-called Eastern Question that dominated international relations in the Balkans and the Black Sea area during that 'long nineteenth century' (1789–1914).[93] Jockeying for influence in the Balkans were, first and foremost, the Austrians and Russians, but – with an eye on their interests in the wider Muslim world – Britain and France played a decisive role as well.

Although the term was only coined in the 1830s, in *Bosnian Chronicle*, the Ottoman Empire is already depicted as the 'sick man of Europe', with Andrić's dramatic portrayals of the new vizier of Travnik and his entourage. Ousted as grand vizier after the fall of Selim III and appointed governor of Bosnia by way of a face-saver, Ibrahim Halimi Pasha cuts a tragic, ailing and indolent figure; he is 'a walking ruin' (185), 'a physical freak and spiritual mummy' (220). His retainers too are described as disease-ridden individuals suffering from a variety of afflictions. Although the vizier's secretary and confidante, 'the benign and exceptionally intelligent' Tahir Bey, had been a child prodigy and was therefore considered the 'brains of the residence' (189), at only thirty-six years of age he too was already 'a sickly, heavy, elderly man' (190). The residence's treasurer,

Baki, is not just yet another 'physical and mental freak'; as a malicious, eccentric and 'inveterate miser' (193) he also is the polar opposite of Tahir Bey. The more marginal figures in both the vizier's retinue and in the novel's narrative included his personal physician Eshref Effendi, who not only lacked even the most rudimentary medical expertise, but was 'almost completely paralysed by rheumatism' (191). Moving a few decades ahead to the middle of the nineteenth century, in *The Bridge on the Drina*, Andrić characterises the Empire as being 'consumed by a slow fever' (106) and Višegrad as a 'remote district of Turkey, the rotten-ripe Turkey of the nineteenth century (152).

As both outside foreign powers and subjugated peoples, such as the Serbs and Greeks, ate away at its territorial expanse, the Ottoman government responded with a two-pronged approach, combining repression of provincial attempts at secession by military means with a new reform policy known as the *Tanzimat* (1839–76), so as to fend off the danger of sedition in the metropole. When these proved insufficient or unsuccessful, an increasingly paranoid Sultan Abdulhamid II turned the Ottoman Empire into the police state and surveillance society depicted by Ismail Kadare in *The Palace of Dreams* and *The Blinding Order*, but also noted by Ivo Andrić, who describes these dynamics thus:

> For those who rule and must oppress in order to rule must work according to reason; and if, carried away by their passions or driven by an adversary, they go beyond the limits of reasonable action, they start the slippery slope and thereby reveal the commencement of their own downfall. (93–4)

Aside from territorial disintegration, the onslaught of modernity came also in the form of an influx of new ideas. The threat posed by nineteenth-century European imperialism to the Ottomans has emanated not so much from the world of Christendom (although Austria and Russia may have continued to self-identify as Christian countries) as from a Europe that has rediscovered its civilisational roots in antiquity, extending from the Renaissance through the Enlightenment era into the industrial age.

Contrasting Dispositions: Closed World-views versus Cosmopolitan Attitudes

The influx of modern ideas is a recurring theme in the novels of Ivo Andrić, which are predominantly set in the nineteenth century. He illustrates this influx by contrasting the closed world-views of the traditional Muslim establishment and Ottoman officialdom with the dispositions of other educated figures, who are more open to technological and scientific advances as well as new knowledge in the fields of philosophy, religion and politics that had been evolving elsewhere in Europe throughout the Renaissance, Reformation and Enlightenment eras.

Combining stubborn conservatism with an innate suspicion of outsiders and resistance to external influences, Ivo Andrić's depictions of Bosnia's local beys offer an apt illustration of the prevailing atmosphere in nineteenth-century small-town Ottoman Bosnia and the mentality of its population. Already in the prologue to *Bosnian Chronicle*, a gathering of a dozen or so notables from Travnik agree that they do not appreciate the presence of foreigners: 'We've lived for hundreds of years without consuls, and that's how we'll go on' (2). However, the Travnik beys are greatly disturbed when it becomes clear that, with the arrival of the Vizier Husref Mehmed Pasha, his enthusiasm for the French and his personal admiration for Napoleon Bonaparte, '*the days of the Consuls* had begun' (12). Consequently, they regarded the French military presence in Dalmatia and Napoleon's diplomatic representatives in Travnik with the same suspicion as all other 'Bosnian Turks' (41). As opponents of the reform efforts of Selim III, they welcomed his fall from power in 1807, anticipating that 'now the time has come to wash away the filth that has clung to the pure faith and true Turks' (43) and that also the disgraced former grand vizier of the 'Giaour Sultan', who was 'hated in Bosnia as a friend of the French and supporter of the reforms' (44), would be recalled, and with him the consul as well.[94]

Comparable passages from later time periods in *The Bridge on the Drina* evince that the same attitude persisted during the Austrian occupation. One of the most admired men in Višegrad was Shemsibeg Branković, who had ordered that 'not a new tool or a new word was allowed to enter the Branković house. Not one of his sons had any connection with the new authorities and his grandchildren were not allowed to go to school' (160). In Višegrad, opposition to foreign intervention was usually limited to this type of hostile and passive resistance, as its inhabitants 'never had the reputation of being enthusiastic fighters' (131). So when the mufti of Plevlje, located in present-day Montenegro, arrived in town to recruit for an armed rebellion against the Austrians, he found his staunchest opponent in Alihodja Mutevelić, a scion of the mutevelia family and formally still in charge of a now very decrepit caravanserai. 'Frequently at odds with the local *ulema* and the Moslem notables', he nonetheless agreed with the majority of Višegrad's Muslims to refrain from armed resistance, although in his particular case there was 'no question of cowardice or religious lukewarmness' (132). Ever the consummate diplomat safeguarding the status quo, Andrić notes how Alihodja's belligerence towards the mufti and his deputy commander

Osman Effendi Karamanli was 'a boon to the begs and agas for the question of their participation in the insurgence remained unanswered and they themselves were not compelled to take sides at once' (134). With time, Alihodja's persistent rejection of anything novel – Austrian and foreign – turned into 'a sort of calm meditation' as he 'withdrew into a tiny closet behind the shop which he called his coffin' (249). In a way, Alihodja's isolation from 'all that this life could bring him, this life which in his opinion had long become rotten and proceeded along evil ways' (250), resembles Nuruddin's seclusion in his tekke, locking up his mind in a traditional Islamic world-view. Although Andrić depicts his literary character more kindlily and with greater compassion than Selimović's merciless dissection of the dervish's moral cowardice, Alihodja too succumbs to fatalist resignation:

> At one time my late lamented father heard from Sheik Dedije and told me as a child how bridges first came to this world and how the first bridge was built. When Allah the Merciful and Compassionate first created the world, the earth was smooth and even as a finely engraved plate. That displeased the devil who envied man this gift of God. And while the earth was still just as it had come from God's hands, damp and soft as unbaked clay, he stole up and scratched the face of God's earth with his nails as much and as deeply as he could. Therefore, the story says, deep rivers and ravines were formed [...] And Allah felt pity when he saw what the Accursed One had done [...] So men learned from the angels of God how to build bridges, and therefore, after fountains, the greatest blessing is to build a bridge and the greatest sin is to interfere with it, for every bridge, from a tree trunk crossing a mountain stream to this great erection of Mehmed Pasha, has its guardian angel who cares for it and maintains it as long as God has ordained that it should stand. (252)

Such closed world-views associated with conservative attitudes were not restricted to the local Muslims; in *Bosnian Chronicle* they extend to the local Christian clergy and the microcosm of the Travnik diplomatic corps as well. The wives of both the Austrian and the French consuls were devout Catholics, and Colonel Joseph von Mitterer himself was a minor aristocrat representing the reactionary Austrian Habsburgs. Although his French counterpart, Jean Daville, is presented as protégé of the statesman and master political survivor Talleyrand and a careerist under the Jacobins, Andrić also writes that 'the Consul had grown up before the revolution and been educated along classical lines' (73). Consequently, his intellectual and literary tastes contrast strongly with those of his deputy Des Fossés, who belonged to the generation that reached maturity under the Empire:

> The 'world of ideas' which was for Daville's generation their only spiritual homeland and their real life, appeared not even to exist for the new men.

> Consequently, what existed for them was 'living life', the world of reality, the world of tangible facts and visible measurable successes and failures, a terrible new world which was opening up in front of Daville like an icy desert. (70)

Both Daville and Des Fossés are based on historical figures, namely Pierre David (1772–1846), a parliamentarian and former consul to Naples and Smyrna, and the geographer and diplomat Amédée Chaumette des Fossés (1782–1841).[95] Des Fossés had learned Turkish at the Collège de Louis le Grand, and his communicative flair enabled him to speak to everyone – Ottoman officials, Muslim bazaar merchants, and also the Franciscan friars operating in the area – except for one group: 'only the Travnik beys remained inaccessible' (73). Commentators have noted Andrić's sympathy for this fictionalised character, but I would go a step further and suggest that he considered Des Fossés as his literary alter ego.[96] I do not attribute this only to the vice-consul's knack for collecting both political intelligence and scholarly data or his 'intention to write a book about Bosnia' (73) – which the real des Fossés indeed has done as well.[97] Also, the inappropriate relationship between the novel's character and the Austrian consul's spouse reads like a brutally honest hint by the otherwise very private Andrić of his own adulterous affair with the wife of one of his subordinates during his time as envoy in Berlin.[98] While Andrić's Des Fossés is capable of maintaining cordial relations, his progressive ideas clash with the deeply ingrained traditionalism of both Travnik's Muslims and Catholic clergy. This becomes clear in a lengthy debate he has with Friar Julian, who blames the wretched lives of Bosnians of all faiths on Turkish rule:

> Des Fossés did not conceal the fact that he was surprised at the obstinacy with which in Bosnia not only the Turks but people of all the other faiths too, resisted every influence, even the best, opposed every innovation, every advance, even what was possible in the present circumstances and depended on no one but themselves. He pointed out all the harm done by this 'Chinese' rigidity, the way they cut themselves off from life.
>
> 'How is it possible', asked Des Fossés, 'for this country to become stable and orderly and adopt at least as great a degree of civilization as its closest neighbours, if its people are divided as nowhere else in Europe? Four faiths live in this narrow, mountainous and meagre strip of land. Each of them is exclusive and strictly separate from the others. You all live under one sky and from the same soil, but the centre of spiritual life of each of these four groups is far away, in a foreign land, in Rome, Moscow, Istanbul, Mecca, Jerusalem, and God alone knows where, but at any rate not here where the people are born and die. And each group considers that its well-being is conditioned by the disadvantage of each of the other three faiths, and that they can make progress only at their cost. Each of them made intolerance the greatest virtue [...].' (283)

Friar Julian is not convinced that the acceptance of rationality will not result in a loss of faith. Instead, Des Fossés' Franciscan interlocutor insists that, without their 'Chinese rigidity', his Catholic 'parishioners Petar and Anton would today be called Muhammad and Hussein' (284).

The most remarkable local exception to this attitude is the 'Illyrian doctor' (315). According to his own life story, Giovanni Mario Cologna was born on the Ionian island of Cephalonia to a Venetian father and Dalmatian mother. Raised by his grandfather in Greece and later educated as a physician in Italy, 'he had lived the rest of his life in the Levant, in Turkish and Austrian service' (272). It was not so much Cologna's biography that made him a cultural hybrid in Travnik; it was predominantly his personal disposition, intellectual curiosity and spiritual inquisitiveness regarding religious traditions that put him in the interstices of Travnik's various faith communities:

> Cologna was a man of up-to-date views, a 'philosopher,' a free and critical spirit, devoid of all prejudice. But this did not prevent him from studying the religious life not only of various Christian churches but also of Islamic and other Eastern sects and faiths. (273)

The passage goes on to unpack Cologna's approach to these investigations. Rather than instances of dispassionate scholarly analysis, his research came with a combination of 'attacks of religious fervour and phases of practical piety' (273). Having spent time with the Franciscan monks in the monastery of Guča Gora, and having acquired learning based on comparative studies of the liturgies of the Greek and Serbian Orthodox churches, he

> carried on scholarly discussions about the history of Islamic beliefs with the learned Travnik Muderris Abdusalam Effendi, for Cologna knew well not only the Koran but also all the theological and philosophical trends from Abu Hanif to Al Gazali. Whenever he had the opportunity, he would shower all the other learned gentlemen of the Travnik ulema tirelessly and inconsiderately with quotations from Muslim theologians whom, for the most part, they did not know. (274)[99]

In a rare reference to Sufism, in a later chapter of *Bosnian Chronicle*, Cologna invokes Rumi: 'For I cannot know myself. I am neither Christian, nor Jew, nor Parsee, nor Muslim. I am neither from the East, nor the West, neither from the land, nor the sea' (314). As a man interested in 'all religious and philosophical movements in the history of mankind' (275), Cologna took an attitude towards religious diversity that in today's language would be called pluralist, making him a proponent of the theologies of religions developed by the likes of Paul Knitter. However, his irresistible urge 'to penetrate into the destiny of human thought, wherever it appeared and whatever form it took' (275), also created problems, as his obsessive and intense engagement with one religious tradition after another 'set him apart and alienated him from people' (276) – except for Des Fossés. When showing the vice-consul round the grounds of the Yeni Mosque, which used to be the church dedicated to St Catherine and before that a temple of the Roman deity Mithras, Cologna emphasises that 'it is all connected' (274), and that there is hope in the words of the Qur'an: 'Perhaps one day God will reconcile you and your opponents and establish friendship between you. He is powerful, mild and merciful' (317).[100]

Although such a disposition creates opportunities for cultural brokerage and mediation between religions, the Illyrian doctor was acutely aware of the challenges resulting from such liminality, which Andrić lets him articulate with lucidity and in great detail:

> That is the fate of the man from the Levant, for he is 'poussière humaine', human dust, drifting painfully between East and West, belonging to neither and beaten by both. These are people who know many languages, but none is their own, who know two faiths, but are steadfast in neither. These are the victims of the fatal division of humanity into Christians and non-Christians, eternal interpreters and go-betweens. (314)

He calls Levantines like himself 'people from the frontier', 'a small separate humanity' inhabiting a 'third world', where all malediction settled as a result of the division of the earth into two worlds, 'where there should not be any boundaries' (314). And indeed, things do not end well for the Illyrian doctor, as he died under mysterious circumstances after embracing Islam in order to take under his protection a Catholic man who is about to be murdered by a Muslim lynch mob.

The Bridge on the Drina features a similar debate, but there it is transposed a century further in time to Višegrad on the eve of the First World War. It engages two budding intellectuals who belong to the same generation as Ivo Andrić himself, studying at universities in Vienna. In this case, the discussion involves Fehim Bahtijarević, son of a kadi in the nearby town of Rogatica and a woman belonging to the local Osmanagić beys, and Toma Galus, whose father had come from Burgenland in Austria to work in Bosnia, where he married the daughter of a local landowner, Hadji Toma Stanković. Although this title clearly indicates a Muslim origin, all their children were baptised in the Serbian Orthodox Church. Over several pages, Andrić rolls out a debate in which Toma tries to dissuade Fehim from his plan to study oriental languages in Vienna, suggesting an alternative, more suitable field of study instead:

> You Moslems, you begs' sons, often make a mistake. Disconcerted by the new times, you no longer know your exact and rightful place in the world. Your love for everything oriental is only a contemporary expression of your 'will to power'; for you the eastern way of life and thought is very closely bound up with a social and legal order which is the basis of your centuries of lordship. That is understandable. But it in no way means that you have any sense for orientalism as a study. You are orientals but you make a mistake when you think that you are thereby called upon to be orientalists. In general you have not got the calling or the true inclination for science. [...] you are the only nobles in this country, or at least you were; for centuries you enlarged, confirmed and defended your privileges by sword and pen, legally, religiously and by force of arms; that has made of you typical warriors, administrators and landowners [...] the true studies for you are law and economics, for you are men of practical knowledge. Such are men from the ruling classes, always and everywhere. (296)

When Fehim retorts that he no longer belongs to a ruling class, because 'today we are all equal' (296), Toma insists that even when conditions or circumstances change 'a class remains what it is' (297). Although the discussion then expands to take in the merits of Mehmed Pasha Sokolović and the ills of both the Ottoman Empire and the Austrian-Hungarian monarchy, Toma's advocacy of modern nationalism that will 'triumph over religious diversity and outmoded prejudice' (299) cannot mask his own – and with that also Andrić's! – blind spots, consisting in what seems to me a combination of rigid Marxist class consciousness and cultural stereotyping. As a member of the revolutionary youth movement, Toma Galus describes the merits of a new national state which was 'to rally the Southern Slavs around Serbia as a sort of Piedmont on the basis of complete national unity, religious tolerance and civil equality' (299). Interpreting the silence with which Fehim greets Toma's proposition as a rejection of this alternative future for a united Yugoslavia, Andrić then imagines what is going on in the taciturn Muslim's head. Projecting onto Fehim's mind that 'the foundations of the world and the bases of life and human relationships in it have been fixed for centuries', and that therefore 'it is not human desires that dispose and administer the things in the world', Andrić concludes that this young Muslim from one of Bosnia's noble family also subscribes to a world-view in which 'lasting deeds are realized on this earth only by God's will, and man is only His blind and humble tool' (301).

Unlike Ivo Andrić's elaborate dialogues between religious conservatives and more free-thinking progressives, Ismail Kadare only alludes to such oppositions. In *The Palace of Dreams*, the battle for control over the surveillance agency in question, the *Tabir Sarrail*, pitches the Quprilis, supported by 'the banks and the owners of the copper mines', against the 'Sheikh-ul-Islam faction' (113). Translated in terms of Ottoman politics in the second half of the nineteenth century, this represents the rivalry between, on one side, the proponents of the Tanzimat reform programme and a modern market economy and, on the other, a reactionary religious establishment rallying around Sultan Abdulhamid's Pan-Islamism. Writing during those war years when the tide was turning in favour of Tito's Partisans, Andrić's modernisers exude ambition and optimism. Kadare's novel from the Hoxha years is more depressing: Dispirited by the Sheikh-ul-Islam's constant 'warnings against the weaking of religious feeling among the younger generation' (186), Mark-Alem eventually 'gave in to the call of life and left his refuge, the spell would be broken: the wind would turn against the Quprilis and the men would come for him' (190).

Epilogue: The Ottoman Balkans and Europe

Although far from flattering, the characterisation of the Ottoman Empire as the 'sick man of Europe' stands in marked contrast to present-day discussions as to whether Turkey is a European country – and therefore eligible for EU membership – or not.[101] Aside from such political debates, when regarded from a cultural-historical rather than a topographic viewpoint, the very notion of Europe is ambiguous to begin with. The roots of Ancient Greek civilisation, thought to be one of the cornerstones of European culture, lie in Asia Minor, now western Anatolia. Moreover, according to mythology the very name of the continent refers to the daughter of King Agenor of Phoenicia, a polity located in what is now Lebanon. Moving forward in time, the efforts of the Abbasid House of Wisdom in ninth-century Baghdad, translating philosophical and scientific knowledge from Greek into Arabic, and the reverse exercise translating from Arabic into Latin and other Romance languages by the twelfth- and thirteenth-century Translation School of Toledo, reflect a cultural and intellectual exchange and osmosis between the worlds of Islam and Christendom dating back centuries.

Still, the separation of the Balkans from the rest of Europe runs like a red thread through Ismail Kadare's Ottoman cycle.[102] In his chronicle of the three-arched bridge, the Monk Gjon already reports how 'the lineaments of a new order that would carry the world many centuries forward had faintly, ever so faintly, begun to appear in this part of Europe' (94). In *Three Elegies for Kosovo*, the Great Lady deplores how the rope connecting Europe to the ancient Greek world had been 'cut in places by waves of fate' (76), and that as a result 'the eleven peoples of the peninsula had to stumble along within a communal shell named "Balkan", and it seemed that nobody gave them a second thought' (77). Also, the lament of Sultan Murad's soul speaks of 'the Balkan people's madness', a people who 'instead of trying to build something together, attack each other again like beasts freed from their iron chains' (86). Several literary characters have served as mouthpieces for Kadare's own fascination with the Hellenic legacy. It is again the noblewoman in the second elegy who regards the genre of the Greek tragedy as 'the greatest wealth of mankind' (71); in *The Siege* it is Sirri Selim and his familiarity with Homer's *Iliad*; in *The Palace of Dreams*, the Quprilis are 'the only great family left in Europe, probably in the world, who are the subject of an epic' (58). In all instances, it points at a dichotomous world-view, in which Europe forms a key element of a cultural self-definition in binary opposition to Ottoman otherness that goes back to the East–West rhetoric of the Renaissance Humanists.[103]

Ivo Andrić's nurturing of the idea of the Balkans as an integral part of Europe is not so much connected with its legacy from antiquity as dependent on the acceptance of new knowledge and the politics of modernity shaped by a European sense of cultural and intellectual superiority first formulated by the Renaissance Humanists.[104] Especially in episodes set in the nineteenth century this sense of European belonging is explicitly articulated. Envisioning the Ottoman Empire's collapse, in *Bosnian Chronicle*, Vice-Consul Des Fossés tries to convince Brother Julian that the 'peoples who are now under Turkish rule, called by different names and confessing different faiths, must find a common basis for their existence, a broader, better, more rational and humane formula' (352). When the latter retorts that the 'Catholics have had that formula for a long time', Des Fossés criticises the Franciscan's continuing allegiance to 'the feudal and conservative policies of reactionary European powers' (350). Striking both an optimistic and a cautionary note, the prediction of Andrić's literary alter ego sounds remarkably prophetic:

> There is no doubt your country will join the European community, but it could happen that it joins it divided and burdened with inherited ideas, habits and instincts which you won't find anywhere else any more. And, like ghosts, they will hinder its normal development and create of it an outdated monster which would be prey to anyone. (351)

Some fifteen years after his death, Ivo Andrić writings about Muslim Bosnia received a second lease of life. On the occasion of the one-hundredth anniversary of Ivo Andrić's birth, and a little over three decades after he had won the Nobel Prize for literature, Stanford University hosted a conference on his work: the very year in which Yugoslavia fell apart and descended into civil war. Around the same time, one of Andrić's short stories became the subject of outright political manipulation, when Radovan Karadžić, the ultra-nationalist Serb leader in Bosnia who was later convicted of war crimes, distributed a misleading translation of the story 'A Letter from 1920'. Citing a particular passage on hatred being an inherent part of the Bosnian Muslim soul completely out of context, Karadžić used his contentious interpretation to justify the Serbian struggle in Bosnia, thus insinuating that Yugoslavia's main man of letters would have condoned the inevitable orgy of violence. Unfortunately, this reading was picked up and uncritically repeated by influential writers and even academics, such as Robert Kaplan, Noel Malcolm and Fouad Ajami. This in turn influenced also the perceptions of political leaders, including President Clinton, the British Prime Minister John Major and the EU representative in Bosnia Paddy Ashdown.[105] Such views were only reinforced by the discovery in Andrić's literary estate of plans dating back to 1948 for a revised story under a new title: 'Letter from the Year 1992'. However, what was purposely left out or conveniently forgotten in all these discussions is the end of Andrić's story: there, the author-protagonist flees the hatred and violence of his home country, only to end up dying in the Spanish Civil War. Karadžić's intentional misrepresentation, but also the facile misreadings by those accepting his translation, are diametrically opposed to everything Andrić stood for. The posthumous treatment of Andrić confirms an observation by another Yugoslav writer, Danilo Kiš (1935–89), that 'about dead writers one can write any sort of nonsense'.[106] In fact, Andrić had already noted down something similar himself: 'Neither in life nor after your death are you protected and safe. Anything can happen to you'.[107]

The Balkans: Cacophonic Cultural Hybridity

In all his writings, Andrić has not just dissected hatred in all its variations with surgical precision; as a creative writer he certainly also recognised its cathartic role and productive potential. Andrić's historical novels and stories show that the fate of the land of his birth was not determined in Sarajevo, Banja Luka or Travnik, let alone in Višegrad, but in Istanbul, Vienna, and later also in Belgrade and – eventually – Brussels. At the same time, his empathy was always towards the victims of ethno-religious violence. However, that does not mean he can be presented as a proponent of multiculturalism, because that would be anachronistic too. I have intended to show that while his immediate engagement with Islam as a religious tradition may have been limited to providing the political-historical canvas for the psychological portrayals of the characters populating his novels and stories, his 'thick descriptions' of Bosnian life are of a richness and humanity that is altogether lacking from the reductionist interpretations to which his work has fallen victim. However, it has come at a price:

> Ivo Andrić has posthumously suffered more than any other writer in the former Yugoslavia: his monument in Višegrad has been dynamited by Muslim extremists, his works have been banned from Croatian school programs, and his foundation in Belgrade has been robbed of its assets by Serbian politicians.[108]

The poisonous political climate making this possible is already prefigured in an exchange between the dervish Nuruddin and the religious-scholar-turned-cattle-drover Hassan written by Meša Selimović more than twenty-five earlier, in which they discuss the fate of a poor local cripple named Jemail:

> 'Jemail is the true face of Bosnia,' Hassan said [...]
> 'So what are we then? Lunatics? Wretches?
> The most complicated people on the face of the earth. [...] We've been torn away from our roots, but haven't become part of anything else. [...] We are despised both by our kinsmen and by newcomers, and we defend ourselves with pride and hatred'. (408)

In both Ivo Andrić and Meša Selimović's prose, the words 'hate' and 'hatred' occur with frequent regularity. Still, I do not believe that this is driven by insurmountable sentiments of misanthropy. Both writers portray their protagonists without great expectations regarding people's behaviour, but with astute psychological insight and great humanity. Their subtle dissections of a protagonist's character also show how literary representations can provide room for the ambiguities of identity. They can be taken as a hermeneutics of alterity, providing a counter-narrative to the binaries and dichotomies that dominate the readings of many historians from the Balkans who project misleading and sometimes patently false interpretations onto the Ottoman past: as a totally alien system of governance, repression and violence purposely directed against local populations of Slav Christians, combined with a fanatical adherence to Islamic law.

In terms of their politics, Andrić and Kadare must be considered complex – even problematic – writers. Andrić managed to survive two World Wars, served an inter-war monarchy as diplomat in Nazi Germany, and then became a celebrated writer in post-War Communist Yugoslavia (even though Tito himself was not a fan of his). Ismail Kadare too was a political chameleon, maintaining an ambiguous relationship with the Hoxha regime and jumping on the nationalist bandwagon in the course of the 1990s.[109]

Both Andrić and Kadare wrote novels about bridges as symbols of the Balkans' liminal position between East and West. In contrast to what the anthropologist Christian Bromberger calls the 'polyphonic' Mediterranean exemplified in particular by the *Convivencia* projected onto Muslim Spain, he considers the only Yugoslav Nobel Prize laureate, Ivo Andrić, and the many-times-nominated Albanian Ismail Kadare as representing a 'cacophonic' alternative projecting a much more adversarial and dichotomous relation.[110] South-Eastern Europe is located not only on an east–west fault line between the historical worlds of Christendom and Islam, but also at the crossroads between the Teutonic and Slavic domains, while encompassing territories inhabited by speakers of Albanian, Greek, Hungarian and Romance languages as well. The resulting cultural diversity appears to make the region's margins and interstices much more prone to antagonistic liminalities that are also mirrored in the way Islamic references are used.

Andrić's depictions of Islam and Muslims in his novels and short story collections are certainly impregnated by Orientalist motifs and tropes, but I find myself agreeing with Tomislav Longinović that these are different from what Edward Said meant by Orientalism. In the latter case, the Orient and Orientals function as constructs of 'the other' primarily manufactured in English and French cultures as part of their global imperialist projects. In the case of the Ottoman Balkans, Orientalism concerns

> the effects of colonization by an Asian power on the formation of cultural identity in small European nations. The reversal in the usual colonial roles creates conditions for a specific subspecies of 'Orientalism,' conceived from the point of view of the Westerners who are being colonized by an Eastern power. The Oriental is therefore portrayed as a conqueror whose culture and religion are perceived as alien, inferior, and degrading.[111]

Andrić had already said as much himself in his doctoral thesis, which 'is not to be taken as criticism of Islamic culture as such but only of the consequences of its transfer into a country that was Christian and Slavic' (76). Although concerned with Albanians instead of Slavs, the concomitant alternative Orientalism of this kind of critique in its artistic-literary manifestations also applies to Ismail Kadare. In concrete terms, Turkish political domination over Albanians and Slavs (as well as Greeks, Hungarians and Romanians) has produced

> a hybrid culture where clear distinctions between the Eastern and Western elements gradually became indistinguishable. While the two religions (which later defined national alliances) drifted apart, the two cultures were blended imperceptibly together.[112]

For centuries, this cultural hybridisation of foreign influences emanating from Byzantium, Rome and the Muslim East has isolated Albanians and Bosnians and hindered their emancipation into the wider European context. All three authors have used the Ottoman past as a foil for where they thought their home countries should be heading. Whereas Andrić and Selimović looked for the answer in the idea of a union of South Slavs, Kadare became an advocate of a form of Albanianism that is conscious of its ancient Homeric legacy in order to make a case for Albania as an integral part of Europe. There is a certain irony to Kadare's treatment of the Ottoman past. It challenges the tendency of certain nineteenth-century Albanian nationalists to point at their own Bektashi roots in order to argue that Albanians were only superficially Islamised or even to suggest a degree of religious indifference. This was actually a projection of their own exposure to the secularising influence of nationalism as the emergent political ideology of the century.[113] Instead, Kadare's Ottoman Cycle demonstrates that, for centuries, the Ottoman territories inhabited by Albanians had formed an integral part of the Sunni Muslim world, not least through the involvement of a disproportionately large number of Albanians in the administration of the realm.

In general, I don't think it's a good idea to learn about Islam by reading the Koran, unless of course you take the trouble to learn Arabic and read the original text.

Michel Houellebecq, *Submission*, 218

Massacres of others are always less awkward, memory is always selective and history always official.

Mathias Énard, *Zone*, 201

God has deserted, conscience has gone its way and identity along with it – I am what I have read, I am what I have seen, I have as much Arabic in me as Spanish and French, I have been multiplied in those mirrors until I have been lost or rebuilt, fragile image, image in motion.

Mathias Énard, *The Street of Thieves*, 260

Wagner is a calamity for music, Nietzsche asserts. A disease, a neurosis. The remedy is Carmen, *the Mediterranean, and the Spanish Orient.*

Mathias Énard, *Compass*, 330

Chapter 5

New Humanisms

This final chapter deals with a set of French novels that offer vastly different literary treatments of Islam and Muslims. The writers of these novels made their international breakthroughs at the beginning of the new millennium and are both recipients of the Prix Goncourt, France's most prestigious literary prize. As writers, however, the erudite scholar Mathias Énard and the almost anti-intellectual Michel Houellebecq are each other's polar opposite. These different dispositions are also borne out in their treatment of Islam, in particular where it concerns its political aspects. In several of his novels, Houellebecq has latched on to those political discourses projecting a global Islamic threat to the new world order of the twenty-first century. Political Islam is a returning theme in Énard's writings too, but there it is emphatically contextualised in relation to Europe's cultural history. In both instances, however, it has also led the authors to the formulation of distinctly new forms of humanism.

Between Erudition and Anti-intellectualism: Two French Novelists on Islam

Mathias Énard (b. 1972) shares Navid Kermani's academic background in Oriental studies. Like Kermani, instead of pursuing a scholarly career, Énard too opted for a life as a literary writer. However, as their careers progressed, Kermani became increasingly politically engaged, while in the case of Énard the inverse is true. Where his early novels focused on overtly political themes in relation to the Middle East, he has moved towards a more 'decentered writing style, a crossroads of history and geography', inspired by his readings of the brothers Jean and Olivier Rolin, two former Maoist student activists turned writers.[1] Trained at the National Institute for Eastern Languages and Civilisations (Institut national des langues et civilisations orientales, INALCO), Énard graduated with a thesis on post-war Arabic and Persian poetry and their connections with European literature. After spending an extended period of time in the Near East and North Africa (including military service in Syria), in 2000, he settled in Juan Goytisolo's city of birth, Barcelona, where he became a lecturer in Arabic language in the faculty of translation and interpretation of Catalonia's Universitat Autònoma de Barcelona. His literary breakthrough came in 2008, with *Zone*, a long, stylistically experimental novel consisting of a single sentence. The title refers to the theatres of war and other conflict areas in North Africa and the Eastern Mediterranean where the main character, a French secret agent of Croatian origin, plied his trade.

Seven year later, Énard won the Prix Goncourt with *Boussole* (*Compass*, 2015), another massive tome where his erudition is in full display: not only in terms of his expertise in oriental studies or his wide readings in history and philosophy, but through his detailed knowledge of music as well.[2] Also, the Islam-related themes are more clearly developed in *Compass* than in *Zone*. Literary scholars have categorised both novels as works of historiographic meta-fiction, as theorised by Ansgar Nünning.[3] In both cases the autodiegetic narration of the novel's story unfolds in the course of a single night. Commentators on this shared feature of *Zone* and *Compass* have pointed at the parallel with the narrator of the *Arabian Nights*, or analysed it under the aspects of insomnia and the night watch.[4] None, however, has made the connection with the Night Journey of Muhammad, which – as discussed in the chapter on Abdelwahab Meddeb – influenced Dante's *Divine Comedy*. Between these two epic accounts, Énard wrote two shorter novels: a fictive account of Michelangelo's stay at the Ottoman Court in Istanbul, *Tell Them of Battles, Kings and Elephants* (2010); and *The Street of Thieves* (2012). The latter, a novel addressing Islamic radicalisation and the migration crisis through the eyes of a young Moroccan emigrating to Spain during the Arab Spring of 2011, appears to have been written in haste and cannot compare to *Zone* or *Compass* in terms of multi-layered richness and narrative elaboration. In spite of these shortcomings, it is thematically relevant and also parallels Houellebecq's preoccupation with Islamism.

Michel Houellebecq (pen name of Michel Thomas, b. 1956) is the son of a French mountain guide and an Algerian-born physician of Corsican descent.[5] Born on the Indian Ocean island of Réunion (now still an overseas dominion of France), he first lived with his maternal grandmother in Algeria, until he was packed off to France in 1961, in order to be further raised by his paternal grandmother (whose maiden name he later adopted as his pseudonym) – while his parents continued to pursue what the later author described as their hippie lifestyles. On account of his high-school results, Michel qualified for admission to France's prestigious École Normale Supérieure, but failed to take the required oral entrance exams. Instead he obtained a degree in agronomics and then went on to briefly study film, while dabbling in literary publishing and writing poetry on the side. Until the early 1990s, he worked as a civil servant in IT departments of the Ministry of Agriculture, the city of Paris and the French National Assembly. During this period he also experienced periods of unemployment and received psychiatric treatment for depression. In 1992, he was awarded the Tristan Tzara Prize for his poetry; two years later he published a first novel, entitled *Extension du domain de la lute* (appearing in English translation in 1998 under the title *Whatever*). His literary breakthrough came in 1998 with *Les Particules élémentaires* (translated as *Atomised*). A bestselling commercial success, the novel established Michel Houellebecq as France's new – turn-of-the-century – literary celebrity. However, the novel's frank – frequently vulgar – passages about sex, as well as a very public dispute with his mother about the novel's autobiographical elements, also caused scandal and upheaval.

With three subsequent novels written over a time span of fifteen years, Houellebecq further cemented his controversial reputation with unflattering depictions of Muslims and disconcerting scenarios featuring political Islam.[6] The uncanny timing of the release of these books only added to the author's notoriety, with *Platform* (2001) appearing in the same year as the attacks on New York's World Trade Center and the Pentagon in Washington, *The Possibility of an Island* (2005) coming out in the wake of the bombings of Madrid and London's public transport systems, and the publication of *Submission* (2015) coinciding with the shooting spree at the offices of the satirical magazine *Charlie Hebdo*.[7] In contrast with this latter novel's sketch of a France that falls under the control of Muslim politicians, the role of Islam in the other two novels is only tangentially relevant to their main themes. *The Possibility of an Island* is a futuristic novel covering a time span of a millennium and fits within a sub-genre of speculative fiction dealing with what in philosophy is referred to as the posthuman. Its chief protagonist, a stand-up comedian, occasional actor and screenwriter by the name of Daniel1, uses Muslims and events in the Islamic world for the sake of provocation in both his comedy routines and film scripts. Also, *Platform*'s scattered references to the prevailing social conservativism in Muslim countries and the occurrence of terrorist attacks on southern Thai tourist resorts by radicalised Muslims are of only marginal importance to the examination of its main topic: the burgeoning sex tourism industry in the Global South.

Incisive book-size studies of Michel Houellebecq and his oeuvre have been appearing in French under the Rodopi label since the early 2000s.[8] However, for the purposes of this book, only the literary criticism and other analyses that include the novel *Submission* afford the necessary comprehensive treatment of Houellebecq's stance towards Islam and Muslims in relation to the present European context. I will therefore assess developments in Houellebecq's attitude towards Islam primarily in conversation with Russell Williams' monograph *Pathos, Poetry and Politics in Michel Houellebecq's Fiction* (2020) and an essay collection specifically concerned with *Submission* published under the title *Michel Houellebecq, the Cassandra of Freedom* (2022). While its editors, Kochin and Spektorowski, opine that 'no other work of fiction published in the last fifty years has had the impact of Houellebecq's *Submission*', Williams has stressed a need for moving away from Houellebecq's 'extra-literary reputation' to 'refocus critical discussion of Michel Houellebecq on his texts'.[9] Challenging accusations that Houellebecq's novels lack style and that his success must be attributed to hype, provocation and vulgarity, Williams asserts that a careful examination of Houellebecq's writings will show that 'poetry is at the very heart of his literary style'.[10] Evidence of Houellebecq's acceptance as a literary writer and public figure, while he retained his reputation as the *enfant terrible* of the French cultural scene, is evinced by several prize awards and honours, including the 2010 Prix Goncourt for the novel *The Map and the Territory*, the first Oswald Spengler Prize in 2018, and, a year later, the Legion d'Honneur.

Comte, Lovecraft, Schopenhauer: The Early Readings and Writings of Michel Houellebecq

Although Michel Houellebecq's fame as a writer rests on his novels, his first book-length publication was an essay volume on the American fantasy and horror fiction writer H. P. Lovecraft (1890–1937). It was originally published in French in 1991; an English translation with an introduction by Stephen King first appeared in 2005 and was reissued in 2019. According to Houellebecq expert Agathe Novak-Lechevalier, these essays are already suffused with the influence of the German philosopher Arthur Schopenhauer (1788–1860), whose work Houellebecq had been reading since the early 1980s.[11] Although he later shifted away from the German pessimist towards the writings and ideas of the French positivist August Comte (1798–1857), Houellebecq returned to Schopenhauer in 2005, translating and commenting on selected passages from *The*

World as Will and Representation and from the essay 'Aphorisms on the Wisdom of Life', only to abandon the project again until it was finally brought to fruition in 2016 (with an English translation appearing in 2020).

Readers of the Lovecraft volume may be forgiven for taking the title *H. P. Lovecraft: Against the World, Against Life* on face value as affirmation of Houellebecq's and Lovecraft's shared misanthropic outlook on human existence. Closer inspection of the various essays, however, shows that the affinity between today's most prominent French writer and the American cult author cannot be simply reduced to a commonly-held nihilist world-view; Houellebecq's identification with Lovecraft is more complex and multifaceted than that.[12] First of all there is a tension between what Houellebecq has called Lovecraft's 'absolute materialism' (32) and the latter's adamant rejection of literary realism. Also, the total absence in Lovecraft's stories of any allusions 'to the two realities to which we generally ascribe great importance: sex and money' (71) stands in marked contrast to Houellebecq's own preoccupations with precisely these two subjects. Houellebecq says as much himself in the volume's eponymous essay:

> The value of a human being today is measured in terms of his economic efficiency and his erotic potential – that is to say, in terms of the two things that Lovecraft most despised.[13]

Whereas Lovecraft accepted living in dignified poverty, after initially struggling to make a living, Houellebecq is now not only a bestselling author – one critic has even categorised him as a 'finance novelist'.[14] On the other hand, it is not difficult to see Houellebecq agreeing with Lovecraft's view of 'religions as so many sugar-coated illusions made obsolete by the progress of science' (40), arguing that their founding mythologies are indeed grounded in theogonies that must be considered as 'purely imaginary creations' (32). Also significant in this regard is the connection Houellebecq has signalled between Lovecraft's racism and 'its essential and most profound core: *fear*' (32, original italics).[15] Together with a fascination for Lovecraft's orientalist demonisation of Arabs and his use of other tropes that seem clearly inspired by the tales of the *Arabian Nights*, this makes for an intriguing link with Houellebecq's own literary exploitation of Islamophobia. However, here it is again important to caution against reductionist interpretations and to recognise the aesthetics that underlie Houellebecq's interest in poetics: 'To transform perceptions of ordinary life into an infinite source of nightmares is the wild hope of every writer of weird fiction' (88).[16]

With just over fifty pages, *In the Presence of Schopenhauer* is about half the length of the Lovecraft volume. However, when commenting on the impact of this cantankerous nineteenth-century thinker, Houellebecq notes that, although already widely read in both French and foreign literature, with regard to philosophy he had not gone any further than Nietzsche, but that his 'reading of Schopenhauer changed everything' (2). From the volume's first two chapters, it quickly becomes clear that – for Houellebecq – the attraction of Schopenhauer's philosophy lies first and foremost in the quality of his 'aesthetic contemplation' (13):

> Peaceful contemplation, detached from all thought and desire, of all the objects of the world: this is Schopenhauer's aesthetic, as simple as it is profoundly original, as far removed from classicism as from romanticism. (24)

Further reading shows that Houellebecq's appreciation of Schopenhauer is somewhat more complex. Sharing the latter's unsentimental conviction of the absurdity of all life, human, animal and plant alike, Houellebecq cites Schopenhauer's exclamation 'what an execrable thing is this nature of which we are part!' (32), before sarcastically dedicating the chapter in question to ecologists and dispelling any illusions of some kind of serene world-view. Whereas on the one hand, another chapter called 'The Theatre of the World' exudes resignation to the fact that our existential plane merely forms a stage on which the tragedy of human life – whether the result of malice or blind fate – unfolds, the next one offers a Buddhist-like guideline for practical wisdom in a 'purely immanent sense' (41). It is the compassion shining through in Schopenhauer's 'Aphorisms' that also informs the changing view in Houellebecq's later novels regarding the utility of religion – albeit with the caveat that humans remain inescapably bound to their individuality and constricted by their innate intellectual abilities. Here Houellebecq quotes a line from Schopenhauer containing an Islamic referent that aligns well with some of his own pronouncements about Muslims and Islam: '*until the end of his days a fool remains a fool, a moron remains a moron, even if he is in paradise and surrounded by* houris' (45, original italics).[17]

Although Houellebecq never wrote an essay volume on the third major influence on his thinking and writing, in the opening pages of his Schopenhauer text he confesses that his encounter with Auguste Comte in the early 1990s constituted a 'second philosophical shock' (3). Later, Houellebecq showcased his interest in the father of positivism through *Platform*'s main character. Also named Michel, this official in the Ministry of Culture is an enthusiastic reader of Auguste Comte's *Course in Positive Philosophy*:

> I liked the tedious, dense book; often I would reread a page three or four times. It took me almost three weeks to finish Lesson Fifty: 'Preliminary Considerations on Social Statics, or the General Theory of the Spontaneous Order of Human Society'. I certainly needed some theory to help me take stock of my social status. (178)[18]

Summarising the influence of the two philosophers on Houellebecq, Guillermo Graíño Ferrer estimates that, when it comes to dealing with the individual human condition, Houellebecq is 'at his most Schopenhauerian', but shows himself 'at his most Comtean' in relating these experiences to the historical moment in which they unfold.[19]

Spectres of Jihad

Even though it is only mentioned explicitly (and even then just briefly) towards the end of the novel, *Platform*'s story unfolds against a background of violent Islamism. More persistent attention is actually paid to the prevailing social mores of Muslims towards sex, a matter that is also at the centre of the satirical treatment of Islam and its followers in *The Possibility of an Island*. Moreover, in *Platform*, opinions and views of Islam are primarily refracted through the lenses of three characters with Arab-Muslim backgrounds: Aicha, the housekeeper of the protagonist's father; an expatriate Egyptian biochemist whom the protagonist encounters during a holiday in Egypt; and a Jordanian banker whom he meets on his final trip to Thailand. Houellebecq thus uses insider voices to air critical or openly negative opinions about Muslims and their religion.

Platform begins with chief protagonist (also named Michel) settling the affairs of his father, a murder victim who turns out to have been killed by his housekeeper's brother. This twenty-something woman of North African origin appears to have been in an – according to the son highly unlikely – intimate relationship with the retired septuagenarian: 'she seemed like a serious girl, and my father was hardly a ladies' man' (21). Ostracised by her family, Aicha complains that, after performing Hajj two years earlier, her father had become detached and withdrawn ('you can't get a word out of him'), while her brothers are drunk idiots who 'encourage each other's stupidity' (22). These revelations trigger the first Islamophobic sentiments on the part of the emotionally awkward loner Michel, uncomfortable with Aicha's candidness about her personal life:

> At that moment I had a vision of migratory flows crisscrossing Europe like blood vessels; Muslims appeared as clots that were only slowly reabsorbed. (22)

There is a lot of subtext to this phrase. Likening streams of migrants entering Europe to a blood flow conjures up uncomfortable associations with other notions loaded with blood symbolism, such as the sinister nationalist *Blut und Boden* ('blood and soil') slogan adopted by the Nazis, or the notorious 1968 'Rivers of Blood' speech by the ultra-conservative British MP Enoch Powell (1912–98).[20] The same is true of the comparison of Muslims to blood clots potentially hindering or inhibiting the cardiovascular system. Such turning of immigrants into pathogens has remained a persistent trope that was also employed by Donald Trump during a 2023 election rally in New Hampshire, when he accused immigrants of 'poisoning the blood of the country'.[21]

For the next diatribe against Islam Houellebecq introduces another Muslim character, this time an Egyptian who had moved to England immediately after having graduated as a biochemist. While he 'could not find words harsh enough to revile Islam', the expatriate also attached great importance to stressing that 'Egyptians were not Arabs' (250). The scientist's rejection of Islam hinged mainly on two arguments, the first being that the religion's genesis must be attributed to its arid environment:

> '[...] Islam was born deep in the desert amidst scorpions, camels and wild beasts of every order. Do you know what I call Muslims? The losers of the Sahara. That's what they deserve to be called. Do you think Islam could have been born in such a magnificent place?' (with genuine feeling, he motioned again to the Nile valley). 'No, *monsieur*. Islam could only have been born in a stupid desert, among filthy Bedouins who had nothing better to do than [...]' [there follows an allegation of bestiality] (251)

The second argument concerning its further development is more theological in nature. Insistence that, since its emergence, Islam has remained locked in 'an intellectual vacuum, an absolute void' leads the biochemist to reason that

> the closer a religion comes to monotheism [...] the more cruel and inhuman it becomes; and of all religions, Islam imposes the most radical monotheism. From its beginnings, it has been characterised by an uninterrupted series of wars and invasions and massacres; never, for as long as it exists, will peace reign in the world. Neither, in Muslim countries, will intellect and talent find a home; if there were Arab mathematicians, poets and scientists, it is simply because they lost the faith.[22] Simply reading the Koran, one cannot help but be struck by the regrettable tautology which typifies the work. (251)

Whereas the biochemist's scientific background might warrant the assumption that he subscribes to the kind of positivism advocated by August Comte, this passage actually reads more like a vulgarisation of

Ernest Renan's thesis that the only thing the Semitic peoples have had to offer to humankind was their monotheist religion.[23]

Throughout *Platform*, however, the main reason for criticising Islam is Muslim attitudes towards sex, in terms of both sexual orientation and the act of intercourse outside of wedlock. At various instances, Michel and his tourism business executive friends Valérie (also his lover) and Jean-Yves return to the problems they expect in Muslim countries with rolling out their plans for a worldwide network of resorts catering to adult travellers willing to pay for sex during their holidays.[24] This episode confirms an observation by the political scientists Ronald Inglehart and Pippa Norris that '"eros" not "demos" is the main point of contention between Islamic and Western societies'.[25] Only in the instance of the kidnapping of a German tourist and his female Thai companion in the southern Thai town of Hat Yai is an explicit connection made between interaction between the sexes and religiously-inspired political violence:

> the two young people would be executed for behaviour in contravention of Islamic law. For some months there had indeed been an increase in the activities of Islamic movements, supported by Libya, in the border area with Malaysia; but this was the first time that they had attacked people. (309)[26]

The subsequent assault on another Thai resort by 'three men wearing turbans, moving swiftly in our direction, machine-guns in hand' (331), which leaves Valérie dead, Jean-Yves injured and Michel in a state of catatonic trauma, is no longer directly linked to the trio's plans for their envisaged niche market of international leisure and tourism; instead the focus has indeed shifted to concerns about a worldwide jihad. The Thai police, French embassy officials and American intelligence officers are all anxious to determine 'whether an international terrorist network had established a foothold in Thailand, or whether they were dealing with Malay separatists' (339). Under the pressure of his traumatic experience and subsequent interrogations by the authorities, Michel becomes virulently Islamophobic:

> Islam had wrecked my life, and Islam was certainly something which I could hate; in the days that followed, I devoted myself to trying to feel hatred for Muslims. I was quite good at it, and I started to follow the international news again. Every time I heard that a Palestinian terrorist, or a Palestinian child or pregnant Palestinian woman had been gunned down in the Gaza Strip, I felt a quiver of enthusiasm at the thought that it meant one less Muslim. Yes, it was possible to live like this. (349)

Hiding behind the screen of literary characters as mouthpieces for dismissive and negative portrayals of Islam and Muslims has not convinced all commentators. Russell Williams cites the Moroccan poet and scholar of literature Abdel-Ilah al-Salhi, who maintains that the viewpoints expressed by Aicha and the Egyptian biochemist are Houellebecq's 'own unframed opinions' and that, on account of their literary stature, authors like him actually make shameful hate speech *salonfähig*.[27] Moving away from the opinion and editorial pages in the media, Williams does make a valid point by noting that isolating passages in a novel from their literary context 'is ultimately a reductive analysis since it negates any critical claims for parody, satire or criticism present in the novel, ultimately denying the text's literary status, turning it into little more than a political or ideological pamphlet' (31).[28] Moreover, it is actually the third Muslim character who facilitates a corrective of the uncompromisingly negative depictions of Muslims in *Platform* and the resulting abject Islamophobia on the part of the main protagonist. It is the alternative scenario sketched by a Jordanian banker that allays Michel's fear of Islam. In the former's estimation:

> The problem with Muslims, he told me, was that the Paradise promised by the prophet already existed here on earth: there were places on earth where young, available, lascivious girls danced for the pleasure of men, where one could become drunk on nectar [...] To gain admission, there was absolutely no need to fulfil the seven duties of a Muslim, nor to engage in holy war; all you had to do was pay a couple of dollars. (350)

Aside from echoing Schopenhauer's *houri* aphorism, the financier is evidently also a proponent of free market dynamics, as he goes on to explain that – realising capitalism would triumph in the end – increasing numbers of his fellow Arabs 'were turning their backs on Islam'. This also convinces Michel that 'Islam was doomed' (351). An avid reader of Comte's *Course in Positive Philosophy*, he adds that 'this simple thought was sufficient to dispel my hatred' (351). Although it leaves anti-religious attitudes intact, and indeed also a space for further satirising Islam, this observation on the part of Michel at least deflects the outright dehumanisation of its adherents. Exhibiting a degree of forgiveness that Houellebecq appears to have taken away from his readings about Schopenhauer's take on compassion, it indicates a shifting disposition vis-à-vis religions that also distinguishes his subsequent novels about Islamism.[29]

Written a full decade later than Houellebecq's *Platform*, Mathias Énard's *The Street of Thieves* is a story of radicalisation and migration told in three parts against the background of the 2011 uprisings in the Arab world that became known as the 'Arab Spring'.[30] The title refers to a street in an immigrant neighbourhood of Barcelona and is also the name of the novel's final part. The first part, entitled 'straits', is set in Tangier proper and what used to be its International Zone, while the middle part takes place on board a ferry operating between Tangier and Spain, and in the Spanish port city of Algeciras. Interspersed are digressions into the travels of Ibn Battuta (1303–68/77), a scholar from Tangier who for more than thirty years traversed the wider Muslim world, crossing the Indian Ocean and even continuing to the Far East.[31] The novel's main character is a young Moroccan who falls in the hands of an Islamist organisation after having been ostracised by his family following a sexual liaison with a female cousin. However, he gets second thoughts when it dawns on him that the group is implicated in acts of terrorism. That his own convictions do not tally with the organisation's Salafi leanings is illustrated not only by his reading interests, which range from French and American crime novels to the classical poetry of Abu Nuwas and al-Mutannabi or the scholarship of al-Jahiz and Ibn Kathir, but also by the symbolic meaning of his name:

> Lakhdar. As he later explains to his Spanish girlfriend: 'Lakhdar had two meanings, "green", but also "prosperous". Green is the colour of Islam. Maybe that's why my father chose it. There's also a prophet who was important to mystics. Khidr the Green. He appears in the Cave Sura'. (102)[32]

Making such a mystical connection would not sit well with the Group for the Propagation of Koranic Thought which he had joined. That Sufism is clearly at odds with the views of the group's leader Sheikh Nureddin and his entourage is evinced by the following passage, in which they criticise the sermon given at a Tangier mosque:

> Like every Friday, they were going over the sermon of the detested Imam, whom they would end up calling a *mystique*, in French. For Sheikh Nureddin, *mystique* was an insult even worse than *miscreant* [...] Sufis or those who were suspected of being so were his bête noire, almost as bad as Marxists. Right now, the conversation centred on the Cave, and on its commentary; one was asking why the Imam hadn't insisted on the first verses, that attack against the Christians, and the fact that God had no son; the other was worried about the emphasis placed on the dog, the guardian of the Seven Sleepers, who watched over them during their sleep; a third found that there really were more pressing matters to concern oneself with than the land of Gog and Magog and the Two-Horned Alexander. (64)

A very different individual from the main character in Selimović's *Death and the Dervish*, this Nureddin turns out to have an impressive international network that enables him to seek out a comfortable refuge in the Persian Gulf when his organisation finds itself in the authorities' cross-hairs following bomb attacks in Marrakesh and Tangier. As Lakhdar tries to disentangle himself from the group, his knowledge of Arabic, French and some Spanish enables him to find work as a translator for a French businessman in Tangier's commercial district. Although it looks at first that he has found an escape, cutting off ties definitively proves difficult, leaving Lakhdar with the ominous feeling that this life is determined by external factors beyond his control:

> I didn't know that I had only four months left there; I didn't know that I would leave for Spain, but I could glimpse the hand of Fate, the power of the interconnectedness of invisible causal series called Fate. Going back to the Group, at nightfall, the world seemed like it was on fire; Morocco, Tunisia, Libya, Syria, Greece, all of Europe, everything was burning. (77)

Lakhdar makes another step towards his dream of moving to Europe, when he is hired as a steward on a ferry service operating between Tangier and Algeciras in Spain. Initially sequestered on the ship, when he is finally granted a temporary visa that allows him to disembark, he initially disappears into the underground world of illegal immigration in Andalusia, but eventually makes it to Barcelona, home town of a Spanish student of Arabic, named Judit, whom he had befriended earlier when she visited Morocco. However, the reappearance of Sheikh Nureddin and his former best friend Bassam give Lakhdar the uneasy feeling that his Islamist association is catching up with him, and he begins to develop an increasing sense of paranoia. In *The Street of Thieves* this is represented by the Sheikh's references to the Battle of Badr, in which the young Muslim community led by Muhammad defeat its more powerful Meccan adversaries, and his repeated invocation of an ominous passage from the thirty-third chapter of the Qur'an:

> *If the people question you about the Final Hour, reply: 'Only God knows about it.' What do you know about it? It could be that the Hour is near. God has cursed the Infidels and has prepared a burning furnace for them, where they will remain for eternity, without finding either ally or aid.* (264, original italics)[33]

Convinced that Bassam, who looks at Sheikh Nureddin 'as if the Prophet himself were appearing' (263), will take this as a signal to spring into action once more, in a momentary lapse of reason Lakhdar stabs his childhood friend to death because, 'eaten way by a necrosis of the soul [...] Bassam was one of those birds of the apocalypse who keep circling' (272). The effect of this act of despair on Lakhdar's own state of mind is captured in a final self-reflection while in custody with the Spanish police as he awaits trial on terrorism charges:

I am not a murderer. I'm more than that.
I'm not a Moroccan, I'm not a Frenchman, I'm not a Spaniard, I'm more than that.
I'm not a Muslim, I'm more than that.
Do what you will with me. (274)

Satirising Islam, Serious about Religion

Indicative of Houellebecq's changing attitude towards Islam and Muslims is the shift of attention in *The Possibility of an Island* from jihadism towards more benign forms of Islamic activism. At the beginning of this futuristic novel, its main character, known as Daniel1, explains that he feels safe enough satirising Islam in his comedy routines because the influence of the violent Islamists is on the wane, comparing them to the Punks of the 1970s and 1980s: 'they had been made obsolete by the appearance of polite, gentle and pious Muslims from the Tabligh movement – a kind of equivalent of New Wave' (34). This refers to the Tabligh Jama'at, a *da'wa* or religious propagation organisation that had first emerged in British India in the late 1920s. With its headquarters still located near the Indian capital New Delhi, it has since morphed into a global phenomenon, becoming one of the most widespread exponents of Islamic revivalism dedicated to the peaceful dissemination of Islam's religious teachings. Members of the movement are expected to spend regular and extensive time on so-called proselytising tours (*khuruj*), ranging from a few days a month to lengthy missions lasting up to four consecutive months.[34]

In spite of this apparent mellowing towards Islam, *The Possibility of an Island* nevertheless ridicules the religion through its chief protagonist, who is gaining fame – and making a fortune – as a stand-up comedian, actor and scenarist by targeting Muslims. To give his novels an air of realism, Houellebecq is in the habit of incorporating actual French politicians and other public figures into the narrative. Showcasing the French-Moroccan comedian Jamel Debbouze as one of Daniel's artistic collaborators makes *The Possibility of an Island* extra-edgy: aged fifteen, Debbouze was involved in the accidental death of another youth hailing from Réunion, the birth island of Houellebecq himself. Although the incident left Debbouze with a disabled right arm, the family of the dead teenager nevertheless sued him for culpability (without success) and also prevented Debbouze from ever performing on Réunion. As in the case of *Platform*, in this novel too the focus is on eros rather than demos. Daniel's satire revolves around the sexual mores in Muslim societies, staging a provocative comedy routine in which 'Arab immigrant girls were once again available in the sexual market places' (34), and producing a film about promiscuous Palestinian girls. Daniel's 'Islamophobic burlesque' is thus extended to the Middle East conflict and even infused with 'a touch of anti-Semitism aimed at counterbalancing the rather anti-Arab nature of the show' (36). With apparent satisfaction, Daniel relates that a critic writing for the periodical *Le Point* noted how 'the religions of the book "were played against each other"'. He goes on to explain that his comedy is ultimately directed against 'all forms of rebellion, of nationalist or revolutionary struggle, and in reality against political action itself', gleefully admitting that it is imbued with 'a vein of *right-wing anarchy*' (45). Driving the provocation even further, he invokes the names of other controversial cultural figures, such as the anti-Semitic writer Louis-Fernand Céline and the irreverent film director Michel Audiard. Daniel even claims taking inspiration from St Paul's premise of divine authority for 'a sombre meditation, not unlike that of Christian apologetics' – albeit for the purpose of 'evacuating any theological notion and developing a structural and essentially mathematical argument, based notably on the concept of "well-ordering"' (46).

This – in itself serious – turn of thought is in line with a confession further on in the novel, where Daniel admits to having 'never held any religious belief' and that his 'atheism was so monolithic, so radical' (221) that he had never been able to entertain the idea of the existence of such entities as souls or spirits. However, again it appears that something has shifted: although when he debated with Christians, Muslims and Jews about matters of faith, it had always been his position that 'their beliefs were to be taken *ironically*', he can imagine that 'they were a sign of recognition, a sort of password allowing them access to the community of believers' (221). This is further elaborated in another passage on Islam, set several decades further in the future, in which one of Daniel1's 'neohuman' successors, named Daniel25, explains how Islam has succeeded in surpassing Christianity as Europe's dominant religion and holding out longest against the rise of a new religious movement called the Elohimite Church:

> This expansion of Islam was only made possible thanks to the introduction of a series of compromises, under the influence of a new generation of imams who, inspired by the Catholic tradition, reality shows and American televangelists' sense of spectacle, developed for the Muslim public an edifying script for life based on conversion and forgiveness of sin. (309)

Such hints at a growing appreciation for Christianity, and Catholicism in particular, were already present in *Platform*, namely in the episode about Michel's meeting with the Egyptian biochemist, whose rejection of Islam on account of its radical monotheism is contrasted with an admiration for the theological subtleties of Catholicism:

> Far from being an attempt at abstraction, as it is sometimes portrayed, the move towards monotheism is nothing more than a shift toward mindlessness. Note that Catholicism, a subtle religion, and one which I respect, which well knew what suited human nature, quickly moved away from the monotheism imposed by its initial doctrine, Through the dogma of the Trinity and the cult of the Virgin and the Saints, the recognition of the role played by the powers of darkness, little by little it reconstituted an authentic polytheism; it was only by doing so that it succeeded in covering the earth with numberless artistic splendours. (253)

In *The Possibility of an Island*, Houellebecq writes that it was only thanks to what he calls the hypocritical adoption by Muslims of Christian 'dogmas that were sufficiently primitive to be grasped by the greatest minds while persevering sufficient ambiguity to seduce the most agile minds' (310) that Islam succeeded in reaching the same hegemonic position in Europe as Christianity had once occupied. However, eventually Islam suffered the same fate as Communism had several decades earlier:

> It then became perfectly clear, in the eyes of the Western populations, that all the countries of the Dar al-Islam had only been kept in their primitive ignorance and constraint; deprived of their bases in the rear, the Western Islamist movements collapsed at a stroke.[35]

These particular passages are a significant departure from the menacing depictions of religiously inspired violence by Muslims and of Islam as the most uncompromising form of radical monotheism in *Platform*. The connection between Islam and the 'eros factor' is maintained, however, because in *The Possibility of an Island* too, Islam's appeal to immigrants from the Maghreb and Africa, as well as 'some "indigenous" Europeans', is attributed to its macho image: 'If the abandonment of machismo had effectively made men unhappy, it had not actually made women happy' (308). The same trope recurs yet again in *Submission*.

Lectures on Islam

The main character in *Submission* works as a scholar of literature specialised in the work of Joris-Karl Huysmans (1848–1907), the French author who was one of the trailblazers of the French Decadent movement before converting to Catholicism. Although working as an academic at the Sorbonne, François is no intellectual and admits so himself at various points in the novel. Professing his ignorance of religion, history, architecture – or France in general for that matter – he is satisfied with a steady but unspectacular rise through the ranks at the Sorbonne. François has no real interest in politics either, and his fascination with the rise to power of Mohammed Ben Abbes and his French Muslim Brotherhood is only triggered by its unusual trajectory. Although bearing the same name as the influential Islamist movement established in Egypt in 1928, which then branched out to other Arab countries, Ben Abbes's organisation only came into being after the 2017 presidential elections in France. It was also founded on very different principles from those of an earlier Islamic Party, the French Muslim Party, which had collapsed on account of its leader's anti-Semitism. Although Ben Abbes's party indeed resembles the Egyptian Muslim Brotherhood in its successful mobilisation of public support via 'a network of youth groups, cultural institutions and charities' (41), ideologically it has nothing to do with its Egyptian namesake. Skilfully navigating between toned-down support for the Palestinian cause and maintaining cordial relations with France's Jewish community, while also courting the Catholics, according to projections for the 2022 elections Ben Abbes is trailing just behind the Socialists. Characterised as a moderate Muslim, he is also described as 'the craftiest, most cunning politician France has known since François Mitterrand'.[36] It is not surprising, therefore, that – in the novel's narrative – he succeeds in getting both the centre-right and left on board for a coalition led by himself. Writing in 2015, Houellebecq is actually describing Islamic moderatism, in Arabic referred to as *wasatiyya*. Over the previous one or two decades this has become an increasingly salient trend throughout the Muslim world, steadily gaining traction in the most diverse Islamic settings. In Indonesia, it has become the most influential strand of politically-engaged Islam, advocated by the country's largest mass organisation of traditional Muslims, while also commanding growing interest in the Persian Gulf States and garnering intellectual support from such figures as the late Yusuf al-Qaradawi (1926–2022).[37]

Faced with the prospect of dismissal from his university job by the new Muslim-led government, François decides to educate himself about things Islamic with the help of two of the novel's auxiliary characters.[38] Initial introductions come from Alain Tanneur, the husband of one of François's colleagues at the Sorbonne, who works at the French internal security service (DGSI).[39] These are followed by conversations with Robert Rediger, a former 'nativist' – *Submission*'s term for identitarians – and convert to Islam. This opportunistic Belgian-born academic is first appointed as the new president of the Sorbonne, then joins the Ben Abbes administration as secretary of universities, before being promoted to foreign minister.[40]

Tanneur having spent almost his entire career monitoring Islamist movements, his lessons provide a subtle insight into the variances found within political Islam, as well as into the motivations of Mohammed Ben Abbes as its most prominent and successful exponent.[41] By way of illustration, I cite a lengthy passage from *Submission* in which the radicalisation expert explains to François the dynamics of Islamism. I will then show how this part of the novel's narrative dovetails with some contemporaneous contributions to the scholarly literature on political thinking in the today's Muslim world. The excerpt begins with a question from François about a spree of political violence:

> 'Do you know who was behind the attacks?'
> 'Who do you think?'
> 'The nativists?'
> 'Yes, partly. And partly young jihadists. It was roughly half and half.'
> 'These jihadists were working for the Muslim Brotherhood?'
> 'No.' He shook his head firmly. 'I've spent fifteen years of my life on this – and I've never found the slightest connection, the slightest contact, between the two groups. The jihadists are rogue Salafists. They may have resorted to violence, instead of prayer, but they're Salafists all the same. For them, France is a land of disbelief – Dar al-Kufr. For the Muslim Brotherhood, France is ready to be absorbed into the Dar al-Islam. More to the point, for the Salafists all authority comes from God. To them the very idea of popular representation is sacrilege. They'd never dreamt of founding, or supporting, a political party. Still, even if they're obsessed with global jihad, the young extremists do want Ben Abbes to win. They don't want to believe in him – for them jihad is the one true path, but some belonged to the National Front before they were radicalised. They'd never actively oppose it. From the beginning, both the National Front and the Muslim Brotherhood have chosen the way of the ballot. They've always wagered that they could take power *and* play by the rules of democracy [...]'[42]

Tanneur's distinction between the Islamist agenda of Ben Abbes's party and jihadists, and – even more importantly – his characterisation of jihadists as 'rogue Salafists', is remarkably similar to the taxonomy proposed by Quintan Wiktorowicz, an actual former CIA officer and White House national security advisor specialising in violent extremism and radicalised Muslims. In a landmark article published in *Studies in Conflict and Terrorism* under the title 'Anatomy of the Salafi Movement' (2006), Wiktorowicz divides Salafis into purists, politicos and jihadis, not only setting the politically quietists purists apart from those translating their convictions into a political ideology, but also taking care to distinguish the latter from violent extremists. Such subtleties are by no means common knowledge in the international intelligence and security community, where all too often religious puritanism and radicalisation are painted with the same brush.

Also, the contrast between Salafist claims of divine authority and their rejection of democratic representation and Ben Abbes's decision to seek power through the ballot box reflects another strand of Islamic political thought that seemed to gain traction in the wake of the uprising in the Arab world in 2011 and 2012. In *The Caliphate of Man* (2019), the political scientist Andrew March offers a dense but lucid analysis of the transformation of Islamists, such as the leader of Tunisia's Ennahda Party Rached Ghannoushi, into proponents of popular sovereignty, willing to adhere to the same rules for the democratic process as Houellebecq's fictional character Mohammed Ben Abbes.[43] Tanneur's observation that Salafists still regard France as part of the *Dar al-Kufr*, whereas the Muslim Brotherhood considers it all but part of the *Dar al-Islam*, strikes a kind of triumphant tone. It also presents a binary opposition that the Swiss-Egyptian Muslim intellectual Tariq Ramadan has tried to overcome by proposing that European democracies neither are Abodes of Unbelief nor belong to the lands of Islam, but constitute a third category, which he calls *Dar al-Shahada*, or 'Abode of Testimony', where Muslims can profess their faith freely on account of the constitutional right to freedom of religion.[44] Tariq Ramadan is also mentioned by name in *Submission*. In one of his fictional lectures to François, Tanneur contrasts this grandson of the founder of the 'real' Muslim Brotherhood, Hasan al-Banna, with Mohammed Ben Abbes:

> Unlike his sometime rival Tariq Ramadan, who'd been tainted by his old Trotskyite connections, Ben Abbes had kept his distance from the anti-capitalist left. He understood that the pro-growth right has won the 'war of ideas,' that the young people today had become *entrepreneurs*, and that no one saw any alternative to the free market. But his real stroke of genius was to grasp that elections would no longer be about the economy, but about values, and that there too, the right was about to win the 'war of ideas' without a fight. Whereas Ramadan presented himself as forward-looking, even revolutionary, Ben Abbes restored its reassuring, traditional value – with a perfume of exoticism that made it all the more attractive. (175–6)[45]

By keeping equidistant from both the Ultra-Right and the 'progressive mummified corpses' still committed to the ideas of 1968 on the extreme Left, Ben Abbes could pursue political options that were not open to others. Whereas the Left was 'paralysed by his multi-cultural background', the National Front could not raise any real objections against Ben Abbes's social conservativism.

The set of values advocated by the Muslim Brotherhood actually points towards an accordance with the ideas operating in nativist circles. Here Tanneur's lectures are complemented with what François learns from his meetings with a fellow academic, Godefroy Lempereur. A self-confessed 'intellectual of the right' and expert on the work of Léon Bloy, the reactionary Catholic and contemporary of Huysmans so admired by Carl Schmitt and Ivo Andrić, Lempereur was quick to point out that there is no such thing as a nativist bloc. Instead it is better regarded as an amalgam of 'Catholics, followers of Bruno Mégret, royalists, neo-pagans [and] hard-core secularists from the far left' (55). It was for a long time powerless owing to internal rivalries and infighting, but this changed with the arrival of what in *Submission* are called the 'indigenous Europeans', who are not just worried about a Muslim takeover, but are also opposed to corporate America and the emerging economic powers India and China. Such reservations towards capitalism also mirror Huysmans' aversion to the Industrial Age and the bourgeoisie it produced, as well as the disdain for money displayed by Houellebecq's own favourite, H. P. Lovecraft. Not unlike the nativists, Ben Abbes's Muslim Brotherhood too is more interested in demographics and education than in economics, or, as Tanneur formulated it, 'if you control the children, you control the future' (66). Tanneur further speculates that Ben Abbes will introduce a two-tier education system by slashing the budget for public education and creating opportunities for privately-funded faith-based schools. This would be dominated, of course, by Muslim charter schools, but open to all French children. Not only would co-education be abolished, but also,

> every teacher would have to be Muslim, No exceptions. Schools would observe Muslim dietary laws and the daily prayers; above all the curriculum itself would have to reflect the teachings of the Koran. (66–7)

This satirised dystopian or utopian – depending on one's viewpoint – scenario gets a darker, more menacing twist. Warned about the prospect of a civil war between proponents and opponents of the new government, François follows Lempereur's advice to leave the capital and seek refuge in the countryside of southern France. In the town of Martel, he unexpectedly runs into Alain Tanneur, who turns out to be a native of the region. This next meeting with the now ex-intelligence officer (who has been forced into early retirement) turns symbolic as he educates François about the history of the town named after Charles Martel, founder of the Carolingian dynasty, who had also continued to fight the invading Muslim armies from North Africa in the decades after defeating them at Poitiers.[46] Tanneur concludes his history lesson with the observation:

> It's true that Christianity and Islam have been at war for a very long time; war has always been one of the major human activities. As Napoleon put it, war is human nature. But with Islam, I think the time has come for accommodation, an alliance. (121–2)

This is where Houllebecq brings the politician François Bayrou into the narrative as an object of ridicule. In *Submission*, this long-serving mayor of Pau and failed presidential candidate is appointed prime minister of the new coalition government, which Tanneur judges a stroke of genius on the part of Ben Abbes:

> If you are looking for a politician who can embody the humanist spirit, he's perfect: he thinks he's Henri the Fourth bringing peace through interfaith dialogue. Plus he plays well with the Catholic base, who find his stupidity reassuring. He's exactly what Ben Abbes needs, since he wants above all to embody a new humanism, and to present Islam as the best possible form of this new, unifying humanism – and by the way, he happens to mean it when he proclaims his respect for the three religions of the book. (125)

At this point it becomes clear how the ideas of the French nativists and the Muslim Brotherhood actually converge. The key notions to pay attention to in this regard are their shared interest in a 'new, unifying humanism' and the 'three religions of the book' (125). Leon Bloy expert and 'intellectual of the right' Godefroy Lempereur had already said as much in an earlier passage. Although the nativists were bracing themselves for a confrontation with the Muslims, anticipating even a full-blown civil war, he is perceptive enough to note that both sides share the conviction that 'atheist humanism – the basis for any "pluralist" society – is doomed' (56), and that followers of the religions of the book subscribe to similar patriarchal values while rejecting the hedonism and individualism that characterises atheists and agnostics. During a press conference, such sentiments are also expressed by Ben Abbes himself:

> Everyone had to admit that times had changed. More and more families – whether Jewish, Christian or Muslim – wanted their children's education to go beyond the mere transmission of knowledge, to include spiritual instruction in their own traditions. This return to religion was deep, it crossed sectarian lines, and state education cold no longer afford to ignore it. It was time to broaden the idea of republican schooling, to bring it into harmony with the great spiritual traditions – Muslim, Christian or Jewish – of our country. (88)

Where nativists and the Muslim Brotherhood differ is in how to go about this. In contrast to nativists like Empereur, who appear to subscribe to Samuel Huntington's 'clash of civilisations' thesis, Ben Abbes remains committed to the existing political system from which he – by his own admission – had benefited more than anyone else.[47] In a similar vein,

Tanneur underscores that 'for all Ben Abbes's ambitions – and he's hugely ambitious – his plans had nothing to do with Islamic Fundamentalism' (127). Houellebecq even lets the former intelligence officer venture into some detailed predictions about the future of France under Ben Abbes's leadership:

> There's an idea you hear in far-right circles, that if the Muslims came to power, Christians would be reduced to second-class citizens, or dhimmis. Now dhimmitude is part of the general principles of Islam, it's true, but in practice the status of dhimmis is a very flexible thing. Islam exists all over the world. The way it is practiced in Saudi Arabia has nothing to do with the Islam you find in Indonesia or Morocco. In France, I promise you, they won't interfere with Christian worship – in fact, the government will increase spending for Catholic organisations and the upkeep of churches. And they'll be able to afford it, since the Gulf States will be giving so much more to the mosques. For these Muslims, the real enemy – the thing they fear and hate – isn't Catholicism. It's secularism. It's laicism. It's atheist materialism. They think of Catholics as fellow believers. Catholicism is a religion of the Book. Catholics are one step away from converting to Islam – that's the true, original Muslim vision of Christianity. (127)[48]

While Ben Abbes's overtures to the Vatican fit within this projection, his personal ambitions extend beyond France, as Houellebecq allows Tanneur to speculate further:

> The first thing you notice is that he's always going on about the Roman Empire. For him, European integration is just a means to this glorious end. The main thrust of his foreign policy will be to shift Europe's centre of gravity to the south. There are already organisations pursuing this goal, like the Union of the Mediterranean. [...] At the same time, we'll see European institutions – which are now anything but democratic – evolve toward more direct democracy. The logical outcome would be a president of Europe elected by the people of Europe. That's when the integration of populous countries with high birth rates, such as Turkey and Egypt, could be key. Ben Abbes's true ambition, I'm sure of it, is eventually to be elected president of Europe – greater Europe, including all the Mediterranean countries. (128–9)

If François needed any more convincing as to which way the political wind was blowing and how to turn it to his own benefit, this was done through the additional nudges he received from Robert Rediger. A skilful manipulator, the newly-appointed president of the Sorbonne appeals to both François's vanity and his venality. After arranging his appointment as editor for the publication of the collected works of Huysmans in the prestigious Pléiade series, Rediger receives François at his opulent Parisian residence, offering him drinks from a choice collection of wines and whiskies. Aside from blatantly displaying the material benefits to be gained from a return to the Islamic Sorbonne (now owned by Saudi Arabia), by way of final seduction, a supposedly accidental glimpse that François is allowed of Rediger's fifteen-year-old second wife serves to showcase the prospects offered by the now legalised polygamy for middle-aged men like themselves. With that, in *Submission* too, Houellebecq returns once again to the eros-over-demos trope. Sensing François's venality, Rediger praises François's thesis on Huysmans, comparing it favourably to his own – allegedly less impressive – dissertation on the French traditionalist René Guénon, but then offers him a copy of his own bestselling book *Ten Questions about Islam.*[49] When opening Rediger's primer on Islam at home, François admits that 'like most men, probably, I skipped the chapters on religious duties, the pillars of wisdom and child-rearing and went straight to chapter seven: "Why polygamy?"' (224). Although, in his recollection, the conversation with Rediger strikes him in hindsight as 'a *well-rehearsed speech*' (226, original italics) and although in his *Ten Questions about Islam* Rediger 'made lots of concessions to the humanist reader' (225), François is suddenly struck by the realisation that '[f]or the first time in my life I'd started thinking about God' (219). Expanding his readings of Rediger's publications to the latter's – bolder – articles about the future of Islam in Europe, François felt himself increasingly drawn to the latter's Guénonian side:

> The nativists and Muslims were in perfect agreement. When it came to rejecting atheism and humanism, or the necessary submission of women, or the return of patriarchy, they were fighting exactly the same fight. And today this fight, to establish a new organic phase of civilisation, could no longer be waged in the name of Christianity. Islam, its sister faith, was newer, simpler and more true. (230)

As was also already the case in *Platform* and *The Possible of an Island*, after that the final chapters of *Submission* seem rushed. Seeing Rediger's scenarios indeed unfold in the policies of Ben Abbes, both domestically and on the European stage, François converts to Islam, thus opening the way for his reappointment as professor at the Islamic University Paris IV-Sorbonne and the prospect of marrying multiple wives.

New Humanism: Satire, Provocation, Prophecy?

Michel Houellebecq may be a more tormented – even damaged – individual than the other writers discussed in this book, but that subtracts nothing from the significance of his writings for the place of Islamic referents in contemporary European literature. Moreover, his descriptions of Islam and Muslims tend to be treated more in the context of his reputation as the *enfant terrible* of contemporary French literature than on account of their artistic merits. To a large extent this must be attributed to Houellebecq's own provocative statements in the media, such as the characterisation of Islam as 'the most stupid religion' during an interview with the literary magazine *Lire* on the occasion of the publication of *Platform*.[50] Such remarks were bound to turn both novel and author into a *cause célèbre*. It appears that Houellebecq is fully aware of the effects of such pronouncements, given what he wrote in the essay on Schopenhauer:

> it indicates the limits that can be accorded to *interviews* with artists; if these artists are endowed with a rich conceptual imagination (and this is sometimes the case), they can amuse themselves by inventing this or that interpretation of their work; but they will never take the exercise altogether seriously. (24–5)[51]

In the light of this observation, interviews such as the one given to *Lire* pose, therefore, a considerable challenge to determining what serves the purpose of literary satire and what constitutes Houllebecq's actual opinion of religions and their followers. Adding to the confusion are the differences between the centrality and serious treatment of Islam in the narrative of *Submission* and the only occasional and disparaging mention of the religion and its followers in *Platform* and *The Possibility of an Island*.

The visionary qualities which some commentators began attributing to Houellebecq in the wake of the 9/11 attacks and subsequent atrocities on Bali and in Thailand's Muslim south must not only be dismissed as gross exaggerations on account of the benefit of hindsight. The explosion of so-called Muslim extremism at the beginning of the twenty-first century forms part of a worldwide upsurge of increasingly radical, uncompromising and also violent exponents of political Islam that had already been going on for decades.[52] That is why I have argued elsewhere that it is more accurate and correct to speak of a greater salience of the political use of Islam than of an Islamic resurgence supposedly appearing out of nowhere.[53] If anything, the references in *Platform* to kidnappings and assassinations in southern Thailand evince detailed research on the part of Houellebecq, rather than the author being endowed with the gift of prophecy. This is even more clearly borne out in *Submission*, the only novel in which the political use of Islam does constitute the main theme. Here, Houellebecq moves from a concern with violent Islamism to a depiction of a culturally hybridised Islam: a kind of 'Euro-Islam' that indeed adheres to the rules of the democratic project, but ultimately only for the sake of implementing the reactionary agenda of an ambitious politician from a Muslim background. The political programme of Mohammed ben Abbes consists of a mix of conservative family values, a re-appreciation of faith-based education, and an economic policy driven by the protection of small-scale entrepreneurship that depends on the thriftiness of family-owned businesses. The prospect of such an alternative future lends itself to an ironic treatment of both European identitarians and Salafi Muslims who find themselves outmanoeuvred by the political savviness of the son of North African migrants. Eager to re-establish the Mediterranean as Rome's *Mare Nostrum* with himself as leader, Ben Abbes models himself more after Emperor Augustus than the Prophet Muhammad.

That Michel Houellebecq's literary output is also affected by the religious turn in philosophy, which I have mentioned in the Introduction, is first discernible in *The Possibility of an Island*, where a cult called the Elohimite church, modelled on the really existing cult of the Raëlians, occupies a central place in the story. It becomes more salient in *Submission* with its academic milieu populated with academics specialising in reactionary Catholics, such as Leon Bloy and Joris-Karl Huysmans, or admirers of the traditionalism of René Guénon. In recent years, Houellebecq has also expressed a growing interest in – and sympathy for – Christianity, and Catholicism in particular.[54] This appears to have developed in tandem with a tendency to increasingly and unambiguously identify with the positions of the political Far Right, something borne out further by the subject matters of the subsequent novels *Serotonin* and *Annihilation*, which no longer feature Islam or Muslims.

The Night Journeys of Mathias Énard

The novel *Zone* tells the professional life story of Francis Servain Mirković, a French intelligence officer of Croatian extraction travelling by overnight train with a suitcase full of secrets collected during fifteen years of service as a spy handler, which he intends to sell to the Vatican. It is an epic novel running over five hundred pages without a full stop, the narrative nonetheless divided in twenty-four chapters – the same number as Homer's *Iliad*, as Énard observed himself.[55] Various themes and tropes from previous chapters recur and come together in this modern-day political history of the Mediterranean. Mirković's reminiscences connect the dots between disparate elements of the fragmentation of Yugoslavia, featuring maverick mercenaries such as the Bolivian-Hungarian-Croatian convert to Islam Eduardo Rózsa-Flores (1960–2009), but including also:

an exposé of Ivo Andrić's schoolfriend Gavrilo Princip; events in the Levant, such as the Arab–Israeli conflict in Palestine and the Lebanese civil war; and the upheavals on the Mediterranean's southern shore, in Meddeb's – and Goytisolo's – Maghreb. Although these reminiscences are predominantly a long reflection by Mirković on his involvement in all kinds of unsavoury political manoeuvrings, he also unveils a passion for reading literature: 'a remnant from Venice, from Marianne great devourer of books, a way to forget to disappear wholly into paper' (149). This twist in the protagonist's interests allows Énard to insert his own erudition into the novel and make reference to such authors as the Alexandrian-based Greek and Italian poets Constantine Cafavy, Stratis Tsirkas and Giuseppe Ungaretti; the Moroccan novelist Mohamed Choukry (who also features in *The Street of Thieves*); his adopted fellow Tangerine Jean Genet (spiritual guide to Juan Goytisolo); and other French writers, including Ferdinand Céline and Marcel Proust. It also enables excursions into Syria and Turkey during the First World War, the Spanish Civil War and the war for independence in Algeria, as well as further back in time to the naval confrontation between the Ottoman Empire and the Holy League at Lepanto: 'another battle between East and West, between North and South, without anyone knowing very clearly who the barbarians were' (48). Also heralding the end of the age of chivalry in the 'maze of modernity' (224), it inspired the Spanish arquebusier Miguel de Cervantes Saavedra to write what is widely regarded as the first modern novel, *Don Quixote*. Another passage records the 'first mass deportation from the Mediterranean' of 1609, when, at the instigation of the Inquisition under Philip III, 'the Mudejars, the poor Moors' were expelled from Spain and 'transported in galleys from all ports of the kingdom to African coasts' (261). It is easy to imagine how many of these passages, as exercises in intertextuality, could have been written by Goytisolo or Meddeb.

That everything is connected is also true of *Compass*. The novel's title refers to a compass that used to belong to Ludwig van Beethoven. Instead of pointing to the north, this device, described as a 'Suhrawardian artifact. A mystical diviner's wand' (323), has an eastern orientation (which sounds tautological). Énard uses it to reintroduce yet again the twelfth-century Persian esotericist, whose thinking was unlocked for Europeans and modern-day Iranians alike by Henri Corbin:[56]

> As Muslim metaphysics was dying out, in the darkness of the West, with the death of Averroes (and Latin Europe died with him), it continued to shine in the East in the mystical theosophy of the disciples of Suhrawardi. This is the path shown by my compass, according to Sarah, the path of Truth, in the rising sun. The first Orientalist in the strict sense of the word was the

> decapitated man of Aleppo, sheikh of Oriental illumination, of *Ishraq*, the Enlightenment of the East. (324)

In *Compass*, the main character, Franz Ritter, learns from an Iranian poet-friend that the ideas of the executed mystic are more interesting and subversive than the 'reading of Shiism as a revolutionary weapon' by the contemporary Iranian philosopher and sociologist Ali Shariati. On further reflection, Ritter realises that 'this philosophical, mystical Iran was always there, flowing like an underground river below the feet of indifferent mullahs; the holder of *erfan*, spiritual knowledge, pursued the tradition of practice and commentary' (325).

Compass too unfolds in the course of a single night and consists of the reminiscences of Franz Ritter, an ailing musicologist specialised in the reception of European music in the late Ottoman Empire. Many of these memories concern the object of his unrequited love, a French cultural historian and literary scholar named Sarah. With this, Énard's focus shifts from the political upheavals in today's Mediterranean dominating the narratives of *Zone* and *The Street of Thieves* to nineteenth- and twentieth-century Central and Western European culture, connecting the novel with the thematic concerns of Navid Kermani in such books as *Between Quran & Kafka* and *Über den Zufall.*

Orientalism as Humanism: Fixing the Ontological Fissure between East and West

This transition from writing about politics to cultural history is already prefigured in *The Street of Thieves*, in an episode in which Lakhdar reunites with Judit, the Spanish student of Arabic and Middle Eastern studies whom he had befriended in Morocco. An enthusiast of modern Arabic literature, she had recommended Lakhdar to read *For Bread Alone* by the Moroccan author Mohamed Choukri – a book that, initially, is not at all to his taste. Moreover, Judit's frustration with the way Arabic is taught at her university in Barcelona leaves Lakhdar confused:

> Through her, I began to hate these puny Arabic scholars in colonial shorts who every day regretted the fact that Spain had for a few centuries been Arabic, sighing over Andalusian texts in which they saw nothing but lexical difficulty. She told me look, we're studying such-or-such a poem by Ibn Zaydún, such-or-such fragment by Ibn Hazm whom they called Abenhazam, and I would rush to a bookshop to find the book in question; most of the time it was a wonder to me, a jewel from another time whose Arabic filled my mouth and eardrums with unprecedented pleasure. (108–9)

In this passage, Énard shows how a Moroccan youth lacking formal education appears more capable than Judit of appreciating not only that cultural hybridity refers to a porosity of geographical borders, but that it is also the product of temporal continuity, which is obscured by the segmentation of cultural history into distinct time periods. Lakhdar's ability to recognise these connections between the past and the present is already illustrated by the earlier episode about his time as a steward on the ferry operating between Morocco and Spain. On board this ship, named *Ibn Battuta*, Lakhdar shows himself astutely aware of the parallels between the travels of this fourteenth-century fellow Tangerine and his own prospects in emigrating to Spain.

In *Compass* too, Énard uses a love-story to introduce his critical reflections on the academic field that used to be called Oriental Studies. In this case it is Franz Ritter's infatuation with Sarah that had motivated him to follow her and travel further east from his own research base in Istanbul to Syria. In Damascus he found himself in a milieu of eccentric scholars that appears very similar to the one sketched in *The Street of Thieves*:

> You found all kinds in Syria, from Swedish specialists in female Arabic writers to Catalan exegetes of Avicenna, most were connected in some way to one of the western research centres housed in Damascus [...] All were trained together, in the purest Orientalist tradition: future scholars, diplomats and spies sat side by side and immersed themselves together in the joys of Arabic grammar and rhetoric. (142)

The parallels do not end there. While his illegal status prevents Lakhdar from enrolling at Barcelona's university, he educates himself in the library, improving his Spanish and learning some Catalan, while also keeping up his French. His readings in Spanish and European history also lead to reflections on the relations between the West and the Muslim world:

> It was strange to think that all our religions were essentially tales: fables in which some believed and others not, an immense storybook, where everyone could choose what he liked – there was a collection called *Islam* which didn't entirely tally with the versions contained in *Christianity*, which itself differed from the *Judaism* collections. (208)

That blindness to the geographical and temporal connectivities of cultures affects not only privileged university students of Arabic from the West is demonstrated in *Compass*. Not abandoning Middle Eastern politics altogether, Énard uses the rise of IS to unpack what later in the novel is referred to as an 'ontological fissure' (347) between East and West. The mouthpiece is one of *Compass*'s minor characters: the mentally unstable archaeologist Bilger. As he drifts between hyperactive megalomania and drug-induced depression, his neurotic diatribes against the average Syrian's lack of interest in their own, particularly pre-Islamic, history are in themselves not inaccurate:

> Europe sapped Antiquity under the Syrians, the Iraqis, the Egyptians. Our triumphant nation appropriated the universal with their monopoly on science and archaeology, dispossessing the colonised populations by means of this pillage of a past that, as a result, they readily experienced as alien: and so brainwashed Islamist wreckers drive tractors all the more easily through ancient cities since they combine their profoundly uncultivated stupidity with the more or less widespread feeling that this heritage is an alien, retroactive emanation of foreign powers. (70)

Shining through in these passages is Mathias Énard's frustration as an erstwhile lecturer of Arabic at the Autonomous University of Barcelona about the disconnect within his own specialist field: between scholars specialising in the modern Middle East and philologists working on the classical heritage of the Arabs. Such compartmentalisation of the study of non-Western cultures may be inevitable owing to the pressures of academic specialisation, but Enard's – and Kermani's – decision to opt for literature can be interpreted as a refusal to give in to this, but instead to offer an alternative way of engagement with the cultures of others. In *Compass* this is further voiced through the cultural historian Sarah, who is showcased as a thoughtful articulator of a holistic, and what she calls humanist, take on Orientalism.

The unwillingness of scholars to see how the compartmentalisation of scholarly fields creates the kind of tunnel vision that hinders an appreciation of the connections and continuities between different aspects of their field of study is already addressed at the very beginning of *Compass*. In the opening pages, Ritter quotes extensively from Sarah's – of course fictional – doctoral thesis, written fifteen years earlier and submitted under the title *Visions of the Other between East and West*.[57] In the three-page excerpt she relates Omar Khayyam to the contemporary novelists Sadegh Hedayat (1903–51) and Julian Gracq (pen name of Louis Poirier, 1910–2007). The former's most renowned novella, *The Blind Owl*, reached a kind of cult status after its posthumous publication following the author's suicide in Paris, in 1951. Its appearance a year later coincided with the release by the same publisher, José Corti, of Julian Gracq's *Le Rivage des Syrtes* (translated as *The Opposing Shore*). It was honoured with the Prix Goncourt, but the author refused to accept the award. This third and most famous novel by Gracq revolves around a decades-long lull in a confrontation that has been going on for centuries between two fictive countries on opposite sides of the

Mediterranean: (Christian?) Orsenna and (Muslim?) Farghestan. While its dream-like descriptions betray the influence Surrealism has exercised on Gracq's superb stylism, its concern with apocalyptic foreboding reflects a widespread thematic concern in contemporary literature with the topos of 'waiting for the barbarians'.[58] Énard and – with him – Kermani too would appreciate this kind of intertextuality, just as they would subscribe to Sarah's proposal at the end of this prologue to her dissertation to research 'this between-space, this bardo, this *barzakh*, the world between worlds into which artists and travellers fall' (16). Énard and Kermani would therefore also share Sarah's anger at the verdict of the 'vexed Orientalists and sleepy mandarins' examining her thesis, who reproached Sarah 'for the "romantic" tone of her preamble and for her "absolutely irrelevant" parallel with Gracq and Kafka'.[59]

The feistiness of this all-too-rare dissenting feminine voice in the world of Orientalist philology is further underscored by the difference in Sarah's and Ritter's dispositions towards their field of study. Elsewhere in *Compass*, Ritter characterises Sarah's thesis as 'a catalogue of melancholics, the strangest catalogue of adventurers into melancholia, of different kinds and from different countries, Sadegh Hedayat, Annemarie Schwarzenbach, Fernando Pessoa, to mention only her favourites' (64).[60] However, critical interrogator that she is, Sarah insists that it is in fact Ritter himself who pines for romantic nostalgia. Ritter is an admirer of Claudio Magris's landmark book *Danube*, a work Sarah condemns as 'terribly "Austro-centrist"' and therefore 'terribly unfair to the Balkans' (30), especially since 'the Danube is the river that links Catholicism, Orthodoxy and Islam'. Although Magris himself was a native of the Friuli border region between Austria, Italy and Slovenia, in Sarah's estimation 'Magris is like you, he's nostalgic. He's a melancholy Trieste native who misses the empire' (31). Ritter and Sarah's diverging viewpoints become clear also from their debates about where the West ends and the East begins. Pushing back at her suggestion that Vienna could be considered a *Porta Orientalis* with the argument that two Ottoman sieges do not make the former Habsburg capital the gateway to the Orient, Sarah retorts:

> That's not the question, the question isn't in the reality of the idea, what interests me is understanding why and how so many travellers have seen Vienna and Budapest as the first 'Oriental' cities, and what that can teach us about the meaning they give to the word. And if Vienna is the *gateway* to the Orient, to what Orient does it lead? (24)

Although he seems to be partially swayed, Ritter nonetheless continues to stubbornly resist:

> There may have been in the cosmopolitanism of Imperial Vienna something of Istanbul, something of the *Öster Reich*, the Empire of the East, but it seems remote, very remote today. It's been a very long time since Vienna was the capital of the Balkans, and the Ottomans no longer exist. (24–5)

These different interpretations of the cultural-historical status of the Vienna of the Habsburgs are replicated in Ritter and Sarah's respective views concerning the place of the Ottoman Empire and Constantinople/ Istanbul in the cultural history of Europe, which Ritter summarises as follows:

> Whether you regard Constantinople as the easternmost city in Europe or the westernmost city in Asia, as an end or a beginning, as a bridge or a border, this mixed nature is fractured by nature, and the place weighs on history as history weighs on humans. For me it was the limit of European music, the most Oriental destination of the indefatigable Liszt, who had drawn its outlines; for Sarah it was the beginning of the land where her travellers had wandered, in both directions. (73)

In a further delineation between the implicit patronising patriarchy of Ritter and the defiant feminine – yet inclusivist – alternative represented by Sarah, Énard describes how Ritter's experimentations with smoking opium in Istanbul had brough him 'closer to Novalis, Berlioz, Nietzsche, Trakl' (80), whereas Sarah dealt not only with Schwarzenbach, Isabella Eberhardt or Gertrude Bell. In an – again fictive – article entitled 'Orientalism is a Humanism' (133), she had also engaged with the Oriental Judaism of Ignaz Goldziher and Gershom Scholem, as well as writing (non-existent) articles on Germain Nouveau (1851–1920), a friend of both Arthur Rimbaud and Paul Verlaine, who – after a mental breakdown – (re)discovered Catholicism and lived the rest of his life as an ascetic. Énard turns Sarah into the mouthpiece for a very critical estimation of the significance of Edward Said's *Orientalism* critique:

> The question was not whether Said was right or wrong in his vision of Orientalism: the problem was the breach, the ontological fissure his readers had allowed between a dominating West and a dominated East, a breach that, by opening up well beyond colonial studies, contributed to the realisation of the model it created, that completed a posteriori the scenario of domination which Said's thinking meant to oppose. Whereas history could be read in an entirely different way, she said, written in an entirely different way, in sharing and continuity. She spoke at length on the postcolonial holy trinity – Said, Bhabha, Spivak: on the question of imperialism, of difference, of the twenty-first century when, facing violence, we needed more than ever to rid ourselves of this absurd idea of the absolute otherness of Islam and to admit not only the terrifying violence of colonialism, but also all that Europe owed to the Orient – the impossibility of separating them from each other, the necessity of changing our perspective. We had to find, she said, beyond

the stupid repentance of some or the colonial nostalgia of others, a new vision that includes the other in the self. On both sides. (347–8)

Reading this passage through the lens of Hamid Dabashi establishes Sarah as his virtual interlocutor. The rejection by Dabashi, himself an admirer and self-proclaimed brother-in-arms of Edward Said, of dichotomous world-views as false binaries that have been rendered obsolete by our 'post-everything' world resonates with Sarah's concern about the 'ontological fissure' between East and West, unwittingly extended by readers of Said's *Orientalism*.[61] Whether one calls it Post-Orientalism (Dabashi) or affirmative Orientalism (King), Sarah's apocryphal article 'Orientalism is a Humanism' (133) chimes with Said's acknowledgement of the commonalities between 'the best Orientalist work' and 'the best humanistic scholarship', as well as Dabashi's appreciation of the likes of Ignaz Goldziher.[62] Similarly, Europe's cultural debt to the East signalled by Sarah finds its counterpart in Hamid Dabashi's *Persophilia*, which describes the fascination of eighteenth- and nineteenth-century European intellectuals with the classical Persian poets, whom Dabashi regards as the embodiment of literary humanism and worldly cosmopolitanism.[63] Dabashi's hermeneutics of alterity, finally, is echoed verbatim in Sarah's remark regarding 'the necessity of accepting alterity as an integral part of ourself, as a fertile contradiction' (136). Moreover, Sarah's assertion – occurring a few lines before the quoted passage above – that writers such as Hedayat and Schwarzenbach 'bring to light the rhizomes of the common construction of modernity' (347) inserts a key notion of Gilles Deleuze into the narrative of *Compass* as well.[64] Aside from underscoring Sarah's insistence at the beginning of the novel that 'there is no such thing as chance, everything is connected' (13), Gilles Deleuze's philosophy of difference also served as a major source of inspiration for Dabashi's hermeneutics of alterity.

In an episode about Franz Ritter's student years in Tübingen, *Compass*'s autodiegetic narrative maps Ritter's own Orientalist trajectory. Ritter had chosen the University of Tübingen over Paris, Rome or Barcelona, because Tübingen was the city where Hölderlin had ended his days locked up in a tower and where Ernst Bloch had lived and worked from 1961 until his death in 1977. It was also the alma mater of the Orientalist Julius Euting (1839–1919) and the last place where another translator of the *Arabian Nights*, Enno Littmann (1875–1959), had taught. Therefore, in Ritter's estimation, 'the prospect of joining Hölderlin's poetry, Enno Littmann's Orientalism, and Ernst Bloch's musical philosophy together seemed a good programme to me' (199). Tübingen was also where Ritter had first read Muhammad Asad's *Road to Mecca*, the book that had driven him from Istanbul to Syria and that he had 'read as if it were the Koran itself' (197). I will expand on this seemingly minor section (taking up only four pages in *Compass*), because it too is an illustration of a kind of humanist Orientalism that makes some unexpected connections:

> In Tübingen, I could see three possible paths: religion, as of Leopold Weiss alias Muhammad Asad; utopia, as in Bloch's *The Spirit of Utopia* or *The Principle of Hope*; or the madness and seclusion of Hölderlin. (198)

This passage forms part of a section in which Franz Ritter looks back on his failed love life and futile search for spirituality after he returned to Tübingen from a conference on Arabic literature and occultism, where he had first met Sarah. The conference was held in the Rhineland town of Hainsfeld: 'the home of Joseph von Hammer Purgstall, first great Austrian Orientalist, translator of the *Arabian Nights* and of Hafez's *Divan*, historian of the Ottoman Empire' (36). Everything is connected, or as Ritter put it: 'fate changes course, bends, makes a detour' (196). Two of these three individuals, Ernst Bloch and Friedrich Hölderlin, already feature in the chapter on Navid Kermani. In *Compass*, Énard brings the Romantic poet and Marxist philosopher back together again, but then pairs this duo with a Jewish convert to Islam.

The Placeless Cosmopolitanism of Leopold Weiss, alias Muhammad Asad

The writings and ideas of Muhammad Asad, born Leopold Weiss (1900–92), have exercised such an extraordinary influence on the way Islam is viewed by Muslims and non-Muslim westerners alike that they deserve some further elaboration in the present context.[65] Originating from Lemberg, then capital of the Kingdom of Galicia, a crown domain within the dual monarchy of Austria-Hungary, and now the city of Lviv (or Lvov in Polish) in Ukraine, Leopold Weiss spent his early childhood in what Joseph Roth later characterised as a 'city of erased borders', a kind of 'little Vienna' where German was spoken alongside Polish, Ukrainian and Yiddish.[66] The grandson of a rabbi and son of an assimilated Jewish lawyer, Weiss was later educated in Vienna, but dropped out of university (to the great dismay of his father) in order to pursue a career in journalism and to live a Bohemian lifestyle.[67] Already before his conversion to Islam in 1926–7, at which time he adopted the name Muhammad Asad (Asad being Arabic for lion – a reference to his birth name Leopold), Weiss had made his name as a Middle East correspondent, writing travel reports from Palestine, Egypt, Syria, Iraq, Iran and Afghanistan for quality newspapers in Germany and the Netherlands. It was at the behest of the editors of the *Frankfurter Zeitung* (where Ernst Bloch too worked as a columnist) that he wrote his first book in 1924, *Unromantisches Morgenland: Aus dem Tagebuch einer Reise* (translated into English in 2004 and published under the title *The Unromantic Orient*).[68] The very title is an evident nod to Oswald Spengler's seminal *Untergang des Abendlandes* (*The Decline of the West*), the book that captured like no other the cultural pessimism prevailing in German-speaking Europe during the Weimar Republic years (1918–33), and standing in marked contrast to 'Roaring Twenties' inter-war Berlin or New York.[69] Aside from deploring the interbellum's maldevelopment and nihilism, Weiss's early writings also evince a vehement rejection of Zionism and a kind of 'reverse culture shock' that made him regard the Muslim East as a viable alternative.[70] Consequently, Weiss resolved to seek out a new future in the Muslim world, first embracing Islam in Berlin, in 1926. It also awakened in him an awareness of the 'Oriental origins' of the Jews. Gravitating around the figure of Abraham as the primordial monotheist, this notion was not only advocated by the likes of Martin Buber, Hans Kohn and Jacob Wassermann, but also exploited by anti-Semites.[71] Formalising his conversion a year later in Cairo in order to obtain the required documentation to perform his first pilgrimage to Mecca, for the next three decades Muhammad Asad lived almost exclusively in the Muslim world, except for a few brief visits to Europe, including a failed attempt to save his father, sister and stepmother from the Holocaust. The first five of these years were spent in the Arabian Peninsula (1927–32), where his son, the later anthropologist Talal Asad, was born. He regarded the nascent Kingdom of Saudi Arabia as a modern-day manifestation of the authentic Islamic lifestyle he then associated with the nomadic existence of the pastoral Bedouin rather than the decadent urbanity of Muslim city-dwellers.[72] This was followed by a twenty-year residency in British India (including internment as an enemy alien during the Second World War) and early independent Pakistan, of which he became a citizen. After a brief career as a senior civil servant and diplomat, Asad resigned as the country's permanent representative to the UN in New York, because of the Pakistani government's objection to his marrying the American-Polish convert Pola Hamida as his fifth wife. Initially living an itinerant life between America, Germany, Lebanon, Pakistan and Syria, the couple settled in Switzerland (1959–64), where Asad collaborated closely with the exiled Egyptian Said Ramadan, son-in-law of te Muslim Brotherhood founder Hasan al-Banna and father of

Tariq Ramadan.[73] Next, Asad and his wife lived for almost twenty years in Tangier, before spending their twilight years in Portugal (1983–7) and southern Spain (1987–92). It is a life story that warrants Dominik Schlosser's characterisation of Leopold Weiss/Muhammad Asad as a polyglot intellectual and independent scholar of Islam, a 'placeless cosmopolitan' (23), 'cultural mediator' and 'border crosser between East and West' (377–8).[74]

Disenchantment with the direction in which Western modernity was moving led Muhammad Asad to project a binary opposition between the inevitable secularisation of the world of Christendom, which he attributed to the dominance of Pauline theology and its concomitant body–soul dichotomy, and Islam's alternative religious anthropology, which retains an integral view of human nature and denies such a division between the physical-material and mental-spiritual domains.[75] Aside from their sharing similar views on masculinity and patriarchy as Houellebecq's fictional character Robert Rudiger in *Submission*, it is also possible to draw a further parallel between Asad's pessimism and Houellebecq's disappointment at the impoverishing effects of modern-day hedonism and empty materialism on Europe's civilisational achievements; except that Houellebecq's use of irony and satire, whereby Islam functions as a pharmakon in the Derridean sense of the word, stands in marked contrast to Asad's turn to Islam as a genuine panacea for these afflictions.[76] Throughout his years in the Muslim world, first as a cheerleader for Arabia's Wahhabi leader Abd al-Aziz Ibn Saud, and later as an advocate of Pakistan as a blueprint for a modern Islamic community, as well as a scholar of Islam sponsored by the Saudi-based Muslim World League, Asad propagated Islam of a total way of life – or *manhaj*, as Islamist ideologues, such as Pakistan's Abu'l-Ala Mawdudi and the Egyptian Sayyid Qutb, had called it.[77]

In *Compass*, the musicologist Franz Ritter is not so much interested in Muhammad Asad's Islamist agenda as attracted by the aesthetics of the Islamic call to prayer as described by Asad in *The Road to Mecca*:

> I remember precisely the phrases that had taken my breath away and brought tears to my eyes: 'This sonorous, solemn mingling and parting of voices is unlike any other chant of man. And as my heart pounds up to my throat in excited love for this city and its sounds, I begin to grasp that all my wanderings have always had but one meaning: to grasp the meaning of this call …' The meaning of the call to prayer, of the *Allah Akbar* ululated at the top of all the minarets in the world since the age of the Prophet, the meaning of this unique melody that had overwhelmed me as well when I heard it for the first time in Istanbul, the city where nevertheless this *adhan* is among the most discreet, drowned in the racket of modernity. (197–8)

Muhammad Asad's description resonated in Ritter's later discovery of *Songs of the Infatuated Muezzin* by the Polish composer Karol Szymanowski (1882–1937), in particular 'his '*Allah Akbar*' right in the middle of Polish verses' (201). Aside from adding another layer to the shared Polish connection of the composer and the convert formerly known as Leopold Weiss, Énard's introduction of Asad's impressions of the sounds of the Muslim world does not just serve to explain Ritter's interest in the musical connections between Europe and the East: it also connects with Navid Kermani's attention to the aural aspects of the aesthetics of the Qur'an discussed in the first chapter of this book.

Avicennan Illuminations in Ernst Bloch's Speculative Materialism

Ultimately, Franz Ritter noted that he felt 'condemned to the utopian materialism of Ernst Bloch, which in my case is a resignation, the "Tübingen paradox"' (198). It is a paradox because, in his book of aphorisms called *Traces* and in *Avicenna and the Aristotelian Left*, Bloch 'took the Muslim mystic by the hand, reconciled Hegel with Ibn Arabi, and everything in music' (200).[78] However, where Muhammad Asad's Salafi leanings precluded any sympathies for Sufism, Bloch's writings about Islam led Ritter also to 'René Guénon, who became Sheikh Abd el-Wahid Yahya in Cairo' (200), the very same French-born traditionalist who had also captivated Robert Rediger and François in Houellebecq's *Submission*.[79] In spite of its brevity and therefore seemingly modest place in the author's voluminous body of writings, Bloch's *Avicenna and the Aristotelian Left* is an important text, as the translator Loren Goldman has explained:

> In addition to offering an unsurpassed précis of Bloch's own speculative materialism, it also presents itself as a testament to Bloch's extraordinary learning and imaginative genius; as early as 1952, he was insisting on *the intertwined* nature of Arabic and Western thought in the medieval period and beyond, a perspective that has only become common among specialists in the field in recent years. Moreover, by situating the world's emancipatory possibilities in the Islamic interpretation of Aristotle, this small book provides a provocative reconstruction of the sources of modern philosophy that both confounds standard binaries of East/West and Premodernity/Modernity [...] (xi)[80]

In little over twenty thousand words, Bloch explains why the philosophers from the Muslim world must not be simply regarded as transmitters of Aristotelian metaphysics, in which the ancient Greek identifies the four operational terms of his philosophy: matter, form, potentiality and actuality. Instead, he suggests that, beginning with Avicenna, Muslim thinkers were partisan to a 'leftist' strand of Aristotle's metaphysics – a term Bloch borrows from the division between left- and right-wing Hegelians in European thought.[81] Of central importance is Bloch dissection of Aristotle's notion of potentiality, or *dynamis*, into a structured – fixed, mechanical – variant (*kata to dynaton* in Greek) and an unstructured – open, unfinished – variant (*dynamei-on*). In Bloch's often obscure German, these two understandings of potentiality are rendered as *Nach-Möglichkeit-Sein* and *In-Möglichkeit-Sein* respectively, which Goldman and Thompson translate as 'what-is-considered-possible' and 'what-may-become-possible'.[82] In developing his utopian materialism as the basis for his philosophy of hope, Bloch dismisses 'what-is-considered-possible', because the resulting conservative actuality, or entelechy, makes change unthinkable, leading therefore to what Bloch considers a hopeless abstraction of utopia. Only a genuinely dynamic understanding of dialectics holds out the prospect of a concrete utopia of open-ended possibility. Bloch embeds this transposition of Aristotle's ontology in the social-political and intellectual-historical context of the Muslim world. In his account of Islamic Aristotelianism, the rightist variant is represented by the religious discourses dominated by the Ghazalian modus of theological thinking, whereas the leftist variant, in which 'natural science outweighs theology' (5), begins with Avicenna. Also referred to by Bloch as 'my friend Ibn Sina', as an exponent of the 'broad and progressive culture of the Near East, with its Iranian-Arabic brilliance', the Bukhara-born ethnic Tajik is credited with developing a 'most singular materialist vitality' (3) of non-Christian origin that forms an important source for the European Enlightenment.

The 'Avicennan light' (198) that captivates Franz Ritter in *Compass* alludes to Bloch's association of Ibn Sina with the 'Iranian reverence for light' (4) and its 'cosmological metaphysics of light' (8). Eventually culminating in Suhrawardi's Illuminationism, this light metaphysics had already been absorbed into the unified Arab-Persian culture of Ibn Sina's time, and was then transmitted throughout the Islamic realm, reaching its intellectual heights in the Muslim west thanks to contributions of such figures as the Arabised Jew Avicebron (Ibn Gabirol) and Averroes. This, which Bloch calls the 'worldly culture' (5) of Islam, has a very different conceptualisation of the relationship between faith and knowledge from that found in medieval Christendom. The Islamic alternative was all the more appealing to a Marxist materialist like Bloch, because most important Muslim thinkers 'were doctors rather than monks, naturalists rather than theologians' (5). This led philosophers such as Avicenna and Averroes to deviate from dogmatic Islamic views about the body–soul connection, in that they denied the resurrection of the body and the surviving sentience of the human soul. Also, they privileged the universality of reason over both faith and the human intellect. Although sceptical about the Neoplatonic emanation theory to which the likes of Ibn Sina had to have recourse in order to create the 'fantastical constructs' (18) necessary for reconciling this universal reason with the rational faculties of the individual human, Bloch appreciated Ibn Sina's leftist Aristotelian elaboration of the matter–form relationship whereby 'divine power is to be found in nature, with no need for a transcendental God' (20). Paralleling the condemnation of Ibn Sina and Ibn Rushd's philosophies as heresies on the part of Ghazalian theologians, Bloch insists that in Christendom too, the Aristotelian left was not represented by Albertus Magnus or Aquinas, but had to be sought in what he calls the 'anti-Church' (9) of the Amalricians and Albigensians, as well as in the writings of Joachim Fiore, Meister Eckhart and – especially – Giordano Bruno, who was a devotee of Avicebron and Averroës.[83]

The materialist underpinnings of leftist Aristotelian understandings of dynamic entelechy in both cultural and epistemological terms as a 'world-of-becoming' or world-as-becoming' point towards an aesthetics that does not just explain Franz Ritter's sense of being condemned to utopian materialism. The prerequisites of human agency and freedom for its poiesis, which directed Ernst Bloch's gaze towards religion as 'being brought to morality' (33) and art as 'releasing matter-form' (42), are also relevant for the broader argument made in this book that Islamic references in literary texts can be taken as sublimations of intellectual-historical abstractions. Religion as ethics 'brings the humane, deep element in great religious documents out of myth and to the earth' (37), while aesthetics is 'creatively giving shape to the indicated perfection of norms and dimensions of matter-nature' (44). Together they contribute concretely to the actualisation of utopia, which thus 'stops being abstract' (42).

Summary Findings

The novels of Michel Houllebecq and Mathias Énard's *Zone* are situated in the 'post-everything' world which Hamid Dabashi has laid out in his hermeneutics of alterity for interpreting a global order in which the colony is as much in the metropole as the metropole used to be in the colony and is therefore premised on the assertion that the 'Islam versus the West' binary also is obsolete. While in Houellebecq's *Submission* Islam also serves the function of satire, it is no longer Houellebecq's objective to mock Islam. Instead he targets France's vain and opportunistic intellectuals and politicians. Tropes of right-wing-inspired Islamophobia may dismiss multiculturalism, but the references to a Muslim presence in Europe are nonetheless markers of cultural hybridity.

If awarding the first Oswald Spengler Prize in 2018 to Michel Houellebecq is regarded as affirmation of and recognition for his dystopian scenarios of a decline of the West, then Mathias Énard's use of the trope of the night journey in both *Zone* and *Compass* could also be read as symbolising a similar pessimistic prospect for the cultural achievements of both East and West receding into darkness. Muhammad Asad's disenchantment with the West in the 1920s is mirrored in the nihilism bred by the empty materialism of European modernity in the postmodern novels of Michel Houellebecq. However, in the latter case Islam is used as a foil, while for Asad it provides the answer. The Muhammad Asad of Énard's *Compass* shares Houellebecq's concern for the decline of the West, but where Houellebecq sees this in Europe's impotence to stem the rise of Islamism, according to Asad, Islam is the solution to European decadence, excessive individualism and disregard of a common good.

One detail concerning which Asad and Houellebecq appear to see eye to eye, however, is in the stance of the male characters in *Submission* towards polygamy and Asad's apologetics for the same institution, as well as their closely related defences of patriarchy and traditional understandings of masculinity. This, then, brings me to a final point: the growing prominence of women characters in the novels of Mathias Énard, from the rather subdued role of women in *Zone* to the still largely passive Spanish student of Arabic in *The Street of Thieves*, but ending with the assertive Sarah's affirmative Orientalism in *Compass*. This contrast also stands for the different new humanisms developed in by Houellebecq and Énard in their novels, whereby Islamic referents point to a new unifying humanism celebrating socially conservative values (Houellebecq) or a reading of the scholarly field of Orientalism as a form of open and inclusive humanism (Énard). Similarly, Ernst Bloch's idiosyncratic reading of Avicenna enabled him to merge the philosophy of this Persianate thinker with his own Marxist-inspired speculative materialism into an open-ended philosophy of hope that qualifies as humanist, because it is not based on a metaphysical theology or dependent on an emanation theory, but grounded in the kind of worldly immanence that has also been explored by post-structuralists such as Gilles Deleuze and Gianni Vattimo, and to an extent also by those operating in the interstices of philosophy and theology, such as John Caputo, Richard Kearney and Mark C. Taylor.

it is all connected, one thing with another, and it is only apparently lost and forgotten, scattered, haphazard. It is all moving, even without realizing it, towards the same goal, like converging rays towards a distant, unknown focus. You should not forget that it is expressly written in the Koran: 'Perhaps one day God will reconcile you and your opponents and establish friendship between you. He is powerful, mild and merciful.' So there is hope.

Ivo Andrić, *Bosnian Chronicle*, 317.

A share of Fate like a burden on my shoulders, everything connects …

Mathias Énard, *Zone*, 343.

There is no such thing as chance, everything is connected …

Mathias Énard, *Compass*, 13.

Final Thoughts: Everything is Connected

From the intermittent conclusions and cross-references in the various chapters, it already becomes clear that this book itself is an exercise in intertextuality too. The various case studies of this book have sketched the contours of a how a scholar of Islam with Iranian roots can also self-identify as a literary writer who is as German as Kafka; how a descendant from a lineage of Tunisian religious scholars managed to carve out a place for himself within the Francophone Maghrebian literary milieu of 1960s Paris; or how a gay Catalan *mudejar* with Cuban roots navigated the highbrow intellectual circles of the *Quartier Latin* and the working-class quarters of Barcelona and Murcia, Marrakesh and Tangier. Literature was also the medium through which an Albanian, a Catholic Croat and a Bosniak could deal with their Ottoman past, reconciling their belonging to an Eastern Mediterranean culture partly shaped by Islam with the idea of South Slav solidarity or nostalgia for a Homeric past. A misanthrope born on an island in the Indian Ocean may deplore the decline of the West and rail against the humanism undergirding French Republicanism or the cosmopolitanism of the country's intellectual elite, but his satirising of these contested notions is to be preferred to the political manipulation of so-called strong identities based on religion, ethnicity or a supposedly shared national past. Finally, there is the French Orientalist who uses his erudition to tie together history and contemporary political concerns, the cultural and intellectual achievements of people living around the Mediterranean and in the continent's interior as a shared legacy of those calling Europe home and those knocking at its gates.

First among the recurring themes is the legacy of Muslim spirituality we refer to as Sufism, with certain key contributions making repeated appearances: the rapturous statements of Abu Yazid (Bayezid) al-Bistami and al-Hallaj; the intellectualism of Ibn Arabi's theosophy; and Suhrawardi's Illuminationism. In the cases of Navid Kermani,

Abdelwahab Meddeb and Juan Goytisolo, these are presented as exponents of a dogmatically unconstrained and therefore tolerant, but also provocative, strand within the Islamic tradition. The relationship between the former religious scholar-turned-caravaneer Hassan and Shaykh Ahmad Nuruddin, as sketched in Meša Selimović's *Death and the Dervish*, puts Sufism in a very different light from that in the other chapters. It also seems possible for non-Muslims to be endowed with a Sufi disposition, witness Kermani's characterisation of Friedrich Hölderlin as the Sufi of German literature and Goytisolo's comparison of the French vagabond poet Jean Genet with the antinomian Malamatiyya. Several authors have juxtaposed Islam and Muslims with Christianity, more particularly Catholicism and its sacred arts: various chapters feature (former) Franciscan Anselm Turmeda and Ramon Llull, or their missionising confraters in Bosnia, the discalced Carmelite Juan de la Cruz, as well as modern-day reverts like the beatified former soldier Charles de Foucauld and Louis Massignon, Pope Pius XI's 'Muslim Catholic'. To some, the groundbreaking and at times idiosyncratic work of the former Heideggerian Henri Corbin has proven useful in unlocking the mystical thought of Ibn Arabi and Suhrawardi. Énard not only expounded on the vehemently anti-Sufi Jewish convert to Islam Muhammad Asad, but also found a useful interlocutor in the speculative materialist Ernst Bloch, an interest he shares with Kermani. Both are also partial to the constructive strand of affirmative Orientalism that inhabits the writings of Goytisolo and Meddeb.

The image that emerges from the use of Islamic referents by the various featured authors is anything but uniform. In that sense, the answer to the question of whether it is possible to discern a distinct kind of Euro-Islam must be negative, with the exception of the ironic scenario sketched in Houellebecq's *Submission*. Navid Kermani's West-Eastern affinities are closely bound up with the cultural and intellectual heritage of Germany. Abdelwahab Meddeb's double genealogy and the Mudejarism of Juan Goytisolo reflect the connectivities between the Mediterranean's northern and southern shores, but also the respective influences of the laicism of French Republicanism and the hegemonic historiography of Spain. The cosmopolitanism of Mathias Énard is an admixture of Mediterranean and Central European cultures, which also touches on the Ottoman-Turkish influences that dominate the Islamic references of Andrić, Kadare and Selimović. The impressions left by the literary elaboration of the writers' thematic interests through Islamic references is therefore one of heteroglossia and, in the case of some of the authors, also what in Gianni Vattimo's *The Transparent Society* is called heterotopia.

Another shared theme is the political use of Islam in the past and the present: from the invasions and occupations of the Iberian Peninsula and the Balkans, to inverse interventions and increasingly incisive incursions of European states into the Muslim world and subsequent Islamist responses to that. The novels of Ivo Andrić, Ismail Kadare, Meša Selimović and Michel Houellebecq are about prejudice and threat perceptions, and – specifically in relation to Islam and Muslims – the connection between the two. The effects of the European expansion overseas and subsequent decolonisation, but equally, the inverse occupation of the Balkans by the Ottoman Turks, make all the writers in this book acutely aware of the ambiguities of our own postcolonial time and its resistance to binary or dichotomous representations of 'us and them'.

So what do the various authors discussed in this book have in common? What unites their use of Islamic referents for literary purposes? If anything, it would be an emphasis on their own individuality and a claim to freely express their own personal interpretation of religious traditions. Whether we call it critical or post-foundational Islam, or give it no name at all, when writers decide to use Islamic referents or feature religion as a theme in their literary output, even if only for the purpose of satire, it means they find religion/Islam worthy of their attention, and that they therefore take it seriously. In that sense literature can become theology. I insert here an immediate word of caution regarding this return to religion. It is true that totalising secular ideologies of both the left and right have inescapably become derailed into the totalitarianism of Stalinism, Maoism and Fascism; but also, the death toll of Europe's wars of religion erupting in the wake of the Reformation and Counter-Reformation or – more recently – the rise of sectarianism in various Muslim countries, pitching Muslims against Christians and Sunnis against Shi'is, teaches that strong identities grounded in religions can be equally disastrous.

The works of the authors featured in each of the chapters of this book can be read using the conceptual toolbox outlined in the introduction. All the authors discussed in this book have themselves dealt with cultural hybridity and the accompanying disposition of cosmopolitanism: accepting it with generous enthusiasm (Kermani, Meddeb, Énard); acknowledging it grudgingly (Andrić, Kadare, Selimović, Houellebecq); or embracing it with provocative defiance (Goytisolo and – to a degree – Houellebecq). Cultural hybridity and associated concepts, such as liminality or interstitiality, in-betweenness or *entre-deux*, acknowledge the porosity of geographical borders and temporal segmentations. They are accommodative of ambiguities and are therefore more accurate reflections of the realities of the human condition. As for the epistemological dimensions, the merger of weak and nomad thought in a hermeneutics of alterity acts as a counter-narrative to the strong identities and associated truth claims of what Hamid Dabashi calls the politics and metaphysics of identity. As such, it provides an alternative interpretative lens for understanding the use of Islamic referents in literary contexts. Cultural hybridity and liminality are fuzzy concepts, weak and nomad thought represent modest epistemologies, but together they can capture the complexity of what it means to be human more accurately and honestly. They are safer options for making sense of and giving meaning to who we are than religiously-inspired or nationalist ideologies. One can look at the world through the eyes of a believer, a poet or a scholar, but one should not remain locked up in just one of these perspectives. Instead, a cosmopolitan disposition rooted in the in-between seems preferable to strong identities of any kind that lead to the dehumanisation of the other.

I have tried to show that the abstract notions and theoretical concepts used in this book can help capture the literary realities of the various case studies, reflective of what in the Introduction I have called a shift from abstraction to sublimation. If not all, then at least most of the authors discussed in this book have turned the act of writing into a theme in itself. In their literary outputs they have also deployed the Islamic referents in which I am interested as a scholar of religion as vignettes and tropes in the service of their experimentations with language and narration. I maintain that, although these are different objectives, scholars of religion can gain new insights into their object of study from literary texts, while literary critics – but, perhaps even more so, those reading the work of the writers featured in this book for their own reasons – may also take something away from it in terms of knowing a bit more about Muslims and their religion. Without having to read a book like this.

Notes

Acknowledgements

1. Financed by the Slovenian Research Agency (ARIS) as projects J6-5565 and P6-0279.
2. Financed under the BOFZAP scheme of the Flemish Government in Belgium.

Introduction

1. Gould 2016: 32.
2. Cf. Giorgio Agamben's *The Kingdom and the Glory: For a Theological Genealogy of Economy and Government* (Italian original 2007); *The Sacrament of Language: An Archeology of the Oath* (Italian original 2008); *The Highest Poverty: Monastic Rules and Form-of-Life* (Italian original 2011); *Opus Dei: An Archaeology of Duty* (Italian original 2012). Aside from the short monographs, *Belief* (Italian original 1996) and *After Christianity* (2002), Vattimo also collaborated with other deconstructionists, such as John Caputo, Jacques Derrida and René Girard, as well as the hermeneutician Hans-Georg Gadamer and the neo-pragmatist Richard Rorty. This has resulted in joint publications, such as: *After the Death of God* (Caputo and Vattimo 2007); *Religion* (Derrida and Vattimo. 1998); *The Future of Religion* (Rorty and Vattimo. 2005); *Christianity, Truth and Weakening Faith: A Dialogue* (Vattimo and Girard, 2010).
3. In a way, this path of exploration lines up with that of the Germanist Joseph Twist. Although inspired by the innovative Muslim scholars of Islam discussed in my *Cosmopolitans and Heretics: New Muslim Intellectuals and the Study of Islam* (2011), his book *Mystical Islam and Cosmopolitanism in Contemporary German Literature* (2018) moves in a different direction: 'in contrast to the political and theological discourses of the new Muslim intellectuals, the literary works under consideration here are arguably free to be more imaginative, more radical, and less pious' (9). In that sense, the present project can be considered an extension and expansion of such a line of investigation, except that, instead of writing a literary critique, I will pursue the specific Islamic referents used by the authors in question.

4. Cf., for example, Bassam Tibi's *Euro-Islam: die Lösung eines Zivilisationskonfliktes* (2009) and *The Idea of European Islam* (2020) by Mohammed Hashas.
5. Bisaha 2004: 86.
6. In my view, The West/New World refers not only to the Americas, but also to the white settler cultures in the southern hemisphere (South Africa, Australia and New Zealand).
7. For Goethe's interest in Islam, cf. Katherina Mommsen's *Goethe und der Islam* (2001) and Kuschel and Alam's *Goethe und der Koran* (2021).
8. Of course, this leaves me open to another challenge: that of a 'Europe and the rest' approach. But then one cannot make everybody happy. Besides, as the argument of the present volume unfolds, it will become clear that I am on the side of the critics of dichotomous world-views informed by thinking in terms of binary opposites.
9. For example, at the time of writing *Cosmopolitans and Heretics*, I had never considered myself a Deleuzian until I read Nicolas Tampio's 'The Politics of the Garden', where he calls the book an exercise in comparative political theory in the vein of Deleuze and Guattari (Tampio 2013). This triggered an interest not just in the epistemological investigations of Deleuze, but also in other post-structuralist thinkers or philosophers of difference, especially Gianni Vattimo.
10. Bugeja 2012: 102.
11. Bugeja 2012: 3.
12. Peters 2021: 58–9.
13. The son of an Azeri and Shi'a Muslim father while connected to Georgian nobility on his mother's side, Daryush Shayegan (1935–2018) received his secondary education in England and then went on to pursue university studies in Geneva and at the Sorbonne. Trained as a philosopher and a Sanskritist, he is a cultural in-betweener on account of both his biography and his academic work.
14. Shayegan 1997: ix. Also, I want to draw attention to the different subtitles of the French and English versions of *Cultural Schizophrenia*. The original French reads: '*pays traditionnels face à la modernite*' (traditional countries in the face of modernity), but in the English translation this has been narrowed down to 'Islamic societies confronting the West', cf. Kersten 2020: 14.
15. Shayegan 2013: 335–46. The underlying text by Sohrawardi, which was first translated into French by Shayegan's doctoral adviser at the Sorbonne, the former Heideggerian-turned-scholar of Islam Henri Corbin, will be further discussed in Chapter 2.
16. Shayegan 2013: 192ff.
17. These notions recur in the writings of Juan Goytisolo and Abdelwahab Meddeb respectively, and will be discussed further in the relevant chapters.
18. Cf. Kersten 2011: 37–8; Kersten 2015: 9, 52.
19. I am grateful to John O. Voll for bringing this important variant in the theorising of cosmopolitanism to my attention. For more on its relevance in Islamic contexts, past and present, cf. Bruce Lawrence's *Islamicate Cosmopolitan Spirit* (2021).
20. Tarrow 2005: 39.

21. Waldron 1992: 752.
22. Waldron 2000: 229.
23. Marramao 2012: 33. Marramao's cosmopolitanism and its implications for his wider philosophical project is discussed in more detailed in my forthcoming book chapter, 'Hermeneutics of Alterity: A Muslim Challenge of Continental Philosophy of Religion' in Michael Staudigl et al. (eds) *Bonds of Separation: Community, Religion, Violence* (New York: Columbia University Press, 2025).
24. Cf. Dabashi's *The World of Persian Literary Humanism* (2012) and *Persophilia: Persian Culture on the Global Scene* (2015a).
25. *Theology of Discontent: The Ideological Foundation of the Islamic Revolution in Iran* (Dabashi 1992); *Truth and Narrative: The Untimely Thoughts of Ayn al-Qudat al-Hamadhani* (Dabashi 1999).
26. Cf. also my 'Islam Versus the West? Muslim Challenges of a False Binary', especially Kersten 2017: 82–8.
27. Cf. my article in the periodical *Critical Muslim*, entitled 'Post-Everything' (Kersten 2016).
28. Vattimo 1991: 145–62.
29. Vattimo in turn is quoting the anthropologist Remo Guidieri. For a detailed discussion, cf. Kersten 2024: 82.
30. Dabashi 2013: 15.
31. For a detailed discussion, cf. Kersten 2017: 88 and 2022b: 165.
32. *Weak Thought* is also the title of the 1983 essay collection, which Vattimo co-edited and in which he introduces the term (Vattimo 2012: 39–52). Cf. also *Weakening Philosophy: Essays in Honour of Gianni Vattimo* (Zabala 2007).
33. Vattimo 1999: 48–9.
34. Dabashi 2008: 22. I think that here we also have an affinity with how Colby Dickinson has described Giorgio Agamben's take on evil: namely as 'the act of reducing the wonder of each singular existence to the "facts" of reality, as if each thing could simply fit within a given representational scheme' (Dickinson 2011: 147).
35. Deleuze and Guattari 2004: 387–467, also published separately in 1986 by Semiotext(e) as *Nomadology: The War Machine*.
36. Note in this regard the following observation also: 'The nomad is not at all the same as the migrant; for the migrant goes principally from one point to another [...]. But the nomad goes from point to point only as a consequence and as an actual necessity; in principle points for him are relays along a trajectory' (Deleuze and Guattari 2004: 419). Deleuze has repeated this also in an eight-hour-long interview with Claire Parnet, for the documentary *L'Abécédaire de Gilles Deleuze*, where he rejects literal nomadism, remarking that 'nobody moves less than a nomad: the nomad just stands still while the world revolves under their feet'. Cf. http://www.film-documentaire.fr/4DACTION/w_fiche_film/30863_0, also available online at https://youtu.be/SlNYVnCUvVg?si=Lmoj2lsBAnRwoVHp (last accessed 4 December 2024). I thank Ziad Elmarsafy for this reference.
37. Deleuze and Guattari 2004: 402.
38. Cf. Deleuze and Guattari 2004: 389 and 458–9. For an entirely different and pragmatic application of these Deleuzian notions of space in strategic

studies: cf. Shimon Naveh, *In Pursuit of Military Excellence* (1997) and a critique of the latter in Eyal Weizman's *Hollow Land: Israel's Architecture of Occupation* (2007). Cf. also my (unpublished) presentation 'Speculative realism in the Middle East: rethinking war and terror after Operation Desert Storm' in the seminar of the Institute of Middle East Studies (IMES), King's College London, 26 January 2021, https://www.kcl.ac.uk/events/speculative-realism-in-the-middle-east-rethinking-war-and-terror-after-operation-desert-storm (last accessed 4 December 2024).

39. Cf. Bataille 1991: 81ff.
40. Cf. specifically the essay 'Le rhizome et la pensée nomade' (Shayegan 2013: 145–54). The figure of the nomad is also found in the writings of literary authors, for example Bruce Chatwin's posthumously published *Anatomy of Restlessness* (1997), and in the intellectual nomadism and the geopoetics of Kenneth White, laid out in the essay collection *The Wanderer and his Charts* (2004).
41. Braidotti 2011: 7–8.
42. Dabashi uses 'worldly' on purpose and consciously avoids 'secular' because of its Latin and concomitant European Christian connotations; cf. Kersten 2017: 87.
43. Marramao 2012: 67.
44. Dabashi 2013: 35–9.
45. Barber 2014: 2.
46. Taylor 1987: 75.
47. Dabashi 2008: 22.
48. Taylor 1987: 79.
49. Dabashi 2013: 20.
50. Said 1995: 339.
51. Cf. Dietrich Jung's *Orientalists, Islamists and the Global Public Sphere* (2011); Hamid Dabashi's chapter on Ignaz Goldziher in his book *Post-Orientalism* (2008: 17–122).
52. Said 1995: 9, 258, 331. Cf. also Irwin 2006: 279.

Chapter 1

1. Kermani 2014a: 341–9; Kermani 2016a: 15–33; Ulrich 2016.
2. For a detailed study of nationalism in the Iranian context, cf. Arshin Adib-Moghaddam's *Psycho-nationalism: Global Thought, Iranian Imaginations* (2018). In his *Intellectual Discourse and the Politics of Modernization: Negotiating Modernity in Iran* (2000), Ali Mirsepassi traces also the German antecedents of Iranian nativism: cf. in particular Chapter 5, 'German Intellectuals and the Culture of Modernity'.
3. Kermani 2017: 138. Lene Rock even borrowed this characterisation for the title of her book (Rock 2019: 4).
4. In a rare acknowledgement of German Orientalism, Edward Said also named the orchestra he co-founded with the Argentine-born Israeli composer and conductor Daniel Barenboim after Goethe's poetry collection: cf. https://west-eastern-divan.org/founders/edward-w-said (last accessed 4 December 2024).

5. I have decided to work with the German originals. All translations are therefore mine. The same applies to Kermani's other writings.
6. Joseph Twist too has recognised the significance of Kermani's scholarship for his later creative writing. However, where Twist's literary-critical examination focuses more generically on Kermani's cosmopolitan outlook, the present chapter seeks a more in-depth pursuit of the religious referents he has employed.
7. The fate suffered by Amin al-Khuli (1895–1966), Muhammad Khalafallah (c. 1916–98) and Nasr Hamid Abu Zayd (1943–2010) illustrates that approaching the Qur'an as a literary (read: human) text is not without risks in the Muslim world. The academic careers of Cairo University scholars al-Khuli and his student Khalafallah were cut short in 1948, when the latter's doctoral thesis on the narrative art of the Qur'an was rejected following protests and accusations of apostasy by scholars at Al-Azhar Islamic University. As a result, Khalafallah's doctoral adviser al-Khuli also had his own credentials as an *ʿālim* (traditionally trained religious scholar, plural: *ʿulamāʾ*) withdrawn. In the 1990s, the story repeated itself, when Nasr Hamid Abu Zayd's application for promotion to a full professorship in Arabic literature on the basis of his text-critical and discursive-analytic examinations of the Qur'an met with similar objections from a reactionary Al-Azhar scholar. The case was picked up by Islamist activists, who filed charges of apostasy and petitioned the courts to forcibly divorce Abu Zayd from his wife, arguing that a Muslim woman cannot remain married to a non-Muslim spouse. In Egypt's charged and polarised political atmosphere at the end of the twentieth century, when even Nobel Prize laureate Naguib Mahfouz was almost fatally stabbed by a violent extremist, the couple's life was in danger. With the help of German and Dutch Arabists Stefan Wild and Fred Leemhuis, Abu Zayd was given asylum in Germany and then appointed to a professorship at Leiden University in the Netherlands.
8. Aside from publishing a study of Abu Zayd's conceptualisation of revelation as communication (Kermani 1996 and 2004), he also acted as ghost writer for Abu Zayd's autobiography (Abu Zayd 1999). Cf. also Carool Kersten, 'Nasr Hamid Abu Zayd: An Introduction to his Life and Work' in the first integral translation of one of Abu Zayd's books into English.
9. Kermani 1999: 17.
10. Kermani mentions Arab and Iranian poets, such as Nizar Qabbani, Ardonis and Sohrab Sephri, as well as Western authors, including Jorge Luis Borges, Paul Celan, Octavio Paz, Rainer-Maria Rilke and Paul Valéry.
11. With regard to the Qur'an's intertextuality and self-referentiality, cf. also Neuwirth's references to John Wansbrough's work and to Kermani as 'the most recent scholar to have taken up arms in defence of the Qur'an's essentially poetic nature' (Neuwirth 2014: 37, also 281).
12. Referencing both Abu Zayd and Kermani, Ayman El-Desouky has made an attempt to connect the Qur'an's *iʿjaz*, composition and poetics to the philosophical hermeneutics of Heidegger, Gadamer and Ricoeur and the kerygmatic and existential theologies of Barth and Bultmann (El-Desouky 2013).

13. Cf. Chapter 2, p. 84.
14. Kermani 2014a: 19–43. Elsewhere, Kermani drew a parallel between the prophet's objections and Adorno's dislike of poetry (Kermani 2012: 14).
15. The names refer to Layla bint Mahdi and the poet Qays ibn al-Muwalla, both of the central Arabian 'Āmir tribe, whose love-story constitutes a Middle Eastern version of that of Romeo and Juliet, and later captivated in particular the imagination of the classical Persian poets; cf. the chapter 'ideal love couples' in Annemarie Schimmel's *Two-Colored Brocade* (1992: 129–36).
16. Introduced in *The Idea of the Holy*; originally published in German as *Das Heilige* (1917) and first appearing in English in 1923.
17. Kermani 1999: 392, cf. also Schimmel 1975: 44.
18. For example: Annemarie Schimmel's *Mystical Dimension of Islam* (1975), her student Carl Ernst's *Sufism: An Essential Introduction to the Philosophy and Practice of the Mystical Tradition of Islam* (1997); or the translations of Michael Sells presented under the title *Early Islamic Mysticism: Sufi, Qur'an, Mi'raj, Poetic and Theological Writings* (Sells 1996).
19. Schimmel 1975: 112ff.
20. Hodgson I 1974: 238.
21. Schimmel 1975: 58ff.
22. Kermani 2005: 208, 220ff.
23. Cf. Hamid Dabashi 2011.
24. For a more detailed discussion of Kermani's interest in the biblical, Jewish and Christian interpretations of theodicy, cf. von Stosch 2016.
25. Kermani 2005: 42.
26. Rumi referred to himself as 'a planet orbiting the Sun Attar' (Kermani 2005: 42).
27. Helmut Ritter (1892–1971) was a German Orientalist who worked for many years in Istanbul as a contemporary of Erich Auerbach (1892–1957), the author of *Mimesis: The Representation of Reality in Western Literature* (1946). Referred to as 'magisterial' (248) by Edward Said in his book *Orientalism*, he took Auerbach as one of his 'role models' (Irwin 2006: 279), but completely ignored Ritter.
28. 'In Sufism, forty is the numeral of perseverance, patience, acceptance of suffering' (Kermani 2005: 52). It also matches the forty-day period during which the human soul is thought to remain in limbo around the grave, a state for which the Muslims use the Persian word *barzakh*; cf. also the chapters below discussing Juan Goytisolo and Mathias Énard (pp. 142–4 and 249).
29. Goldman 2019: xii.
30. To make it fit the Islamic context, Kerman replaced the original word 'Christian' with 'believer'. The original phrase features in an epigraph from Bloch's *Atheism in Christianity*.
31. Cf the final chapter in this book.
32. Hoffmann 2018b: 14.
33. Hoffmann 2018b; Peters 2021: 288–2.
34. Hoffmann 2018b: 16; Peters 2021: 289.
35. Hoffmann 2018b: 18–19; Peters 2021: 288–9.

36. Kermani 1999: 365.
37. Kermani 1999: 376–8.
38. For an English translation, cf. Shaykh al-Islam Abdullah al-Ansari (2011), *Stations of the Wayfarers*. Translated by Hisham Rifaʿi. Paris: Éditions Albouraq. For a detailed study of al-Ansari, cf. Farhadi 1996.
39. Schimmel 1975: 89.
40. Anjum 2010: 161.
41. Anjum 2010: 167. The American scholar of Islam Carl Ernst has presented a complete breakdown of Ansari's one hundred stations, juxtaposing them with those of his contemporary Abu'l-Qasim al-Qushayri (d. 1072); cf. Ernst 1997: 104–6.
42. Anjum 2010: 187.
43. Anjum 2010: 168.
44. Von Stosch 2016: 85. Such non-resolution also resonates with an expression of hope by the theologian Klaus von Stosch that – one day – Kermani too 'will devote his own book-length study of working out how the notion of *Tawhid* allows us to accept both the terror and the beauty of God at the same time'.
45. Al-Ansari 1988: 88.
46. Kermani 2014b: 107.
47. Jordan 2012: 251.
48. Adorno 2000: 38.
49. Also known as Jalāl al-Dīn al-Balkhī (1207–73), Rumi wrote in Persian, but ended up living in the central Anatolian town of Konya, in present-day Turkey, where he founded the Mevlevi or 'whirling dervishes' order. Thanks to translation projects such as those of Coleman Barks, Rumi has become a bestselling poet in English. Cf. Franklin Lewis's *Rumi: Past and Present, East and West* (2000).
50. Machtans 2016: 97.
51. '[Mozes said to the people:] 'Do not fear, for God has come to test you, that the fear of him may be before you, that you may not sin', https://www.biblegateway.com/passage/?search=Exodus+20&version=ESV (last accessed 1 April 2022).
52. It appears that von Stosch has chosen to ignore this story altogether, because he only refers to 'ten short stories about abusive love between a man and a woman' (von Stosch 2016: 81).
53. Kermani 2014b: 335.
54. Kermani 2014b: 361.
55. Jordan 2012: 254.
56. Although homosexuality continues to be a difficult issue for socially conservative believers from both Muslim and non-Muslim backgrounds, there has been some movement on the issue: cf. Habib 2010; Kugle 2010; De Sondy 2014.
57. Mohagheghi 2012: 259; von Stosch 2016: 81.
58. Althaus-Reid 2002. An Argentinian-born theologian and community worker schooled in the methods of the Brazilian pedagogue Paulo Freire, Althaus-Reid moved to Scotland in 1986 for postgraduate studies at St Andrews and later taught at the University of Edinburgh.
59. Althaus-Reid 1993.

60. Cf. also Althaus-Reid's *The Queer God* (2004), as well as Thia Cooper's *Queer and Indecent: An Introduction to the Theology of Marcella Althaus-Reid* (2021).
61. Sigmund Freud had first developed this notion of the death drive (*Todestrieb*) in *Beyond the Pleasure Principle*, but given Kermani's predilection for *Minima Moralia*, it seems in this context also appropriate to gesture towards Adorno's essay 'This Side of the Pleasure Principle' (Adorno 2005: 60–3).
62. Most religious references in *Text Message* are of a different order from in the early short story collections. Dealing more with cultural identity questions, the position of Muslims as minorities in non-Muslim countries, and developments in the Muslim world, *Text Message* is therefore best read in conjunction with Kermani's essays on Muslims in Germany, *Who Is We? Germany and its Muslims* (Kermani 2017).
63. Kermani 2014b: 394.
64. Kermani 2011a: 270; Kermani 2014b: 399.
65. Hoffmann 2016: 122.
66. Kermani 2011a: 1,112.
67. Druxes 2016: 164–5.
68. Kermani 2015c: 291.
69. These are English translations of the titles of the German originals which I have used. Cf. Kermani 2012, 2015b, 2015c in the Bibliography. For the English translations of the latter two, cf. Kermani 2018b and Kermani 2019b.
70. Kermani 2012: 54–5.
71. Druxes 2016: 171–2.
72. Hoffmann 2018b: 19; Kermani 2011a: 395.
73. Peters 2021: 330–1.
74. Kermani 2011a: 31–2.
75. (Q 4:135), cf. Kermani 2011a: 33, 35. Hossein Ali Rasched (Husayn Ali Rashid, 1905–80) was an enlightened cleric and respected orator before the revolution (Kermani 2011a: 48).
76. Kermani's grandfather had remained a supporter of the nationalist Prime Minister Mohammed Mosaddegh (1882–1967), who had been ousted in the 1953 coup orchestrated by the USA (Kermani 2011a: 33–4). Kermani also found out that his grandfather was personally acquainted with Mehdi Bazargan (1907–95), the first prime minister of the transitional government put in place after the 1979 revolution. By then, Kermani himself had already written an introduction to the translation of Bazargan's book on Jesus, Mary and Christians in the Qur'an (Bazargan 2006).
77. Kermani 2011: 602.
78. Cf. *A Culture of Ambiguity: An Alternative History Islam* by Thomas Bauer, first published in German in 2011, appearing in English translation in 2021.
79. Kermani 2011a: 93 and 397. For more on the ambiguities surrounding the consumption of intoxicants/substance abuse (depending on one's perspective), cf. Shahab Ahmed's *What Is Islam?* (Ahmed 2015).
80. Kermani 2011a: 54; Kermani 2012: 41.
81. Kermani 2011a: 181–2; Kermani 2012: 63.

82. Kermani 2011a: 181.
83. Kermani 2011a: 182; Kermani 2012: 64.
84. Cf. Otto's earlier-mentioned *The Idea of the Holy* and Barth's *The Epistle to the Romans* (1933; a translation of the heavily revised second edition of *Der Römerbrief* from 1922).
85. Kermani 2011a: 181; Kermani 2011: 65. The quotation comes from Hyperion's ninth letter to Bellarmin, cf. Hölderlin 2019: 36.
86. Persian rendition of the Arabic *baqā' fī'l-fanā'*.
87. Kermani 2011a: 184; Kermani 2012: 65.
88. Kermani 2012: 72.
89. Hölderlin 2009.
90. Kermani 2012: 144.
91. Sohrawardi refers to Shihāb al-Dīn Yahya Suhrawardī al-Maqtūl (1154–91), a leading exponent of Persian Illuminationism (*ishrāq*). Nicknamed *al-maqtūl*, 'the Slain', Suhrawardī will make frequent reappearances in other chapters in this book.
92. His full name in Arabic transliteration reads: Muhyī al-Dīn Abū 'Abd Allāh Muḥammad ibn 'Alī ibn Muḥammad ibn al-'Arabī. That *Love Writ Large* accords such prominence to Ibn Arabi should come as no surprise: the study of this Andalusian-born theosophist has grown into a veritable academic industry, where his writings are translated, analysed and interpreted not only in English and French, through the seminal contributions of William Chittick (b. 1943) and Michel Chodkiewicz (1929–2020), but also in Arabic by, among many others, Nasr Hamid Abu Zayd. There is even an international Muhyiddin Ibn Arabi Society (MIAS), founded in 1977 and jointly administered from Oxford and Berkeley.
93. Schimmel 1975: 311.
94. Schimmel 1975: 43.
95. Kermani 2014c: 75, 88, 91, 100.
96. Kermani 2014c: 45, 63, 85.
97. Schimmel 1975: 59.
98. Schimmel 1975: 142 (original italics).
99. Kermani 2014c: 83.
100. Kermani 2014c: 84.
101. Schimmel 1975: 80; Kermani 2014c: 94. For a detailed study cf. *A Soaring Minaret: Abu Bakr al-Wāsiṭī and the Rise of Baghdadi Sufism* by Laury Silvers (2010). Al-Wasiti also features in Kermani's study of the history of Christian art, *Wonder Beyond Belief* (2019b). In an essay on Francis of Assisi's visit to the Ayyubid ruler of Egypt and Syria during the fifth Crusade, Kermani speculates that Sultan al-Malik al-Kamil (1177–1238) may have taken the friar for a Sufi, because he matched the ideal type of the Islamic mystic in every detail. Aside from his appearance, the mendicant's attitude and behaviour, which sometimes also bordered on the scandalous, were 'associated in the East with ascetics like al-Wasiti' (Kermani 2015c: 284).
102. Kermani 2014c: 73, 69.
103. Schimmel 1975: 88–9. Hamid Dabashi mentions him too in his *Being a Muslim in the World* (Dabashi 2013: 140).
104. Schimmel 1975: 296. Cf. also Hamid Dabashi's *Truth and Narrative: The Untimely Thoughts of 'Ayn Al-Quḍāt Al-Hamadhānī* (1999).

105. A detailed recent study of Baqli is Kazuyo Murata's *Beauty in Sufism: The Teachings of Rūzbihān Baqlī* (2017).
106. Schimmel 1975: 280–1.
107. Kermani 2014c: 4, 12, 14, 42, 49, 57, 68, 82, 97. Schimmel 1975: 353.
108. Kermani 2014c: 66.
109. The 'Creative Feminine' is discussed in great detail in Corbin's *Alone with the Alone: Creative Imagination in the Sūfism of Ibn 'Arabī* (Corbin 1997: 157–75).
110. Cf. Corbin 1994: 39–60. Henry Corbin (1903–78) was a former Heideggerian philosopher turned Persianist and scholar of Islam. For a detailed study of his place in the field of French Islamic studies, cf. Elmarsafy 2021: 59–92.
111. Corbin 1989.
112. Peters 2021: 307. As a scholar of literature rather than expert on religious studies, Peters also deserves to be commended for signalling the debate among scholars of Islam concerning the designation 'Islamic mysticism' as an equivalent of or synonym for Sufism, Peters 2021: 295–9.
113. Peters 2021: 335–6.
114. Peters 2021: 307.
115. Kermani 2014c: 40, 48, 60.
116. Kermani 2014c: 29, 40, 48, 73.
117. Kermani 2014c: 60. In this context he also notes the importance of the contributions of Sohrawardi.
118. Kermani 2014c: 13. The German word used by Kermani for *qabḍ* in *Love Writ Large* is *Einschnürung*, which can also be translated as 'constriction'.
119. Kermani 2014c: 13, 14; Kermani 2014a: 122, also 129.
120. Kermani 2014a: 121, 141. The English is based on Edward Dowden's translation (Goethe 1914).
121. The centrality of the notion *qabḍ wa basṭ* is not confined to the traditional theorising of Sufism by the likes of Ibn Arabi and Suhrawardi: it also extends to modern and contemporary Islamic thinking. For example, the Iranian philosopher Abdolkarim Soroush used it in the title of one of his most important works: *Theoretical Contraction and Expansion of Religion: The Theory of Evolution of Religious Knowledge* (Soroush 1994).
122. Aldous Huxley (1894–1963), most renowned for his dystopian social science fiction novel *Brave New World* (1932), also wrote a book on perennialism: *The Perennial Philosophy*. Robert Zaehner (1913–74) was a polyglot and former intelligence officer with experience in Iran; he served as Spalding Professor in Eastern Religions and Ethics at Oxford (1952–74). Himself partial to both gin and opium, Zaehner was later involved in the 1953 coup, which must make him an ambiguous individual for Kermani (Bellaigue 2012: 193–4).
123. Huxley 1954.
124. Kermani 2014c: 82. Cf. also Peters 2021: 301.
125. Kermani 2014c: 82; Zaehner 1957: 206.
126. Kermani 2014c: 82.
127. Cf Coury 2013; Coury 2014; Coury 2016; Machtans 2015; Segelcke 2016; Seibt 2018.

128. Kermani 2014a: 7. The German *Stellvertreter* can be translated as either 'representative' or 'successor'. In this context, 'successor' is better, because positing a twenty-first-century writer as representing nineteenth-century cosmopolitanism is anachronistic. *Stellvertreter* resembles both the English 'deputy' and the Arabic *khalīfa*, from which 'caliph' is derived. Depending on whether the Caliph is regarded as *khalīfa rasūl Allāh* (Deputy of the Prophet of God) or *khalīfa Allāh* (God's Deputy), the appropriate translations also read 'successor' and 'representative' respectively.
129. Kermani 2014a: 9.
130. Stegman 2016: 207, quoting Deleuze and Guattari 1994: 16 (originally published in 1975 as *Kafka: Pour une littérature mineure*, cf. Damrosch 2003: 188).
131. Kermani 2014a: 216, 219.
132. Kermani 2017: 135; Coury 2013.
133. Kermani 2014a: 15.
134. On Shiʿa Muslims as the mustadaʿifin, cf. Hamid Dabashi's *Shiʿism: A Religion of Protest* (2011).
135. Kermani 2014a: 15.
136. Kermani 2014b: 405.
137. Kermani 2014b: 417.
138. Machtans 2015; Druxes and Machtans 2016: 10.
139. Kermani 2014b: 409, 418, 421–2, 450–1.
140. Kermani 2017: 32–3.
141. Cf. in particular the first two volumes of Giorgio Agamben's *homo sacer* project: *Homo Sacer: Sovereign Power and Bare Life* (1995) and *State of Exception* (2003).
142. Kermani 2011a: 1,195.

Chapter 2

1. After Meddeb's death, the presentation of this programme was taken over by the philosopher Abdennour Bidar (b. 1971); cf. Kiwan 2020: 129.
2. In his first novel, Meddeb explains that the surname Meddeb is a Gallicised corruption of the Arabic *mu'addib*, which in the dialect of his native Tunisia is used to refer to a teacher in a Qur'an school (Meddeb 2011: 207–9). The accompanying passive participle, *mu'addab*, means refined, cultured, well-mannered. Both words are taken from the root *adab*, which refers not just to belles-lettres, but also to the humanities in general, as well as to *Bildung*, etiquette, *humanitas* and *paideia*. As a consequence of this ambiguity, '*adab* resists semantic or conceptual codification' (El Shakry 2020: 17, original emphasis). As an aside I also want to mention that in his *Dune* Trilogy, the science fiction writer Frank Herbert used 'Muad'Dib' as the name later adopted by his chief protagonist Paul Atreides. Through his acquaintance with the work of Ibn Khaldun, Herbert borrowed liberally from the Arabic-Islamic vocabulary.
3. Casanova 2004: 87ff.
4. The Maghreb or Maghrib encompasses the western parts of the historical Dar al-Islam or 'Abode of Islam'. Aside from Morocco, Algeria, Tunisia

and the Libyan province of Tripolitania, until the end of the fifteenth century it also used to include the Islamised Iberian Peninsula, referred to as Al-Andalus in Arabic.

5. Khatibi 1983 and 1985. Cf. also Waïl Hassan's introduction to his translation of Abdelfattah Kilito's *Thou Shalt Not Speak My Language* (Kilito 2008).
6. Mehrez 1991: 259; cf. also Idriss Jebari's use of the notion of '*dissensus*' as theorised by the philosopher Jacques Rancière, Jebari 2018: 55.
7. Abdel-Jaouad 1991: 61 cf. also Sellin 1988: 166–7.
8. Abdel-Jaouad 1991; 62.
9. For Mohammed Arkoun, cf. Kersten 2011: 177–237. For the relevance of Jean-Luc Nancy's views of religion in relation to Islam, cf. Joseph's Twist's discussion of Nancy's 'Deconstruction of Monotheism' (Twist 2018: 11–12). Remaining at Paris-X Nanterre until his death in 2014, Meddeb also held visiting appointments at the University of Geneva (1989–90, 1994–2002), Yale (1993–4) and the Free University of Berlin (2012).
10. Meddeb's interests were not limited to the Muslim world; he also engaged with Japanese poetry and religion. Cf. *Saigyô. Vers le vide* (2004), which he wrote in collaboration with Hiromi Tsukui.
11. Abdel-Jaouad 1991 62.
12. Cf. also Sellin 1988: 166–7.
13. Abdel-Jaouad 1991: 72. Cf., for example, Meddeb 2005: 19–34.
14. Abdel-Jaouad 1991: 67, 70. For the 'trace' in Meddeb's work, cf. Lauro 2020.
15. Mincheva 2016: 83.
16. Cf. Mehrez 1991: 160; Jebari 2018: 58; Fieni 2020: 141–2. Cf. also Kersten 2024: 95.
17. Abdel-Jaouad 1991: 59; cf. also Sellin 1988: 172.
18. Abdel-Jaouad 1991: 63.
19. *Les Temps Modernes* (1945–2019) was founded by Jean-Paul Sartre and first edited by Maurice Merleau-Ponty; the journal's editorial board also included Simone de Beauvoir and Raymon Aron.
20. Jebari 2018: 58–60.
21. Casanova 2005: 89.
22. Casanova 2005: 88.
23. Cf. Introduction, pp. 13–14 above.
24. Khatibi 1985: 171; Scharfman 1986: 41.
25. Djedid 2014: 735; El Shakry 2020: 63; Stétié 1997: 200. Salah Stétié (1929–2020) was a Francophone Lebanese writer and former diplomat, highly preoccupied with the cultural mediation between East and West.
26. Elmarsafy 2020: 104.
27. Meddeb 2014: 66. The French original reads as follows:

    telle que l'a cerné Kindî
    le premier philosophe des Arabes
    qui a appris des Grecs
    ce que *phantasia* veut dire
    Il en verse le sense au *khayêl*

28. Gauch 1998: 124.
29. Gauch 1998: 125–6.

30. Connolly 2020: 136–7.
31. Elmarsafy 2020: 102.
32. Scharfman 2001: 105; Kuntz 2011: vii. Cf. also Rahma 2008; Urbani 2014. Cf. Chapter 3, p. 122 above.
33. Mehrez 1991: 260.
34. Mehrez 1991: 270.
35. Meddeb 2005: 9.
36. Kuntz 2011: vi. cf. also Scharfman 1986 and 2001; Alami 2000; Rahma 2008; Djedid 2014; El Shakry 2019; Fieni 2020.
37. Al-Kassim 2010: 183–4.
38. The most detailed and authoritative biography of Huysmans in English is Robert Baldick's *The Life of J.-K. Huysmans* (2006).
39. Meddeb 2011: 5 and 261.
40. Cf. Chapter 1, pp. 34–43 and 45 above.
41. Meddeb 2011: 17.
42. Cf. El Shakry 2020: 29, 60–9.
43. The Iranian revolution and the less well-known violent occupation of the Great Mosque of Mecca by Muslim militants in 1979 coincided with the start of the fifteenth century of the Islamic, Hijri, calendar.
44. Meddeb 2003: 18.
45. Connolly 2020: 139.
46. Meddeb 2003: 43–4 (original italics).
47. Meddeb 2003: 115–18.
48. Also known as Yunus the Dervish (1238–1320); an Anatolian folk poet, who played a pioneering role in the emancipation of Turkish as a language of culture.
49. Meddeb 2011: 236.
50. Cf. Hall 1996.
51. Cf. pp. 13–14 and 62. Cf. also Kersten 2024. 95.
52. Meddeb 2011: 81–2.
53. Scharfman 1986: 45–6.
54. Scharfman 1992: 87.
55. Scharfman 2002: 97.
56. Cf. Braidotti 2000: 156–72; Braidotti 2011: 213–44; MacCormack 2020: 522–39.
57. Kearney 2002: 232.
58. Kearney 2002: 7, 5; cf. also Paul Ricoeur's *Oneself as Another* (1992).
59. Kearney 2002: 88 (original italics).
60. Scharfman 1996: 95.
61. Meddeb 2011: 83. Zemzem or Zamzam refers to the well located in the Grand Mosque of Mecca; its waters are thought to have healing qualities. Fitra is the Qur'anic notion of humankind's innate religiosity.
62. The Blind Man of Maʿarra refers to Abu'l-ʿAlāʾ al-Maʿarrī (973–1057), a famous poet and equally controversial philosopher from Syria.
63. El Shakry 2020: 67.
64. Hints at such a shift are already present in *Talismano*; witness Meddeb's observation that 'those who adopted Islam practiced more calligraphy than they did painting', and the more provocative statement that 'painting is potentially the core of monotheism' (Meddeb 2011: 113 and 115).

65. Meddeb 2003: 28.
66. Massignon 1986: 36; Krokus 2016: 190. Although Edward Said singled out Massignon's scholarship as an example of 'the best Orientalist work done during the interwar period' (258), he criticises him for amplifying and exaggerating the importance of a figure like al-Hallaj. Said's profiling of the French Sufi expert is hugely reminiscent of that of the image he sketched of Ernest Renan (271–2).
67. Meddeb 2003: 28–9.
68. Elmarsafy 2020: 100–2.
69. Cf. Filiz 2020: 400–3. Marion's silence on things Islamic came to an end in 2015; after a brief article about the Charlie Hebdo massacre of that year, in *A Brief Apology for a Catholic Moment*, the French original of which appeared two years later, Marion resorts to the usual clichés about Islam as a violent religion (Marion 2021).
70. Cf. Marion 2002.
71. Elmarsafy 2020: 100. The references come from Mitchell's book *Picture Theory: Essays on Verbal and Visual Representation* (1994).
72. Connolly 2020: 137.
73. Elmarsafy 2020: 100; Connolly 2020: 140.
74. Connolly 2020: 148. On grounds of the image used for the cover of *Phantasia*'s 2003 Seuil edition, Connolly speculates that the book may have been Mohammed Aziza's 1961 book *La Calligraphie arabe*. Cf. n. 19.
75. Meddeb 2003: 20.
76. Recent additions include: Saif, Leoni, Melvin-Koushki and FaroukYahya, *Islamicate Occult Sciences in Theory and Practice* (2021); Garcia Probert and Sijpesteijn, *Amulets and Talismans of the Middle East and North Africa in Context* (2022).
77. Meddeb 2011: 143.
78. Meddeb 2011: 151.
79. The *Hamsa/Khamsa* is found in both the Judaic and Islamic traditions, said to refer to the Pentateuch and Five Pillars of Islam respectively. For a recent study of its significance in the Islamic tradition, see von Kemnitz and Inloes's *The Hand of Fatima* (2022).
80. Massignon 1963, I: 550–72.
81. El Shakry 2020: 71.
82. El Shakry 2020: 71–3. Cf. Chapter 5, p. 302, n. 77.
83. Massignon 1913.
84. Meddeb 2011: 113 (original italics). This reference to al-Hallaj's 'theory of the point' has commanded the interest not only of scholars of Islam, but also of philosophers and theologians; cf., for example, a comparative study of al-Hallaj and Nicolas of Cusa in Bunyazade 2013.
85. Cf., for example: *The Way and Its Power: Lao Tzu's Tao Tê Ching and Its Place in Chinese Thought* (Waley 1958).
86. Meddeb 2011: 201 (original italics).
87. Martin Palmer's translation *The Book of Chuang Tzu* provides a slightly different translation of the cited phrase: 'The abuse of the true elements to make artefacts was the crime of the Craftsman' (Palmer 1996: 73).
88. Meddeb 2011: 117.
89. Meddeb 2003: 156.

90. Al-Kassim 2010: 267, n. 54; El Shakry 2020: 80.
91. Cf. Vattimo 1992: 8–9.
92. Meddeb 2011: 229.
93. Hoda El Shakry 2020: 15.
94. Meddeb 2011: 118, 129, 132.
95. Meddeb 2011: 239.
96. For a discussion of this question, cf. Angelika Neuwirth's 'From the Sacred Mosque to the Remote Temple: *Sūrat al-Isrā'* (Q. 17), between Text and Commentary' (2014: 216–52).
97. Schrieke and Horovitz 1993: 99–100.
98. Cf. Wronecka 1984 and Morris 1987 and 1988 respectively.
99. Meddeb 1985.
100. Cf. *La escatología musulmana en la 'Divina Comedia'* (multiple editions: Asín Palacios 1943); *Dante y el islam* (Asín Palacios 1927); 'Nuove luce sulle fonti islamiche della Divina Commedia'. *Al-Andalus: revista de las Escuelas de Estudios Árabes de Madrid y Granada* (Della Vida 1949); 'Dante dans et l'Islam d'après des travaux récents' (Rodinson: 1951). The significance of Meddeb's contribution to this discussion is evinced by the inclusion of his essay, alongside these luminaries, in the bibliography of the entry on the Night Journey in the second edition of the prestigious *Encyclopaedia of Islam* (Bencheikh 1993: 103).
101. Bencheikh 1993: 102. For an edited version of this translation, cf. Wunderli 1968. An English translation was published in 1997 under the title *The Prophet of Islam in Old French* (Hyatte 1997).
102. Cf. Echevarria 2005.
103. Meddeb returns again to the Night Journey in an essay entitled 'Blanches traverses du passé', first published in 1997 and reprinted in *L'exil occidental* (2005: 117–41); an English translation was included in *Tombeau of Ibn Arabi and White Traverses* (2010: 77–107).
104. Aside from the Fata Morgana edition, the French version of *Tombeau of Ibn Arabi and White Traverses* was also included in *L'Exil Occidental* (2005).
105. Elhariry 2016: 257. Cf. also Djedid 2014: 724.
106. Jambet 2015: 10. Jambet mentions the *Tabaqāt al-Sūfiyya* of Sulāmī (937–1021), but it also applies to Attar's *Tadhkirat-ul-Awliyā*, mentioned in the previous chapter.
107. Elmarsafy 2021: 4.
108. Elmarsafy 2021: 94–5.
109. Smith and Whistler 2010: 1–24.
110. Meddeb 2015: 31.
111. Meddeb: 2015: 31–2. Adonis is a pseudonym of Ali Ahmad Saʿīd Asbar; cf. his *The Static and Dynamic: An Investigation into the Arabs' Creativity and Mimesis* (1974–8) and *Sufism and Surrealism*.
112. Meddeb 2011: 57.
113. Meddeb 2015: 151.
114. Elmarsafy 2021: 52.
115. Elmarsafy 2021: 95.
116. 'là où le peril croît, grandit ce qui sauve'. The German original reads: 'Wo aber Gefahr ist, wächst / Das Rettende auch'. The phrase is taken from the hymn *Patmos*.

117. Meddeb 2015: 86. Cf. also p. 44 above.
118. For *lāhūt* and *nāsūt* and their connections with the exoteric/apparent (*ẓāhir*) and esoteric (*bāṭin*) respectively, cf. Corbin 1997: 119–20 and 304–5.
119. Meddeb 2011: 28; Meddeb 2003: 28. This last phrase is found in a footnote in Massignon's *The Passion of Al-Hallāj* (Massignon 1986 I: 13, n. 62).
120. Meddeb 2003: 27.
121. Elmarsafy 2021: 26.
122. Elmarsafy 2021: 16–17.
123. Meddeb 2011: 56
124. Massignon 1972: 3.
125. Meddeb 2011: 28.
126. Meddeb 2010: 15. The Comoros is an archipelago in the Southern Indian Ocean, just north of Madagascar, inhabited by a predominantly Muslim island population.
127. Gude 1996: 47, quoting from 'Voyelles sémitiques et sémantique musicale' (Massignon 1983: 345). In her biography of Massignon, Marie-Louise Gude goes on to explain that, in Massignon's mind, the pigeons remained for ever associated with his conversion to Catholicism following a psychotic episode he had suffered in Iraq, in the wake of a homosexual liaison with the Spanish aristocrat and Islam scholar Luis de Cuadra: 'The truth of my pardon came out of the broken talisman, from the veil of the torn Name' (Gude 1996: 47, quoting from Daniel Massignon's 'Le Voyage en Mésopotamie et la conversion de Louis Massignon en 1908' in *Islamochristiana* 14 (1977)).
128. Elmarsafy 2021: 33.
129. Elmarsafy 2021: 19, 27–8.
130. Elmarsafy 2021: 59.
131. Corbin 1997: 88.
132. El Shakry 2020: 25.
133. Meddeb 2015: 62–5. Two were octogenarians from Seville in his native Spain (Shams Umm al-Fuqarā' and Nūna Fātima bint Ibn al-Muthanna); the others he met in Mecca. One was a slave woman who had mastered and internalised the qualities of *futuwwa*; the other, named Zaynab al-Qal'iyya, accompanied Ibn 'Arabi on a journey to Jerusalem and is said to have had the capacity to levitate during *dhikr* sessions.
134. Meddeb 2015: 71–2.
135. Meddeb 2003: 145–6 (original italics).
136. Meddeb 2015: 78.
137. Meddeb 2011: 136 (original italics).
138. Meddeb 2015: 144.
139. Meddeb 2011: 158 (original italics).
140. Meddeb 2011: 231; Meddeb 2003: 44 (original italics).
141. Ibn 'Arabi 1978: 67.
142. Meddeb 2010: 74.
143. Nancy 2010: 109–10.
144. Khatibi 1085; Casanova 2005: 88.
145. Elhariry 2016: 259.
146. Ibn al-'Arabi 1978: 148–9.

147. Meddeb 2015: 140.
148. Cf. Deleuze and Guattari 2004: 423; Bataille 1991: 81ff.
149. Meddeb 2008: 52 and 120.
150. Levett 2020: 85ff; Abdel-Jouad 1991. Cf. p. 61 above.
151. Khalil 2020: 180.
152. Meddeb 2005: 57. On the literary value of the original text by al-Suhrawardi, cf. Hämeen-Anttila 2011.
153. Corbin 1994: n.p. For a recent study of Suhrawardi's Illuminationism, cf. Kaukua 2022.
154. Meddeb 2011: 56–7 (original italics).
155. Meddeb 2011: 234–5.
156. Jara Kaukua has criticised such anti-Aristotelian readings of Suhrawardi, suggesting a re-appreciation of the Peripatetic elements in Suhrawardi's philosophical thinking (Kaukua 2022: 231–5).
157. Meddeb 2011: 260.
158. The Bani Murra are a tribe inhabiting the massive sandy expanse in the eastern part of the Arabian Peninsula known as 'the Empty Quarter'.
159. Q. 79:34. The title of *Sura al-Nāziʿāt* has been translated as 'Those Who Tear Out' (Ali) and 'The Pluckers' (Arberry).
160. Elmarsafy 2020: 109.
161. The same hadith is also quoted as one of the epigraphs in *Instants Soufis* (Meddeb 2015: 115).
162. Elhariry 2020: 64.
163. 'Je plaçai la lampe dans la bouche d'un Dragon qui habitait dans le château de la roue hydraulique; au-dessous se trouvait certaine Mer Rouge; au-dessus il y avait des astres dont personne ne connaît les lieux d'irradiation hormis leur Créateur et "ceux qui ont une ferme expérience dans la connaissance"' (Corbin 1976: 276–7).
164. 'Je mis la lampe dans la gueule du dragon habitant la tour de la roue hydraulique. Il y avait, au-dessous, une Mer Rouge; au-dessus, des astres dont personne ne connaît le foyer d'irradiation hormis leur créateur et *ceux qui sont très-savants*' (Meddeb 2005: 65, original italics).
165. Benjamin 1968: 69–82.
166. Ricoeur 1992: 8.
167. Meddeb 2015: 171.
168. Jambet 2015: 23. Cf. also Massignon's article 'Étude sur une courbe personnelle de vie: le Cas de Hallaj, martyr mystique de l'Islam (Massignon 1963, II: 167–90).
169. *The Malady of Islam* (2003; the French original had appeared a year earlier) and *Islam: The Challenge of Civilization* (2013, French original 2009).
170. For the Empedocles–Hölderlin connection and the 'accursed fields', cf. Krell 2009: 21–3 in *The Death of Empedocles: A Mourning-Play* (Hölderlin 2009). Cf. also Navid Kermani's remark in the previous chapter concerning the importance of Empedocles' theory of four elements for Sohravardi's Philosophy of Illumination. Cf. Chapter 1, pp. 37–9 above.
171. Meddeb 2006: 14–19.
172. There are also literary, philosophical and theological excursions on George Bataille and his relevance for poetic transgressions and heterogeneity (Meddeb 2006: 73–87), and on the significance of Goethe's interest

in Islam and the Persian poet Hafiz for the emergence of world literature (258, 470); and essays about the *shataḥāt* of al-Bistami (297), the controversial position of the Muʿtazila on the createdness of the Qurʾan (383), and blasphemy (457).

173. Mincheva 2016: 13.
174. Cf. *Figuring the Sacred: Religion, Narrative and Imagination* (Ricoeur 1995).
175. In an interview with *Libération*, published 6 May 2006, cited in Fieni 2020: 141.
176. Abdel-Jaouad 1991; Fieni 2020: 141, 154.
177. Qadiri 2013: 49–50.
178. Cf. also the chapter 'Abdelwahab Meddeb: Postfoundational Islam' in Nadia Kiwan's *Secularism, Islam and Public Intellectuals in Contemporary France* (Kiwan 2020: 20–51).
179. Qadiri 2013: 60 (italics added).
180. El Shakry 2020: 3.
181. For a comparison between Abdelwahab Meddeb and Daryush Shayegan, cf. Kersten 2020.

Chapter 3

1. Casanova 2004: 87.
2. Both Juan Goytisolo's elder and younger brothers became writers too: José Agustín Goytisolo (1928–99) made a name as a poet and translator of Catalan and Italian poetry, while Luis Goytisolo (b. 1935) is best known for the tetralogy *Antagony* (1973–81).
3. Aside from Miguel Cervantes, other medieval and Renaissance writers who have influenced Goytisolo, and who are frequently referenced or featured in his writings, include Juan Ruiz (1283–1350); the Jewish convert poet and dramatist Fernando de Rojas (d. 1541); the chief representative of the baroque *Culteranismo* School, Luis de Góngora (1561–1627), and his rival from the sparser *Conceptismo* School, Francisco Quevedo (1580–1645). Later influences include the Spanish-Irish theologian and political thinker José María Blanco Crespo (1775–1841), who later adopted the name Joseph Blanco White, and who has often functioned as Goytisolo's literary alter ego, and the philosopher-writer Miguel de Unamuno (1864–1936) as well as the poets Antonio Machado (1875–1922) and Federico García Lorca (1898–1936).
4. Despite being banned in Spain, by 1963, Spanish-language editions published in Latin America, and foreign-language versions released in London, New York and Paris, had turned Goytisolo into the second most translated Spanish writer after Cervantes (Goytisolo 2003a: 248).
5. Goytisolo became close friends with the Latin American writers Mario Vargas Llosa and Carlos Fuentes; the relationship with Gabriel García Márquez was less warm (Goytisolo 2003a: 317).
6. Cf. also the book *Fille d'* (2011), written by Monique Lange's daughter from an earlier relationship, Carole Achache (1952–2016). Carole's daughter,

the French-Moroccan cinéaste and screenwriter Mona Achache, used the extensive written and audio-visual archive material she discovered after her mother's suicide to make a film about her mother and grandmother, *Little Girl Blue* (2023).

7. Living as a couple but sleeping in separate bedrooms (Goytisolo 2005: 19). After Monique's death in 1996, Goytisolo gave up their apartment on 33 rue Poissonnière in Paris's second *arrondissement*, which without her presence felt to him as a 'kind of tomb' (Jaggi 2000).
8. Goytisolo 2003a: 199.
9. Goytisolo 2003a: 252ff.
10. Goytisolo 2003a: 276. Already acquainted with Genet before his introduction to Goytisolo, Monique Lange too had fallen under the vagabond poet's spell, describing herself as 'his slave in the years 1947–1948' (Kirkup 1996, citing from Lange's contribution to a special issue of *Magazine Littéraire* on Gene, no. 113, from September 1993). After the premiere of Mona Achache's film at the Cannes Film Festival, press releases reported that the files of Carole Achache also revealed how Monique Lange had not protected her daughter from abuse by her friends, including Jean Genet.
11. It is thought to have been on the 27th day of Ramadan in 610 CE. Unfortunately for Goytisolo, in 1955, 8 October did not coincide with that holy month, corresponding instead with 22 Safar 1375 AH).
12. Goytisolo 2003a: 143.
13. Ricoeur 2004: 15.
14. Ugarte 1982: 23.
15. Black 2001a: 34–5.
16. Deleuze and Guattari 2004: 387–466. Cf. also Pope 1995: 36–8; Epps 1996: 14, 139ff.
17. Shayegan 2013: 217. 326, 339. Cf. Introduction, p. 9.
18. Goytisolo 1992: 4 and 95; cf. also Goytisolo 2003a: 23–4. For a detailed discussion of the term 'al-Andalus', see 'The Reception of Al-Andalus 1821–2021: Two Hundred Years of Study and Debate' (Fierro and García-Sanjuán 2022).
19. Goytisolo 2003a: 48.
20. Castro 1948: 371ff. An adapted translation in English by Edmund L. King appeared in 1954 under the title *The Structure of Spanish History* (Castro 1954). While it contains the term *mudejares*, the abstract Mudejarism is missing.
21. Ugarte 1982: 75.
22. Chalmeta 1993: 286.
23. Chalmeta 1993: 287.
24. The full titles read *Ornament of the World: How Muslims, Jews, and Christians Created a Culture of Tolerance in Medieval Spain* (Menocal 2002) and *The Myth of the Andalusian Paradise: Muslims, Christians, and Jews under Islamic Rule in Medieval Spain* (Férnandez Morera 2016).
25. Márquez Villanueva 2009: 27–8.
26. The characterisation is taken from Michael Ugarte (Ugarte 1979).
27. 'Mudejarism Today' (Goytisolo 1992: 1–5) and 'Vicissitudes of Mudejarism: Juan Ruiz, Cervantes, Galdós' (Goytisolo 1992: 93–112).

28. Goytisolo 1992: 2–4.
29. Goytisolo 2003a: 23.
30. Before moving to Paris, Juan Goytisolo had already made a name for himself with the novels *Young Assassins* (*Juego de Manos*, 1954) and *Duel in Paradise* (*Duelo en el Paraiso*, 1955). These were followed by a trilogy, *The Ephemeral Tomorrow* (*El Mañana Efímro*), and a further four novels and travelogues.
31. The dates in this overview refer to the original publications in Spanish.
32. Goytisolo 1992: 212–28.
33. *Forbidden Territory* was first published in Spanish in 1985, and was followed a year later by *Realms of Strife*. The latter's Spanish title actually reads *En los reinos de Taifa*, which is more accurately translated as 'In the Realms of the Moorish Kings' (Lee Six 1990: 5). English translations by Peter Bush from 1989 were reissued in a single volume in 2003. *Saracen Chronicles* (1992) is a collection of translations of essays which had appeared in Spanish between 1977 and 1985; *Cinema Eden* is composed of a collation of translations of articles written in 1990 and 1992 (Goytisolo 2003b).
34. Goytisolo 2005: 22–4. *The Blind Rider* was written in Marrakesh and Tangier between November 1996 and August 2002.
35. Following Monique's passing, Goytisolo gave up their apartment on 33 rue Poissonnière in Paris's second *arrondissement*, which without her presence felt to him a 'kind of tomb'. (Jaggi 2000).
36. Cf. also Black 2001a: 3 and 27.
37. Pope 1995: 7. Cf. also: 'the excretory functions of the "men of flesh and bone" (suspiciously reminiscent of Unamuno) becomes a tool of resistance' (Ugarte 1982: 136).
38. Goytisolo 2003a: 232.
39. 2003a: 204–5; 232; 248–9.
40. Black 2001a: 37. Cf. Chapter 2, pp. 61 and 79–84 above.
41. Schulman 1984: 153.
42. This refers to the Islamic realms that continued to be governed by Muslim rulers following the collapse of the Umayyad Caliphate of Cordoba in 1031.
43. Goytisolo 2011a: 133.
44. Aside from José Ortega y Gasset (1883–1955), Goytisolo mentions Herman Keyserling (1880–1946), the Swiss theorist of culture Denis de Rougemont (1906–85) and the later promoter of European federalism, Emmanuel Mounier (1905–50).
45. Goytisolo 2011b: 2.
46. Another of the epigraphs at the beginning of *Count Julian* comes from a chronicle commissioned by the Castilian king already mentioned in the previous chapter. Alfonso X, *El Sabio* was the patron of the translation school of Toledo, where *The Book of Mohammed's Ladder* was first translated from the Arabic. However, another text commissioned by this monarch, *Crónica General*, curses 'the traitor Julian', accusing him of being 'incapable of loyalty', consumed by hatred and 'guilty of many misdeeds against his own people' (Goytisolo 2011b: n.p.).
47. Despite vast differences in concerns and writing styles, the only ones that come to mind in this respect are Norman Lewis (1908–2003) and Cees

Nooteboom (b. 1933), in whose oeuvres of fiction and travelogues Spain also features prominently.

48. Goytisolo 2011b: 204.
49. For an overview of Islamic references in *Count Julian*, cf. the article by Bernard Loupias, which provides a useful categorisation of the Arabic lexicon employed bv Goytisolo (Loupias 1978).
50. These include histories and chronicles by Ibn Abd al-Hakam of Egypt (d. 871), the Cordoban Abu Bakr Ibn Qūṭiyya (d. 977), the Tunisian Ibn al-Kardabus (d. 1179), Shams al-Din al-Dhahabi of Damascus (1274–1348) and the Algerian Aḥmad ibn Muḥammad al-Maqqarī al-Tilmisānī (1577–1632).
51. Denise Filios has examined both early Arabic and Hispanic text material concerning Count Julian's role as a 'border crosser' and depictions of the Straits of Gibraltar as 'either a bridge between two cultures or as a bridge that connects al-Andalus and the Maghreb' (Filios 2009: 376, 378).
52. Although it is not at all certain, some sources allege the sons of Wittiza even went to Damascus, probably as part of the triumphant return of Musa ibn Nusair upon his recall to the Umayyad Capital in 715 (Hitchcock 2014: 20).
53. If true at all, it would not have been for educational purposes as suggested in Arabic sources, but as a hostage to ensure Julian's continuing loyalty to Roderic as the new King of Hispania (Kaegi 2010: 256–7).
54. Hitchcock 2014: 17.
55. Filios 2009: 378.
56. For a detailed account, cf. Elizabeth Drayson's *The King and Whore: Roderic and La Cava* (2007). An alternative explanation for the designation 'la Cava' suggests that it is a corruption of the Arabic rendition of Eve: Hawwā.
57. Black 2001a: 8; cf. also Goytisolo 2011b: 5.
58. Epps 1996: 23.
59. Goytisolo 2011b: n.p.
60. Cf. Black 2001a: 84–91; Ugarte 1982: 91ff.
61. Goytisolo 2011b: 72. Taken from *The Spaniards: An Introduction to their History* (Castro 1971: 354).
62. Cf. p. 109 above.
63. Goytisolo 2011b: 104, cf. also pp. 6, 73, 113, 203–4.
64. Cf. Chapter 2, pp. 67 and 76–7 above.
65. *Gebal-Tariq* or *Jabal Tariq*: Arabic for Tariq's Mountain, which in European languages has been corrupted to Gibraltar.
66. Black 2001a: 110.
67. Aïdi 2017. Cf. Chapter 2, p. 65 above.
68. Albrecht 2005: 190.
69. Cf. also the section on Michel Houellebecq (pp. ?–?) in the final chapter of this book.
70. Cf. Chapter 5, pp. 223, 229, 237, 242–3 below.
71. Goytisolo 2003a: 126. Cf. his observation a few pages further: 'My fervor for slum areas, which urged me on for years, was incomprehensible and even shocking to most of my friends' (138).
72. From the article 'Why I Have Chosen to Live in Paris' (1981), cited in Lee Six 1990: 124.
73. Vattimo 1991: 29.

74. Ugarte 1982: 119.
75. Epps 1996: 129.
76. Goytisolo 1990: 71–2.
77. Goytisolo 1990: 74.
78. He does feature prominently in Asín Palacios's *Huellas del Islam: Santo Tomas de Aquino, Turmeda, Pascal, San Juan de La Cruz* (1941). In recent years, a number of medievalists and scholars of Islam have started to write about Turmeda. Cf. Alvarez (2002); Gugel (2015); Thomas (2017); Hackenburg (2020).
79. Meddeb 2010: xi. Cf. Chapter 2, p. 95 above. For a detailed recent study of Llull, cf. Leblanc 2024.
80. This name translates as 'the Rightly-Guided Mallorcan Abdallah the Interpreter'.
81. Goytisolo 1990: 206–7 (original capitalisation).
82. Pope 1995: 43.
83. Randolph Pope signals what he calls a 'precarious "in-betweenness" that becomes a scandal [...] for groups whose claims to centrality and superiority are questioned' (Pope 1995: 44–5).
84. Goytisolo 1990: 104–5. Several biographers have written about Lawrence's sexuality, the most detailed being *A Prince of Our Disorder: The Life of T. E. Lawrence* (1976) by the American psychiatrist John E. Mack, for which he was awarded a Pulitzer Prize.
85. Goytisolo 1990: 107 (italics added).
86. *Almocri* is the Spanish rendition of the Arabic *muqrī'* – a Qur'an reciter.
87. Goytisolo 1987: 1.
88. For the expansion of real estate holdings by the Persian Gulf States in Paris (and other European metropoles), see also Michel Houellebecq's novel *Submission*. Cf. Chapter 5, pp. 241–2 below.
89. Bhabha 1994: 183.
90. Barbès is also the area where Goytisolo went for his encounters with working-class men of North African extraction.
91. In her study of topology and intertextuality in *Landscapes after the Battle*, Lucille Braun explains that L'Sa Monammu is a pun, a phonetic rendition of 'Elsa Mon Amour', which Goytisolo uses to parody Louis Aragon's poem *L'Fou d'Elsa*, dedicated to his wife Russian wife Elsa Triolet. According to Braun, Goytisolo wanted to ridicule the poem's intolerable Orientalism 'with its jumble of Boabdil, the last days of Granada, and a poet crazy with love for a woman named Elsa' (Braun 1989: 23). This Orientalising figure of Elsa is very similar to Abdelwahab Meddeb's muse Aya in *Phantasia* and in the poetry collection *Aya dans les villes*. Cf. Chapter 2, pp. 86 and 94 above.
92. Cf. the essay included in *Saracen Chronicles*: 'The Language of the Body (Octavio Paz and Severo Saduy)' (Goytisolo 1992: 113–32); Epps 1996: 150, 152; Lee Six 1990: 23, 100; Ugarte 1982: 127. 130.
93. Goytisolo 2003a: 152–3; 334–5; 344. Cf. also *State of Siege*, Goytisolo's *roman à clef* set in Sarajevo and based on his own visit to the besieged city during the Bosnian War.
94. On account of his travels through Arabia and expeditions to East and Central Africa in search of the sources of the Nile, Burton is regarded as one of the most prominent explorers of the Victorian Age. A gifted

linguist, he spent most of his final diplomatic posting to the Adriatic port city of Trieste (1872–90) translating and writing. Burton had begun his career as a military intelligence officer in British India, where his services were terminated in 1847 on account of his research into homosexual practices in the places where he was stationed. The fact that, after his sudden death in Trieste, his widow burned all his papers and manuscripts only fuelled speculations about Burton's own sexuality. Detailed discussions of these aspects of Burton's life can be found in Fawn Brodie's biography, *The Devil Drives: A Life of Sir Richard Burton* (1967).

95. Goytisolo 2003a: 155.
96. Black 2001a: 145.
97. Epps 1996: 147–50.
98. Goytisolo 1992: 6–13.
99. Kersten 2017: 88 (quoting from Giovanna Borradori's essay 'Weak Thought and Postmodernism').
100. Goytisolo 2003a: 347.
101. Goytisolo 1987: 60, 114. The battle at Poitiers is also referred to as the Battle of Tours and – by the Arabs – as the Battle of the Court of Martyrs. Charles Martel and the town named after him (Martel means 'hammer') also make an appearance in Michel Houellebecq's novel *Submission*; cf. Chapter 5, pp. 239 and 300, n. 46 below.
102. Goytisolo 1987: 157; Vattimo 1991: 29 and 1992: 8.
103. Lee Six 1990: 106. Cf. Introduction, p. 9 above, and Chapter 2, pp. 96–8 above.
104. Introduction, pp. 13–14 above.
105. Epps 1996: 298–9.
106. Cf. Introduction, p. 16 above.
107. Goytisolo 1987: 85.
108. Goytisolo 1987: 41.
109. Lee Six 1990: 191.
110. Cf. Kersten 2016.
111. Epps 1996: 150 (original emphasis).
112. Goytisolo 1993: 50.
113. Taylor 2002: 36.
114. I note that *Landscapes after the Battle*, published between *Makbara* and *Quarantine*, also features a hecatomb.
115. Peter Bush, 'Translator's Note on Ibn Arabi, Asín and the *Miradj* and Other Islamic References' in Goytisolo 1994: 7.
116. The word itself is taken from the Italian *cuarantina*, meaning a forty-day isolation practice to prevent the spread of contagious diseases and ward off the outbreak of pandemics. Its first recorded use was by the Venetians in medieval Ragusa, the Adriatic port city in South Croatia currently known as Dubrovnik.
117. Referred to in Arabic as Al-Qarāfa and located at the foot of the Muqattam Hills, these massive necropolises stretch out for miles along the eastern walls of the old city of Cairo (and thus form part of the UNESCO Heritage Site of 'Historic Cairo').
118. Goytisolo 2003b: 55–137. The original Spanish versions appeared in *Aproximaciones a Gaudi en Cappadocia*.

119. Goytisolo 1992: 4.
120. Goytisolo 1994:11. Most of the references in this passage have been encountered before in this book; the mystic Miguel de Molinos (1628–96) was a key figure in a religious revival movement know as Quietism.
121. Goytisolo 1992: 4; Goytisolo 1993: 241–70.
122. For an English translation of what in Arabic are called *Al-hikāyāt al-ʿajība waʾl-akhbār al-gharība* in Arabic, cf. the translation by Malcolm C. Lyons with an introduction by Robert Irwin, published by Penguin Classics in 2014.
123. First appearing in Spanish in an essay collection entitled *De la ceca a la Mecca* (1997), it is also the opening chapter of *Cinema Eden* (Goytisolo 2003b: 7–12).
124. Goytisolo 2003b: 7–8. The passage also includes a mention of '[Elias] Canetti's fertile visit' – meaning the Nobel Prize laureate's book *Die Stimmen von Marrakesh*.
125. Goytisolo 1993: 33 and 42; cf. also Goytisolo 1993: 105.
126. Cf. also the chapter in *Landscapes after the Battle*: 'in the Paris of forking paths' (Goytisolo 1987: 87–8).
127. For the distinction between nomocracy and theocracy in Islamic contexts, cf. Kersten 2019: 104.
128. The English translation 'European halaiquí' does not quite capture the original Spanish *halaiquí nesrani*, which combines the Moroccan dialect word for storyteller with another Arabic word used to designate Christians.
129. Lee Six 1990: 86.
130. Cf. especially Stanley Black's elaboration of a section of his analysis of *Makbara* entitled 'Critical utopia' (Black 2001a: 165–8).
131. This conflation on the part of Goytisolo is extensively discussed in the secondary literature I have cited so far. It also has been a point of criticism in the generic literature on Orientalism, especially in relation to nineteenth-century novelists such as Gustave Flaubert (cf. Said 1995: 188–90).
132. Goytisolo 1984: 109–19, later reprinted in *Saracen Chronicles* (1992: 212–28). A Spanish version had appeared in *Crónicas sarracinas* (1981). Cf. also Luce López Baralt's article '*Makbara*: Juan Goytisolo's Fictionalised Account of "Orientalism"'. Both appeared in the same issue special issue of the *Review of Contemporary Fiction* on *Makbara*.
133. Said 1985: 105; 1993: xxii.
134. Goytisolo 1992: 215. These later writings also evince a less dichotomous approach to the East–West divide on Edward Said's part. *Orientalism* is as guilty of totalising the West as the Western scholarship put under scrutiny by Said – a point eloquently made by the Syrian philosopher Sadik al-Azm in his 'Orientalism and Orientalism in Reverse' (Al-Azm 2014: 27–55).
135. Goytisolo 1992: 215.
136. Cf. also Abigail Lee Six: 'Goytisolo never purports to depict Arabs as they really are, but rather to breathe life into the traditional image of the Arab, a process that emerges most clearly in the character of the North African of *Makbara* [...] The Moor may be apprehended both as inherent to the Spanish self and in opposition to it' (Lee Six 1990: 56); and Stanley Black: 'Unlike his non-fictional writings, in which he defends the cause of the real-life Arab, the novels are directed at a European audience and are

meant as an attack on European values. Part of those values is the mythology surrounding the Arab as an image of "the Other" – both a threat and a seduction' (Black 2001a: 31).

137. Epps 1996: 373.
138. Goytisolo 1993: 243.
139. The secondary literature on *Quarantine* is relatively sparse. The most extensive study I have been able to find is a long article in Spanish by Luce Lopéz-Baralt, 'Narrar después de morir: *La cuarentena* de Juan Goytisolo' (1995).
140. Pierre Joris, the Luxembourg-American poet and translator of Meddeb, published a collection of poems written between 2000 and 2012 under the title *Barzakh* (Joris 2014). Although concerned with his own cultural liminality as a poet in a generic sense, the choice for this Arabic-Islamic title can be explained by Joris's sustained interest in and engagement with North African literature following a stint at the University of Constantine in Algeria during the 1970s.
141. Watt 1977: 160.
142. Cf. Abu Zayd's explanation: 'Ibn al-ʿArabī developed an Islamic pantheistic system of thought, according to which the existence of this world is an imaginative one, parallel to the dream-images: this world does exist in the Divine Imagination (*al-khayāl al-mutlaq*; sometimes called *al-khayāl al-munfaṣil, al-barzakh al-kabīr, al-barzakh al-ḥaqīqī* or *barzakh al-barāzikh*). Here we find an ontological interpretation of Q 55:19–20; the image of the merged seas separated by a *barzakh* alludes to the impossibility of distinguishing between existence and non-existence as well as distinguishing between the absolute existence, *al-wujūd al-mutlaq*, and conditional existence, *al-wujūd al-muqayyad*' (Abu Zayd 2011: 64).
143. Burge 2012: 45; cf. also 190–1 for a listing of references to Munkar and Nakīr in classical sources collected by the fifteenth-century religious scholar al-Suyuti (1445–1505).
144. Wensinck 1993: 577.
145. Goytisolo 1994: 11–12 (original italics). Compare this with Abu Zayd's explanation as given in n. 142 above.
146. Goytisolo 1994: 27. This text has been translated into English by Angela Jaffray and published by Anqa in its series of mystical treatises of Ibn Arabi (Ibn Arabi 2006).
147. Cf. the note on Abu Zayd's explanation above, and also Abdelwahab Meddeb's poem in *Portrait du poète en soufi*. See Ch. 2, p. 64 above.
148. Chittick 1989: 118, translated from the introduction to *Futūḥāt al-Makkiyya* (I, 304:16).
149. For descriptions of Munkar and Nakīr's appearances as (bluish-) black, cf. Burge 2012: 54.
150. 'Didn't Ibn Arabi experience a similar apparition on his circumambulations around the Kaaba?' (49). For this episode, cf. Henry Corbin's *Alone with the Alone* (Corbin 1997: 279) and Stephen Hirtenstein's biography, *The Unlimited Mercifier: The Spiritual Life and Thought of Ibn ʿArabi* (Hirtenstein 1999: 151–2).
151. Goytisolo 1994: 32, 37–8, 43, 45, 53, 63–4, 115.

152. The translator Peter Bush has remained close to the Spanish *macabre* and its Arabic original *maqbara*.
153. The translator Helen Lane has decided to retain the Spanish spelling.
154. Goytisolo 1987: 157. In *Quarantine*, Cairo's City of the Dead features in episodes four, twenty-six and thirty-six.
155. Goytisolo 1987:111–12.
156. De Jong 1991: 223.
157. Algar 1991: 225.
158. Goytisolo 2003b: 36.
159. Goytisolo 2003b: 99, 105.
160. First appearing in the travelogue *De la ceca a la meca aproximaciones al mundo islámico* (1997); an English translation was included in *Cinema Eden: Essays from the Muslim Mediterranean*. Also, the earlier-mentioned Luxembourger-American poet and Meddeb translator Pierre Joris writes about Jean Genet in a poem called 'In Larache', which was included in his *Barzakh* collection (Joris 2014: 164–7).
161. For the seven holy men associated with Marrakesh, cf. Goytisolo's essay 'The Popular Worship of Saints in North Africa' (Goytisolo 2003b: 40).
162. Goytisolo's and López-Baralt's working relationship is symbiotic, with the novel *The Virtues of the Solitary Bird* benefiting from López Baralt's scholarship on Juan de la Cruz, while her appreciation for Goytisolo's literary writings have resulted in articles about *Makbara* (1984) and *Quarantine* (1995). Whereas the latter has only appeared in Spanish, the former was reprinted under the slightly different title 'Toward a "mudejar" reading of Juan Goytisolo's *Makbara*' in López-Baralt's *Islam in Spanish Literature: From the Middle Ages to the Present Day* (1992). Tellingly, the title of the originally Spanish book, *Huellas del Islam en la literatura española. De Juan Ruiz a Juan Goytisolo*, also pays homage to Asín Palacios's *Huellas del Islam: Santo Tomas de Aquino, Turmeda, Pascal, San Juan de La Cruz* (1941).
163. Aside from a monograph, *San Juan de la Cruz y Islam*, the bird as a religious and philosophical symbol is also discussed in a chapter about Saint John of the Cross in *Islam in Spanish Literature*.
164. López-Baralt 1992: 69.
165. Goytisolo 1991: 146.
166. López-Baralt 1992: 87.
167. Goytisolo 1991: 7.
168. Epps 1996: 399; cf. also Westerveld 2016: 226–33.
169. Kubra refers to Najm al-Din Kubra; Algazel is al-Ghazali.
170. Ibn Taymiyya (1263–1328) was an important scholar from the Hanbali law school whose ideas continue to influence present-day Salafis; Tomás de Torquemada (1420–98) was the first head of the Spanish Inquisition; Marcelino Pelayo Menéndez (1856–1912) was a historian and literary critic advocating strict adherence to Catholic orthodoxy, and a staunch supporter of Ultramontanism (spiritual and civil papal authority).
171. Goytisolo 2005: 22.
172. Cf. my presentation 'Speculative realism in the Middle East: Rethinking war and terror after Operation Desert Storm' in the seminar of the Institute

of Middle East Studies (IMES), King's College London, 26 January 2021, https://www.kcl.ac.uk/events/speculative-realism-in-the-middle-east-rethinking-war-and-terror-after-operation-desert-storm (last accessed 4 December 2024).

173. Baudrillard 1995: 86.
174. Virilio 2002: 8.
175. Goytisolo 1994: 34–5. In his essay 'The Oral Patrimony of Humanity', Goytisolo mentions how he followed the unfolding of the Gulf War in the now closed Café Matich on Marrakesh's Djemaa el Fna (Goytolo 2003b:11).
176. Goytisolo 2003c: 141–55.
177. *The Blind Rider* was published in English translation in 2005; the English version of *Landscapes of War* appeared in 2000.
178. Cf. the essay 'Tolstoy and the War in the Caucasus: Hadji Murad' in *Landscapes of War* (Goytisolo 2000: 168–73), and Goytisolo's repeated reflections on a line from *Hadji Murad* that also serves as a epigraph in *The Blind Rider*: 'The crushed thistle I saw in the middle of the countryside reminded me of his death'.
179. Goytisolo 2005: 25.

Chapter 4

1. Cf. the third volume of his magisterial *The Venture of Islam* (Hodgson 1974, III).
2. *Balkan* is in fact a Turkish word meaning 'wooded mountains'.
3. Cf. Lukács 1962.
4. For the relevant historical data in this chapter, I have relied on *A Concise History of Albania* written by Bernd Fischer and Oliver Schmitt (2022) and Noel Malcolm's historical surveys of Bosnia and Kosovo (1994, 1998), augmented by details from Jason Goodwin's history of the Ottoman Empire (1998), as well as relevant lemmas from the new edition of the *Encyclopaedia of Islam* and the *Encyclopedia of the Ottoman Empire* (Ágoston and Masters 2009).
5. 'Kosovo' is the Serbian word for blackbird.
6. Malcolm 1994: 45; 1998: 95.
7. Note that the designations Ottoman Albania and Bosnia are anachronisms, as the Ottomans did not use these topographical terms. I use them here to identify the territories concerned by their political-geographical names.
8. The name Sarajevo is thought to be a contraction of the Turkish word for palace or mansion, *saray*, and the Slavic suffix *evo*, thus 'City of the Palace'.
9. Malcolm 1998: 58ff.
10. Celia Hawkesworth, who has translated several of Andrić's works into English, has also produced a biography. However, Michael Martens' *Im Branden der Welt: Ivo Andrić, ein europäisches Leben* is generally regarded as the most authoritative account of Andrić's life (Martens 2022).

11. Tito is the *nom de guerre* of Josip Broz (1892–1980), commander of the Communist Partisans during the Second World War and political leader of Yugoslavia from 1943 until his death.
12. A cultural feature that has also been highlighted by the Bosniak scholar of Islam Smail Balić (1968: 124).
13. Cf. also Andrić 2016: 210. Translating as 'crafty', it is derived from the Arabic word *muzawwir*, meaning 'forger'.
14. As the most senior diplomat in Nazi Germany, Ernst von Weizsäcker (1882–1951) after the war was charged and convicted of war crimes, but eventually released early in 1950. His son Richard went on to become President of the Federal Republic of German (1984–94), while his other son, Carl Friedrich, made a name as a physicist and philosopher.
15. Martens does not hesitate calling Tito a 'mass murderer' (310), whose relentless killing machine 'ate hundreds of thousands' (461) in the first years of his rule.
16. Malcolm 1994: 100.
17. Cf. also the critical remarks by the editors of the English translation (Juričić and Loud 1990: xvii–ix) and John Loud's contribution to *Ivo Andrić Revisited: The Bridge Still Stands* (Loud 1995).
18. Andrić himself alludes to this in the dissertation: 'In content and basic idea, the present treatment is related to other work that I have composed in a different form and on a different occasion' (Andrić 1990: 1).
19. An English translation by Lenore Grenoble has appeared in *The Damned Yard and Other Stories* (Andrić 2012: 183–201).
20. A fourth novel, which was only published posthumously and formally not part of the Bosnian trilogy, is *Omer Pasha Latas*. Covering the period between the French presence in Bosnia and Dalmatia and the Austrian occupation, it tells the story of an Ottoman military officer taking command of Sarajevo in 1850 (Andrić 2018).
21. It was also the first of Andrić's writings read by Carl Schmitt, triggering his enthusiasm for Ivo Andrić's prose style. It has been translated into English and included in *The Damned Yard and Other Stories* (Andrić 2012: 79–91).
22. Himself of Bosnian-Serbian origin, Vucinich (1913–2005) was a specialist in Byzantine and Slavic studies as well as in the history of the Balkans, and the author of *The Ottoman Empire: Its Record and Legacy* (1965).
23. Cooper 1996: xii–xiii.
24. While Šefkija, Mehmed and a third brother, Tewfik, were all Communist Partisans themselves, suggestions were made that Mehmed and Tewfik had not done enough to save their elder brother (Cooper 1996: ix–xi).
25. Antić 2019: 51–3.
26. Antić 2019: 53–62.
27. Cooper 1996: xiii.
28. King Zog ruled from 1928 up until 1939. A scion of a landowning family (during Ottoman times referred to as *beys*), his original name was Ahmed Muhtar Zogollo (1895–1961).
29. For an insight into Ismail Kadare's own explanation (and evasions!) regarding his literary and political manoeuvrings, cf. the interview he gave to Stephane Courtois in February 2006. An English translation by

David Bellos has been included in the British edition of the novel *Chronicle in Stone* under the title 'Truths, Secrets and Lies' (Kadare 2018c: 313–63).

30. Baldwin 2010: n.p.; Ossewaarde 2015: 715.
31. Ossewaarde 2015: 716, 718.
32. Martens 2022: 355. After all, the chief protagonist in the first instalment of Kadare's Ottoman cycle, *The Siege*, is a war chronicler by the name of Mevla Çelebi.
33. As detailed in Nancy Bisaha's *Creating East and West: Renaissance Humanists and the Ottoman Turks* (2004).
34. Written between 1973 and 1977; cross-references between *The Palace of Dreams*, *The Traitor's Niche* and *The Three-Arched Bridge* turn these three novels into an Ottoman trilogy of their own.
35. Kadare 2013: 25.
36. The 'Inn of the Two Roberts' is also mentioned in *The Traitor's Niche*, which Kadare had already completed before he began writing *The Three-Arched Bridge*.
37. Malcolm 1998: 59.
38. Malcolm 1998: 58–80.
39. Fischer and Schmitt 2022: 42.
40. Malcolm 1998: 70, 75.
41. This particular form of corporeal punishment makes a return in the novella *The Blinding Order* from 1984.
42. The *lahuta* and *gusla* are single-stringed instruments used to accompany the singing of epic poetry.
43. This echoes an earlier excuse: challenged that while 'the Turks are marching on us [...] you are singing the same old songs', the minstrels had responded with 'our models need at least a century to adapt' (Kadare 2013: 16).
44. For details, cf. Şentop 2009: 305.
45. Malcolm 1994: 50.
46. Fischer and Schmitt 2022: 57ff.
47. For details cf. Dávid 2009: 13–17.
48. Masters 2009a: 383–4.
49. Among the irregulars, *The Siege* distinguishes the following units: foot soldiers known as *azab*; mounted scouts or raiders (*akinxhis*); and a cavalry specifically recruited for the campaign (*eshkunxhis*). These are augmented by Muslim volunteers (*müslüman*), as well as Kurdish, Persian, Tatar and Caucasian mercenary units. Among the regular forces were the *dalkiliç*, or swordsmen, and the so-called soldiers of death or *serder geçti* – in effect, kamikaze or suicide storm troopers (Kadare 2018a: 7–8).
50. Children from certain ethnic groups were considered ineligible. These included Georgians, Hungarians and Croats living north of Belgrade (on account of their unreliability), as well as Kurds and the peoples living between Erzurum and Karaman (because of their mixed Turkoman-Muslim origins). Also exempt were the children of headmen, shepherds and herdsmen (considered too wild and savage); boys who had already been to Istanbul (!); married teenagers (too worldly-wise); and town dwellers (unsuitable for military discipline). Collectors also had instructions not the take more than one child per family and not to consider boys with

physical and mental defects, or in ill health. For more details cf. Ágoston 2009: 183–5.

51. Malcolm 1998: 96; cf. also Fischer and Schmitt 2022: 57–8.
52. Ágoston 2009: 184.
53. Veinstein 2012: 706; Andric 2021: 15–17.
54. Malcolm 1998: 110. Cf. also Veinstein 2012: 706 and 708.
55. Veinstein 2012: 708. Mehmed Pasha's continued contacts with his Bosnian homeland and family show that the boy levy did not always mean a complete severance of any connection with one's origins.
56. Veinstein 2012: 709.
57. Veinstein 2012: 710. Two even more recent sources about the Hamzevis and their Shaykh include 'The Hamzeviye: A Deviant Movement in Bosnian Sufism' (Algar 1997) and 'A Subaltern Hero: The 1573 Execution of Sheikh Hamza Bali as part of the "Sunnitisation" of the Ottoman Empire' (Asceric-Todd 2022). This particular order is also mentioned in *Death and the Dervish*: 'Abdullah-effendi is a mystic. He belongs to the Bayramiyya order' (Selimović 1996: 36).
58. For a detailed study of Sokollu Mehmed Pasha/Mehmed-Paša Sokolović's place in the writings of Ivo Andrić, cf. the article by Kim Sang Hun (2018).
59. Andrić 2021: 75.
60. The originally Georgian Husref (Hüsrev) Mehmed Pasha (1769–1855) and Ibrahim Halimi (Hilmi) Pasha (1747–1825) were relieved of their positions in Bosnia on account of their failure to quell the Serbian uprising of Karađorđe.
61. The Köprü connection was only established after Köprülü Mehmed Pasha had become a *sipahi* with a *timar*, or landholding, in the Sancak of Amasya; cf. the entry on Köprülü in the *Encyclopedia of Islam* (Gökbilgin and Repp 1986: 256).
62. Cf. Gökbilgin and Repp 1986: 256–63.
63. Cf. Nathalie Clayer's 'Religious Pluralism in the Balkans During the Late Ottoman Imperial Era' (2017).
64. Nock 1933.
65. Clayer 2017: 104–5; Fischer and Schmitt 2022: 91–2; Malcolm 1998: 132–3.
66. Cf. also Endresen 2012: 79–80; Fischer and Schmitt 2022: 91.
67. Because of shared elements of Manichean dualism, there are also connections between Bogomils and the twelfth- and thirteenth-century Albigensians or Cathars of southern France.
68. For a detailed discussion, cf. Malcolm 1994: 27–41.
69. The Ottomans tended to be more tolerant towards Eastern Orthodox Churches than towards Roman Catholics, because of the latter's allegiance to the Papal State and other Catholic political powers in Europe (Malcolm 1994: 55).
70. See p. 174 above.
71. Cf. Gould 2012: 213–21.
72. Cf. 'The Journey of Ali Đerzelez' on the website of the Ivo Andrić Foundation, https://www.ivoandric.org.rs/english/worksen/short-stories/176-the-journey-of-alija-đerzelez (last accessed 1 March 2024).

73. Fischer and Schmitt also note how a 'Sunni counter narrative' challenging this depiction was not formulated until 1975 by Hasan Kaleshi (59–60). For detailed studies of the continuing 'Europeanization' of Islam in Albania in the twentieth century, cf. Nathalie Clayer's 'Der Balkan, Europa und der Islam' (2003), 'Behind the Veil' (2008) and 'Adapting Islam to Europe' (2010).
74. Cf. also Clayer 2017.
75. The most nuanced scholarship on Sufism in the Balkans, past and present, is provided by Nathalie Clayer and Alexandre Popovic.
76. Adapted from Rebecca Gould's notion of 'transgressive sanctity', introduced in her valuable study of Sufi militancy in the literatures of the Caucasus (Gould 2016: 3).
77. Cf. my discussion of Leo Tolstoy's *Hadji Murad* in the previous chapter, p. 155. Novels about Sufi resistance in the Caucasus and the Sudan will be discussed in another volume on Islam and contemporary literature.
78. Halveti is the Turkish rendition of the Arabic Khalwati. Although its exact origins are obscure, it is named after Umar al-Khalwati, a mystic from Herat, but its ideas received wider circulation through the efforts of its second master Yahya Shirvani (d. 1457), who lived in Azerbaijan. Cf. Nathalie Clayer's monograph about the history of this order in the Balkans (1994).
79. For their continuing relevance cf. Popovic's 'Les turuq balkaniques à l'épreuve de la modernité' (2006).
80. Masters 2009b. For their continuing relevance today, cf. Nathalie Clayers 'Bektashi Institutions on Southeastern Europe' (2012).
81. Fischer and Schmitt 2022: 138–9; Malcolm 1998: 217–20. Cf. also Abazi and Doja 2013.
82. Fischer and Schmitt 2022: 59 and 139. For a detailed study of Albanianism in the present-day context, cf. Cecilie Endresen's *Is the Albanian's Religion really 'Albanianism'?* (2012).
83. For detailed studies of these episodes, cf. Mona Hassan's *Longing for the Lost Caliphate* (2016) and *Caliphate Redefined* by Hüseyin Yilmaz (2018).
84. Although the Ottomans made no formal claim to the Caliphate, there was an implicit recognition that the Ottoman Sultans had effectively become Caliphs. While this was made explicit in the 1774 Treaty of Küçük Kaynarca between the Ottoman Empire and Russia, only from 1876 onwards would Sultan Abdulhamid II lay claim to the title 'Caliph' as part of his Pan-Islamism agenda.
85. Note that in Albania, the word *kanun* is actually used to refer to orally transmitted, customary law traditions that must not be confused with the Turkish *kanun*, which refers to written Ottoman law proclaimed through imperial decrees and edicts. The various regional customary law traditions provide a system for adjudicating conflicts and regulating blood feuds in the largely stateless Albanian highlands (the Kanun of Skanderbeg in central Albania, that of his rival Leka Dukagjin in the north, and the Kanun of Labëria in the south; cf. Fischer and Schmitt 2022: 66–7).
86. For a detailed study of the late Ottoman view of this Greece legacy, cf. *Homer, Troy and the Turks: Heritage and Identity in the late Ottoman*

Empire, 1870–1915 by Günay Uslu (2017), former deputy minister of culture in the Netherlands (2022–3).

87. Marina Antić has argued that Selimović's Hasan is modelled after the seventeenth-century Bosnian poet Hasan Kamija (Kaimi), but with the caveat that 'this is enacted primarily in terms of his popular image, brief historical record, and secondary sources on this Ottoman-era poet revolutionary' (Antić 2019: 50).
88. *Muderris* is an Ottoman-Turkish rank accorded to a teacher at a higher Islamic college.
89. Antić 2019: 51, quoting from Jameson 1981: 59–61.
90. For charms, amulets and talismans, cf. also Chapter 2, pp. 79–82 above.
91. *Kapia* is the name for the widened terraced part in the middle of the bridge.
92. The full name was Sanjak of Novi Pazar; it covered a border region between Serbia, Montenegro and Kosovo.
93. Coined by the Soviet writer Ilya Ehrenburg, it was given wider currency through the work of another Marxist, the British historian Eric Hobsbawm.
94. Cf. the architect Giaour in Kadare's *The Siege*, p. 200 above.
95. Cf. Martens 2022: 269–70.
96. Cf. Wachtel 1995: 85.
97. Cf. Chaumette des Fossés, *Voyages en Bosnie dans les années* 1807 et 1808 (1822).
98. Cf. Martens 2022: 207 and 334–5.
99. Abu Hanif refers to Abu Hanifa (d. 767), founder of the eponymous Hanafi School of Islamic Law. Established in Abbasid Baghdad, Hanafi jurists displayed a greater degree of cosmopolitanism than others. The Hanafi School became the predominant law school in the Turkish-speaking parts of the Muslim world, including the Ottoman Empire.
100. Andric 2016: 317. From the chapter 'The Woman Tested' (*Sura al-Mumtahana*, Q 60.7). Cf. also Wachtel 1995: 86, 94, 100.
101. Cf. Endresen 2012: 79–80.
102. It has also formed the subject of a polemical debate with Rexhep Qosja, a Montenegrin-born Albanian novelist and literary historian. Cf. Endresen 2012: 79 and Lika 2020.
103. Cf. Bisaha 2004: 7 and 83–7.
104. Cf. Bisaha 2004: 86, 179.
105. Martens 2022: 444, 448–51; cf. also Malcolm 1994: xx.
106. Martens 2022: 449.
107. Martens 2022: 453.
108. Longinović 1995: 136–7.
109. Cf. Florence Noiville's obituary in the English edition of *Le Monde*, on the occasion of Ismail Kadare's death in July 2024, which pays attention to his political ambiguity: https://www.lemonde.fr/en/obituaries/article/2024/07/01/ismail-kadare-the-great-albanian-writer-dies-aged-88_6676315_15.html (last accessed 31 July 2024).
110. Bromberger 2007: 291.
111. Longinović 1995: 125.

112. Longinović 1995: 124.
113. Cf. President Moisiu's claim, in a speech he gave in 2005 in Oxford, that Islam has only affected Albanians superficially and that it was the result of foreign interference, that is, 'political abuse' at the hands of the Ottomans, Endresen 2012: 80.

Chapter 5

1. Asholt and Viart 2020: 5. Énard specifically mentions Olivier Rolin's *Méroé* (1998), an atmospheric novel set in Sudan, and *L'invention du monde* (1993), an experimental work of metafiction that describes one day, 21 May 1989, on the basis of newspaper reports from across the world. Neither has yet been translated into English.
2. This aspect of Énard's oeuvre was also the topic of the first colloquium dedicated to the writer, which was held at the Centre Marc Bloch of Humbold University in Berlin and published under the title *Mathias Énard et l'érudition du roman* (2020).
3. Asholt and Viart 2020: 21–5. Cf. Nünning's *Von historischer Fiktion zu historiographischer Metafiktion* (1995). Cf. also Chapter 1, p. 34 above.
4. Cf. Bung 2020; de Senarclens 2020.
5. Initially Houellebecq gave 1958 as his birth year, but in 2005 the biographer Denis Demonpion established that 1956 was the correct year (Demonpion 2005).
6. For part of this period, Houellebecq lived in a kind of self-imposed exile in Ireland (2000–2) and the southern Spanish region of Andalusia (2002–12).
7. Cf. also Russell Williams's observation that viewing Houellebecq's novels as *romans à thèse* must be considered 'ambiguous since it is problematic to navigate the line between satire and didactic intent in his fiction' (Williams 2020: 30).
8. Van Wesemael 2004; Clément and van Wesemael 2007 and 2011.
9. Kochin and Spektorowski 2022: 1; Williams 2020: 2.
10. Williams 2020: 3.
11. Novak-Lechevalier 2020: ix.
12. The essay volume has drawn quite some attention from literary critics, including Lovecraft specialists; worth mentioning are Louis Betty's monograph *Without God: Michel Houellebecq and Materialist Horror*, although it falls short in its treatment of the novel *Submission* (Betty 2016), and two articles in the *Lovecraft Annual*, including one by the leading authority on Lovecraft and editor of his collected works, S. T. Joshi (Spaulding 2015; Joshi 2018).
13. Houellebecq 2019: 136.
14. Cf. 'Michel Houellebecq: Finance Novelist' (de Boever 2018: 129–51).
15. Cf. also the essay 'Racial Hatred' (Houellebecq 2019: 123–9). For a critical assessment of Houellebecq's treatment of Lovecraft's racism, cf. S. T. Joshi's article 'Why Michel Houellebecq is Wrong about Lovecraft's Racism' (Joshi 2018).
16. Cf. also Williams 2020: 46–8 and 61–6.

17. *Houris* are mentioned four times in the Qur'an, in much-debated verses generally interpreted as referring to virgins made available for the pleasure of dead souls once they have entered heaven; cf. Bell and Watt 1977: 161–2.
18. Cf. also *In the Presence of Schopenhauer*, where Houellebecq remarks that rereading Comte gives him a kind of 'perverse pleasure', but immediately adds that 'no philosopher, to my knowledge, is so immediately agreeable and reinvigorating to read as Arthur Schopenhauer' (Houellebecq 2020: 4).
19. Graíño Ferrer 2022: 108. This is not necessarily in contradiction with Houellebecq's own observation that 'I became a positivist; to the same degree I ceased to be a Schopenhauerian' (Houellebecq 2020: 4).
20. https://anth1001.wordpress.com/wp-content/uploads/2014/04/enoch-powell_speech.pdf (last accessed 4 December 2024).
21. 'Trump revives "blood and soil" rhetoric at New Hampshire rally', reported in *The Independent*, 16 December 2023, https://www.the-independent.com/news/world/americas/us-politics/trump-blood-new-hampshire-hitler-rhetoric-b2465378.html (last accessed 13 May 2024).
22. Cf. Houellebecq's remark in his essay volume on H. P. Lovecraft about the 'half-crazed Arab' Abdul Al-Hazred 'returning around the year 731 after ten years of utter solitude. Having grown indifferent to the practices of Islam, he devoted the year that followed to writing an impious and blasphemous book, the repugnant *Necronomicon*' (Houellebecq 2019: 57–8).
23. Much has been written about Renan's role in the development of the study of religion as a field of scholarly inquiry. For a recent assessment see Guy Stroumsa's *The Idea of Semitic Monotheism: The Rise and Fall of a Scholarly Myth*, in particular Chapter 5, 'Semitic Monotheism: Renan on Judaism and Islam' (Stroumsa 2021: 111–31).
24. 'It doesn't really work for Muslim countries, your idea ...' (242); 'The Arab countries were the quickest to deal with. In view of their absurd religion, all possible sexual activity seemed to be ruled out' (249).
25. Cited by Sam Cherribi in his contribution to *Houellebecq, the Cassandra of Freedom* (Cherribi 2022: 76, quoting from *Rising Tide*).
26. In the early 2000s, there was indeed a rise in Islamist activity in southern Thailand; cf. my article 'The Predicament of Thailand's Southern Muslims' (Kersten 2004).
27. Williams 2020: 31.
28. Cf. also the observations in the previous chapter (pp. 162–5) concerning the literary quality, as opposed to the scholarly accuracy, of Ivo Andrić's depictions of Ottoman Turks and Bosnian Muslims.
29. It may be another instance of Houellebecq's satire, but in the final paragraph of *Platform*, the character Michel is blatantly wrong when he states that '[unlike] other Asian peoples, the Thai don't believe in ghosts, and have little interest in the fate of corpses; most of them are buried in communal graves' (Houellebecq 2003: 362). In fact, in the case of Thailand the very opposite is the case. Thais are very much concerned with funerary rites and the correct disposal of the dead through cremation. This is also directly connected with the fascination, obsession even, in Thai culture with ghosts (witness their thriving horror movie industry).

30. Translated by Charlotte Mandell in 2015, I have worked with the 2023 edition.
31. Upon his return he put his memories on paper under the title *al-riḥla*, 'Travelogue', which also became the eponym for a genre of Arabic literature. A scholarly translation of selected parts was made in 1929 by Hamilton Gibb (later Professor of Arabic at Oxford and Harvard) and published under the title *Travels in Asia and Africa 1325–1354*. An equally erudite but much more entertaining version is the trilogy by Tim Mackintosh-Smith, published by John Murray as *Travels with a Tangerine* (2001), *The Hall of a Thousand Columns* (2005) and *Landfalls* (2010).
32. For two recent publications concerning the place of Khidr in the Islamic tradition, cf. Patrick Franke's entry in *The Encyclopaedia of Islam* (Franke 2022) and the monograph by Irfan A. Omar, published as *The Prophet al-Khiḍr: Between the Qur'anic Text and Islamic Contexts* (Omar 2022).
33. These lines come from the Qur'an chapter 'The Parties' (*Sura al-Aḥzāb*), which refers to another armed confrontation with the Meccans known as the Battle of the Trench.
34. For a recent book-length study of this movement, cf. *A Sociological Study of the Tabligh Jama'at* (Ali and Sahib 2022).
35. Houellebecq 2006: 311.
36. Houellebecq 2015: 126.
37. Cf. Kersten 2019: 105 and 134.
38. This section's title is a nod to one of the seminal works of the Hungarian scholar of Islam Ignác Goldziher (1850–1921), *Vorlesungen über den Islam* (1910), which has also been translated into English and published under the title *Introduction to Islamic Theology and Law* (1981).
39. *Direction générale de la sécurité intérieure*: the branch of the French intelligence community responsible for counter-espionage and for monitoring activities considered a threat to the republic's national security, as well as for fighting terrorism and cyber-crime.
40. The first book-length study of this 'ethnocultural transnational movement' is José Pedro Zúquete's *The Identitarians: The Movement against Globalism and Islam*. First published in 2018, it mentions Houellebecq's *Submission* by name (Zúquete 2021: 358–9).
41. As Tanneur claims in *Submission*: 'I've spent ten years on the Ben Abbes file, I can honestly say that only a few people in France know him better than I do' (Houellebecq 2015: 127).
42. Houellebecq 2015: 116–17.
43. Cf. also *On Muslim Democracy: Essays and Dialogues* (Ghannouchi and March 2023).
44. Ramadan 2004: 63–77. Cf. also the contextualisation of this notion in *Contemporary Thought in the Muslim World* (Kersten 2019: 105, 177).
45. Already before his fall from grace following allegations of sexual misconduct, Tariq Ramadan was considered controversial, facing accusations of being a wolf in sheep's clothing and that his political correctness was just a cover for the stealthy introduction of an Islamist agenda. Two such portrayals are Caroline Fourest's *Frère Tariq: discours, strategie et méthode de Tariq Ramadan* (2004) and *Tariq Ramadan und die Islamisierung Europas* by Ralph Ghadban (2006).

46. Also called the Battle of Tours and Battle of the Court of Martyrs. For its significance for the nativists/anti-Islamic identitarians, cf. Zúguete 2021: 179–80.
47. The late Samuel Huntington was a professor of International Relations and frequent adviser to the US government. His 1993 article 'The Clash of Civilisations?' in *Foreign Affairs* – later expanded into a bestselling book – effectuated a similar paradigm shift in thinking about the post-Cold War world order as George Kennan's legendary 'X' had done for the Atomic Age.
48. For an inverse scenario of a future France dominated by a reinvigorated Catholicism with Islam as the second most influential religion, cf. Spektorowski 2022: 41–66.
49. René Guénon (1886–1951) was a French writer from a Catholic background who eventually converted to Islam and settled in Egypt. For a detailed study of his place within traditionalism, cf. Mark Sedgwick's *Against the Modern World: Traditionalism and the Secret Intellectual History of the Twentieth Century* (2004).
50. Williams 2020: 1–2 and 237–8.
51. Cf. also Claudia Brühwiler's contribution to the *Houellebecq, the Cassandra of Freedom* volume (Brühwiler 2020: 26–40).
52. The list is long: It can be traced back to the 1990s, from al-Qaeda's bombings of the US embassies in Kenia and Tanzania (1998) and of a housing complex for American military personal in Saudi Arabia (1996) to the killing of foreign tourists at the archaeological sites in the southern Egyptian city of Luxor (1997), as well as an earlier botched attempt on New York's WCT in 1993. A decade earlier, it included the attack on the US Marines barracks in Beirut during the Lebanese civil war (1983) and the assassination of the Egyptian President Sadat (1981). Also, in fact, the Islamic revolution in Iran, the occupation of the Grand Mosque of Mecca by zealous Muslims from within Saudi Arabia itself, and the response to the Soviet invasion of Afghanistan by organised resistance under the banner of Islam at the end of the 1970s – and even the much earlier violent confrontations between the Egyptian Muslim Brotherhood and the Nasser regime back in the 1950s and 1960s – are all part of the same phenomenon: the politicisation of religion in the Muslim world, initially referred to as Islamic fundamentalism, and later renamed Islamism.
53. Kersten 2019: 2, 17, 28.
54. Kochin and Spektorowski 2022: 16–18. Cf. also the chapters 'Western Decline and the Overcoming of the Metaphysical Stage in Houellebecq's Fiction' (Graiño Ferrer 2022: 105–22) and 'Michel Houellebecq's Comparative Science of Religion' (Rogachevsky 2022: 123–40) and articles in the leading English-language Catholic periodical *The Tablet*, 'Michel Houellebecq: An Unlikely Catholic Writer' (Phillips 2019) and in *The Critic*: 'Houellebecq, Joy and Jesus' (Adubato 2023).
55. Asholt and Viart 2020: 6; Evenson 2010: ix, a reference that also recalls Ismail Kadare's celebration of Europe's Greek literary legacy.
56. Cf. also Chapters 1 and 2 on Kermani and Meddeb respectively, pp. 45, 48, 87 and 96–9 above.

57. For Énard's use of fictive academic writings, cf. Vallat and Vuilleumier 2020.
58. Boletsi 2015: 358.
59. Énard 2017: 16–17. In a latter passage, the narrator-protagonist relates how 'Kafkaesque *displacement* is closely linked to his border identity, to his critique of an Austrian Empire that is coming to an end and, beyond that, to the necessity of accepting alterity as an integral part of ourself, as a fertile contradiction' (136).
60. Annemarie Schwarzenbach (1908–42) was a Swiss-born, Berlin-based photographer and journalist. A Bohemian and an inveterate traveller (her destinations included Persia, Afghanistan and Morocco), she had been raised in an androgynous manner by her bisexual mother. Fernando Pessoa (1885–1931) was one of the most important Portuguese writers of the early twentieth century. He used a number of pen names and is considered a leading exponent of modernism. A translator by profession, like Kafka he spent his working life mostly in modest office jobs.
61. For Hamid Dabashi's view of Edward Said, cf. his *On Edward Said: Remembrance of Things Past* (2020).
62. Cf. Said 1995: 258; Dabashi 2009: 17–123.
63. Pursued further in Dabashi's more recent book on the subject, *The Persian Prince* (2023).
64. Cf. also Bung 2020: 56–7.
65. Although most of these writings are in English, detailed and extensive research into the life and thought of Muhammad Asad has primarily been conducted in German. Two of the best studies are: *Leopold Weiss alias Muhammad Asad* (2008) by Günther Windhager and Dominik Schlosser's *Lebensgesetz under Vergemeinschaftungsform: Muḥammad Asad (1900–1992) und sein Islamverständnis* (2015).
66. Windhager 2008: 39–40.
67. As part of these exploits, in Berlin Weiss began a relationship with the woman who would become his first wife, the twenty-two-year-old German painter Else Schiemann-Specht (1878–1927). She too converted to Islam and eventually died of malaria after performing Hajj, leaving the young Muhammad Asad in charge of her son from an earlier marriage, the later science journalist Heinrich Schiemann (1916–2002).
68. Muhammad Asad (trans. Elma Ruth Harder), *The Unromantic Orient: A Journey in the Middle East* (2004). Petaling Jaya: Islamic Book Trust Malaysia.
69. Windhager 2008: 100–2; Schlosser 2015: 120–1.
70. Schlosser 2015: 103.
71. Windhager 2008: 193; Schlosser 2015: 161–8. The Muslims have a similar notion of Abraham as *ḥanīf* or 'primordial monotheist'.
72. Schlosser 2015: 90–4. Also signalled in *Compass*: 'the humility of nomadic life was one of the strongest images in Islam, the great renunciation, the stripping away of worldly trappings in the nakedness of the desert' (Énard 2017: 199).
73. Schlosser 2015: 307–10.
74. *Compass* also features another interlocutor of Ritter who has the same family name, but is no relation of Leopold Weiss/Muhammad Asad: Julien

Jalâl Eddine Weiss (1953–2015), musician and composer, founder of the Al-Kindi Assemble (Énard 2017: 207).

75. Schlosser 2015: 122; 343–6.
76. For Asad's attitude towards marriage, cf. Schlosser 2015: 146, 159–60.
77. Kersten 2019: 28; cf. also John Calvert's *Sayyid Qutb and the Origins of Radical Islamism* (2010) and Jan-Peter Hartung's *A System of Life: Mawḍūdī and the Ideologisation of Islam* (2013). Whereas Sayyid Qutb had read an Arabic translation of *Islam at the Crossroads* (1934), the first book written by Muhammad Asad as a Muslim (Schlosser 2015: 123, 205), Mawdudi showed himself critical of Asad's later Qur'an translation and exegesis (Schlosser 2015: 319).
78. Written in 1936, but first published in 1952 under the title *Avicenna und die aristotelische Linke*, it was translated in 2019 by Loren Goldman and Peter Thompson.
79. Énard 2017: 200.
80. For a detailed and wider analysis of Bloch's speculative materialism in English, cf. Cat Moir's *Ernst Bloch's Speculative Materialism: Ontology, Epistemology, Politics* (2020).
81. Bloch 2019: 14–15.
82. Bloch 2019: 20–1; Goldman 2019: xviii.
83. Bloch 2019: 29–31.

Bibliography

Abazi, E. and Doja, A. (2013). 'Further Considerations on the Politics of Religious Discourse: Naim Frashëri and his Pantheism in the Course of Nineteenth-Century Albanian Nationalism'. *Middle Eastern Studies*, 49(6), 859–79. doi: https://doi.org/10.1080/00263206.2013.836495.

Abdel-Jouad, H. (1991). 'The Dialectics of the Archaic and the Post-Modern in Maghrebian Literature Written in French'. *Studies in 20th Century Literature*, 15(1), 59–76.

Abu Zaid, N. (1999). *Ein Leben mit der Islam: Erzählt von Navid Kermani*. Freiburg: Herder.

Abu Zayd, N. (2011). 'Towards Understanding the Qur'an's Worldview: An Autobiographical Reflection'. In G. S. Reynolds (ed.), *New Perspectives on the Qur'an: The Qur'an in its Historical Context* 2 (pp. 47–87). London and New York: Routledge.

Adib-Moghaddam, A. (2018). *Psycho-nationalism: Global Thought, Iranian Imaginations*. Cambridge and New York: Cambridge University Press.

Adorno, T. W. (ed. B. O'Connor) (2000). *The Adorno Reader*. Malden, MA: Blackwell.

Adorno, T. W. (trans. E. Jephcott) (2005). *Minima Moralia: Reflections from Damaged Life*. London and New York: Verso.

Adubato, S. (2023). 'Houellebecq, Joy and Jesus: A Morbid Pessimist Reminds Us of the Purity of Faith'. *The Critic*, 19 June. https://thecritic.co.uk/houellebecq-joy-and-jesus/.

Agamben, G. (trans. K. Attell) (2005). *State of Exception*. Chicago and London: University of Chicago Press.

Agamben, G. (trans. L. Chiesa) (2011). *The Kingdom and the Glory: For a Theological Genealogy of Economy and Government*. Stanford: Stanford University Press.

Agamben, G. (trans. A. Kotsko) (2011). *The Sacrament of Language: An Archaeology of the Oath*. Stanford: Stanford University Press.

Agamben, G. (trans. A. Kotsko) (2013). *Opus Dei: An Archaeology of Duty*. Stanford: Stanford University Press.

Agamben, G. (trans. A. Kotsko) (2013). *The Highest Poverty: Monastic Rules and Form-of-Life*. Stanford: Stanford University Press.

Ágoston, G. (2009). 'Devşirme'. In G. Ágoston and B. Masters (eds), *Encyclopedia of the Ottoman Empire* (pp. 183–5). New York: Facts on File.

Ahmed, S. (2015). *What Is Islam? The Importance of Being Islamic*. Princeton, NJ: Princeton University Press.
Aïdi, H. (2017). *Juan Goytisolo*. https://merip.org/2017/12/juan-goytisolo/.
Alami, A. E. (2000). *Métalangage et philologie extatique. Essai sur Abdelwahab Meddeb*. Paris: L'Harmattan.
Al-Kassim, D. (2010). *On Pain of Speech: Fantasies of the First Order and the Literary Rant*. Los Angeles: University of California Press.
Al-Azm, S. J. (2014). *Is Islam Secularizable? Challenging Political and Religious Taboos*. Berlin: Gerlach Press.
Albrecht, A. (2005). 'Im Zeichen der Dissidenz. Juan Goytisolos "Rückforderung des Conde don Julián"'. *Monatshefte*, 97(2), 184–212.
Algar, H. (1991). 'Malāmatiyya 2. In Iran and the Eastern Lands'. In C. E. Bosworth, E. van Donzel, B. Lewis and C. Pellat (eds), *The Encyclopaedia of Islam – New Edition* (Vol. VI, pp. 224–5). Leiden: Brill.
Algar, H. (1997). 'Hamzeviye: A Deviant Movement in Bosnian Sufism'. *Islamic Studies*, 36(2–3), 243–61. https://www.jstor.org/stable/23076196.
Ali, J. A. and Sahib, R. (2022). *A Sociological Study of Tabligh Jama'at: Working for Allah*. Cham: Palgrave Macmillan.
Althaus-Reid, M. (1993). 'Paul Ricoeur and the Methodology of the Theology of Liberation: The Hermeneutics of J. Severino Croatto, Juan Luis Segundo and Clodovis Boff'. Unpublished PhD thesis, University of St Andrews.
Althaus-Reid, M. (2002). *Indecent Theology: Theological Perversions in Sex, Gender and Politics*. London and New York: Routledge.
Althaus-Reid, M. (2003). *The Queer God*. London and New York: Routledge.
Alvarez, L. M. (2002). 'Anselm Turmeda: The Visionary Humanism of a Muslim Convert and Catalan Prophet'. In A. Classen (ed.), *Meeting the Foreign in the Middle Ages* (pp. 172–91). London and New York: Routledge.
Anderson, P. (2004, 23 September). 'Union Sucrée'. *London Review of Books*, 26(18).
Andrić, I. (ed. Ž. Juričić and J. F. Loud) (1990). *The Development of Spiritual Life in Bosnia under the Influence of Turkish Rule*. Durham and London: Duke University Press.
Andrić, I. (trans. C. Hawkesworth) (2012). *The Damned Yard and Other Stories*. Belgrade: Dereta.
Andrić, I. (trans. C. H. Rakić) (2016). *Bosnian Chronicle*. London: Apollo.
Andrić, I. (trans. C. Hawkesworth) (2018). *Omer Pasha Latas: Marshal to the Sultan*. New York: New York Review of Books.
Andrić, I. (trans. L. F. Edwards) (2021). *The Bridge on the Drina*. New York, London, Toronto: Everyman's Library, Alfred A. Knopf.
Anjum, O. (2010). 'Sufism without Mysticism? Ibn Qayyim al-Ǧawziyya's Objectives in "Madāriğ al-Sālikīn"'. *Oriente Moderno*, 90(1), 161–88.
Ansari, A. a.-H. (1988). *Kitāb Manāzil al-Sā'irīn*. Beirut: Dar al-Kutub al-Ilmiya.
Ansari, A. a.-H. (trans. H. Rifaʿi) (2011). *Stations of the Wayfarers*. Paris: Éditions Albouraq.
Antić, M. (2019). 'Historical Hasan: Poetry and Revolution in Selimović's Death and the Dervish'. *Dialogue – Journal for Philosophy and Social Theory*, 3–4, 48–72. doi: 10.5644/DIJALOG.2019.3-4.05.

Aresu, B. (2020). 'Abdelwahab Meddeb, or the Plenitude of Heterology'. *Expressions maghrébines*, 19(2), 27–44.

Asceric-Todd, I. (2022). 'A Subaltern Hero: The 1573 Execution of Sheikh Hamza Bali as Part of the "Sunnitization" of the Ottoman Empire'. In A. J. Newman (ed.), *Iranian / Persianate Subalterns in the Safavid Period: Their Role and Depiction* (pp. 193–210). Berlin: Gerlach Press.

Asholt, W. and Viart, D. (2020). 'L'oeuvre de Mathias Énard, les Incultes et le roman contemporain français: regards croisés'. In M. Messling, C. Ruhe, L. Seauve and V. de Senarclens (eds), *Mathias Énard et l'érudition du roman* (pp. 4–30). Leiden and Boston: Brill Rodopi.

Asín Palacios, M. (1927). *Dante y el islam*. Madrid: Editorial Voluntad.

Asín Palacios, M. (1941). *Huellas del Islam: Santo Tomas de Aquino, Turmeda, Pascal, San Juan de la Cruz*. Madrid: Espasa-Calpe.

Asín Palacios, M. (1943). *La escatologia musulmana en la Divina Comedia sequida de la historia y critica de una polemica*. Madrid: Consejo superior de investigaciones scientíficas.

Baldick, R. (2006). *The Life of J.-K. Huysmans* (2nd edition edited by Brendan King). Sawtry: Dedalus.

Baldwin, B. (2010). *Review of Ismail Kadare: The Writer and the Dictatorship 1957–1990 by Peter Morgan*. https://www.islamicpluralism.org/2097/ismail-kadare.

Balić, S. (1968). 'Der bosnisch-herzegowinische Islam'. *Der Islam: Zeitschrift für Geschichte und Kultur des islamischen Orients*, 44, 116–37.

Barber, D. C. (2014). *Deleuze and the Naming of God*. Edinburgh: Edinburgh University Press.

Bataille, G. (trans. R. Hurley) (1991). *The Accursed Share: An Essay on General Economy. Volume 1: Consumption*. New York: Zone Books.

Baudrillard, J. (trans. P. Patton) (1995). *The gulf war did not take place*. Bloomington and Indianapolis: Indiana University Press.

Bauer, T. (2011). *Die Kultur der Ambiguität: Eine andere Geschichte des Islams*. Berlin: Insel Verlag.

Bauer, T. (trans. H. Biesterfeldt and T. Tunstall) (2021). *A Culture of Ambiguity: An Alternative History of Islam*. New York: Columbia University Press.

Bazargan, M. (trans. M. Gerhold) (2006). *Und Jesus ist sein Prophet: Der Koran und die Christen* (edited and with an introduction by Navid Kermani). Munich: C. H. Beck.

Bellaigue, C. (2012). *Patriot of Persia. Muhammad Mossadegh and a tragic Anglo-American coup*. New York: HarperCollins.

Bencheikh, J. E. (1993). 'Miʿrādj - 2. In Arabic Literature'. In C. E. Bosworth, E. van Donkel, W. P. Heinrichs and C. Pellat (eds), *Encyclopaedia of Islam – New Edition* (Vol. VII, pp. 100–3). Leiden: Brill.

Benjamin, W. (1968). 'The Task of the Translator'. In W. Benjamin and H. Arendt (eds), *Illuminations, Essays and Reflections* (pp. 69–82). New York: Schocken.

Betty, L. (2016). *Without God: Michel Houellebecq and Materialist Horror*. University Park, PA: Pennsylvania State University Press.

Bhabha, H. (1994). *The Location of Culture*. London and New York: Routledge.

Bieder, M. (1984). 'Cárcel Verbal: Narrative Discourse in Makbara'. *Review of Contemporary Fiction – Juan Goytisolo Reader*, 4(2), 120–7.

Bisaha, N. (2004). *Creating East and West: Renaissance Humanists and the Ottoman Turks*. Philadelphia: University of Pennsylvania Press.
Black, S. (2001a). *Juan Goytisolo and the Poetics of Contagion: The Evolution of a Radical Aesthetic in the Later Novels*. Liverpool: Liverpool University Press.
Black, S. (2001b). 'Mysticism, Postmodernism and Transgression in La Cuarentena by Juan Goytisolo'. *Bulletin of Hispanic Studies*, 78(2), 241–57.
Bloch, E. (1959). *Das Prinzip Hoffnung*. Frankfurt am Main: Suhrkamp.
Bloch, E. (1969). *Spuren*. Frankfurt am Main: Suhrkamp.
Bloch, E. (trans. L. Goldman and P. Thompson) (2019). *Avicenna and the Aristotelian Left*. New York: Columbia University Press.
Boletsi, M. (2015). 'Waiting for the Barbarians after 9/11: Functions of a Topos in Liminal Times'. In C. Moser and M. Boletsi (eds), *Barbarism Revisited: New Perspectives on an Old Concept* (pp. 355–75). Leiden and Boston: Brill.
Braidotti, R. (2000). 'Teratologies'. In I. Buchanan and C. Colebrook (eds), *Deleuze and Feminist Theory* (pp. 156–72). Edinburgh: Edinburgh University Press.
Braidotti, R. (2011). *Nomadic Subjects: Embodiment and Sexual Difference in Contemporary Feminist Theory*. New York: Columbia University Press.
Braidotti, R. (2012). 'Becoming World'. In R. Braidotti, O. Blaagaard and P. Hanafin (eds), *After Cosmopolitanism* (pp. 29–66). London and New York: Routledge.
Braidotti, R. (2012). *Nomadic Theory: The Portable Rosi Braidotti*. New York: Columbia University Press.
Braun, L. V. (1987). 'The "Intertextualization" of Unamuno and Juan Goytisolo's "Reinvindicacion del Conde Don Julian"'. *Hispanofili*, 89, 39–56.
Bria, G. (2022). 'Nationalism, Post-Secular and Sufism: The Making of Neo-Bektashism by Moikom Zeqo in Post-Socialist Albania'. *Religions*, 13(9), 828. doi: https://doi.org/10.3390/rel13090828.
Bromberger, C. (2007). 'Bridge, Wall, Mirror; Coexistence and Confrontations in the Mediterranean World'. *History and Anthropology*, 18(3), 291–307. doi: 10.1080/02757200701389030.
Brühwiler, C. F. (2022). 'Submission and Decline: Houellebecq as Cassandra and Jester'. In M. Kochin and A. Spektorowski (eds), *Houellebecq, the Cassandra of Freedom: Submission and Decline* (pp. 24–40). Leiden and Boston: Brill.
Bugeja, N. (2012). *Postcolonial Memoir in the Middle East: Rethinking the Liminal in Mashriqi Writing*. London and New York: Routledge.
Bung, S. (2020). 'Ni roman historique, ni roman à thèse: comment lire Boussole?'. In M. Messling, C. Ruhe, L. Seauve and V. de Senarclens, *Mathias Énard et l'érudition du Roman* (pp. 51–62). Leiden: Brill.
Bunyazade, K. (2013). 'The Path of Truth: From Absolute to Reality, From Point to Circle'. In A.-T. Tymieniecka (ed.), *Phenomenology and the Human Positioning in the Cosmos: The Life-World, Nature, Earth Book One* (pp. 245–58). Dordrecht: Springer.
Burge, S. (2012). *Angels in Islam: Jalāl al-Dīn al-Suyūṭī's al-Ḥabā'ik fī akhbār al-malā'ik*. London and New York: Routledge.
Calasso, R. (trans. G. Brock) (2005). *K*. London: Penguin.
Calvert, J. (2010). *Sayyid Qutb and the Origin of Radical Islamism*. London: Hurst.

Caputo, J. D. and Vattimo, G. (ed. J. W. Robbins) (2007). *After The Death of God*. New York: Columbia University Press.
Carra de Vaux, B. (1986). 'Barzakh'. In P. Bearman, T. Bianquis, C. E. Bosworth, E. van Donzel and W. Heinrichs (eds), *Encyclopaedia of Islam, Second Edition* (Vol. I, pp. 1,071–2). Leiden: Brill.
Casanova, P. (trans. M. DeBevoise) (2004). *The World Republic of Letters*. London and Cambridge MA: Harvard University Press.
Casanova, P. (2005). 'Literature as World'. *New Left Review*, 31 (January–February), 71–90.
Cassirer, E. (1944). *An Essay on Man: An Introduction to a Philosophy of Human Culture*. New Haven and London: Yale University Press.
Castro, A. (1948). *España en su historia: Cristianos, Moros y Judios*. Buenos Aires: Editorial Losada.
Castro, A. (trans. E. L. King) (1954). *The Structure of Spanish History*. Princeton, NJ: Princeton University Press.
Castro, A. (trans. W. F. King and S. Margaretten) (1971). *The Spaniards: An Introduction to their History*. Berkeley, Los Angeles and London: University of California Press.
Chalmeta, P. (1991). 'Mudéjar'. In C. E. Bosworth, E. van Donzel, W. P. Heinrichs and C. Pellat (eds), *The Encyclopaedia of Islam – New Edition* (Vol. VII, pp. 286–9). Leiden: Brill.
Chatwin, B. (1990). *What Am I Doing Here?* London and New York: Penguin.
Chatwin, B. (ed. J. Borm and M. Graves) (1997). *Anatomy of Restlesness: Selected Writings 1969–1989*. London and New York: Penguin.
Cherribi, S. (2022). 'The Mother of Invention: Theo van Gogh in Houellebecq's Rearview Mirror'. In M. Kochin and A. Spektorowski (eds), *Houellebecq, the Cassandra of Freedom: Submission and Decline* (pp. 67–84). Leiden and Boston: Brill.
Chittick, W. C. (1989). *The Sufi Path of Knowledge: Ibn al-'Arabi's Metaphysics of Imagination*. Albany: State University of New York Press.
Clayer, N. (1994). *Mystiques, État et Société: Les Halvetis dans l'aire balkanique*. Leiden: Brill.
Clayer, N. (2003). 'Der Balkan, Europa und der Islam'. In K. Kaser, D. Gramshammer-Hohl and R. Pichler (eds), *Wieser Enzyklopädie des Europäischen Ostens* (Vol. 11: Europa und die Grenzen im Kopf, pp. 303–28). Klagenfurt: Wieser Verlag.
Clayer, N. (2008). 'Behind the Veil: the Reform of Islam in Inter-war Albania or the Search for a "Modern" and "European" Islam'. In N. Clayer and E. Germain (eds), *Islam in Inter-War Europe* (pp. 128–55). London: Hurst.
Clayer, N. (2010). 'Adapting Islam To Europe: The Albanian Example'. In C. Voss and J. Telbizova-Sack (eds), *Islam und Muslime in (Südost) Europa im Kontext von Transformation und EU-Erweiterung* (pp. 53–69). Munich: Otto Sagner.
Clayer, N. (2012). 'The Bektashi Institutions in Southeastern Europe: Alternative Official Islamic Structures and their Limits'. *Welt des Islams*, 52(2), 183–203.
Clayer, N. (2017). 'Religious Pluralism in the Balkans during the late Ottoman Era: Towards a Dynamic Model'. In R. Murphey (ed.), *Imperial Lineages and Legacies in the Eastern Mediterranean* (pp. 101–14). London and New York: Routledge.

Clément, M. L. and van Wesemael, S. (2007). *Michel Houellebecq sous la loupe*. Amsterdam and New York: Rodopi.
Clément, M. L. and van Wesemael, S. (2011). *Michel Houellebecq à la Une*. Amsterdam and New York: Rodopi.
Connolly, T. C. (2020). 'Corporeal Fantasies, False Bodies: Ways of Seeing in Abdelwahab Meddeb's Phantasia'. *Expressions maghrebines*, 19(2), 135–55.
Cooper Jr., H. R. (1996). 'Introduction'. In M. Selimović, *Death and the Dervish* (pp. ix–xvii). Evanston, IL: Northwestern University Press.
Cooper, T. (2021). *Queer and Indecent: An Introduction to the Theology of Marcella Althaus-Reid*. London: SCM Press.
Corbin, H. (1976). *Shihâboddîn Yahyâ Sohravardî, Shaykh al-Ishrâq: L'Archange empourpré: Quinze traités et récits mystiques*. Paris: Fayard.
Corbin, H. (ed. and trans. A. Schimmel) (1989). *Die smaragdene Vision: der Licht-Mensch im persischen Sufismus*. Munich, Diederich.
Corbin, H. (trans. N. Pearson) (1994). *The Man of Light in Iranian Sufism*. New Lebanon, NY: Omega.
Corbin, H. (trans. R. Manheim) (1997). *Alone with the Alone: Creative Imagination in the Sufism of Ibn 'Arabi*. Princeton, NJ: Princeton University Press.
Coury, D. N. (2013). 'Enlightenment Fundamentalism: Zafer Şenocak, Navid Kermani and Multiculturalism in Germany Today'. In E. Jeremiah and F. Matthes (eds), *Edinburgh German Yearbook 7: Ethical Approaches in Contemporary German-Language Literature and Culture* (pp. 139–57). Camden House, NY: Boydell & Brewer.
Coury, D. N. (2014). 'Ways of Belonging: Navid Kermani and the Muslim Turn in Contemporary German Literature'. *Colloquia Germanica – Themenheft, Framing Islam: Faith, Fascination, and Fear in Twenty-First-Century German Culture*, 47(1/2), 9–29.
Coury, D. N. (2016). 'Kafka and the Quran: Patriotism, Culture, and Post-National Identity'. In H. Druxes, K. Machtans and A. Mihailovic (eds), *Navid Kermani* (pp. 49–67). Oxford: Peter Lang.
Dabashi, H. (1999). *Truth and Narrative: The Untimely Thoughts of 'Ayn Al-Quḍāt Al-Hamadhānī*. London and New York: Routledge.
Dabashi, H. (2008). *Islamic Liberation Theology: Resisting the Empire*. London and New York: Routledge.
Dabashi, H. (2009). *Post-Orientalism: Knowledge and Power in a Time of Terror*. New Brunswick, NH: Transaction.
Dabashi, H. (2011). *Shi'ism: A Religion of Protest*. Cambridge MA: Belknap Press.
Dabashi, H. (2012). *The World of Persian Literary Humanism*. Cambridge, MA: Harvard University Press.
Dabashi, H. (2013). *Being a Muslim in the World*. London: Palgrave Macmillan.
Dabashi, H. (2015a). *Persophilia: Persian Culture on the Global Scene*. Cambridge, MA and London: Harvard University Press.
Dabashi, H. (2015b). *Can Non-Europeans Think?* London: Zed Books.
Dabashi, H. (2020). *On Edward Said: Remembrance of Things Past*. Chicago: Haymarket Books.

Dabashi, H. (2022). *The End of Two Illusions: Islam after the West*. Oakland, CA: University of California Press.
Dabashi, H. (2023). *The Persian Prince: The Rise and Resurrection of an Imperial Archetype*. Redwood City, CA: Stanford University Press.
Daftari, F. (1992). *The Ismāʿīlīs: Their History and Doctrines*. Cambridge: Cambridge University Press.
Damrosch, D. (2003). *What Is World Literature?* Princeton and Oxford: Princeton University Press.
Dávid, G. (2009). 'Administration, Provincial'. In G. Ágoston and B. Masters (eds), *Encyclopedia of the Ottoman Empire* (pp. 13–17). New York: Facts on File.
Davis, S. (2003). *Juan Goytisolo and the Institution of the Spanish Canon*. Birmingham: University of Birmingham. https://core.ac.uk/download/pdf/16292863.pdf.
de Boever, A. (2018). *Finance Fictions: Realism and Psychosis in a Time of Economic Crisis*. New York: Fordham University Press.
de Jong, F. (1991). 'Malāmatiyya 1. In the Central Islamic Lands'. In C. E. Bosworth, E. van Donzel, B. Lewis and C. Pellat (eds), *The Encyclopaedia of Islam – New Edition* (Vol. VI, pp. 223–4). Leiden: Brill.
Deleuze, G. (ed. and trans. Anne Boyman) (2001). *Pure Immanence: Essays on Life*. New York: Zone Books.
Deleuze, G. (ed. M. Salemy, trans. T. Yanick, J. Adams and A. Kleinherenbrink) (2015). *What Is Grounding?* Grand Rapids, MI: &&& Publishers.
Deleuze, G. and Guattari, F. (trans. D. Polan) (1994). *Kafka: Toward a Minor Literature*. Minneapolis: University of Minnesota Press.
Deleuze, G. and Guattari, F. (trans. B. Massumi) (2004). *A Thousand Plateaus: Capitalism and Schizophrenia*. London and New York: Continuum.
Demonpion, D. (2005). *Houellebecq Non Autorisé: Enquête sur un Phénomène*. Paris: Maren Sell.
Derrida, J. and Vattimo, G. (trans. D. Webb) (1998). *Religion*. Palo Alto: Stanford University Press.
De Sondy, A. (2014). *The Crisis of Islamic Masculinities*. London: Bloomsbury.
Dickinson, C. (2011). *Agamben and Theology*. London and New York: T. & T. Clark.
Djedid, O. (2014). 'La double absence dans Talismano d'Abdelwahab Meddeb'. *University of Toronto Quarterly* (3), 723–38.
Doja, A. (2006). 'A Political History of Bektashism in Albania'. *Totalitarian Movements and Political Religions*, 7(1), 83–107.
Doja, A. (2013). 'The Politics of Religious Dualism: Naim Frashëri and his Elective Affinity to Religion in the Course of 19th-Century Albanian Activism'. *Social Compass*, 60(1), 115–33. doi: 0.1177/0037768612471770.
Drayson, E. (2007). *The King and the Whore: Roderic and La Cava*. London: Palgrave Macmillan.
Druxes, H. (2016). 'The Crisis of (Re-)Productivity in Dein Name'. In H. Druxes, K. Machtans, Karolin and A. Mihailovic (eds), *Navid Kermani* (pp. 163–79). Oxford: Peter Lang.
Druxes, H. and Machtans, K. (2016). 'Introduction: The Intercultural Project of Navid Kermani'. In H. Druxes, K. Machtans and A. Mihailovic (eds), *Navid*

Kermani (Vol. 3 Contemporary German Writers and Filmmakers, pp. 1–14). Munich: Peter Lang.

Druxes, H., Machtans, K. and Mihailovic, A. (2016). *Navid Kermani* (Vol. 3 Contemporary German Writers and Filmmakers). Oxford: Peter Lang.

Eagleton, T. (2005). 'The Empire Writes Back'. *New Statesman*, pp. 50–1.

El-Desouky, A. (2013). 'Naẓm, Iʿjāz, Discontinuous Kerygma: Approaching Qur'anic Voice on the Other Side of the Poetic'. *Journal of Quranic Studies*, 15(2), 1–21.

El-Desouky, A. (2014). 'Between Hermeneutic Provenance and Textuality: The Qur'an and the Question of Method in Approaches to World Literature'. *Journal of Qur'anic Studies*, 16(3), 11–38.

Elhariry, Y. (2016). 'Abdelwahab Meddeb, Sufi Poets, and the New Francophone Lyric'. *PMLA*, 131(2), 255–68.

Elhariry, Y. (2017). 'Sufis in Mecca: Abdelwahab Meddeb, Ibn Arabi and the New Lyric'. In Y. Elhariry (ed.), *Pacifist Invasions: Arabic, Translation and the Postfrancophone Lyric* (pp. 134–51). Liverpool: Liverpool University Press.

Elhariry, Y. (2020). 'The Birds'. *Expressions maghrébines*, 19(2), 57–76.

Elmarsafy, Z. (2009). *The Enlightenment Qur'an: The Politics of Translation and the Construction of Islam*. Oxford: OneWorld.

Elmarsafy, Z. (2014). *Sufism in the Contemporary Arab Novel*. Edinburgh: Edinburgh University Press.

Elmarsafy, Z. (2020). 'The Sufi, the Idol, and the Icon: Meddeb's Visions'. *Expressions maghrébines*, 19(2), 99–117.

Elmarsafy, Z. (2021). *Esoteric Islam in Modern French Thought: Massignon, Corbin, Jambet*. London and New York: Bloomsbury Academic.

El Shakry, H. (2017). 'Abdelwahab Meddeb and the Po/Ethics of Sufism'. *Expressions Maghrebines*, 16(s), 95–115.

El Shakry, H. (2020). *The Literary Qur'an: Narrative Ethics in the Maghreb*. New York: Fordham University.

El Shakry, H. (2022). 'The Ontology of Becoming'. *Publications of the Modern Language Association*, 137(2), 370–80.

Énard, M. (trans. C. Mandell) (2010). *Zone*. Rochester, NY: Open Letter – Literary Translations from the University of Rochester.

Énard, M. (trans. C. Mandell) (2017). *Compass*. London: Fitzcarraldo Editions.

Énard, M. (trans. C. Mandell) (2023). *Street of Thieves* (2nd edn). London: Fitzcarraldo Editions.

Endresen, C. (2012). *Is the Albanian's Religion Really 'Albanianism'? Religion and Nation According to Muslim and Christian Leaders in Albania*. Wiesbaden: Harrasowitz Verlag.

Epps, B. (1996). *Significant Violence: Oppression and Resistance in the Later Narrative of Juan Goytisolo, 1970–1990*. Oxford and New York: Oxford University Press.

Erhart, W. (2018). 'Grundton überhaupt des Lebens: Navid Kermanis Neil Young'. In T. Hofmann (ed.), *Text + Kritik 217: Navid Kermani*, I(18), 32–9.

Ernst, C. W. (1997). *Sufism: An Essential Introduction to the Philosophy and Practice of the Mystical Tradition of Islam*. Boston: Shambala South Asian Editions.

Evenson, B. (2010). 'Introduction'. In M. Énard, *Zone* (pp. vii–xi). Rochester, NY: Open Letter.

Farhadi, A. (1996). *'Abdullah Ansari of Herat (1006–1080 C.E.): An Early Sufi Master*. Richmond: Curzon Press.

Farley, W. (2016). 'Only Goodness Matters: Reflections on Theodicy with Klaus von Stosch and Jefferey Long'. In M. V. Roberts (ed.), *Comparing Faithfully: Insights for Systematic Theological Reflection* (pp. 126–44). New York: Fordham University Press.

Fernández Morera, D. (2016). *The Myth of the Andalusian Paradise: Muslims, Christians, and Jews under Islamic Rule in Medieval Spain*. Wilmington, DE: ISI Books.

Fieni, D. (2020). 'Virtual Secularization: Abdelwahab Meddeb's "Walking Cure" and the Immigrant Body in France'. In D. Fieni (ed.), *Decadent Orientalisms: The Decay of Colonial Modernity* (pp. 136–58). New York: Fordham University Press.

Fierro, M. and García-Sanjuán, A. (2022). 'The Reception of Al-Andalus 1821–2021: Two Hundred Years of Study and Debate'. In A. Hughes and A. Aghdassi (eds), *New Methods in the Study of Islam* (pp. 36–68). Edinburgh: Edinburgh University Press.

Filios, D. K. (2009). 'Legends of the Fall: Conde Julián in Medieval Arabic and Hispano-Latin Historiography'. *Medieval Encounters*, 15(2–4), 375–90.

Filiz, K. (2020). 'Eine andere Beziehung, eine andere Offenbarung: Berührungspunkte zwischen Jean-Luc Marion und der Islamischen Philosophie'. In M. Staudigl (ed.), *Der Primat der Gegebenheit: Zur Transformation der Phänomenologie nach Jean-Luc Marion* (pp. 398–426). Freiburg and Munich: Karl Alber.

Fischer, B. J. and Schmitt, O. J. (2022). *A Concise History of Albania*. Cambridge: Cambridge University Press.

Franke, P. (2022). 'Khiḍr'. In K. Fleet, G. Kramer, D. Matringe, J. Nawas and D. Steward (eds), *Encyclopaedia of Islam Three Online*. Leiden: Brill. https://doi-org.kuleuven.e-bronnen.be/10.1163/1573-3912_ei3_COM_35534.

Garcia Probert, M. A. and Sijpesteijn, P. (2022). *Amulets and Talismans of the Middle East and North Africa in Context: Transmission, Efficacy and Collections*. Leiden: Brill.

Gauch, S. (1998). 'Phantasmatic Artifacts: Postcolonial Meditations by a Tunisian Exile'. *Mosaic: An Interdisciplinary Critical Journal*, 32(2), 124–45.

Ghannouchi, R. and March, A. F. (2023). *On Muslim Democracy: Essays and Dialogues*. London and New York: Oxford University Press.

Goethe, J. W. (trans. E. Dowden) (1914). *West-Eastern Divan*. London and Toronto: J. M. Dent & Sons.

Gökbilgin, M. T. and Repp, R. C. (1986). 'Köprülü'. In C. Bosworth, E. van Donzel, B. Lewis and C. Pellat (eds), *Encyclopaedia of Islam – New Edition* (pp. 256–63). Leiden: Brill.

Gould, R. (2012). 'Allegories and the Critique of Sovereignties: Ismail Kadare's Political Theologies'. *Studies in the Novel*, 44(2), 208–30.

Gould, R. (2016). *Writers and Rebels: The Literature of Insurgency in the Caucasus*. New Haven, CT: Yale University Press.

Goytisolo, J. (trans. H. Lane) (1987). *Landscapes After the Battle*. London: Serpent's Tail.

Goytisolo, J. (trans. H. Lane) (1990). *Juan the Landless*. London: Serpent's Tail.

Goytisolo, J. (H. Lane) (1991). *The Virtues of the Solitary Bird*. London: Serpent's Tail.

Goytisolo, J. (trans. H. Lane) (1992). *Saracen Chronicles: A Selection of Literary Essays*. London: Quartet.

Goytisolo, J. (trans. H. Lane) (1993). *Makbara*. London: Serpent's Tail.

Goytisolo, J. (trans. P. Bush) (1994). *Quarantine*. Normal, IL: Dalkey Archives Press.

Goytisolo, J. (trans. P. Bush) (2000). *Landscapes of War: From Sarajevo to Chechnya*. San Francisco: City Lights.

Goytisolo, J. (trans. P. Bush) (2000). *The Garden of Secrets*. London: Serpent's Tail.

Goytisolo, J. (trans. P. Bush) (2002). *A Cock-Eyed Comedy: Starring Friar Bugeo Montesino and Other Faeries of Motley Feather and Fortune*. London: Serpent's Tail.

Goytisolo, J. (trans. P. Bush) (2003a). *Forbidden Territory and Realms of Strife*. London and New York: Verso.

Goytisolo, J. (trans. P. Bush) (2003b). *Cinema Eden: Essays from the Muslim Mediterranean*. London: Sickle Moon.

Goytisolo, J. (trans. H. Lane) (2003c). *State of Siege*. London: Serpent's Tail.

Goytisolo, J. (trans. P. Bush) (2005). *The Blind Rider*. London: Serpent's Tail.

Goytisolo, J. (trans. G. Rabassa) (2011a). *Marks of Identity*. London: Serpent's Tail.

Goytisolo, J. (trans. H. Lane) (2011b). *Count Julian*. London: Serpent's Tail.

Graíño Ferrer, G. (2022). 'Western Decline and the Overcoming of the Metaphysical Stage in Houellebecq's Fiction'. In M. Kochin and A. Spektorowski (eds), *Michel Houellebecq, the Cassandra of Freedom: Submission and Decline* (pp. 105–22). Leiden and Boston: Brill.

Gude, M.-L. (1996). *Louis Massignon: The Crucible of Compassion*. Notre Dame and London: University of Notre Dame Press.

Gugel, D. (2015). 'Moor or Mallorquín? Anselm Turmeda's Ambiguous Identity in the Cobles de la Divisió del Regne de Mallorca'. In L. Delbrugge (ed.), *Self-Fashioning and Assumptions about Identity in Medieval and Early Modern Iberia* (pp. 79–115). Leiden Brill.

Habib, S. (2010). *Homosexuality in Islam*. Santa Barbara, Denver and Oxford: Praeger.

Hackenburg, C. (2020). 'Anselm Turmeda/ʿAbd Allāh al-Tarjumān: A Former Mallorcan Franciscan in the Service of the Ḥafṣids of North Africa'. In N. Hurvitz, C. C. Sahner, U. Simonsohn and L. Yarbrough (eds), *Conversion to Islam in the Premodern Age: A Sourcebook* (pp. 294–9). Oakland and Los Angeles: University of California Press.

Hall, S. (1996). 'When Was "The Post-Colonial"? Thinking at the Limit'. In I. Chambers and L. Curti (eds), *The Post-Colonial Question: Common Skies, Divided Horizons* (pp. 242–60). London: Routledge.

Hämeen-Anttila, J. (2011). 'Suhrawardi's Western Exile as Artistic Prose'. *Ishraq: Islamic Philosophy Yearbook*, 2, 105–18.

Hannerz, U. (1990). 'Cosmopolitans and Locals in World Culture'. *Theory Culture Society*, 7, 237–51.

Harrington, K. N. (2012). *Writing the Nomadic Experience in Contemporary Francophone Literature*. New York: Lexington Books.
Hart, K. (1989). *The Trespass of the Sign: Deconstruction, Theology and Philosophy*. Cambridge: Cambridge University Press.
Hartung, J.-P. (2013). *A System of Life: Mawḍūdī and the Ideologisation of Islam*. London: Hurst.
Hashas, M. (2017). *Intercultural Geopolitics in Kenneth White's Open World*. Newcastle upon Tyne: Cambridge Scholars.
Hashas, M. (2020). *The Idea of European Islam: Religion, Ethics, Politics and Perpetual Modernity*. London and New York: Routledge.
Hassan, M. (2016). *Longing for the Lost Caliphate: A Transregional History*. Princeton and Oxford: Princeton University Press.
Hirtenstein, S. (1999). *The Unlimited Mercifier: The Spiritual Life and Thought of Ibn 'Arabi*. Oxford and Ashland: Anqa & White Cloud Press.
Hitchcock, R. (2014). *Muslim Spain Reconsidered: From 711 to 1502*. Edinburgh: Edinburgh University Press.
Hobsbawm, E. and Ranger, T. (1983). *The Invention of Tradition*. Cambridge: Cambridge University Press.
Hobus, J. (2016). 'Down by the River: Music, Love and Memory in Navid Kermani's Work'. In H. Druxes, K. Machtans and A. Mihailovic (eds), *Navid Kermani* (pp. 107–19). Oxford: Peter Lang.
Hodgson, M. G. (1974). *The Venture of Islam: Conscience and History in a World Civilization. Volume One – The Classical Age of Islam*. Chicago and London: University of Chicago Press.
Hodgson, M. G. (1974). *The Venture of Islam: Conscience and History in a World Civilization. Volume Two – The Expansion of Islam in the Middle Periods*. Chicago and London: University of Chicago Press.
Hodgson, M. G. (1974). *The Venture of Islam: Conscience and History in a World Civilization. Volume Three – The Gunpower Empires and Modern Times*. Chicago and London: University of Chicago Press.
Hoffmann, T. (2016). 'Literary Cemeteries: Recalling the Dead in Kurzmitteilung and Dein Name'. In H. Druxes, K. Machtans and A. Mihailovic (eds), *Navid Kermani* (pp. 121–42). Oxford: Peter Lang.
Hoffmann, T. (2018). 'Trennungsprobleme: Navid Kermani's Autofiktionen'. In T. Hoffmann (ed.), *Text+Kritik: Zeitschrift fuer Literatur. 217 Navid Kermani*, 18, 14–22.
Hofmann, M. (2018). 'Scheitern und Glück: Navid Kermanis Liebesdiskurse'. In T. Hofmann (ed.), *Text + Kritik 217: Navid Kermani*, I(18), 23–31.
Hofmann, M. and von Stosch, K. (2012). *Islam in der deutschen und türkischen Literatur*. Paderborn: Ferdinand Schöningh.
Hofmann, M., von Stosch, K. and Schulte Eickholt, S. (2019). *Navid Kermani*. Würzburg: Königshausen & Neumann.
Hölderlin, F. (trans. D. F. Krell) (2009). *The Death of Empedocles: A Mourning-Play*. Albany: State University of New York Press.
Hölderlin, F. (trans. H. Gaskill) (2019). *Hyperion, or the Hermit in Greece*. Cambridge: Open Book Publishers.
Houellebecq, M. (trans. F. Wynne) (2003). *Platform*. London: Vintage.
Houellebecq, M. (trans. G. Bowd) (2006). *The Possibility of an Island*. London: Phoenix.

Houellebecq, M. (trans. L. Stein) (2015). *Submission*. London: Vintage.
Houellebecq, M. (trans. D. Khazeni) (2019). *H. P. Lovecraft: Against the World, Against Life*. Paris: Cernunnos.
Houellebecq, M. (trans. A. B. Novak-Lechevalier) (2020). *In the Presence of Schopenhauer*. Cambridge and Medford MA: Polity Press.
Huxley, A. (1944). *The Perennial Philosophy*. New York: Harper & Row.
Huxley, A. (1954). *The Doors of Perception*. London and New York: Chatto & Windus, Harper & Row.
Hyatte, R. (1997). *The Prophet of Islam in Old French: The Romance of Muhammad (1258) and Muhammad's Ladder (1264)*. Leiden: Brill.
Ibn al-'Arabi, M. (trans. R. A. Nicholson) (1978). *The Tarjuman al-Ashwaq: A Collection of Mystical Odes*. London: Theosophical Publishing House.
Ibn 'Arabi, M. (trans. A. Jaffray) (2006). *The Universal Tree and the Four Birds*. Oxford: Anqa.
Irwin, R. (2006). *Dangerous Knowledge: Orientalism and its Discontents*. Woodstock and New York: The Overlook Press.
Jaggi, M. (2000). 'The Scourge of the New Spain'. *The Guardian*, 12 August.
Jambet, C. (1990). *La Grande Resurrection d'Alamut. Les formes de la liberté dans le shi'isme ismaelien. Lagrasse*. Paris: LaGrasse Verdier.
Jambet, C. (2015). 'Preface'. In A. Meddeb, *Instants Soufis* (pp. 9–27). Paris: Albin Michel.
Jameson, F. (1981). *The Political Unconscious: Narrative as a Socially Symbolic Act*. Ithaca NY: Cornell University Press.
Jebari, I. (2018). 'Rethinking the Maghreb and the Post-colonial Intellectual in Khatibi's Les temps modernes issue in 1977'. *The Journal of North African Studies*, 23(1–2), 53–70.
Jordan, J. (2012). 'Für eine kämpferische Toleranz: der Islam in Navid Kermanis literarischen Schriften'. In M. Hofmann and K. von Stosch (eds), *Islam in der deutschen und türkischen Literatur* (pp. 247–57). Paderborn: Ferdinand Schöningh.
Joris, P. (2014). *Barzakh: Poems 2000–2012*. Boston: Black Widow Press.
Joshi, S. (2018). 'Why Michel Houellebecq Is Wrong about Lovecraft's Racism'. *Lovecraft Annual*, 12, 43–50.
Jung, D. (2011). *Orientalists, Islamists and the Global Public Sphere: A Genealogy of the Modern Essentialist Image of Islam*. Sheffield and Oakville: Equinox.
Juričić, Ž. and Loud, J. F. (1990). 'Introduction'. In I. Andrić, *The Development of Spiritual Life in Bosnia under the Influence of Turkish Rule* (pp. vii–xx). Durham and London: Duke University Press.
Kadare, I. (trans. D. B. Vrioni) (2007). *The Blinding Order*. Edinburgh: Canongate.
Kadare, I. (trans. B. B. Vrioni) (2008). *The Palace of Dreams*. London: Vintage.
Kadare, I. (trans. P. Constantine) (2011). *Three Elegies for Kosovo*. London: Vintage.
Kadare, I. (trans. J. Hodgson) (2013). *The Three-Arched Bridge*. London: Vintage.
Kadare, I. (trans. D. B. Vrioni) (2018a). *The Siege*. Edinburgh: Canongate.
Kadare, I. (trans. J. Hodgson) (2018b). *The Traitor's Niche*. London: Vintage.

Kadare, I. (ed. D. Bellos, trans. D. Bellos and A. Pipa) (2018c). *Chronicle in Stone*. Edinburgh: Canongate.

Kaegi, W. (2010). *Muslim Expansion and Byzantine Collapse in North Africa*. Cambridge and New York: Cambridge University Press.

Kaukua, J. (2022). *Suhrawardi's Illuminationism: A Philosophical Study*. Leiden: Brill.

Kearney, R. (2001). *The God Who May Be: A Hermeneutics of Religion*. Bloomington: Indiana University Press.

Kearney, R. (2002). *Strangers, Gods and Monsters: Interpreting Otherness*. London and New York: Routledge.

Kearney, R. (2011). *Anatheism [Returning to God after God]*. New York: Columbia University Press.

Kemnitz, E.-M. and Inloes, A. (2022). *The Hand of Fatima: The Khamsa in the Arab-Islamic World*. Leiden: Brill.

Kermani, N. (1996). *Offenbarung als Kommunikation: Das Konzept wahy in Nasr Hamid Abu Zayds Mafhum an-nass*. Munich: Peter Lang.

Kermani, N. (1999). *Gott ist schön: Das Aesthetische Erleben des Koran*. Munich: C.H. Beck.

Kermani, N. (2003). *Schöner neuer Orient: Berichte von Städte und Kriegen*. Munich: C. H. Beck.

Kermani, N. (2004). 'From Revelation to Interpretation: Nasr Hamid Abu Zayd and the Literary Study of the Qur'an'. In S. Taji-Farouki (ed.), *Modern Muslim Intellectuals and the Qur'an* (pp. 169–92). Oxford and New York: Oxford University Press with the Institute of Ismaili Studies.

Kermani, N. (2005). *Der Schrecken Gottes: Attar, Hiob, und die metaphysische Revolte*. Munich: C. H. Beck.

Kermani, N. (2011a). *Dein Name*. Munich: Carl Hanser Verlag.

Kermani:, N. (2011b). *The Terror of God: Attar, Job and the Metaphysical Revolt*. Cambridge and Malden: Polity Press.

Kermani, N. (2012). *Über den Zufall: Jean Paul, Hölderlin und der Roman, den ich schreibe*. Munich: Carl Hanser Verlag.

Kermani, N. (2014a). *Zwischen Koran und Kafka: West-östliche Erkundungen*. Munich: C. H. Beck.

Kermani, N. (2014b). *Album: Das Buch der von Neil Young Getöteten; Vierzig Leben; Du Sollst; Kurzmitteilung*. Munich: Carl Hanser Verlag.

Kermani, N. (2014c). *Große Liebe*. Munich: Carl Hanser Verlag.

Kermani, N. (2015a). *God Is Beautiful: The Aesthetic Experience of the Quran*. London and New York: Polity Press.

Kermani, N. (2015b). *Ausnahmezustand: Reisen in eine beunruhigte Welt*. Munich: C. H. Beck.

Kermani, N. (2015c). *Ungläubiges Staunen: Über das Christentum*. Munich: C. H. Beck.

Kermani, N. (2016a). 'Was zählt ist das gesprochene Wort' (What Counts Is the Spoken Word): Bundestagrede Celebrating the 65th Anniversary of the Basic Law, 23. Mai 2014, Berlin. In H. Druxes, K. Machtans and A. Mihailovic (eds), *Navid Kermani* (Vol. 40 Contemporary German Writers and Filmmakers, pp. 15–33). Munich: Peter Lang.

Kermani, N. (trans. T. Crawford) (2016b). *Between Quran & Kafka: West-Eastern Affinities*. Cambridge: Polity Press.

Kermani, N. (2017). *Wer ist Wir? Deutschland Und Seine Muslime* (2nd edn). Munich: C. H. Beck.
Kermani, N. (2018a). *Entlang den Gräben: Eine Reise durch das östliche Europe bis nach Isfahan*. Munich: C. H. Beck.
Kermani, N. (trans. T. Crawford) (2018b). *State of Emergency: Travels in a Troubled World*. Cambridge: Polity Press.
Kermani, N. (trans. A. Booth) (2019a). *Love Writ Large*. Kolkata: Seagull Books.
Kermani, N. (trans. T. Crawford) (2019b). *Wonder Beyond Belief: On Christianity*. Cambridge: Polity Press.
Kersten, C. (2004). 'The Predicament of Thailand's Southern Muslims'. *American Journal of Islamic Social Sciences*, 21(4), 1–29.
Kersten, C. (2011). *Cosmopolitans and Heretics: New Muslim Intellectuals and the Study of Islam*. London and New York: Hurst and Oxford University Press.
Kersten, C. (2015). *Islam in Indonesia: The Contest for Society, Ideas and Values*. London and New York: Hurst and Oxford University Press.
Kersten, C. (2016). 'Post-Everything'. *Critical Muslim*, 20, 122–31.
Kersten, C. (2017). 'Islam vs the West? Muslim Challenges of a False Binary'. In K.-G. Giesen, C. Kersten and L. Skof (eds), *Poesis of Peace: Narratives, Cultures and Philosophies* (pp. 81–96). London and New York: Routledge.
Kersten, C. (2018). 'Nasr Hamid Abu Zayd: An Introduction to his Life and Work'. In N. H. Abu Zayd (ed.), *Critique of Religious Discourse. Naqd al-Khitab al-Dini* (pp. 1–21). New Haven CT and London: Yale University Press.
Kersten, C. (2019). *Contemporary Thought in the Muslim World: Trends, Themes, and Issues*. London and New York: Routledge.
Kersten, C. (2020). 'Religion and Literature, Identity and Individual: Resetting the Muslim–Christian Dialogue'. *Poligrafi*, 99/100(25), 5–26.
Kersten, C. (2022a). 'Critics as Caretakers, Religion as Critique: Muslim Intellectuals and Islam'. In Leif Stenberg and Philip Wood (eds), *What Is Islamic Studies? European and North American Approaches to a Contested Field* (pp. 42–59). Edinburgh: Edinburgh University Press.
Kersten, C. (2022b). 'Hermeneutics and Islamic Liberation Theologies'. In Sylvain Camilleri and Selami Varlik (eds), *Philosophical Hermeneutics and Islamic Thought* (pp. 157–68). Dordrecht: Springer.
Kersten, C. (2024). 'Heritage, Historicity, and Hermeneutics: Pathways in Contemporary Islamic Thought'. In V. LeGrand (ed.), *Histoire, société, et études islamiques au 21e siècle: Directions, connexions, approches*. Berlin: DeGruyter.
Kersten, K. P. L. G. (2009). 'Occupants of the Third Space: New Muslim Intellectuals and the Study of Islam (Nurcholish Madjid, Hasan Hanafi, Mohammed Arkoun)'. PhD thesis. London: School of Oriental and African Studies (SOAS), University of London.
Khalil, A. (2020). 'Privileged Instants: Meddeb's Tombeau d'Ibn 'Arabi'. *Expressions maghrébines*, 19(2), 179–92.
Khalsi, K. (2017). 'Cosmopolitisme et littérature-monde chez Abdelwahab Meddeb: une pensée mystique'. In S. H.-C. Lambert-Perreault (ed.), *Zizanie: Conflits narratifs et politiques dans l'espace francophone*, 1(1), 78–92.

Khatibi, A. (1983). *Maghreb Pluriel*. Paris: Denoël.
Khatibi, A. (1985). 'Incipits'. In J. Bennani, *Du Bilinguisme* (pp. 171–203). Paris: Denoël.
Kia, M. (2020). *Persianate Selves: Memories of Place and Origin Before Nationalism*. Stanford: Stanford University Press.
Kilito, A. (trans. W. S. Hassan) (2008). *Thou Shalt Not Speak My Language*. Syracuse: Syracuse University Press.
Kim, S. H. (2018). 'The Character of Mehmed-paša Sokolović in Ivo Andrić's Work'. *Zeitschrift für Slawistik*, 63(1), 30–51.
King, R. (1999). *Orientalism and Religion: Postcolonial Theory, India and 'The Mystic East'*. London and New York: Routledge.
Kirkup, J. (1996). 'Obituary: Monique Lange'. *The Independent*, 4 December.
Kiwan, N. (2020). *Secularism, Islam and Public Intellectuals in Contemporary France*. Manchester: Manchester University Press.
Kochin, M. S. and Spektorowski, A. (2022). *Michel Houellebecq, the Cassandra of Freedom: Submission and Decline*. Leiden and Boston: Brill.
Konuk, K. (2010). *East West Mimesis: Auerbach in Turkey*. Palo Alto: Stanford University Press.
Krell, D. F. (2009). 'General Introduction'. In F. Hölderlin, *The Death of Empedocles: A Mourning-Play* (pp. 1–23). Albany: State University of New York Press.
Krokus, C. S. (2016). *The Theology of Louis Massignon: Islam, Christ and the Church*. Washington, DC: Catholic University of America Press.
Kugle, S. S.-D. (2010). *Homosexuality in Islam: Critical Reflections on Gay, Lesbian, and Transgender Muslims*. Oxford: OneWorld.
Kuntz, J. (2011). 'Translator's Introduction'. In A. Meddeb, *Talismano* (pp. v–xii). Champaign and London: Dalkey Archive Press.
Kuschel, K.-J. (2021). *Goethe und der Koran*. Olstfildern: Patmos Verlag.
Lauro, R. (2020). 'Abdelwahab Meddeb, interprète des traces, archéologue du contemporain'. *Expressions maghrébines*, 9(2), pp. 119–34.
Lawrence, B. B. (2021). *Islamicate Cosmopolitan Spirit*. Hoboken, NJ: Wiley Blackwell.
LeBlanc, M. (2024). 'The Disputatio Raimundo Christiani et Homeri Saraceni: A Case Study of Medieval Christian–Muslim Exchange'. PhD dissertation. Leuven: Catholic University Leuven.
Lee Six, A. (1990). *Juan Goytisolo: The Case for Chaos*. New Haven: Yale University Press.
Levett, A. (2020). 'Ecstatic Communities: Sufism, Modernism, and Political Possibility in Abdelwahab Meddeb's Talismano'. *Expressions maghrébines*, 19(2), 77–97.
Levi Della Vida, G. (1949). 'Nuove luce sulle fonti islamiche della Divina Commedia'. *Al-Andalus: revista de las Escuelas de Estudios Árabes de Madrid y Granada*, 14(2), 377–407.
Lewis, B. (1938). 'An Ismaili Interpretation of the Fall of Adam'. *Bulletin of the School of Oriental Studies (BSOS)*, 9(3), 691–704.
Lewis, F. D. (2000). *Rumi: Past and Present, East and West: The Life, Teachings and Poetry of Jalâl al-Din Rumi*. Oxford: OneWorld.
Lika, H. (2020). 'The Europeanization of Albanian National Identity: The Identity Debate of Ismail Kadare versus Rexhep Qosja'. *Perspectives of Law*

and Public Administration, 9(2), 64–75. https://www.ceeol.com/search/article-detail?id=932805.

Llored, Y. (2009). *Juan Goytisolo: Le soi, le monde et la création littéraire*. Villeneuve d'Ascq: Presses Universitaires du Septentrion.

Longinović, T. Z. (1965). 'East within West: Bosnian Cultural Identity in the Works of Ivo Andric'. In W. S. Vucinich (ed.), *Ivo Andric Revisited: The Bridge Still Stands* (pp. 123–38). Berkeley: University of California at Berkeley.

López-Baralt, L. (1984). 'Makbara: Juan Goytisolo's Fictionalized Version of "Orientalism"'. *Review of Contemporary Fiction – Juan Goytisolo Reader*, 4(2), 138–45.

López Baralt, L. (1985). *Huellas del Islam en la literatura española. De Juan Ruiz a Juan Goytisolo*. Madrid: Hiperión.

López-Baralt, L. (1990). *San Juan de la Cruz y el Islam*, 2nd edn. Madrid: Hiperión.

López-Baralt, L. (trans. A. Hurley) (1992). *Islam in Spanish Literature: From the Middle Ages to the Present*. Leiden: Brill.

López-Baralt, L. (1995). 'Narrar después de morir: La cuarentena de Juan Goytisolo'. *Nueva Revista de Filología Hispánica*, 43(1), 59–124.

López-Baralt, L. (2010). 'Teresa of Jesus and Islam: The Simile of the Seven Concentric Castles of the Soul'. In H. Kallendorf (ed.), *A New Companion of Hispanic Mysticism* (pp. 175–200). Leiden: Brill.

Loud, J. F. (1995). 'Andrić on Bosnia: The 1924 Dissertation'. In W. S. Vucinich (ed.), *Ivo Andrić Revisited: The Bridge Still Stands* (pp. 187–99). Berkeley: University of California at Berkeley.

Loupias, B. (1978). 'Importance et signification du lexique d'origine arabe dans le "Don Julián" de Juan Goytisolo'. *Bulletin Hispanique*, 80(3–4), 229–62.

Lukács., G. (trans. T. F. Mitchell) (1962). *The Historical Novel*. Boston: Beacon Press.

Lyons, M. C. (2014). *Tales of the Marvellous and News of the Strange*. London: Penguin.

Lyotard, J.-F. (trans. E. Rottenberg) (1994). *Lessons on the Analytic of the Sublime*. Stanford: Stanford University Press.

MacCormack, P. (2020). 'Posthuman Teratology'. In J. A. Weinstock (ed.), *The Monster Theory Reader* (pp. 522–39). Minneapolis: University of Minnesota Press.

Machtans, K. (2015). 'Navid Kermani: Advocate for an Antipatriotic Patriotism and a Multireligious, Multicultural Europe'. In J. E. Twark and A. Hildebrandt (eds), *Envisioning Social Justice in Contemporary German Culture* (pp. 290–311). Camden House, NY: Boydell & Brewer.

Machtans, K. (2016). 'The Beauty and Terror of Love: Große Liebe und Du Sollst'. In H. Druxes, K. Machtans and A. Mihailovic (eds), *Navid Kermani* (pp. 87–105). Oxford: Peter Lang.

Malcolm, N. (1994). *Bosnia: A Short History*. London: Macmillan.

Malcolm, N. (1998). *Kosovo: A Short History*. London: Macmillan.

March, A. F. (2019). *The Caliphate of Man: Popular Sovereignty in Modern Islamic Thought*. Cambridge, MA and London: The Belknap Press of Harvard University Press.

Marion, J.-L. (trans. R. Horner and V. Berraud) (2002). *In Excess: Studies of Saturated Phenomena*. New York: Fordham University Press.
Marion, J.-L. (trans. S. E. Lewis) (2021). *A Brief Apology for a Catholic Moment*. Chicago: University of Chicago Press.
Márquez Villanueva, F. (2009). 'On the Concept of Mudejarism'. In K. Ingram (ed.), *The Conversos and Morisco in Late Medieval Spain and Beyond* (pp. 23–49). Leiden: Brill.
Marramao, G. (2012). *The Passage West: Philosophy After the Age of the Nation State*. London and New York: Verso.
Martens, M. (2022). *Im Brand der Welten: Ivo Andrić ein europäisches Leben*. Munich: BTB Verlag.
Massignon, L. (1913). *Kitâb al-Ṭawâṣîn par al-Hallâj*. Paris: Librairie Paul Geuthner.
Massignon, L. (ed. Y. Moubarac) (1963). *Opera Minora*. Beirut: Dar al-Maaref.
Massignon, L. (trans. H. Mason) (1972). *The Passion of Al-Hallaj, Mystic and Martyr of Islam, Volume 3: The Teaching of al-Hallaj*. Princeton, NJ: Princeton University Press.
Massignon, L. (1983). *Parole Donnée*. Paris: Editions Seuil.
Massignon, L. (trans. H. Mason) (1986). *The Passion of Al-Hallaj: Mystic and Martyr of Islam – Volume 1: The Life of Al-Hallaj*. Princeton, NJ: Princeton University Press.
Massignon, L. (ed. C. Jambet) (2009). *Écrits mémorables – 2 volumes*. Paris: R. Laffont.
Masters, B. (2009a). 'Millet'. In G. Ágoston and B. Masters (eds), *Encyclopedia of the Ottoman Empire* (pp. 383–4). New York: Facts on File.
Masters, B. (2009b). 'Bektaşi'. In G. Ágoston and B. Masters (ed.), *Encyclopedia of the Ottoman Empire* (pp. 88–9). New York: Facts on File.
Matthes, F. (2011). 'Islam in the West: Perceptions and Self-Perceptions of Muslims in Navid Kermani's Kurzmitteilung'. *German Life and Letters*, 64(2), 305–16.
Meddeb, A. (1985). 'Le Palimpseste du Bilingue Ibn 'Arabi et Dante'. In J. Bennani (ed.), *Du Bilinguisme* (pp. 125–44). Paris: Denoël.
Meddeb, A. (1987). *Tombeau d' Ibn Arabi*. Paris: Noël Blandin.
Meddeb, A. (1989). *Les Dits de Bistami: Shatahat*. Paris: Fayard.
Meddeb, A. (1991). *Écriture et Double Généalogie*. Aix-en-Provence: Université de Provence.
Meddeb, A. (1995). *Les 99 Stations de Yale*. Saint Clément de Rivière: Fata Morgana.
Meddeb, A. (1997). *Blanches Traverses du Passé*. Saint Clément de Rivière: Fata Morgana.
Meddeb, A. (1999). *Aya dans les Villes*. Saint Clément de Rivière: Fata Morgana.
Meddeb, A. (2001). *Matière des Oiseaux*. Saint Clément de Rivière: Fata Morgana.
Meddeb, A. (2003). *Phantasia*. Paris: Editions Seuil.
Meddeb, A. (trans. P. Joris and A. Reid) (2003). *The Malady of Islam*. New York: Basic Books.
Meddeb, A. (2005). *L'Exil Occidental*. Paris: Albin Michel.
Meddeb, A. (2006). *Contre-Prêches: Chroniques*. Paris: Seuil.

Meddeb, A. (2008). *Sortir de la Malédiction: L'Islam entre civilisation et barbarie*. Paris: Seuil.
Meddeb, A. (trans. C. Mandell) (2010). *Tombeau of Ibn Arabi and White Traverses*. New York: Fordham University Press.
Meddeb, A. (trans. J. Kuntz) (2011). *Talismano*. Champaign and London: Dalkey Archive Press.
Meddeb, A. (trans. J. Kuntz) (2013). *Islam and the Challenge of Civilization*. New York: Fordham University Press.
Meddeb, A. (2014). *Portrait du poete en soufi*. Paris: Belin.
Meddeb, A. (2015). *Instants soufis*. Paris: Albin Michel.
Meddeb, A. (ed. H. M. Amina Meddeb) (2017). *Le Temps des Inconciliables: Contre-Prêches*, 2 Paris: Seuil.
Meddeb, A. and Story B. (2013). *A History of Jewish–Muslim Relations: From its Origins to the Present Day*. Princeton, NJ: Princeton University Press.
Mehrez, S. (1991). 'The Subversive Poetics of Radical Bilingualism: Postcolonial Francophone North African Literature'. In D. LaCapra (ed.), *The Bounds of Race: Perspectives on Hegemony and Resistance* (pp. 255–77). Ithaca, NY: Cornell University Press.
Menocal, M. R. (2002). *Ornament of the World: How Muslim, Jews, and Christians Created a Culture of Tolerance in MedievaL Spain*. New York, Boston and London: Little, Brown.
Messling, M., Ruhe, C., Seauve, L. and de Senarclens, V. (2020). *Mathias Énard et l'érudition du roman*. Leiden: Brill.
Mincheva, D. (2016). *The Politics of Muslim Intellectual Discourse in the West: The Emergence of a Western-Islamic Public Sphere*. Brighton: Sussex Academic Press.
Mirsepassi, A. (2000). *Intellectual Discourse and the Politics of Modernization: Negotiating Modernity in Iran*. Cambridge and New York: Cambridge University Press.
Mohagheghi, H. (2012). 'Der "Islam" in Navid Kermani's literarischen Schriften'. In M. Hofmann and K. von Stosch (eds), *Islam in der deutschen und türkischen Literatur* (pp. 259–66). Paderborn: Ferdinand Schöningh.
Moir, C. (2020). *Ernst Bloch's Speculative Materialism: Ontology, Epistemology, Ethics*. Chicago: Haymarket Books.
Mommsen, K. (2001). *Goethe und der Islam*. Frankfurt am Main and Leipzig: Insel Verlag.
Morris, J. W. (1987 and 1988). The Spiritual Ascension: Ibn 'Arabî and the Mi'râj. *Journal of the American Oriental Society*, 107–8, 629–52 and 63–77.
Müller-Zähringe, E. and Rahner, J. (2008). 'Nicht Vernunftgemäß zu handelen, ist Gottes Wesen Zuwider: Vernunft und Glaube – Schlüsselbegriffe oder Grenzlinien des interreligiösen Dialogs?'. *Zeitschrift für katholische Theologie*, 130(1), 35–63.
Murata, K. (2017). *Beauty in Islam: The Teachings of Rūzbihān Baqlī*. Albany: State University of New York Press.
Neuwirth, A. (2014). *Scripture, Poetry and the Making of a Community: Reading the Qur'an as a Literary Text*. Oxford and New York: Oxford University Press in association with the Institute of Ismaili Studies in London.

Nock, A. D. (1933). *Conversion: The Old and the New in Religion from Alexander the Great to Augustine of Hippo*. Oxford: Oxford University Press.

Novak-Lechevalier, A. (trans. A. Brown) (2020). 'Preface: The History of a Revolution'. In M. Houellebecq, *In the Presence of Schopenhauer*. Cambridge and Medford MA: Polity Press.

Nünning, A. (1995). *Von historischer Fiktion zu historiographischer Metafiktion*. Trier: Wissenschaftlicher Verlag.

Omar, I. A. (2022). *The Prophet al-Khiḍr: Between the Qur'anic Text and Islamic Contexts*. Lanham: Lexington Books.

Ossewaarde, M. (2015). 'Ismail Kadare's Idea of Europe'. *The European Legacy*, 20(7), 715–30.

Otto, R. (trans. J. W. Harvey) (1958). *The Idea of the Holy*. London Oxford New York: Oxford University Press.

Palmer, M. and Breuilly, E. (1996). *The Book of Chuang Tzu*. London: Penguin Arkana.

Pénicaud, M. (2020). *Louis Massignon: Le 'catholique musulman'*. Toulouse: Bayard.

Perrin, A. (1984). 'Makbara: The Space of Phantasm'. *Review of Contemporary Fiction*, 4(2), 157–76.

Peters, L. (2020). *Religion als diskursive Formation: Zur Darstellung von Religion in der deutschsprachigen Gegenwartliteratur*. Bielefeld: Transcript Verlag.

Phillips, J. (2019). 'Michel Houellebecq: An Unlikely Catholic Thinker'. *The Tablet*. https://www.thetablet.co.uk/features/2/16907/michel-houellebecq-an-unlikely-catholic-thinker.

Pope, R. D. (1995). *Understanding Juan Goytisolo*. Columbia, SC: University of South Carolina Press.

Popovic, A. (2006). 'Les turuq balkaniques à l'épreuve de la modernité'. *Archives de sciences sociales des religions*, 51(135), 141–63.

Qader, N. (2009). *Narratives of Catastrophe: Boris Diop, ben Jelloun, Khatibi*. New York: Fordham University.

Qadiri, S. (2013). 'Abdelwahab Meddeb: A Literary Path toward Atheism?'. *Journal of Romance Studies*, 13(1), 49–64.

Quinn, J. (2024). *How the World Made the West*. London: Bloomsbury.

Rahma. (2008). *L'errance dans l'oeuvre de Meddeb entre islam, soufisme et Occident: lecture d'un interculturel du possible*. Rennes: University of Haute Bretagne.

Rahma, Z. A. (2008). *L'errance dans l'oeuvre de Meddeb entre islam, soufisme et Occident: lecture d'un interculturel du possible*. Rennes: Universite de Haute Bretagne.

Rajchman, J. (trans. A. Boyman) (2001). 'Introduction'. In G. Deleuze, *Pure Immanence: Essays on Life*. New York: Zone Books.

Ricoeur, P. (trans. K. M. Pellauer) (1984). *Time and Narrative. Volume 1*. Chicago: University of Chicago Press.

Ricoeur, P. (trans. K. Blamey) (1992). *Oneself as Another*. Chicago and London: University of Chicago Press.

Ricoeur, P. (ed. M. I. Wallace, trans. M. I. Wallace and D. Pellauer) (1995). *Figuring the Sacred: Religion, Narrative and Imagination*. Minneapolis: Fortress Press.

Ricoeur, P. (ed. and trans. D. Ihde) (2004). *The Conflict of Interpretations*. London and New York: Continuum.

Ricoeur, P. (ed. D. Ihde, trans. D. Ihde and K. McLaughlin) (2004). *The Conflict of Interpretations*. London: Continuum.

Ritter, H. (1955). *Das Meer der Seele: Mensch, Welt und Gott in den Geschichten des Fariduddin Attar*. Leiden: Brill.

Robbins, B. (1993). *Secular Vocations: Intellectuals, Professionalism, Culture*. London and New York: Verso.

Rock, L. (2019). *As German as Kafka: Identity and Singularity in German Literature around 1900 and 2000*. Leuven: Leuven University Press.

Rodinson, M. (1951). 'Dante et l'Islam d'après des travaux récents'. *Revue de l'histoire des religions*, 140(2), 203–36.

Rorty, R. and Vattimo, G. (ed. S. Zabala, trans. S. Zabala and W. McCuaig) (2005). *The Future of Religion*. New York: Columbia University Press.

Safranski, R. (2020). *Holderlin: Komm! Ins Offenem FReund!* Munich: Carl Hanser Verlag.

Said, E. S. (1995). *Orientalism: Western Conceptions of the Orient*. London: Penguin.

Said, E. W. (1985). 'Orientalism Reconsidered'. *Cultural Critique*, 1, 89–107.

Said, E. W. (1993). *Culture and Imperialism*. London: Chatto & Windus.

Saif, L., Leoni, F., Melvin-Koushki, M. and Yahya, F. (2021). *Islamicate Occult Sciences in Theory and Practice*. Leiden: Brill.

Scharfman, R. L. (1986). 'Starting from "Talismano": Abdelwahab Meddeb's Nomadic Writing'. *L'Esprit Créateur*, 26(1) (Maghrebine Literature of French Expression), 40–9.

Scharfman, R. L. (1992). 'Thanatography: Writing and Death in Abdelwahab Meddeb's "Talismano"'. *SubStance*, 21(3), 85–102.

Scharfman, R. L. (2001). 'Nomadism and Transcultural Writing in the Works of Abdelwahab Meddeb'. *L'Esprit Créateur: Villes, modernités et mémoire culturelle*, 43(3) (Cities, Modernity and Cultural Memory), 105–13.

Schimmel, A. (1975). *Mystical Dimensions of Islam*. Chapel Hill: University of North Carolina Press.

Schimmel, A. (1992). *A Two-Colored Brocade: The Imagery of Persian Poetry*. Chapel Hill and London: University of North Carolina Press.

Schlosser, D. (2015). *Lebensgesetz und Vergemeinschaftungsform: Muḥammad Asad (1900–1992) und sein islamverständnis* (Bonner Islamstudien, Vol. 32). Berlin: EB Verlag.

Schmidt-Neke, M. (2010). 'Skanderbegs Gefangene: Zur Debatte um den albanischen Nationalhelden'. *Südosteuropa. Zeitschrift für Politik und Gesellschaft*, 58(2), 273–302.

Schrieke, B. and Horovitz, J. (1993). 'Miʿrādj'. In C. E. Bosworth, E. van Donzel, W. P. Heinrichs and C. Pellat (eds), *Encyclopaedia of Islam – New Edition* (Vol. VII, pp. 97–100). Leiden: Brill.

Schulman, A. (1984). 'Marks of Identity: Identity and Discourse'. *Review of Contemporary Fiction – Juan Goytisolo Reader*, 4(2), 145–57.

Segelcke, E. (2016). 'The Political Anthropology of Navid Kermani's Travelogues'. In H. Druxes, K. Machtans and A. Mihailovic (eds), *Navid Kermani* (pp. 181–200). Oxford: Peter Lang.

Seibt, G. (2018). '"Danke Deutschland". Navid Kermani's Rede "65 Jahre Grundgesetz" vor dem Deutschen Bundestag'. In T. Hoffmann (ed.), *Text + Kritik 217: Navid Kermani* (pp. 43–51). Munch: Richard Boorberg Verlag.

Seigel, J. (2015). *Between Cultures: Europe and its Others in Five Exemplary Lives*. Philadelphia: University of Pennsylvania Press.

Selimović, M. (trans. B. Rakić and S. M. Dickey) (1996). *Death and the Dervish*. Evanston, IL: Northwestern University Press.

Selimović, M. (trans. E. D. Goy and J. Jevinger-Goy) (1999). *The Fortress*. Evanston, IL: Northwestern University Press.

Sellin, E. (1988). 'Obsession with the White Page, the Inability to Communicate, and Surface Aesthetics in the Development of Contemporary Maghrebian Fiction: The Mal de la Page Blanche in Khatibi, Fares and Meddeb'. *International Journal of Middle East Studies*, 20(2), 165–73.

Sells, M. A. (1996). *Early Islamic Mysticism: Sufi, Qur'an, Mi'raj, Poetic and Theological Writings*. New York: Paulist Press.

Senarclens, V. d. (2020). 'L'érudit insomniaque et veilleur, ou Boussole en roman de formation?'. In M. Messling, C. Ruhe, L. Seauve and V. de Senarclens (eds), *Mathias Énard et l'érudition du roman* (pp. 134–49). Leiden and Boston: Brill Rodopi.

Şentop, M. (2009). 'Kadiasker'. In G. Ágoston and B. Masters (eds), *Encyclopedia of the Ottoman Empire* (p. 305). New York: Facts on File.

Shayegan, A. (1968). *Les relations de l'hindouisme et du soufisme d'après le 'Majma' al-Baḥrayn' de Dārā Shokūh*. Paris: doctoral thesis, EPHE, University of Paris.

Shayegan, D. (trans. J. Howe) (1997). *Cultural Schizophrenia: Islamic Societies Confronting the West*. London: Syracuse University Press.

Shayegan, D. (2013). *La lumière vient de l'Occident: Le réenchantment du monde et la pensée nomade*. Paris: Editions L'Aube.

Silvers, L. (2010). *A Soaring Minaret: Abu Bakr al-Wasiti and the Rise of Baghdadi Sufism*. Albany: State University of New York Press.

Smith, A. P. and Whistler, D. (2010). 'What Is Continental Philosophy of Religion Now?'. In A. P. Smith and D. Whistler (eds), *After the Postsecular and the Postmodern: New Essays in Continental Philosophy of Religion* (pp. 1–24). Newcastle upon Tyne: Cambridge Scholars.

Soroush, A. (1994). *Qabd wa Bast-e Te'urik-e Shari'at: Nazariyah-e Takamul-e Ma'rifat-e Dini* (*Theoretical Contraction and Expansion of Religion: The Theory of Evolution of Religious Knowledge*). Tehran: Sirat.

Spaulding, T. (2015). 'Lovecraft and Houellebecq: Two Against the World'. *Lovecraft Annual*, 9, 181–211.

Spektorowski, A. (2022). 'Michel Houellebecq and the "Political Triangle": The Republic, the Radical Right, and "the Ultimate Other"'. In M. Kochin and A. Spektorowski (eds), *Michel Houellebecq, the Cassandra of Freedom: Submission and Decline* (pp. 41–66). Leiden and Boston: Brill.

Stegmann, V. (2016). 'Navid Kermani's Literary Reflections: On Kafka, Brecht, and the Koran'. In T. W. Rippey (ed.), *The Brecht Yearbook 40* (pp. 200–16). Woodbridge and London: Boyden & Brewer with C. Hurst.

Stétié, S. (1997). *Hermès défénestré*. Paris: José Corti.

Stewart, D. J. (2011). 'The Mysterious Letters and Other Formal Features of the Qur'an in Light of Greek and Babylonian Oracular Texts'. In G. S. Reynolds

(ed.), *New Perspectives on the Qur'an: The Qur'an in its Historical Context 2* (pp. 323–48). London and New York: Routledge.
Stroumsa, G. G. (2021). *The Idea of Semitic Monotheism: The Rise and Fall of a Scholarly Myth*. Oxford: Oxford University Press.
Tampio, N. (2013). 'The Politics of the Garden (Pairadaeza)'. *Theory and Event*, 16(2). muse.jhu.edu/article/509905.
Tarnow, S. (2005). *The New Transnational Activism*. Cambridge: Cambridge University Press.
Taylor, M. C. (1984). *Erring: A Postmodern A/theology*. Chicago and London: University of Chicago Press.
Taylor, M. C. (1987). *Altarity*. Chicago and London: University of Chicago Press.
Taylor, M. C. (2002). *Grave Matters*. London: Reaktion.
Thomas, D. (2017). 'Conversion out of Personal Principle: 'Ali b. Rabban al-Tabari (d. c. 860) and 'Abdallah al-Tarjuman (d. c. 1430), Two Converts from Christianity to Islam'. In A. Peacock (ed.), *Islamisation: Comparative Perspectives from History* (pp. 56–68). Edinburgh: Edinburgh University Press.
Tibi, B. (2009). *Euro-Islam: die Lösung eines Zivilisationskonfliktes*. Darmstadt: Wissenschaftliche Buchverlag.
Todorov, T. (trans. C. Cosman) (1990). *Imperfect Garden: The Legacy of Humanism*. Princeton and Oxford: Princeton University Press.
Touda, A. (2016). 'Hybridité et hybridation dans la littérature postcoloniale dans l'œuvre d'Abdelwahab Meddeb'. *Dalhousie French Studies*, 110 (special issue: Du colonial et du postcolonial en littératures française et francophone), 73–82.
Twist, J. (2018). *Mystical Islam and Cosmopolitanism in Contemporary Germany Literature*. Rochester, NY: Camden House.
Ugarte, M. (1979). 'Juan Goytisolo: Unruly Disciple of Americo Castro'. *Journal of Spanish Studies: Twentieth Century*, 7(3), 353–64.
Ugarte, M. (1982). *Trilogy of Treason: An Intertextual Study of Juan Goytisolo*. Columbia, MO: University of Missouri Press.
Ulrich, B. (2016). 'Navid Kermani? Einige wollen ihn zum rot-rot-grünen Bundespräsidenten machen. Eine reizvolle Idee – und eine falsche'. *Der Zeit*, https://www.zeit.de/2016/32/bundespraesident-navid-kermani-kandidat.
Unamuno, M. de (trans. J. C. Flitch) (1954). *Tragic Sense of Life*. London: Dover.
Urbani, B. (2014). 'Les errances d'Abdelwahab Meddeb entre orient et occident'. *Multilinguales*, 2(1), 79–94.
van Wesemael, S. (2004). *Michel Houellebecq*. Amsterdam and New York: Rodopi.
Varsico, D. M. (2007). *Reading Orientalism: Said and the Unsaid*. Seattle and London: University of Washington Press.
Vattimo, G. (trans. J. R. Snyder) (1991). *The End of Modernity*. Cambridge: Polity Press.
Vattimo, G. (trans. D. Webb) (1992). *The Transparent Society*. Cambridge and Malden, MA: Polity Press.
Vattimo, G. (trans. D. Webb) (1997). *Beyond Interpretation: The Meaning of Hermeneutics for Philosophy*. Cambridge: Polity Press.

Vattimo, G. (trans. D. Webb) (1999). *Belief*. Palo Alto: Stanford University Press.

Vattimo, G. (trans. L. D'Isanto) (2002). *After Christianity*. New York: Columbia University Press.

Vattimo, G. and Girard, R. (ed. P. Antonello, trans. P. Antonello and W. McCuaig) (2010). *Christianity, Truth, and Weakening Faith*. New York: Columbia University Press.

Vattimo, G. and Rovatti, P. A. (trans. P. Carravetta) (2012). *Weak Thought*. Albany: State University of New York Press.

Veinstein, G. (2012). 'Soḳollu Meḥmed Pasha'. In P. Bearman, T. Bianquis, C. Bosworth, E. van Donzel and W. Heinrichs (eds), *Encyclopaedia of Islam Second Edition* (pp. 706–11). Leiden: Brill.

Virilio, P. (trans. M. Degener) (2002). *Desert Screen: War at the Speed of Light*. London and New York: The Ahtlone Press.

von Stosch, K. (2012). 'Mit Gott ringen: eine theologische Auseinandersetzung mit Navid Kermani'. In M. Hofmann and K. von Stosch (eds), *Islam in der deutschen und türkischen Literatur* (pp. 267–78). Paderborn: Ferdinand Schöningh.

von Stosch, K. (2016). 'Kermani's Writings on Islamic Religion'. In H. Druxes, K. Machtans and A. Michailovic (eds), *Navid Kermani* (pp. 69–85). Oxford: Peter Lang.

Vries, H. de (1999). *Philosophy and the Turn to Religion*. Baltimore, MD: Johns Hopkins University Press.

Vucinich (ed.), W. S. (1995). *Ivo Andrić Revisisted: The Bridge Still Stands*. Berkeley: University of California at Berkeley.

Wachtel, A. (1995). 'Imagining Yugoslavia: The Historical Archeology of Ivo Andrić'. In W. S. Vucinich (ed.), *Ivo Andrić Revisited: The Bridge Still Stands* (pp. 82–102). Berkeley: University of California at Berkeley.

Waldron, J. (1992). 'Minority Cultures and the Cosmopolitan Alternative'. *University of Michigan Journal of Law Reform*, 25 (3, 4), 751–93.

Waldron, J. (2000). 'What Is Cosmopolitan?'. *Journal of Political Philosophy*, 8(2), 227–43.

Waley, A. (1958). *The Way and Its Power: Lao Tzu's Tao Tê Ching and Its Place in Chinese Thought*. New York: Grove Press.

Wallace, M. I. (1992). 'Introduction'. In P. Ricoeur, *Figuring the Sacred: Religion, Narrative and Imagination* (pp. 1–32). Minneapolis: Fortress Press.

Watkin, C. (2011). *Difficult Atheism: Post-Theological Thinking in Alain Badiou, Jean-Luc Nancy and Quentin Meillassoux*. Edinburgh: Edinburgh University Press.

Watt, W. M. and Bell, R. (1977). *Bell's Introduction to the Qur'an*. Edinburgh: Edinburgh University Press.

Wensinck, A. J. (1993). 'Munkar wa-Nakir'. In C. E. Bosworth, E. van Donzel, W. P. Heinrichs and C. Pellat (eds), *Encyclopaedia of Islam – Second Edition* (Vol. VII, pp. 576–7). Leiden: Brill.

Westerveld, G. (2016). *Muslim History in the Region of Murcia (715–1080) Volume I*. Valle de Ricote: Academia de Estudios Humanísticos de Blanca.

Westphal, B. (1997). 'La ville de destins croisés perception littéraire de Tunis au XX siècle'. *Francofonia*, 33, 3–22.

White, K. (2004). *The Wanderer and His Charts: Essays on Cultural Renewal*. Edinburgh: Polygon.
Whiteman, M. T. (2020). *The Invisible Muslim: Journeys through Whiteness and Islam*. London: Hurst.
Wiktorowicz, Q. (2006). 'Anatomy of the Salafi Movement'. *Studies in Conflict and Terrorism*, 29(3), 207–39. doi: 10.1080/10576100500497004.
Williams, R. (2020). *Pathos, Poetry and Politics in Michel Houellebecq's Fiction*. Leiden and Boston: Brill & Rodopi.
Windhager, G. (2008). *Leopold Weiss alias Muhammad Asad*. Vienna, Cologne, Weimar: Böhlau.
Wronecka, J. (1984). 'Le Kitāb al-isrā' ilā al-maqām al-asrā d'Ibn 'Arabī'. *Annales islamologiques*, 20, 15–27.
Wunderli, P. (1968). *Le Livre de Eschiele Mahomet: Die französische Fassung einer alfonsinischen Übersetzung*. Bern: Francke.
Yilmaz, H. (2018). *Caliphate Redefined*. Princeton and Oxford: Princeton University Press.
Zabala, S. (2007). *Weakening Philosophy: Essays in Honor of Gianni Vattimo*. Montreal, Kingston and Ithaca: McGill-Queen's University Press.
Zaehner, R. C. (1957). *Mysticism: Sacred and Profane*. Oxford: Clarendon Press.
Ziolkowski, E. (1998). 'History of Religions and the Study of Religion and Literature: Grounds for an Alliance'. *Literature & Theology*, 12(3), 305–25.
Ziolkowski, E. (2008). 'Religion, Literature, and the Climate of Fear: Intimations of a Polynomous Culture'. *World Literature Today*, 82(2), 38–42.
Zoppellari, A. (2017). 'Une approche au motif urbain dans l'oeuvre d'Abdelwahab Meddeb'. *Il Tolomeo*, 19, 121–32.
Zúquete, J. P. (2021). *The Identitarians: The Movement against Globalism and Islam*. Notre Dame, IN: University of Notre Dame Press.

Index

www.ingramcontent.com/pod-product-compliance
Lightning Source LLC
LaVergne TN
LVHW052015230825
819359LV00004B/122

* 9 7 8 1 4 7 4 4 9 2 6 7 6 *